# Human Rights in Crisis

**Procedural Aspects of International Law Series**

Richard B. Lillich, Editor (1964–1977)
Robert Kogod Goldman, Editor (1977–)

A complete list of the books in this series appears at the back of this volume.

# Human Rights in Crisis

The International System for Protecting
Rights During States of Emergency

Joan Fitzpatrick

Volume 19, Procedural Aspects of International Law Series

University of Pennsylvania Press

Philadelphia

Library of Congress Cataloging-in-Publication Data
Fitzpatrick, Joan.
   Human rights in crisis: the international system for protecting rights during states
of emergency / Joan Fitzpatrick.
      p.   cm. — (Procedural aspects of international law series: v. 19)
   Includes bibliographical references (p.      ) and index.
   ISBN 0–8122–3238–0
   1. Human rights.   2. War and emergency legislation.   3. International law.
4. Treaties.   I. Title.   II. Series.
K3240.4.F534   1994
341.4′81—dc20                                                                93–30873
                                                                                    CIP

# Contents

# Editor's Foreword

*Human Rights in Crisis* is the most recent book in the Procedural Aspects of International Law Series and the first to be published by the University of Pennsylvania Press. Its author, Joan Fitzpatrick, Professor of Law at the University of Washington, is a respected scholar who has a particular expertise in the subject of states of emergency and their impact on the protection of human rights. From 1985 to 1991 she was Rapporteur to the Committee on the Enforcement of Human Rights Law of the International Law Association. In that role, Professor Fitzpatrick prepared three important analytical reports for the Committee on monitoring human rights during emergency situations.

While there is no dearth of scholarly publications on states of emergency, most published material on the subject generally focuses on a particular study or on the effects of an emergency situation in a particular country or region. In contrast, Professor Fitzpatrick's work is thoroughly global in scope and addresses the most recent developments in the field.

She begins by defining and categorizing various kinds of emergency situations, and then examines the adverse effects that such situations typically have on the protection of human rights and the rule of law in a particular society. In a chapter on standard setting, Professor Fitzpatrick does a comparative analysis of treaty-based standards applicable to states of emergency and discusses the efforts of official and private groups, confronted with the gaps and deficiencies in existing law, to elaborate new, non-treaty-based guidelines to protect the basic rights of those affected by emergency situations.

The remainder of the book is devoted to an in-depth examination of the effectiveness of various treaty implementation bodies and other institutions in monitoring states of emergency. This encompasses a critical assessment of the performance of all relevant UN treaty and non-treaty-based organs, including the Human Rights Committee, the Human Rights Commission and its Sub-Commission on the Prevention of Discrimination and Protection of Minorities, various *ad hoc* investigative mechanisms, and the controversial advisory services program. The innovative use of "theme" mechanisms having a global mandate to monitor specific human rights abuses is also assessed.

On the regional level, the author similarly critiques the operations and impact of the supervisory machinery established by the Organization of American States, (i.e., the Inter-American Commission on Human Rights and the Inter-American Court of Human Rights) and of the principal human rights organs of the Council of Europe (i.e., the European Commission on Human Rights and European Court of Human Rights).

Professor Fitzpatrick devotes a full chapter to describing the substantial and important contributions of non-governmental human rights organizations in the study, documentation, and exposure of gross abuses by governments during emergency situations, as well as their efforts to set new standards in the field. Unlike many other writers on the subject, Professor Fitzpatrick does discuss the unique mandate and operations of the International Committee of the Red Cross in assisting victims of internal armed conflicts and lesser forms of civil strife. Given Professor Fitzpatrick's exhaustive treatment of the subject, *Human Rights in Crisis* should prove to be an invaluable source of information for students and practitioners of human rights law.

\*   \*   \*

On a personal note, I wish to acknowledge with thanks the very considerable contributions made by my Dean's Fellow, Paul A. Barkan, in editing this volume.

Robert Kogod Goldman
Washington, D.C.

# Acknowledgments

This study is the culmination of more than a decade of work on the problem of protecting human rights during states of emergency, which began with the preparation of a thesis under the supervision of Maurice Mendelson, then of St. John's College, Oxford. Special thanks go to Professor Richard Lillich of the University of Virginia for his constant encouragement and assistance throughout the drafting of the three reports for the Committee on the Enforcement of Human Rights Law of the International Law Association, which led up to the present study. The comments of other members of the Committee, especially Subrata Roy Chowdhury, are gratefully acknowledged.

I am extremely thankful for financial support for research provided by the University of Washington Law School Foundation and the Ford Foundation. The Ford Foundation also provided funding that enabled me to obtain the services of three extremely fine research assistants, Alice Miller, Laurie Powers, and Matthew Miller. Their help and that of my secretary, James Thompson, were indispensable for the completion of this work.

I am also grateful to Professor Robert Kogod Goldman of American University, the editor of the Procedural Aspects of International Law Series, for his valuable help in revising the manuscript.

# Chapter I
# Defining the Problem

## A. Introduction

That human rights may be imperiled during states of emergency[1] is self-evident. Whether patterns of human rights abuse during states of emergency are sufficiently in a class by themselves to justify, or even to demand, distinct monitoring[2] is far less clear. Yet enough people have thought so, and even attempted to do so, that there is a wealth of material to analyze in this study.

Indeed, the major problem with an examination of systems for

1. The most useful terminology is a matter of debate. "States of exception" is a more general term which emphasizes the fact that exceptions are being made to the normal legal regime, thus stressing the formal legal aspect of the phenomenon and the notion that there is a preexisting paradigm of normality during which rights are protected to a higher degree. But this phrase has the drawback of describing more accurately the situation in civil law systems and is not a particularly apt term for emergencies in common law systems or in more chaotic *de facto* situations of crisis. Likewise, "derogation" implies that the state is a party to a particular human rights treaty whose provisions it is temporarily suspending to some degree. Since universal ratification of the key treaties has not occurred, this term has obvious defects. "States of emergency" has the drawback of having a technical legal meaning in certain civil law systems, as a state of exception of lesser gravity than the "state of siege." The term "state of siege" shares this drawback if used as a generic term. However, "states of emergency" possesses the advantages of breadth of reference to a wide variety of factual circumstances, de-emphasis upon any particular pattern of formal legal alterations, stress upon the temporary crisis aspect of the situation, and a hint of danger. "States of emergency" thus will be used throughout this book in its generic rather than technical sense.

2. The term "monitoring" is intended to encompass scrutiny by a variety of organs, including treaty implementation bodies such as the European or Inter-American Commissions on Human Rights and the Human Rights Committee; non-treaty-based intergovernmental bodies such as the United Nations Commission on Human Rights; nongovernmental organizations concerned with human rights matters; the press, and so on. The term "enforcement" overstates the capacity of these bodies to force compliance by governments with their human rights obligations.

monitoring human rights abuse during states of emergency is that one must canvass essentially *all* of the human rights monitoring mechanisms that have emerged in the past half-century, and some of even earlier origin. The phenomenon of human rights abuse during emergencies is a matter of concern to all human rights monitors, from those with the most broadly defined agendas to those with the narrowest, but not necessarily because of the correlation of the abuse with the emergency. One undercurrent that will run throughout this study is the question whether these monitors should behave in a distinct manner when they encounter human rights abuses coincident to states of emergency. No single answer will fit every monitor.

Two major obstacles bedevil any attempt to devise special monitoring mechanisms for states of emergency: first, the difficulty in defining a coherent and predictably determinable category of situations that fall under the heading of "states of emergency," to the clear exclusion of other situations in which human rights abuses also might be occurring; and, second, the fact that only some, but not all, emergencies produce human rights abuses of especial severity or of distinct types. As one writer noted, "Hitler could shout 'necessity!' as easily as Lincoln,"[3] and both did. Yet one could argue that the human rights abuses of a Hitler call for monitoring on an order entirely different from the abuses of a Lincoln, despite the common context of emergency.

Thus, the first task of this introductory chapter is to attempt to define and categorize states of emergency, to see if a usable, reasonably coherent concept will be available for emergency-specific monitoring. Second, patterns of human rights abuse that tend to be associated with states of emergency (though without any perfect congruence) will be described, in order to set the stage for analyzing the proper roles of human rights monitors.

Looking at the pieces of the puzzle individually can be a useful prelude to determining whether the pieces, when placed together, form any pattern. The creation of a typology of emergency situations has been attempted several times. Three such attempts will be examined here: (1) that offered by the Committee on the Enforcement of Human Rights Law of the International Law Association (ILA), for which the author acted as rapporteur;[4] (2) the "reference model" and various

---

3. C. Rossiter, Constitutional Dictatorship: Crisis Government in the Modern Democracies 12 (1948) [hereinafter Rossiter].

4. The author prepared three reports for the Committee on the Enforcement of Human Rights Law on the question of monitoring human rights abuses during states of emergency: the Interim Report to the Sixty-Second Conference of the International Law Association in Seoul in 1986 (hereinafter 1986 Seoul Report), the Second Interim Report to the Sixty-Third Conference of the International Law Association in Warsaw in 1988

"deviations" therefrom identified by Nicole Questiaux in her 1982 study for the United Nations Sub-Commission on the Prevention of Discrimination and the Protection of Minorities;[5] and (3) Clinton Rossiter's study of the wartime regimes in the United Kingdom, Germany, France and the United States in which he notes interesting differences among the civil law and common law traditions of emergency powers.[6]

## B. The ILA Study

The ILA has a long-standing interest in the problem of protecting human rights during states of emergency, going back at least as far as 1976, when one of its subcommittees began to examine regional difficulties in implementing human rights norms.[7] This subcommittee concentrated upon the elaboration of substantive standards to which states should conform even during times of emergency. In 1984, after the adoption of the Paris Minimum Standards of Human Rights Norms in a State of Emergency,[8] the ILA's Committee on the Enforcement of Human Rights Law turned its attention to problems in the monitoring of human rights abuses during states of emergency. A rough survey at the time of the 1986 ILA report revealed approximately seventy states

(hereinafter 1988 Warsaw Report), and the Final Report on Monitoring States or Emergency: Guidelines for Bodies Monitoring Respect for Human Rights During States of Emergency to the Sixty-Fourth Conference of the International Law Association in Queensland in 1990 (hereinafter Queensland Report). This book draws upon those studies, which were funded by several grants from the Ford Foundation, the University of Washington Law School Foundation, the European Human Rights Foundation and the University of Virginia Center for Law and National Security.

5. N. Questiaux, *Study of the Implications for Human Rights of Recent Developments Concerning Situations Known as States of Siege or Emergency,* U.N. Doc. E/CN.4/Sub.2/1982/15, at 22–28 (1982) [hereinafter Questiaux Report].

6. *See supra* note 3.

7. The Subcommittee on Regional Problems in the Implementation of Human Rights, under the chairmanship of Subrata Roy Chowdhury, prepared a series of three reports concerning states of emergency which were presented to the ILA conferences in Manila in 1978, Belgrade in 1980, and Montreal in 1982. The work of this Subcommittee was merged into the Committee on the Enforcement of Human Rights Law, which drafted the Paris Minimum Standards of Human Rights Norms in a State of Emergency (hereinafter Paris Minimum Standards) adopted by the ILA in 1984. The work of the ILA in drafting substantive standards for protection of human rights during states of emergency is described briefly in the 1986 Seoul Report, *supra* note 4, at 108–110. *See* S.R. Chowdhury, RULE OF LAW IN A STATE OF EMERGENCY: THE PARIS MINIMUM STANDARDS OF HUMAN RIGHTS NORMS IN A STATE OF EMERGENCY (1989) (providing extensive background information and analysis of the ILA's standard-setting work in this area).

8. *See supra* note 7. The Paris Minimum Standards were drafted under the chairmanship of Professor Richard Lillich of the ILA Committee on the Enforcement of Human Rights Law. Paris Minimum Standards, *reprinted in* 79 AM. J. INT'L. L. 1072 (1985).

that were undergoing some type of emergency with varying consequences for the enjoyment of human rights.[9] Not all of these emergencies follow upon an official proclamation under procedures laid out formally in the national constitution or basic law and for a limited duration. The ILA Committee chose not to confine its attention to such narrowly and formally defined emergencies out of concern that many serious human rights abuses may occur in other contexts that nevertheless merit the label of state of emergency.

Moreover, a restriction to formally declared emergencies would itself be problematic. For example, Brunei has repeatedly extended a formal emergency originally imposed on 12 December 1962 in reaction to a revolt on 8–12 December by the North Borneo National Army, which opposed a plan to federate with Malaysia. Although the revolt was completely quelled by British troops under Brunei's security agreement with the United Kingdom, the Sultan has formally renewed the state of emergency every two years, and several persons involved in the 1962 events remained under detention until January 1990. The 1962 Emergency Orders and the Internal Security (Detained Persons) Order of 1964 permit executive detention, expulsion, and exile, and effectively, but not formally, suspend portions of the 1959 Constitution.[10] These measures remain in effect despite the fact that "[s]ince 1962 there have been no disturbances or agitation in Brunei."[11] Defining what is the normal and what is the emergency legal regime of Brunei thus challenges the imagination. The Brunei example has been replicated in a number of other countries around the globe, including Egypt,[12] Turkey,[13] and Paraguay.[14]

9. 1986 Seoul Report, *supra* note 4, at 112, 112 n.7.

10. 1988 Warsaw Report, *supra* note 4, at 143, 143 n.87. *See* COUNTRY REPORTS ON HUMAN RIGHTS PRACTICES FOR 1990, U.S. DEP'T OF STATE REPORT SUBMITTED TO THE SENATE COMM. ON FOREIGN RELATIONS AND THE HOUSE COMM. ON FOREIGN AFFAIRS, 102d Cong., 1st Sess. 816 (Joint Comm. Print 1991) [hereinafter COUNTRY REPORTS FOR 1990].

11. COUNTRY REPORTS FOR 1990, *supra* note 10, at 816.

12. AMNESTY INTERNATIONAL, EGYPT: ARBITRARY DETENTION AND TORTURE UNDER EMERGENCY POWERS 3–4 (1989) ("an almost continuous state of emergency" since 1967, with a brief hiatus between 15 May 1980 and 6 October 1981). At the time of a three-year extension in May 1988, "the Prime Minister stated to the People's Assembly that its purpose was to protect democracy, and that an end to terrorism in the near future was not foreseen." *Id.* at 3.

13. At a workshop on states of emergency held at Queen's University in Belfast, Northern Ireland, on 5–6 April 1991, Professor Mehmet Semih Gemalmaz of the University of Istanbul noted that for almost thirty of the sixty-seven years of the existence of the Turkish Republic, the nation had been under some kind of state of exception (martial law, state of siege or state of emergency). *See* M.S. Gemalmaz, *State of Emergency*

But recognizing the inadequacy of a purely formal definition of states of emergency does not significantly advance inquiry. For one thing, there are varying degrees of formality. Sometimes a new regime will carry over the emergency laws of a predecessor without any formal declaration or suspension of constitutional provisions. For example, in the Occupied Territories under the control of Israel, the powers of administrative detention, deportation, curfews, summary military trials, and the use of force by the Israeli Defense Forces are based upon 1945 Defence (Emergency) Regulations (EDR) issued under the British Mandate in Palestine.[15] Israel asserts that the 1945 EDR were continued by the proclamation of a Jordanian military commander on 24 May 1948, by Jordanian annexation law,[16] and by the 1952 Jordanian Constitution.[17] Israel claims that when it seized the West Bank it simply maintained these provisions in force. Answering the question whether Israel or the Occupied Territories are under any formal state of emergency can be quite vexing.[18]

---

*Rule in the Turkish Legal System: Perspectives and Texts,* 11–12 Turk. Y.B. Hum. Rts. 115 (1989–90).

14. The repeatedly renewed state of siege in Paraguay was allowed to lapse in 1987. Country Reports on Human Rights Practices for 1988, U.S. Dep't of State Report Submitted to the Senate Comm. on Foreign Relations and the House Comm. on Foreign Affairs, 101st Cong., 1st Sess. 669 (Joint Comm. Print 1989) [hereinafter Country Reports for 1988]. The Inter-American Commission on Human Rights (IACHR) noted in 1987 that implementing legislation required by Article 79 of the Constitution had never been adopted, and that "the provisions of the state of siege have been applied broadly and in an *ad hoc* manner, according to the specific needs of the political moment and the assessment thereof by the executive power." Inter-Am. C.H.R., Report on the Situation of Human Rights in Paraguay 20, OEA/Ser.L/V/ II.71, doc. 19, rev. 1 (1987). Even more interestingly, the IACHR observed after an onsite visit to Paraguay in February 1990, following General Alfredo Stroessner's fall from power in 1989, that "habits and customs that hamper the full observance of human rights" remain because of the "heavy legacy of three decades of authoritarian government systematically violating human rights." Inter-Am. C.H.R., 1989–90 Annual Report 168, OEA/Ser.L/V/II.77, doc. 7, rev. 1 (1990) [hereinafter IACHR 1989–90 Annual Report]. Thus, the Paraguayan example raises serious questions as to the relevance of the formal state of emergency as a factor in the enjoyment of human rights.

15. [1945] *Palestine Gazette* (no. 1442) (Supp. 2) 1055.

16. On 24 April 1950, a joint session of the Jordanian parliament adopted a resolution proclaiming the unity of the East and West Banks into the Hashemite Kingdom of Jordan. Y.Z. Blum, The Juridicial Status of Jerusalem 16–17 (1974).

17. *See* International Commission of Jurists, Israel National Section, The Rule of Law in the Areas Administered by Israel (1981).

18. Two additional factors muddy the waters in the context of the Occupied Territories. When East Jerusalem was annexed by Israel, apparently one result was that the Israeli Defense Forces were no longer regarded as an occupying power and thus lost responsibility for enforcing the EDR in the city. In January 1988, in the early stages of

Common law states, particularly those without written constitutions, may not require a formal proclamation of emergency in order to permit the imposition of extraordinary security laws in times of crisis. Yet, when such states are parties to human rights treaties, they may be required to file formal notices of derogation under the terms of the treaties.

For example, the United Kingdom is a party both to the European Convention on Human Rights[19] and the International Covenant on Civil and Political Rights.[20] The long-standing crisis in Northern Ireland has been dealt with through application of a series of statutes granting wide powers of arrest, internment without trial, trial in special courts, investigatory detention, and restrictions on media coverage of proscribed organizations.[21] Parliamentary enactment (perhaps long

---

the intifada, this anomalous situation was highlighted when the police in Jerusalem were secretly authorized to exercise special emergency powers similar to those enforced on the West Bank, including the imposition of a curfew in one Arab neighborhood and actions to break a strike by shopowners. The new police powers were reported to have been announced only over the Arab-language radio station in Jerusalem, and the government appeared to be reluctant to admit the new arrangement or to make any kind of formal proclamation. *Israelis Impose Curfew on East Jerusalem Area*, N.Y. Times, Jan. 23, 1988, at 6, col. 5.

The status of emergency powers in Israel and the Occupied Territories is made even more ambiguous by the fact that a state of emergency was declared in Israel on 21 May 1948, and the 1945 EDR were absorbed into Israeli law. *See* Leon v. Gubernik, H.C. 5/48, 1 Piskei Din 58 (1948) and Ziv v. Tel Aviv District Commissioner, H.C. 10/48, 1 Piskei Din 85 (1948), *cited in* H. Rudolph, *The Judicial Review of Administrative Detention Orders in Israel*, 14 Isr. Y.B. on Hum. Rts. 148, 149 (1984). Apparently, the application of the EDR does not depend upon the proclamation of a state of emergency. S. Shetreet, *A Contemporary Model of Emergency Detention Laws: An Assessment of the Israeli Law*, 14 Isr. Y.B. on Hum. Rts. 182, 184 (1984). However, the 1979 amendments to the provisions for administrative detention (Regulations 108 and 111, Emergency Powers [Detention] Law, 5739/1979) do apparently depend on the existence of a state of emergency. *See* E. Playfair, Administrative Detention in the Occupied West Bank (1986); M. Saltman, *The Use of the Mandatory Emergency Laws by the Israeli Government*, 10 Int'l. J. Soc. L. 385 (1982).

19. Eur. Comm'n of Hum. Rts., Stock-taking on the European Convention on Human Rights, Supplement 1988, at app. I (1989).

20. *Report of the Human Rights Committee*, 45 U.N. GAOR Supp. (No. 40), U.N. Doc. A/45/40 Annex I (1990).

21. *E.g.*, the Civil Authorities (Special Powers) Act (Northern Ireland), 1922, 12 & 13 Geo. 5, N. Ir. Pub. Gen. Acts of 1922, ch. 5; the Northern Ireland (Emergency Provisions) Act 1987, Public General Acts & Measures of 1987 (pt. II), ch. 30; the Prevention of Terrorism (Temporary Provisions) Act 1974, Public General Acts & Measures of 1974 (pt. II), ch. 56; the Prevention of Terrorism (Temporary Provisions) Act 1976, Public General Acts & Measures of 1976 (pt. I), ch. 8; the Prevention of Terrorism (Temporary Provisions) Act 1984, Public General Acts & Measures of 1984 (pt. I), ch. 8; Prevention of Terrorism (Temporary Provisions) Act 1989, Public General Acts of

before a specific crisis occurs) or issuance of regulations or directives by administrative officials to whom relevant power has been delegated is all that is formally necessary in the British system as a prelude to application of these emergency powers. However, authorities in the United Kingdom have found it necessary because of their treaty obligations to proceed in a more formal manner by issuing or renewing notices of derogation when these emergency laws are actually being applied in a specific crisis, at least if the measures involve suspension of treaty obligations.[22] Scholars of the Northern Ireland situation have noted that recent legislation "has the effect of blurring a distinction . . . between emergency powers and anti-terrorism provisions. . . . [T]hen a permanent emergency state becomes the 'solution' to the emergency."[23] Despite the differences in formalities, therefore, the distinction between states such as the United Kingdom and Brunei also blurs in defining the "normal" versus the "emergency" legal regimes.[24]

But if one moves away from a formal definition of states of emergency, the major line-drawing problem becomes distinguishing between *de facto* emergencies and situations that should not be classified as emergencies at all. Some coherent definition of states of emergency, including both formal and *de facto* emergencies, is a prerequisite to any emergency-specific system of monitoring human rights abuses.

While recognizing that each emergency is factually unique, as well as complex and variable over time, the ILA Committee attempted to

---

1989 (pt. I), ch. 4. *See* Directives issued 19 October 1989 by the Secretary of State under section 29(3) of the Broadcasting Act 1981, *reprinted in* Brind v. Secretary of State for the Home Department, [1991] 1 All E.R. 720, 727 (H.L.).

22. The most recent notice of derogation by the United Kingdom under the European Convention was issued on 23 December 1988, in response to the judgment by the European Court of Human Rights in the case of *Brogan v. United Kingdom*. Brogan v. United Kingdom, 11 Eur. H.R. Rep. 117 (1988) (ser. A, No. 145-B) (judgment of Eur. Ct. H.R.). *Brogan* found that investigative detentions under section 12 of the Prevention of Terrorism (Temporary Provisions) Act 1984 of up to six and a half days, without appearance before judicial authority, violated article 5(3) of the Convention. A similar notice of derogation was filed under the Covenant on 23 December 1988. The U.K.'s previous notices of derogation had been terminated on 22 August 1984. *See* ASSOCIATION OF THE BAR OF THE CITY OF NEW YORK, CRIMINAL JUSTICE AND HUMAN RIGHTS IN NORTHERN IRELAND 24–30 (1988).

23. J.D. Jackson, *The Northern Ireland (Emergency Provisions) Act 1987*, 39 N. IR. L.Q. 235, 257 (1988).

24. Another puzzling example of the difficulties in assessing whether a formal emergency exists is provided by Angola. Angola formally established military courts to try civilians in political cases in areas affected by the conflict with UNITA in 1983, but it did not formally proclaim an emergency or suspend its constitution, nor was it required to notify any human rights treaty body. AMNESTY INTERNATIONAL, ANNUAL REPORT 1985 19 (1985). The Angolan example is replicated in numerous other situations.

divide emergencies into a six-part typology. The two central factors for classification were (1) the distinction between formal (or *de jure*) emergencies and *de facto* emergencies, and (2) whether actual conditions in the country constituted a serious public emergency, threatening the life of the nation, from whatever cause.[25] Several further distinctions are necessary within the category of unjustified *de facto* emergencies. The typology can be illustrated graphically in Table 1. The importance of categorization along these lines can best be explained by use of concrete examples.

## Type 1: The "Good" *De Jure* Emergency

This type of emergency is the one sanguinely envisioned by the drafters of the derogation clauses in the major human rights treaties: actual conditions of public emergency threatening the life of the nation that regrettably, but unavoidably, make extraordinary measures and thus suspension of certain treaty rights necessary. The imposition of emergency measures is accompanied by formal declaration, if required by national law, plus notification to the other states parties under any relevant treaty. Emergencies meeting the criteria of Type 1 would be included under any mechanism of emergency-specific monitoring.[26] However, the criteria for classifying emergencies into Type 1 contain an element of subjectivity, and their application would be open to dispute in specific situations. While determining whether the formalities have been completed may be easy, measuring the gravity of the threat to the nation is difficult because of the possible inaccessibility of reliable and complete data and potential political or other bias in assessment.

Under the ILA Committee's analysis, however, the term "good" should not be taken too literally, because it signifies only that the conditions for a formal emergency have been met. This still leaves open the possibility that the emergency may involve serious human rights abuses, such as violation of non-derogable rights or lack of proportionality between crisis conditions and the specific measures imposed. In fact, the ILA Committee suggested that it would be ex-

25. The threshold of severity is drawn from the three major human rights treaties with derogation clauses: European Convention Article 15(1), ICCPR Article 4(1) and American Convention Article 27(1). The potential causes of serious emergencies are infinitely variable, but can be roughly classed under three headings: war, internal tension, and natural disaster. 1986 Seoul Report, *supra* note 4, at 113.

26. Two such examples are the proposal that the Human Rights Committee request immediate supplemental reports from derogating states under the ICCPR (see Chapter IV) and the Sub-Commission's list of states under formal emergencies (see Chapter V).

TABLE 1.

|  | *De Jure* | *De Facto* |
|---|---|---|
| *Actual Emergency* | (1) "Good" *de jure* emergency<br>Actual emergency conditions<br>Formal declaration and/or notification | (3) "Classic" *de facto* emergency<br>Actual emergency conditions<br>No formal declaration and/or notification |
| *No Actual Emergency* | (2) "Bad" *de jure* emergency<br><br>No real emergency conditions<br>Formal declaration and/or notification | (4) "Ambiguous or potential" *de facto* emergency<br>No real emergency conditions<br>No formal declaration and/or notification<br>Sudden change in application of security laws<br><br>(5) "Institutionalized" emergency<br>No real emergency conditions<br>Lifting of prior formal emergency<br>Simultaneous incorporation of emergency laws in ordinary law<br><br>(6) "Ordinary" repression<br>No real emergency conditions<br>No formal declaration or notification<br>Permanent laws with extreme restrictions on human rights. |

tremely difficult to identify a single concrete instance of a *de jure* emergency that fully complied with all international standards.[27] And even if such a case could be identified, serious human suffering probably still would have occurred during the crisis, since a threat to the life of the nation implies that the population is menaced by some grave danger.

## Type 2: The "Bad" *De Jure* Emergency

This type was also anticipated by the treaty drafters and certainly merits inclusion in any emergency-specific monitoring program. The "bad" *de jure* emergency is invoked by governments that are either acting out of antidemocratic or self-interested motives, or are over-reacting to modest stresses in imposing a formal state of emergency in the absence of a genuine threat to the nation. The European Commission of Human Rights found in 1967, for example, that the military regime in Greece had suspended rights under the European Convention without any plausible or substantial reasons.[28] Long-prolonged emergencies, such as that in Chile[29] and many other states, also fit into this category.

The "bad" *de jure* emergency is frequently and somewhat inaccurately perceived as the paradigm for abuse of human rights associated with states of emergency (the popular stereotype of the Latin American dictatorship). Such abuses are also associated with "good" *de jure*

27. 1988 Warsaw Report, *supra* note 4, at 147.

28. The "Greek" Case, 1969 Y.B. Eur. Conv. on Hum. Rts. 45–76 (Eur. Comm'n of Hum. Rts.). This is the classic example of a treaty implementation body rejecting a derogating government's claim that it faced a genuine emergency. The Commission focused on the actual situation (the level of disturbances to public order, etc.) and not upon the revolutionary character of the Colonels' regime. The question of the relevance of government motive will be discussed further in Chapter II. *See* F. Hassan, *A Juridical Critique of Successful Treason: A Jurisprudential Analysis of the Constitutionality of Coup d'etat in the Common Law*, 20 Stan. J. Int'l L. 191 (1984).

29. Seventeen years of military rule since the coup in September 1973 ended in Chile when an elected civilian government took office on 11 March 1990. IACHR 1989–90 Annual Report, *supra* note 14, at 133–135. According to the IACHR, this "fully reinstated a representative and constitutional democratic system of government." *Id.* at 133. Prior to that time, however, a series of states of siege (*e.g.*, from 7 September 1986 to 6 January 1987), states of emergency and other states of exception had prevailed. 1988 Warsaw Report, *supra* note 4, at 193 n.100. Articles 39, 40, 41 and transitory provisions 15 and 24 of the 1980 Constitution set out elaborate degrees of states of exception for situations of internal or external war, internal disturbances or natural calamity. *Id.* One or the other of these states of exception had been almost continually in force during the military regime.

emergencies and with the various subcategories of *de facto* emergencies. But in "bad" *de jure* emergencies, emergency measures are, almost by definition, disproportionate to the "exigencies" of the situation and frequently result in deprivation of non-derogable rights. The imposition or maintenance of a "bad" *de jure* emergency thus seems to be a reasonably good predictor of human rights abuse and presents the strongest argument for emergency-specific monitoring. The existence of a "bad" formal emergency is not, however, a strong predictor of the *severity* of associated human rights abuses. Long-prolonged formal emergencies may blend gradually into the normal legal regime, and human rights abuses may moderate over time. It may become difficult to distinguish these prolonged formal emergencies from Type 5 ("institutionalized" *de facto* emergencies) or Type 6 ("ordinary" repression). Yet, the government's invocation of emergency powers in these instances merits scrutiny simply because it is likely to cast some light upon the underlying issue of whether there is anything unique about the abuse of human rights in emergency contexts.

## Type 3: The "Classic" De Facto Emergency

As noted in Table 1, which divides *de facto* emergencies into four types, non-formal emergencies require a complex scheme of classification, and all may not be suitable for any targeted program of monitoring. Only one of the four types is "genuine" in the sense that it occurs in the context of actual emergency conditions: that is the "classic" *de facto* emergency.

This "classic" type also merits categorization into four distinct subtypes. The first is where a conflict or other crisis exists but the imperiled government chooses to maintain, both formally and in practice, its ordinary legal regime. The second may be characterized by a conflict or other emergency situation during which the government takes extraordinary measures but without formally declaring or giving notice of an emergency. The third may entail the existence of actual emergency conditions, but the government's "legal" regime may be totally *ad hoc*. And the fourth occurs when a nation is faced with an actual emergency and chooses to respond by incorporating on a permanent basis harsh security laws into its ordinary legislation. Not all of these four subtypes may deserve targeted monitoring.

Looking at the first subtype, in which the government successfully preserves the ordinary legal regime (and enjoyment of human rights) despite extreme stress, little more than admiration or curiosity would seem to justify special monitoring. Genuine examples of this subtype, however, are not immediately apparent. For example, the 1988 Report of the ILA Committee questioned whether the claims of Cyprus[30] and Iraq[31] to have coped with war situations without resort to emergency powers were truly credible.

The second subcategory concerns governments that impose extraordinary measures frequently by decree but without any formal declaration of emergency. Afghanistan[32] at one time fit this category, which

30. The government of the Republic of Cyprus currently controls approximately 60% of the now-divided island, as a result of a 1974 invasion by Turkey. The other 40% under Turkish control unilaterally declared its independence on 15 November 1983 as the Turkish Republic of Northern Cyprus. So far, it has been recognized only by Turkey. COUNTRY REPORTS FOR 1990, *supra* note 10, at 1117. A UN peacekeeping force patrols the volatile "line." It appears that both sides are attempting to bolster their claims to control by not resorting to emergency powers. L. Despouy, *First Annual Report and List of States Which, Since 1 January 1985, Have Proclaimed, Extended or Terminated a State of Emergency,* U.N. Doc. E/CN.4/Sub.2/1987/19, at 23 (1987) [hereinafter 1987 Despouy Report].

31. Leandro Despouy noted that "despite the existence of armed conflicts, in Afghanistan, Iran, and Iraq, *inter alia,* the Special Rapporteur found no indication that a state of emergency had been proclaimed." 1987 Despouy Report, *supra* note 30, at para. 43. He was speaking of course of the situation during the eight-year Iran-Iraq war. At the time of the review of its second periodic report to the Human Rights Committee in 1987, Iraq's representative blithely asserted that "Iraq had not declared a state of emergency nor had it suspended any human rights covered by its obligations under the Covenant. In fact, it had continued to improve the material, economic and social conditions of life and on that basis to develop the human rights of its citizens." *Report of the Human Rights Committee,* 42 U.N. GAOR Supp. (No. 40), U.N. Doc. A/42/40, at para. 347 (1987). Amnesty International reported that during 1987 thousands of political prisoners were arbitrarily detained without trial or after summary trials before the Revolutionary Court, that torture was routinely practiced, and that hundreds of persons had been executed, including children and the relatives of suspected government opponents. AMNESTY INTERNATIONAL, REPORT 1988 236–239 (1989). Indeed, in response to Amnesty's expression of concern, the Iraqi government justified the large number of executions on the grounds that "the society of any country would be bound to defend itself more strongly under certain conditions, such as when it is at war." *Id.* at 238.

32. Special Rapporteur Despouy noted in 1987 that the Afghan government had not declared any emergency. 1987 Despouy Report, *supra* note 30, at para. 43. The Afghan representative who presented his country's report to the Human Rights Committee in 1985 did little to clarify whether Article 4 had been invoked. U.N. Docs. CCPR/C/SR. 603, at para. 58; CCPR/C/Sr. 604, at paras. 6, 27, 43; CCPR/C/SR. 608, at paras. 2–42 (1985). However, after the withdrawal of troops by the USSR, the Afghan government did declare a state of emergency and transfer the authority of the National Assembly under article 81(1) of the Constitution to the Council of Ministers. These powers were reportedly transferred back by presidential decree in October 1989, and the National Assembly continued to function during the emergency. As noted by the Special Rapporteur for the Commission on Human Rights, Prof. Felix Ermacora, in his 1990 report to the Commission, "the state of emergency was still in force but would appear to have had little incidence on the human rights situation in general," which was dismal in areas

also tends to subsume situations under martial law, including foreign military occupation.[33] Martial law situations vary in their relative degree of legal formality. Some, such as that in Jordan, fit the model of a *de jure* emergency[34] which might be "good" or "bad" depending upon the severity of the crisis that triggered the imposition of martial rule. Martial law imposed without any formal declaration of emergency in a situation of genuine national crisis, involving "a suspension of normal civil government in order to restore it . . . [with] civilians for its subjects and civil areas for its loci of operation,"[35] fits the "classic" *de facto* model and should be encompassed in any program of emergency-specific monitoring.

Even more informal is the third subtype, a legal regime which is totally *ad hoc*. Areas occupied by armed opposition groups may fall into this category, such as the portions of Lebanon controlled by militia groups,[36] areas occupied by the Afghan guerrilla factions,[37] and the

controlled both by the government and by the opposition forces. 46 U.N. ESCOR Comm'n on Hum. Rts., at paras. 31–77, U.N. Doc. E/CN.4/1990/25 (1990) [hereinafter Ermacora Report].

33. Clinton Rossiter notes of martial law in England prior to 1914, the "almost complete lack of institutional status . . . the absence of statutory foresight for its initiation and use." ROSSITER, *supra* note 3, at 141. As Rossiter explains: "Given a condition of emergency in England that would call for a declaration of the state of siege in France, the government (or a local magistrate or military commander) has the power to do just about the same things that French officials can do under the state of siege. The authority to adopt whatever arbitrary measures are necessary to restore public order proceeds directly from the common law right and duty of the Crown and its subjects to 'repel force by force in the case of invasion or insurrection, and to act against rebels as it might against invaders' " [citations omitted]. *Id.* at 142.

34. Martial law was declared by Royal Decree on 5 June 1967, in response to the war with Israel. AMNESTY INTERNATIONAL, JORDAN: HUMAN RIGHTS PROTECTION AFTER THE STATE OF EMERGENCY 6 (1990). Martial Law Directives under this declaration provide, *inter alia,* for the appointment of the General Military Governor (currently the Prime Minister) (Art. 2); unappealability of orders by the Martial Law General (Art. 5); and the establishment of a Martial Law Court (Art. 6). Martial law is declared by Royal Decree under Article 125 of the Constitution of the Hashemite Kingdom of Jordan of 1952. *Id.* at 6–9. In 1967, when martial law was declared, Jordan was already under a state of emergency that had been imposed in 1939, "thus effectively introducing a dual state of emergency." *Id.* at 4. Martial law was "frozen" in December 1989, with the announced intention of gradually eliminating it. *Id.* at 1. But by the end of 1990, the parliament had not finished drafting the necessary legislation. COUNTRY REPORTS FOR 1990, *supra* note 10, at 1497. Martial law was formally terminated on 7 July 1991. *Jordanian Cancels Most Martial Law Rules,* N.Y. TIMES, July 8, 1991, at A3 col. 5.

35. ROSSITER, *supra* note 3, at 140.

36. These groups include the Lebanese Forces, Amal, al-Waad, Syrian Social Nationalist Party–Emergency Command, Hizballah, and several Palestinian groups. Portions of Lebanese territory are also under control by foreign armies, including those of Syria and

chaotic war conditions in contested areas in Uganda.[38] Similarly, chaotic conditions may also pertain in situations short of armed conflict. For example, security forces in Haiti at the time of the aborted 1987 elections appear to have engaged in a perhaps calculated loss of control and discipline.[39] In 1989 General Prosper Avril himself referred to his government as *"de facto,"* according to an expert appointed by the United Nations,[40] who found the Avril regime "without legitimate title or a solid legal basis."

These *ad hoc* regimes often entail widespread and grave human rights abuses and a sharp departure from a prior, orderly legal regime. As such, they may present true states of emergency which, in some cases, might even be largely legitimate if the legal chaos is due to factors beyond the control of the government. Thus, it would be important to include them in any targeted program of monitoring. However, it may not always be a simple matter to determine when lawlessness by security forces reaches a level that pushes it beyond an "emergency" threshold.

The fourth subtype of "classic" *de facto* emergency is where a nation confronted with armed conflict or other actual emergency conditions responds to the crisis by adopting harsh national security laws not as a temporary emergency measure but as a permanent one. A somewhat debatable example of this situation occurred in El Salvador, which permitted a state of emergency to lapse while making permanent certain

---

Israel (the latter largely working through the South Lebanon Army). COUNTRY REPORTS FOR 1990, *supra* note 10, at 1522.

37. Special Rapporteur Ermacora noted reports by Asia Watch of serious human rights abuses committed by Afghan guerrillas, and suggested critically that the practice of placing areas under field commanders rather than the Afghan Interim Government "does not guarantee the full respect of basic law and order because full representivity and an effective authority are lacking." Ermacora Report, *supra* note 32, at paras. 46, 48–57 (1990).

38. 1988 Warsaw Report, *supra* note 4, at 195 n.111; COUNTRY REPORTS FOR 1990, *supra* note 10, at 433–42.

39. 1988 Warsaw Report, *supra* note 4, at 195–96 n.112; INTER-AM. C.H.R., REPORT ON THE SITUATION OF HUMAN RIGHTS IN HAITI, 20–21, OEA/Ser.L./V/II.74, doc. 9, rev. 1, at 20–21 (1988).

40. *Report on Haiti by the Expert, Mr. Philippe Texier, prepared in conformity with the Commission on Human Rights Resolution 1989/73,* 46 U.N. ESCOR, Comm'n on Hum. Rts., U.N. Doc. E/CN.4/1990/44 at 12, at para. 53 (1990). Prof. Philippe Texier noted that as of January 1990, General Avril's government had revived some portions of the 1987 Constitution, but continued to suspend "essential provisions about the organization of the State." *Id.* Free elections were held in December 1990. COUNTRY REPORTS FOR 1990, *supra* note 10, at 660. But on 30 September 1991, elected President Jean-Bertrand Aristide was ousted by a military coup. *Haiti's Military Assumes Power After Troops Arrest the President,* N.Y. TIMES, Oct. 1, 1991, at A1, col. 1.

measures on administrative detention.[41] Where emergency conditions exist and the government chooses to make a transition from emergency measures to harsh ordinary legislation, it becomes more difficult to classify the situation as an emergency. In fact, governments may make such transitions, in part, to escape international attention, which is often attracted by declarations of emergency and reassured when emergencies are terminated.[42] Continued monitoring would be essential, however, to determine if the lifting of an emergency actually resulted in improvements in the human rights climate. The ILA Committee recommended that such situations be included in special monitoring if actual emergency conditions still prevailed, or if the revised ordinary laws incorporated a substantial portion of the earlier emergency measures and the new provisions were being applied to a significant extent.[43]

## Type 4: The "Ambiguous or Potential" *De Facto* Emergency

Although in these situations there are no actual emergency conditions and no formal declaration of emergency, they typically entail a sudden increase in the application of harsh, permanent internal security laws. A good example is the sudden crackdown in Singapore in 1987, during which the government placed a number of opposition figures of varying persuasions in administrative detention for periods of up to two years under the Internal Security Act (ISA). Without any change in the formal legal regime, a dramatically new political and human rights situation was created in Singapore by unilateral government action, triggering concern and attracting increased international attention.[44]

41. 1988 Warsaw Report, *supra* note 4, at 150 n.113. The Inter-American Commission on Human Rights reported in 1990 that El Salvador was under a state of siege involving increasing numbers of detentions. IACHR 1989–90 ANNUAL REPORT, *supra* note 14, at 145. *See Final Report to the Commission on Human Rights on the Situation of Human Rights in El Salvador*, 46 U.N. ESCOR Comm'n on Hum. Rts., U.N. Doc. E/CN.4/1990/26 at 6, at para. 20 (1990) (citing Amnesty International data on increased arrests under the state of siege at the time of the late 1989 offensive).

42. *E.g.*, 1990 Queensland Report, *supra* note 4, at 4 n.9 (noting the lifting of "marital law" in Beijing in January 1990; *Taiwan's Leader Ends 43-Year Emergency Rule*, N.Y. TIMES, May 1, 1991, at A6, col. 2.

43. Warsaw Report, *supra* note 4, at 150–51.

44. In May and June 1987, twenty-two people were arrested under the Internal Security Act (ISA) of 1960. AMNESTY INTERNATIONAL, RECENT DETENTIONS UNDER THE INTERNAL SECURITY ACT: REPORT OF AN AMNESTY MISSION IN SINGAPORE, AI Index: ASA 36/11/87 (1987) [hereinafter SINGAPORE MISSION REPORT]. Those arrested were professionals in the media, law, market research, or employed by the Catholic church. *Id.* at 4. Persons may be detained under the ISA (which derives from the British Colonial Preser-

That increased scrutiny of Singapore's human rights situation was justified in 1987 cannot be doubted; what is unclear is whether the situation should be labeled an "emergency."

The 1987 Singapore scenario is replicated in many other countries, particularly those with a British colonial heritage. The common law system places, at best, a modest emphasis upon the formalities of emergency rule, in comparison to the often Byzantine complexity of distinctions in civil law between various states of exception. One legacy of the British Empire was a complex of internal security laws, designed to cope with external threats and internal subversion, including struggles for decolonization. It is a familiar story repeated throughout the world that when those liberation struggles succeeded, the new leaders embraced the same tools of repression that had been used by the colonial masters.[45]

But unlike the United Kingdom, the newly independent states commonly adopted written constitutions. These constitutions typically provide for emergency powers, often with a fair degree of formality.[46]

---

vation of Public Security Ordinance of 1955) for renewable two-year periods. *Id.* at 2–3. The absence of emergency conditions prior to these arrests is underlined by a statement by Foreign Minister Suppiah Dhanabalan: "We are not saying the group was on the verge . . . of starting a revolution. . . . Why should we wait until they are on the verge before we act?" J. Katigbak, *Singapore Insists Communist Threat Is Real*, Reuters, June 2, 1987, *available in* LEXIS, Nexis Library, Reuters File. *See* AMNESTY INTERNATIONAL, CONTINUING DETENTIONS UNDER THE INTERNAL SECURITY ACT: FURTHER EVIDENCE OF THE TORTURE AND ILL-TREATMENT OF DETAINEES, AI Index: ASA 36/09/88 (1988). At the end of 1990, no persons were detained under the ISA; one detainee was released in 1989 after twenty-three years of preventive detention under the ISA. COUNTRY REPORTS FOR 1990, *supra* note 10, at 1021. Singapore itself implicitly acknowledged the significance of these events by describing them to the Sub-Commission's Special Rapporteur on states of emergency. U.N. Doc. E/CN.4/Sub.2/1989/30/Rev.1, at 5 (1990).

45. *See supra* note 10 (noting the example of Brunei); *supra* notes 15–18 (noting the case of Israel in the Occupied Territories); *supra* note 44 (citing the example of Singapore) to South Africa and Zimbabwe.

46. For example, the Governor-General of Fiji asserted power under Section 72 of the Constitution of 1970 to dismiss the Prime Minister and dissolve Parliament, in the face of a coup d'etat in May 1987. This effort to cope with the political crisis was ineffective and was followed in September 1987 by a second coup d'etat by Colonel Sitiveni Rabuka, who abrogated the 1970 Constitution on 1 October 1987. 1988 Warsaw Report, *supra* note 4, at 198 n.121. Prof. F.M. Brookfield questions whether the Governor-General actually possessed authority under the Constitution for his actions. *See* Brookfield, *The Fiji Revolutions of 1987*, 1988 N.Z.L.J. 250.

Sometimes the Constitution offers several alternative sets of extraordinary powers. In 1987, for example, the Punjab was placed under direct presidential rule by the Indian government, invoking Article 356 of the Constitution. Articles 352–355 of the Constitution allow for the suspension of fundamental guarantees in times of emergency. 1988

Such states may also come under martial law regimes, as in Bangladesh and Pakistan.[47] In addition, these Commonwealth nations possess harsh internal security laws, similar to Singapore's ISA. In time of stress, therefore, these governments have a choice between imposing formal emergencies under their constitutions and implementing emergency legislation, or simply invoking the provisions of their permanent national security laws. They seem to alternate between these responses in an unpredictable, haphazard way.[48]

Malaysia presents an especially problematic and complex example. Since independence Malaysia has been under a series of states of emergency, including a nationwide state of emergency declared in 1969 in response to post-election communal violence.[49] During that emergency, Malaysia adopted the Emergency (Public Order and Prevention of Crime) Ordinance, 1969,[50] which permits detention for a maximum of two years of persons suspected of acting or being likely to act in a manner prejudicial to public order. The 1969 emergency has never been terminated, despite the abatement of communal violence.

Malaysia also has an overlay of permanent national security legislation, including the Internal Security Act, 1960 (ISA), which permits persons to be arrested without warrant and detained for renewable two-year periods if they have acted or are about to act "in any manner prejudicial to the security of Malaysia."[51] The government of Malaysia typically invokes the provisions of the ISA in order to crack down on its opponents, particularly suspected communists and Islamic extremists.

---

Warsaw Report, *supra* note 4, at 199 n.124. In April 1990, the Indian Parliament repealed a constitutional amendment that had permitted suspension of the guarantees of life and liberty and direct presidential rule without legislative approval (a provision invoked only in the Punjab). COUNTRY REPORTS FOR 1990, *supra* note 10, at 1432. During 1990 the states of Punjab, Jammu and Kashmir, and Assam were all under direct presidential rule at various times. *Id.* at 1425.

47. 1988 Warsaw Report, *supra* note 4, at 152 and nn.119 & 120.

48. The government of Kenya, for example, orders administrative detention under the Preservation of Public Security Act (PPSA) ("a holdover from colonial days" according to the COUNTRY REPORTS FOR 1990, *supra* note 10, at 169) or criminal prosecution on such charges as sedition. *Id.* at 167. *See* 1988 Warsaw Report, *supra* note 4, at 197 n.118. Many persons are simply detained by the authorities without even being held under the PPSA. AMNESTY INTERNATIONAL, 1987 REPORT 61 (two hundred detained, with fifty eventually held under the PPSA).

49. *See* Warsaw Report, *supra* note 4, at 153–55.

50. The Emergency (Public Order and Prevention of Crime) Ordinance, 1969, *published as* Ordinance 5, H.M. Govt. Gazette as P.U.(A) 187. Malaysia adopted a series of other emergency laws in 1969 as well.

51. 1988 Warsaw Report, *supra* note 4, at 154 n.126; INTERNATIONAL COMMISSION OF JURISTS, STATES OF EMERGENCY: THEIR IMPACT ON HUMAN RIGHTS 204 (1983).

In late 1987, for example, more than 100 persons were detained under the ISA in "Operation Lallang." [52] The ISA was made even harsher in 1989 when detention orders by the Home Minister were completely exempted from judicial review.[53]

And yet the emergency ordinances in Malaysia are far from moribund. They are broadly applied to detain suspected drug dealers and members of secret criminal societies.[54] This is done even though the never-terminated 1969 emergency was premised upon racial and political conflict, and not the drug problem. Singapore also imposes preventive detention on suspected drug offenders, but not in the context of an extended formal emergency.[55]

The Malaysian and Singapore examples thus present a challenge in applying definitional criteria for a "state of emergency." Because Malaysia has retained the formal 1969 emergency, although its original factual premise no longer exists, a plausible argument could be made for including Malaysia in a program of emergency-specific monitoring.[56] In contrast, the sudden increases in the number of detentions under the ISAs in 1987 in both Singapore and Malaysia, though signaling an important change in the human rights climate, do not fit easily under an "emergency" rubric.

If such situations are excluded from monitoring, however, an incentive is created for governments to apply harsh permanent laws to suppress dissent, rather than resorting to theoretically temporary emergency measures. Perhaps such a concern exaggerates the significance of human rights monitoring as a factor in shaping government strategy. But in devising a program for monitoring human rights abuse during states of emergency, the legal formalities are naturally of less interest than the potential for abuse. Thus, the ILA Committee decided that some "ambiguous or potential" *de facto* situations should be

52. 1988 Warsaw Report, *supra* note 4, at 154 and nn.128–29.

53. COUNTRY REPORTS FOR 1990, *supra* note 10, at 954.

54. 1988 Warsaw Report, *supra* note 4, at 154. Although approximately 400 persons were detained under the Emergency Ordinance in October 1986, that number was reduced to 189 as of December 1990. *Id.* The reduction appears to be largely due to the passage of the Dangerous Drugs (Special Preventive Measures) Act of 1985, under which drug suspects can be detained without trial for renewable two-year periods. COUNTRY REPORTS FOR 1990, *supra* note 10, at 954–55. Approximately 1,200 suspects were detained under this law as of December 1990.

55. Singapore detains drug suspects under the Criminal Law (Temporary Provisions) Act. Detentions under this act and Singapore's ISA are not subject to judicial review. COUNTRY REPORTS FOR 1990, *supra* note 10, at 1021–22.

56. As the 1988 Warsaw Report noted, *supra* note 4, at 155, the Special Rapporteur for the Sub-Commission included Malaysia on his 1987 list. *See* U.N. Doc. E/CN.4/Sub.2/1987/19 Annex I, at 18.

counted as emergencies with the key criterion being a "quantum of repression" that would have to be calculated on a case-by-case basis.[57]

## Type 5: The "Institutionalized" Emergency

This applies to a narrowly defined set of circumstances in which a government terminates a formal emergency after having incorporated many control measures into its ordinary law. In many such cases, the government is responding to international criticism for having long maintained a formal emergency in the absence of any genuine crisis.[58] Where real sources of stress remain, however, a government may find such a strategy unworkable. For example, South Africa in 1986 began incorporating portions of its emergency provisions into ordinary legislation in order to deflect virulent international criticism of its emergency, but later decided to extend the emergency.[59] As Nicholas Haysom notes, the attraction of the emergency regulations over ordinary law lay in how they eliminated forms of supervision either by the courts or by the media over the security forces,[60] advantages that could not be gained in ordinary law within the South African legal system.[61]

But in other cases where the government has effective control over the populace, the termination of a formal emergency and its replacement by permanent repressive legislation may be an attractive option that potentially decreases the visibility of the human rights problem. Such a transition presents a painful dilemma for human rights monitors. While no one could logically criticize the lifting of a formal emergency that had no proper basis (because no actual threat to the life of the nation existed), celebration would not be in order where there had been no actual improvement in the human rights situation. Such situations would not be included under any program for emergency-specific monitoring because there would exist neither a "bad" formal emergency nor *de facto* emergency conditions. The only category that might encompass such cases would be the "actual or potential" emergency (Type 4 in the ILA typology), in which ordinary security laws were being widely applied in a manner that created an unusual human

57. 1988 Warsaw Report, *supra* note 4, at 155–56.

58. For example, in 1987 long-prolonged formal emergencies were terminated in Paraguay and Taiwan. 1988 Warsaw Report, *supra* note 4, at 156.

59. *Id.* at 157.

60. N. Haysom, *States of Emergency in a Post-Apartheid South Africa*, 21 Col. Hum. Rts. L. Rev. 139, 147 (1989).

61. Haysom adds, "The State of Emergency regulations can be understood only as an attempt to confer upon the police the capacity to operate in a grey area between an 'extended' legality and wanton illegality, to impose order without law." *Id.* at 148.

rights crisis. Again, the difficult task of measuring a threshold "quantum of repression" would be necessary in assessing borderline cases under this category.

## Type 6: "Ordinary" Repression

Within the ILA typology, this category describes situations that should definitely *not* be included in any emergency-specific program of monitoring, but not because of the absence of serious human rights abuse. Rather, these situations fall outside the concept of state of emergency because no benchmark of normalcy remains, and the severe restrictions on human rights cannot be seen as temporary in any way. One example commonly given is that of the Democratic People's Republic of Korea (North Korea).[62] The existence of this category underlines the fact that emergency-specific monitoring has the drawback of not necessarily correlating with the most extreme forms of human rights abuse. Emergency-specific monitoring is thus "inefficient" from a human rights perspective in including rather mild formal emergencies while excluding some situations involving massive restrictions on fundamental rights, perhaps even non-derogable rights, such as the prohibition on torture or the freedom of conscience and belief.

The ILA typology is complex and multidimensional, stressing the difficulty of the task of defining a coherent single concept of "states of emergency" that could be readily and consistently identified by human rights monitors. Many ambiguous borderline situations exist at the various outer reaches of the concept, especially within the several categories of *de facto* emergencies. The delicacy of the definitional task is underlined by the reluctance of the Sub-Commission's Special Rapporteur to move beyond a purely formal list of emergencies.[63] Yet, in

---

62. 1988 Warsaw Report, *supra* note 4, at 200 n.140. The Human Rights Committee reviewed the "general and brief" initial report by the DPRK government under the ICCPR in 1984, but this review disclosed little about emergency provisions or the actual enjoyment of human rights in North Korea. *Report of the Human Rights Committee*, 39 U.N. GAOR Supp. (No. 40), U.N. Doc. A/39/40, at paras. 364–398 (1984). The second periodic report, due in 1987, is overdue. *Report of the Human Rights Committee*, 46 U.N. GAOR Supp. (No. 40), U.N. Doc. A/46/40 Annex IV (1991). The U.S. State Department's entries on North Korea are highly critical but acknowledge the paucity of information available because of the closed nature of the society. COUNTRY REPORTS FOR 1990, *supra* note 10, at 921.

63. In his 1989 report, the Special Rapporteur urged states to avoid *de facto* emergencies, which he defined as situations "in which emergency measures are taken without an official proclamation or in which, after a state of emergency has been officially repealed, exceptional measures are nevertheless maintained." U.N. Doc. E/CN.4/Sub.2/1989/30/Add.2/Rev.1, at para. 4 (1989). He further noted that "*De facto* states of emergency . . .

the ILA Committee's view, inclusion of *de facto* emergencies is absolutely vital to any effective and realistic program of monitoring human rights abuse during states of emergency. Complexity and difficult line-drawing thus will be inherent in the process. But a moderately restrictive definition will also be crucial for keeping a focus upon states of emergency, and not simply human rights abuse *per se*.

## C. The Questiaux Report

Nicole Questiaux undertook her study at the behest of the United Nations Sub-Commission on Prevention of Discrimination and Protection of Minorities, which had a long-standing interest in administrative detention[64] that was transmuted into a more general concern for risks to human rights during states of emergency. After excluding crises of underdevelopment,[65] natural disaster,[66] and war[67] from the scope of her concerns, Questiaux offered a profile of patterns of national legislation concerning emergency powers, postulating a "reference model" with a high degree of formality.[68] In contrast to this reference model, Questiaux describes various "deviations"[69] that present an interesting contrast to the ILA typology described above.

Questiaux identified five deviations from her reference model: (1)

---

have an extremely adverse effect, not only on the country's internal legal order but also in respect of the most fundamental rights." *Id*. In his fourth annual report, the Special Rapporteur included Iraq, Liberia and Somalia on the basis of press reports, and notes that a *de facto* emergency was reported to exist in an area of Mauritania. U.N. Doc. E/CN.4/Sub.2/1991/28, at 11 (1991).

64. The Sub-Commission expressed concern over practices of administrative detention in the course of its annual review of detention in Res. 7(XXVII) of 20 August 1974, U.N. Doc. E/CN.4/1160, E/CN.4/Sub.2/354 at 52 (1974), and Res. 4(XXVIII) of 10 September 1975, U.N. Doc. E/CN.4//1180, E/CN.4/Sub.2/364 at 59 (1975). The Sub-Commission decided that the situation of persons detained during public emergencies should be studied, in Res. 3A(XXIX) of 31 August 1976, U.N. Doc. E/CN.4/1218, E/CN.4/Sub.2/378, at 46 (1976). In 1977, the Sub-Commission was convinced of the connection between states of emergency and the status of human rights, Res. 10(XXX) of 31 August 1977, U.N. Doc. E/CN.4/1261, E/CN.4/Sub.2/399, at 48 (1977), and Mme. Questiaux began her research into the subject.

65. Questiaux Report, *supra* note 5, at para. 26.

66. *Id*. at para. 27.

67. *Id*. at para. 30.

68. *Id*. at paras. 73–95. The "reference model" has aspects including formal proclamation, legal definition of permissible grounds for exercise of emergency powers, time limits, specification either of non-derogable rights or rights explicitly subject to suspension, measures of control, and formal alterations in the scope of powers of various organs of government.

69. *Id*. at paras. 96–145.

the formal emergency not notified to treaty implementation bodies; (2) the *de facto* emergency, during which rights are suspended without proclamation or notification, or suspension of rights is continued after termination of a formal emergency; (3) the permanent emergency arising out of continual and decreasingly valid formal extensions of the emergency; (4) the complex emergency involving overlapping and confusing legal regimes through partial suspension of constitutional norms and issuance of a large volume of far-reaching decrees; and (5) the institutionalized emergency under which an authoritarian government prolongs an extended transitional emergency regime with the purported, but questionable, aim of returning to democracy and the full reinstitution of constitutional guarantees.

While Questiaux offers apt examples of these categories (*e.g.*, Paraguay as a "permanent" emergency,[70] Turkey and Brazil as "complex" emergencies,[71] Chile and Uruguay as "institutionalized" emergencies[72]), her typology is not comprehensive. In particular, her discussion of *de facto* emergencies is quite cursory and compressed, which may offer some insight into the reasons why the Sub-Commission has failed to come to grips with that concept in a sufficiently serious way.

Moreover, while Questiaux attempted to look beyond her own civil law tradition (bemoaning the lack of useful comparative studies to assist in her task),[73] her typology emphasizes emergencies with a high degree of formality. She does little more than note the proliferation of permanent national security laws as a means of repression as potentially effective as one of her "deviations" from the reference model.[74] She fails to recognize that in a common law system a perceived crisis might be efficiently dealt with either through increased application of prior-enacted permanent national security legislation, or through the rapid passage of new security legislation by a compliant legislature, all without any formal declaration of an emergency, the suspension of constitutional provisions, or formal alteration in the separation of powers.[75] Thus, Questiaux's typology seems inadequate for defin-

70. *Id.* at para. 114.
71. *Id.* at paras. 119–128.
72. *Id.* at paras. 132–145.
73. *Id.* at para. 12. She recommends that the Human Rights Centre of the UN Secretariat assist the Human Rights Committee in its review of state reports under the Covenant on Civil and Political Rights by compiling a file of national laws on emergency powers.
74. *Id.* at paras. 12, 162.
75. Rossiter has described the emergence of "constitutional dictatorships" in the United Kingdom and the United States during the nineteenth and early twentieth centuries. Questiaux's flawed typology, and the analysis's possible ramifications on non-

ing the range of emergency situations with which human rights bodies should be concerned in devising emergency-specific monitoring programs.

## D. Rossiter's Comparative Historical Study

Clinton Rossiter's lively and provocative 1948 study of "constitutional dictatorship,"[76] though limited to several major Western powers at an earlier point in their histories, nevertheless offers useful insights into types of emergency regimes and the potential effects of each model on the enjoyment of human rights and the preservation of basic democratic values. Rossiter's study is especially valuable for its insights into the evolution of emergency powers in the common law countries of the United Kingdom and the United States, which defy Questiaux's reference model. And his contrast of two civil law systems, Weimar Germany and France, sheds important light upon the variations that can exist in, and the relative merits of, more formal systems for declaring emergencies. Such historical studies provide much food for thought, particularly for human rights bodies offering expert advice in the drafting of new national constitutions or devising model standards for such instruments.[77]

Rossiter notes that the problem of elaborating systems of crisis government arises only within states that have previously achieved some level of democracy and retain at least a symbolic, if not real, attachment to its preservation.[78] In Weimar Germany and France, he offers exam-

---

treaty-based programs of special monitoring of emergencies by the Sub-Commission, was brought to the attention of the Sub-Commission in a submission by Professor Tom Hadden of Queen's University, Belfast, in May 1988. Professor Hadden offered an initial framework for analyzing non-declared emergencies, by focusing on three important factors including actual or potential level of disorder, nature of the extraordinary powers, and the extent to which the powers are actually applied. Situations would extend along a continuum, depending upon the presence of each of these factors. Roughly three categories were created including (1) low-level emergencies, in which special powers are introduced to deal with a relatively isolated terrorist or external threat; (2) temporary, generalized emergencies, in which sets of emergency powers are introduced to deal with extensive disorders such as communal conflict; and (3) permanent or preventive emergencies, in which such temporary measures are made permanent to prevent the growth of organized opposition.

76. *See supra* note 3.

77. *See* Chapter III *infra.*

78. As he notes in the case of France: "The history of the state of siege begins with the French Revolution. No civil institution of crisis government existed under the *ancien regime*. It is unnecessary to suspend rights that do not exist or augment powers that are already absolute." ROSSITER, *supra* note 3, at 80. The same observation might be made

ples of two civil law states that created specific mechanisms in their constitutions for formal imposition of emergency powers.[79]

Article 48 of the Weimar Constitution provides an object lesson in loosely written emergency powers, often applied with reactionary aims and without real check from any democratic entity, that became the tool for the destruction of democracy rather than its preservation. On its surface, Article 48 fits Questiaux's reference model:[80] the grounds are specified (though vaguely); a fairly short list of fundamental rights that can be suspended is explicitly enumerated; the President declaring the emergency must immediately inform the legislature, which can demand the revocation of the emergency measures; and national law must set out the details.

But reality turned out to be far different. The Constitution did not prohibit the President from dissolving the Reichstag, the only potential check upon abuse of emergency powers.[81] Judges adopted a highly deferential posture toward the exercise of emergency powers,[82] noting the absence of any specific provision for judicial review. Jurists agreed that essentially all of the Constitution's provisions were suspendible, despite the terms of Article 48;[83] and emergency powers were used extensively in the regulation of the economy over an extended period of time. Rossiter notes that the context of Weimar Germany—an electorate either confused or dedicated to the destruction of the constitutional order, a weak legislature and an absence of long-standing democratic values in the society—essentially invited abuse of Article 48.[84]

The French experience emerges as a happier one in Rossiter's view. In the French state of siege,[85] Rossiter finds the "peak of institutional

---

about modern repressive states that fall into the "ordinary repression" (Type 6) category in the ILA typology.

79. Rossiter also describes the system within the ancient Roman republic, but this is of less interest. *Id.* at 15–29.

80. *See* Questiaux Report, *supra* note 5, at paras. 73–95.

81. ROSSITER, *supra* note 3, at 72. Where the Reichstag had exercised its power under Article 48 to disapprove of emergency measures, nothing prevented the President from dissolving the Reichstag, reissuing the decrees, and then delaying for a substantial period the election of a new Reichstag.

82. *Id.* at 70–71.

83. *Id.* at 68–69. Rossiter notes that German legal theorists had long been interested in an elastic law of necessity. J. KOHLER, NOT KENNT KEIN GEBOT (1915); W. JELLINEK, GESETZ UND VERORDNUNG (1887).

84. ROSSITER, *supra* note 3, at 71.

85. The origins of the term "state of siege" refer to the essentially unlimited powers conferred upon a general in command of a besieged fortress. The military state of siege was gradually extended to a political state of siege in which similar powers could be

and legal perfection" for crisis government.[86] The strong emphasis upon formal legality and reliance upon the legislature (rather than the judiciary) to curb abuse have strongly influenced the structure of emergency powers in other nations.[87] The implementing laws for the state of siege established what has become a familiar pattern: military takeover of ordinary police powers, assumption of jurisdiction by military courts over ordinary crimes by civilians, and increased issuance of regulations by executive authority on topics formerly subject to legislation.[88]

France's rejection of the model praised by Rossiter in Article 16 of its 1958 Constitution casts considerable doubt on the validity of his assessment.[89] The elimination of a legislative power of control over the imposition of the emergency in particular marks a departure from the "perfection" Rossiter had perceived.[90] Other scholars suggest that the

---

exercised over urban populations during both foreign war and internal insurrection. *Id.* at 80–81.

The state of siege described by Rossiter was governed by the laws of 9 August 1849, and 4 April 1878, which placed responsibility for declaring the state of siege on the legislature (except provisionally during foreign war when the legislature was adjourned). *Id.* at 81–83. The 1958 Constitution effected important changes, especially by shifting authority for the imposition of the state of siege to the President of the Republic in consultation with the presidents of the two houses of the legislature, the Premier, and the Constitutional Council. *See* Constitution, art. 16, 4 October 1958. Article 16, however, retains the prohibition on the dissolution of the legislature by the President during a state of siege.

86. *Id.* at 79. Subrata Roy Chowdhury found the French model to have been incorporated into the constitutions of Dahomey (art. 27 of the Constitution of 5 January 1964), Algeria (art. 59 of the Constitution), Morocco (art. 35 of the Constitution) and Tunisia (art. 32 of the Constitution). *See supra* note 7, at 57.

87. Questiaux Report, *supra* note 5, at para. 75. Both Questiaux and Rossiter note that the courts of France have offered only occasional and limited relief to victims of abuse of emergency powers, through review of executive actions for *exces de pouvoir.* Typically, such acts occur only after the state of siege has been lifted. *Id.;* ROSSITER, *supra* note 3, at 97. Questiaux notes that control by the legislature has also become only indirect under the 1958 Constitution, through the provision for trial of the President by the High Court of Justice (composed of members of the legislature) for crimes against the Constitution, should he exceed his very broadly defined powers. Questiaux Report, *supra* note 5, at para. 75.

88. ROSSITER, *supra* note 3, at 86–87. Rossiter notes that these powers are permissive rather than mandatory, and the scope of their exercise varied geographically and temporally during the two wartime crises of the early twentieth century. *Id.* at 86–88, 94–125.

89. For a comprehensive examination of the origins of Article 16 and its application during the Algerian crisis, *see* MICHÈLE VOISSET, L'ARTICLE 16 DE LA CONSTITUTION DU 4 OCTOBRE 1958 (1969).

90. *Id.* at 313–18 (noting departure of Article 16 in this respect from earlier French

French law on the state of siege did not provide an effective check upon executive power,[91] and that legislative control was illusory.[92]

While the exercise of emergency powers achieved increasing formality in the United Kingdom and the United States during the twentieth century, their starting points were far different, and convergence with the civil law model has not yet occurred. In the case of the United Kingdom, great informality and underregulation characterized emergency powers until the First World War.[93] Crises were met by parliamentary action or "independent executive action based on the royal prerogative or the common law," usually taking the form of martial law.[94] The effects of martial law upon enjoyment of liberties were remarkably similar to those resulting from application of the French implementing legislation for the state of siege.[95] The primary curb on abuse of power lay in the courts, but relief could be and often was eliminated through passage of indemnity laws.[96]

Comprehensive emergency legislation was not adopted in the United Kingdom until the Defence of the Realm Act of 8 August 1914,[97] which contained a legislative declaration of martial law, as well as a broad delegation of regulatory authority to the executive. This Act set the model for modern British emergency powers, which "brought the entire scope of English life and liberty under the control of the government, exalted the Cabinet, and deflated Parliament."[98] While Parliament continued to sit, it became subservient to the Cabinet, either passing legislation essentially without change or debate or granting broad authorization for regulations.[99] While executive acts could be challenged in the courts as *ultra vires*, few cases succeeded and then

---

practice). *See also, id.* at 87–118, 231–55, 339–49 (extensive discussion of lack of effective legislative control over emergencies implemented under Article 16). Voisset also finds the substitute, consultation with the Conseil Constitutionnel, to be in reality not an effective check on the President. *Id.* at 225–30.

91. Paul Leroy, L'organisation constitutionnelle et les crises 74–78 (1966) (during the First World War the executive exceeded the powers established in the 1878 law on the state of siege in regulating the economy and the movement of persons).

92. *Id.* at 61, 81, 88–91, 107, 113.

93. Rossiter, *supra* note 3, at 135–39.

94. *Id.* at 136.

95. *See, e.g., id.* at 139, 145–49 (noting the trial of civilians by court martial or summary trials).

96. *Id.* at 138, 142–45.

97. *Id.* at 153; Defence of the Realm Act, 1914, 4 & 5 Geo. 5, ch. 29.

98. Rossiter, *supra* note 3, at 154.

99. *Id.* at 154–72. Rossiter notes: "Whenever downtrodden back-benchers raised serious objections to a particular bill or clause, it was dropped to reappear a few days later in the form of a DORA [Defence of the Realm Act] regulation." *Id.* at 163.

generally only after the crisis had ended.[100] This pattern continued through the Emergency Powers Act of 1920[101] and the legislation and regulations issued during the Second World War.[102]

Despite its written constitution, the United States inherited the British negligence of precise definition of emergency power. Two somewhat contradictory attitudes appear to underlie this initial approach—that the Constitution was adequate to cope with all conceivable emergencies,[103] or that the executive might act illegally and extra-constitutionally during an emergency, with the hope of subsequent indemnity.[104] During the Civil War of the mid-nineteenth century, power was exercised by the President, sometimes without obvious basis in his delegated constitutional powers,[105] and sometimes on the basis of specific ordinary legislation passed by Congress.[106]

During the twentieth century, however, the American model of

100. *Id.* at 158.

101. This statute was passed to deal with an economic crisis involving post-war labor unrest. *Id.* at 172; Emergency Powers Act, 1920, 10 & 11 Geo. 5, ch. 48.

102. ROSSITER, *supra* note 3, at 196–210. Of particular interest are the regulations on administrative detention, which will be discussed in a later chapter. *See* Chapter III *infra.*

103. *See* ROSSITER, *supra* note 3, at 212 (citing the FEDERALIST and Supreme Court decisions in *Ex parte* Milligan, 71 U.S. (4 Wall.) 2, 120–21 (1867), and Home Bldg. & Loan Ass'n v. Blaisdell, 290 U.S. 398, 425 (1934)).

104. Jules Lobel describes eighteenth-century American attitudes as follows: "The Constitution did not grant the executive any general, inherent, constitutional emergency authority. Rather, eighteenth century leaders and philosophers believed that the executive should be required knowingly to act illegally or unconstitutionally when utilizing emergency power. For these thinkers, emergency power was an unconstitutional exercise of power by the executive. Officials risked censure and even impeachment for engaging in activities justified solely by the perception of an emergency context. Courts could impose personal liability on those executive officials who undertook unconstitutional actions, even when such officials acted pursuant to good faith motivations to defuse a crisis. Subsequent to a court's declaration of the unlawfulness of an exercise of emergency power, however, Congress could decide to indemnify the official if it believed the official's actions really were justified by extreme necessity. This system allowed the executive to act without creating inherent emergency power under the Constitution. Furthermore, the identification of crisis activity as unlawful and subject to review reinforced the primary assumption that emergencies were not the norm." J. Lobel, *Emergency Power and the Decline of Liberalism*, 98 YALE L.J. 1385, 1390 (1989).

105. For example, President Lincoln ordered a blockade of Southern ports (later held by the Supreme Court to be an action within his powers as Commander-in-Chief in the Prize Cases, 67 U.S. (2 Black) 635, 670 (1862)), issued the Emancipation Proclamation in 1862 without prior Congressional approval (later "indemnified" by the ratification of the Thirteenth Amendment in 1865), and issued the "Lieber Code" for the armies in the field (though Congress has power under Article 1, Section 8, Clause 14 of the Constitution to make rules for the armed forces). ROSSITER, *supra* note 3, at 226–35.

106. One important example is the Act of 3 March 1863, suspending the writ of habeas corpus in areas under martial law. This Act followed upon Lincoln's controversial

emergency powers began to evolve in a manner similar to that occurring in the United Kingdom: the passage of broadly worded emergency laws that delegated expansive powers to the executive to issue regulations and undertake unusual measures to cope with the crisis. Congress remained in session, but despite the dramatic formal separation of powers between Congress and the President, a high degree of legislative acquiescence resulted in an actual concentration of power in the President. All this occurred without any explicit change in the normal constitutional structure or any formal suspension of liberties. The ordinary courts served as the theoretical check upon abuse of emergency powers, but, as in the British instance, their protections were often illusory or belated.[107]

Though dated and drawn from a narrow range of cultures, Rossiter's study illuminates important differences in the formalities of emergency powers, differences that are replicated in a wide range of contemporary states influenced by these Western societies in the creation of their own emergency regimes. Any accurate typology of states of emergency must be sufficient to embrace not only the highly formal French state of siege, but also the looser and more elusive approaches of states sharing a common law tradition.

---

proclamation of 24 September 1862, suspending the writ on his own inherent authority. *Id.* at 235–36.

107. The classic example of judicial failure to operate as a check upon abuse of emergency powers is the denial of relief to American citizens of Japanese ancestry held in internment camps upon military orders during the Second World War. *Id.* at 252–56, 280–85.

# Chapter II
# Effects of Emergencies on Human Rights

## A. Introduction

Generalizations are dangerous in this area, as in so many others, but certain effects upon the enjoyment of human rights tend to be associated with states of emergency. These effects can be grouped into three categories: changes in the allocation of powers within the government; more frequent invasion of absolute rights; and greater restrictions upon other fundamental rights. Each of these areas will be briefly explored in order to provide a context for understanding why human rights monitors have taken or should take a particular interest in states of emergency. The final portion of this chapter will be devoted to an extended analysis of the uses of administrative detention and its close association with emergencies.

## B. Changes in the Allocation of Powers

Under the classic model of the state of siege, power is concentrated in the hands of the executive, who proceeds to govern by the issuance of decrees pertaining to numerous aspects of civil and economic life, thereby displacing the legislature from its normal role. In some instances, the legislature may be dissolved by executive order.[1] In com-

---

1. *E.g., Pakistan Emergency Declared; Bhutto Out,* L.A. TIMES, Aug. 6, 1990, at P1, col. 4 (noting that the state of emergency declared by the President of Pakistan on 6 August 1990 dissolved the Parliament and removed Prime Minister Benazir Bhutto from power); INTER-AM. C.H.R., REPORT ON THE STATUS OF HUMAN RIGHTS IN CHILE, OEA/Ser.L./V/II.34, doc. 21 (1974) (reporting upon the declaration of a state of siege following the coup d'etat in Chile in 1973, during which the junta assumed "constituent, legislative and executive powers," even though Art. 72 No. 17 of the Political Constitution granted the power to declare a state of siege to the Congress, or if not in session, to

mon law countries, such as the United Kingdom and the United States, the legislature may remain in session, and even go through the processes of normal elections during the crisis, but the effects of the emergency upon the actual enjoyment of power may be profound. The crisis mentality may result in almost supine acquiescence in legislative proposals initiated by the executive, or the parliament may cede its legislative powers in a wholesale manner by authorizing administrative officials to issue regulations to govern national life in the place of ordinary legislation.[2]

On the other hand, the legislature may function as an effective check on abuse of emergency powers or the unreasonable extension of an emergency, especially where public criticism remains possible. For example, a study by the International Commission of Jurists concluded that continuing parliamentary oversight of the emergency in Northern Ireland, in combination with scrutiny by the press and human rights organizations, led to amelioration of emergency measures.[3] The Russian Parliament overrode President Boris Yeltsin's imposition of emergency rule in the Chechen-Ingush region, urging political negotiations.[4] In devising her "reference model" for the Sub-Commission, Nicole Questiaux highlighted systems, such as that in Costa Rica, in which proclamation of an emergency is kept within the control of the legislature and extensions are strictly limited.[5] Among the deviations

---

the President). The Amir of Kuwait dissolved the National Assembly in 1986, relying upon his powers to suspend provisions of the constitution, and subsequently ruled by decree. COUNTRY REPORTS ON HUMAN RIGHTS PRACTICES FOR 1989, U.S. DEP'T OF STATE REPORT SUBMITTED TO THE SENATE COMM. ON FOREIGN RELATIONS AND THE HOUSE COMM. ON FOREIGN AFFAIRS, 101ST CONG., 2D SESS., 1455 (Joint Comm. Print 1990) [hereinafter COUNTRY REPORTS FOR 1989]. On 23 February 1991, the Supreme Commander of the armed forces of Thailand abolished the constitution and Parliament, imposed martial law, promulgated an interim constitution, and appointed an interim prime minister. *Thai Military Overthrows Government,* N.Y. TIMES, Feb. 24, 1991, § I, pt. 1., at 14, col. 1. Martial law was lifted on 3 May 1991. *Thailand Ends Martial Law,* WALL ST. J., May 3, 1991, at A8, col. 4.

2. *See generally* Chapter I, *supra.*

3. "In Northern Ireland, the combined effect of parliamentary debate and questioning of ministers, freedom of the press and the activity of non-governmental organisations and interest groups has encouraged continuing review of government policies and their effects. Abuses have been publicly debated and safeguards designed to prevent their recurrence have been introduced." INTERNATIONAL COMMISSION OF JURISTS, STATES OF EMERGENCY: THEIR IMPACT ON HUMAN RIGHTS 437 (1983) [hereinafter STATES OF EMERGENCY].

4. C. Bohlen, *Legislators Block Yeltsin Rule of Breakaway Area,* N.Y. TIMES, Nov. 12, 1991, at A12, col. 4.

5. N. Questiaux, *Study of the Implications for Human Rights of Recent Developments Concerning Situations Known as States of Siege or Emergency,* U.N. Doc. E/CN.4/Sub.2/1982/15, at para. 91 (1982) [hereinafter Questiaux Report].

from this model, she noted the emergence of "para-legislative" institutions such as the Council of State in Chile and the Commission of
Legislative Assistance in Argentina, which serve in a consultative role
to the decree-issuing executive.[6]

The effects of states of emergency upon the judiciary also vary
considerably. One of the central elements in the classic French state of
siege was the exposure of the civilian population to trial in military
courts.[7] This model was assiduously followed by the military rulers of
Uruguay following the declaration of the "state of internal war" in
1972, with unusual formality.[8] The 1972 Law of National Security
created certain crimes against the state and declared them military
offenses, even if committed by civilians.[9] In 1975, the Council of State
issued a decree that extended military jurisdiction retroactively for acts
committed at any date, even acts committed prior to the passage of the
1972 Law of National Security that defined the offenses.[10] These prosecutions tended to involve serious delays; harsh sentences; evidence
obtained under torture; grossly unfair procedures, including trial in
secret; and judges, prosecutors, and defense counsel who were not
only all military personnel but untrained as lawyers.[11] Independent
civilian defense counsel, though theoretically permitted to participate
in the trials, were impaired both by lack of access to clients and by
intimidation that resulted in many being imprisoned themselves or
forced into exile.[12]

The Uruguayan model, though "classic," is not exclusive. Exposure
of civilians to trial by court-martial is to be expected under regimes of
martial law.[13] But in other types of emergencies, perceived enemies

6. *Id.* at para. 151.

7. *See* Chapter I at note 88.

8. International League for Human Rights, Uruguay's Human Rights Record
11–14 (1982) [hereinafter Uruguay's Human Rights Record].

9. *Id.* at 12 (noting the Law of National Security of 10 July 1972).

10. *Id.* (noting Law 14.493 of 29 December 1975).

11. *Id.* at 12–14. The quality of justice rendered by Uruguay's military courts was
harshly criticized, *inter alia*, by the Inter-American Commission on Human Rights in two
reports in 1978 and 1980 and in a series of decisions by the Human Rights Committee
under the Optional Protocol to the Covenant on Civil and Political Rights. *Id.* at 12–13.
*See, e.g.*, Moriana Hernandez Valentini de Bazzano v. Uruguay, Comm. No. 5/1977,
Views of the Human Rights Committee of August 15, 1979, Selected Decisions under
the Optional Protocol, U.N. Doc. CCPR/C/OP/1, at 40–43 (1985) [hereinafter Selected Decisions] (reprinting the first decision by the Human Rights Committee on the
merits of an application under the Optional Protocol).

12. Uruguay's Human Rights Record, *supra* note 8, at 14.

13. *E.g.*, Amnesty International, Report 1988, at 174 (1989). In Pakistan prior to
the lifting of martial law in 1985, hundreds of persons were convicted by military courts.
Civilian courts were forbidden to examine these verdicts under amendments made to the

might be tried before other types of special courts not of a military character. For example, in Kuwait suspected subversives were given *in camera* trials in the State Security Court, which is convened on an *ad hoc* basis and composed of judges who normally serve on other courts.[14] A similar State Security Court was established in Zaire in 1972.[15] Upon the recommendation of the Diplock Commission, the United Kingdom abolished trial by jury for certain scheduled offenses and modified the common law rules on the admissibility of confessions in Northern Ireland,[16] but otherwise these offenses were tried in the ordinary criminal courts. The victorious Sandinista regime in Nicaragua established the Popular Anti-Somocista Tribunals to try persons associated with the former government. The Tribunals consisted of three-person panels (only one of whom need have legal training) that were appointed by the junta and operated independently of the regular judiciary.[17]

---

Constitution prior to the lifting of martial law. In 1988, however, the Supreme Court permitted certain categories of martial law prisoners to challenge their convictions in civilian courts. In addition, martial law prisoners may seek presidential review. 1989 COUNTRY REPORTS, *supra* note 1, at 1529.

Trials before martial law courts in Kuwait after the withdrawal of the Iraqi invaders were criticized for inadequate procedural protections. Although three of the five judges were civilians and the trials took place in public, the defendants were not permitted to consult with their appointed lawyers, no evidence was presented at trial other than that elicited from the defendants by the judges, the defendants were neither permitted to present defense witnesses nor to cross-examine any persons who may have provided information to the prosecution, and convictions appeared to be based largely upon defendants' confessions, which were alleged to have been coerced under torture. E.A. Gargan, *After the War; At Kuwait Trials, T-Shirt Gets Man 15 Years,* N.Y. TIMES, May 20, 1991, at A1, col. 2.

14. AMNESTY INTERNATIONAL REPORT 1988, *supra* note 13, at 243–44 (1989); COUNTRY REPORTS FOR 1989, *supra* note 1, at 1457. No appeal is permitted from verdicts by the State Security Court. *Id.*

15. STATES OF EMERGENCY, *supra* note 3, at 382–83. No appeals are allowed from its judgments.

16. *Id.* at 232–35. The Diplock Report is formally cited as Cmnd. 5185, Report of the Commission to consider legal procedures to deal with terrorist activities in Northern Ireland, H.M.S.O., 1972. The "Diplock Courts" were constituted in 1973, and the new rules on admissibility of confessions were incorporated in section 8(2) of the Northern Ireland Emergency Powers Act 1978. The ICJ notes that the result was "an increase in the conviction rate in contested cases in which the only evidence consists of a confession allegedly obtained under duress. Increasingly, the courts have convicted on the basis of alleged verbal confessions which the accused denies ever having made." *Id.* at 435. Under the new rules on admission of confessions, judges were to continue to exclude confessions obtained under torture or inhuman or degrading treatment. *See* D.S. Greer, *Admissibility of Confessions and the Common Law in Times of Emergency,* 24 N. IR. L.Q. 199 (1973).

17. R. Steinberg, *Judicial Independence in States of Emergency: Lessons from Nicaragua's Popular Anti-Somocista Tribunals,* 18 COL. HUM. RTS. L. REV. 359, 370–73 (1987). Stein-

Even where ordinary civilian courts retain formal jurisdiction, the independence of the judiciary is often undermined during emergencies by the purging of judges or by the judiciary's own refusal to take jurisdiction over cases involving application of emergency measures. Following the 1967 coup in Greece, the military regime suspended life tenure for judges for a period of three days and then dismissed approximately thirty judges and prosecutors, including the President of the Supreme Court.[18] An even more thoroughgoing purge took place in Argentina after the 1976 coup, involving the removal of the members of the Supreme Court, the Attorney General, district attorneys and members of the superior provincial courts, and a required loyalty oath to the junta by their replacements.[19] A central aspect of the abrogation of constitutional democracy by the elected President of Peru in April 1992 was the dismissal of judges, including members of the Supreme Court, whom he accused of corruption and ineffectiveness in fighting the drug trade and terrorists.[20] When martial law was declared in Bangladesh in 1982, a decree provided that any high court judge could be removed by the Chief Martial Law Administrator "without assigning any reason."[21] Sometimes the same control can be ob-

---

berg notes that the Tribunals have been strongly criticized by human rights groups and the Inter-American Commission on Human Rights for their lack of independence from the executive and for their denial of fair process. *Id.* at 360–61, 371. The Nicaraguan Supreme Court had objected to the creation of the Tribunals on grounds that the ordinary courts could handle the large number of cases against the Somocistas if given adequate resources. However, the Supreme Court later acquiesced in the junta's decision. *Id.* at 370–71.

18. S.R. CHOWDHURY, RULE OF LAW IN A STATE OF EMERGENCY 131–32 (1989). Although the Supreme Administrative Court declared these dismissals illegal, the junta nullified that judgment and placed the president of that court under house arrest, forcing his resignation. The judge, Michael Stasinopoulos, was later elected President of the Greek Republic upon its return to democracy in 1975. *Id.*

19. Article 96 of the Constitution guaranteed the judges of the Supreme Court and the lower courts tenure during good behavior. INTER-AM. C.H.R., REPORT ON THE SITUATION OF HUMAN RIGHTS IN ARGENTINA, OEA/Ser.L./V/II.49, doc. 19, corr. 1, at 220–21 (1980) [hereinafter IACHR ARGENTINA REPORT]; I. GUEST, BEHIND THE DISAPPEARANCES: ARGENTINA'S DIRTY WAR AGAINST HUMAN RIGHTS AND THE UNITED NATIONS 26 (1990).

20. N.C. Nash, *Peru Chief Orders New Mass Arrests*, N.Y. TIMES, Apr. 8, 1992, at A12, col. 1; M. Powers, *Ousted Peru Congressmen Vote to Impeach President Fujimori*, SEATTLE TIMES, Apr. 10, 1992, at A5, col. 2 (thirteen of twenty-three Supreme Court justices were dismissed).

21. F. Nariman, *The Judiciary under Martial Law Regimes*, 14 C.I.J.L. BULLETIN 41, 44 (1984) (citing paragraph 10(4) of the Proclamation First Amendment Order of 11 April 1982, and noting that three judges of the Supreme Court of Bangladesh had been removed under this provision within the span of a few months).

tained through transfers of judges rendering opinions unpalatable to the authorities.[22]

Even where the civilian judiciary retains its tenure of office, key aspects of its jurisdiction over cases involving emergency matters may be formally removed or may simply lie unexercised. In a study of courts in eight common law countries, George Alexander concluded that "in the most serious cases courts have performed badly, will necessarily continue to perform badly and should ideally not be involved."[23] Their poor performance could be explained only in part by explicit removals of their jurisdiction, such as the suspension of *habeas corpus* in India during the 1975 emergency, which was sustained in a questionable judgment by the Supreme Court of India in 1976.[24] Instead, a tendency to defer to executive authority in the exercise of emergency powers appears to characterize courts in many different types of legal systems, democratic as well as repressive.[25] In Ghana, for example, the Supreme Court held in 1961 that *habeas corpus* was not available to challenge detentions under the Preventive Detention Act, 1958, because plenary discretion was vested in the President and because Article 13 of the Constitution, which required the President to respect certain fundamental rights, "does not represent a legal requirement which can be enforced by the courts."[26] While the courts of Argentina retained *habeas corpus* jurisdiction after the 1976 coup, they ordered release in only two cases out of the thousands that were filed on behalf of disappeared persons, frequently declining to exercise jurisdiction where the government responded by denying knowledge of the victim's detention.[27]

22. Chowdhury, *supra* note 18, at 136 (citing events in India).

23. G. Alexander, *The Illusory Protection of Human Rights by National Courts During Periods of Emergency*, 5 HUM. RTS. L.J. 1 (1984). The states examined were Great Britain, South Africa, Ireland, New Zealand, Canada, Australia, India, and the United States.

24. A.D.M. Jabalpur v. Shiv Kant Shukla, 1976 A.I.R. (S.C.) (known as the *Habeas Corpus Case*). Chowdhury notes that the Supreme Court later held that reasonably fair process was necessary and could be supervised through *habeas corpus*, citing the case of Gandhi v. Union of India. 1978 A.I.R. (S.C.) 597. *See supra* note 18, at 138–39. *See also* STATES OF EMERGENCY, *supra* note 3, at 187–88 (noting that the courts could not even inquire on *habeas corpus* whether a detention was *mala fides* or contrary to law and, accordingly, the Supreme Court "suffered severely from self-inflicted wounds").

25. *See* discussion *infra* Section E (noting cases on administrative detention).

26. Baffour Osei Akoto v. The Minister of Interior (re Akoto), Civil Appeal 42/61, *in* STATES OF EMERGENCY, *supra* note 3, at 106–7.

27. One of the two cases was that of prominent journalist Jacobo Timerman, who was ordered by the Supreme Court to be released from house arrest on 17 September 1979, after having been ordered released from detention in 1978. *See* J. TIMERMAN, PRISONER WITHOUT A NAME, CELL WITHOUT A NUMBER (1981). Upon his release from house arrest, Timerman was stripped of his citizenship and sent into forced exile. I. GUEST, *supra* note

The executive power itself may be transformed during the emergency. Questiaux observed a pattern by which the concept of separation of powers was replaced by the "hierarchization of powers," and, at the summit of executive power, civilian authority was subordinated to the military.[28]

## C. Violations of Non-Derogable Rights

Aside from these institutional metamorphoses, emergencies often entail deprivation of fundamental rights of the population. Again, no single pattern of human rights abuse will characterize every emergency, but often a high incidence of very grave abuse will accompany emergencies. Ironically, this appears to be particularly true of non-derogable rights, those that supposedly can never be suspended, even in time of public emergency threatening the life of the nation.[29] Although there is no general agreement on the details of a list of rights that are so fundamental as to never permit suspension,[30] consensus does exist that any such list would include the prohibition on the arbitrary deprivation of life and the prohibition on torture.

Yet, a close correlation has frequently been noted between such practices and states of emergency[31] in states as varied as Argentina, Turkey, Myanmar, South Africa, Bahrain, and China. Deaths may occur through the excessive use of force against demonstrators, by clandestine murder committed by security forces or death squads allied with the authorities,[32] or through summary execution without minimal

---

19, at 284. During the visit of the IACHR in September 1979, the President of the Supreme Court cited the pending Timerman case as "a new expression of its independence." IACHR ARGENTINA REPORT, *supra* note 19, at 221.

28. Questiaux Report, *supra* note 5, at para. 159.

29. This formulation for an emergency is taken from the derogation provisions of the Covenant on Civil and Political Rights and the European Convention on Human Rights.

30. *See* Chapter III *infra* (noting the discussion on efforts to set general standards for protection of human rights during states of emergency).

31. The Questiaux Report originated because of a concern by the Sub-Commission that its annual review of persons under detention revealed "a close correlation between the existence of states of emergency and serious and systematic violations of the rights of detainees, particularly rights which did not allow of any derogation, such as the right to life and the prohibition of torture." U.N. Doc. E/CN.4/Sub.2/1987/19/Rev.1, at para. 55 (1988).

Amnesty International released a study on the incidence of torture and arbitrary deprivation of life during states of emergency in various countries in July 1988, citing the examples of Egypt, Jordan, Pakistan, Peru, South Africa, Sri Lanka, Syria, and Turkey. AMNESTY INTERNATIONAL, AI INDEX: POL 30/02/88.

32. Clandestine murder as a tool of intimidation by emergency regimes can take

due process. Torture is frequently practiced by emergency regimes (as it is by many other governments)[33] and tends to be associated with other human rights abuses characteristic of emergencies, such as incommunicado detention, disappearances, administrative detention, and secret trials in which confessions form the primary evidence of guilt.

Such gross abuses often, but not invariably, receive priority attention by human rights monitors, and the subsequent parts of this study will explore in detail how the various bodies concerned with these grave violations have taken the emergency context into account in their work.[34] The association of emergencies with widespread deprivations of non-derogable rights has acted as the strongest factor in focusing international attention upon the potential link between emergencies and human rights.[35]

## D. Emergency Limitations on Other Fundamental Rights

There is nothing remarkable about the fact that substantial restrictions are placed on other human rights during states of emergency. Indeed, the whole point of recognizing a concept of public emergencies in international human rights law was to provide reasonable limits upon the anticipated restrictions of rights that emergencies would entail.[36]

---

several forms, such as through "disappearances," in which the victim's fate is concealed, and kidnappings and killings, after which the victim's body is dumped in a public place in order to intimidate others.

33. Amnesty International estimated that one-third of the world's governments were practicing torture at the time it published its report. AMNESTY INTERNATIONAL: TORTURE IN THE EIGHTIES (1984).

34. The concern of human rights monitors with other non-derogable rights in the context of emergencies (such as the prohibition on cruel, inhuman, and degrading treatment; or with freedom of thought, conscience and religion) will also be discussed in the ensuing chapters examining the work of specific monitoring bodies.

35. *See* Sub-Commission Res. 10(XXX) of August 31, 1977, *Report of the Sub-Commission on Protection of Discrimination and Protection of Minorities on its Thirteenth Session*, U.N. ESCOR, Hum. Rts. Comm., U.N. Doc. E/CN.4/1261, E/CN.4/Sub.2/399, at 48 (1977).

36. During the earliest drafting stages of the Covenant on Civil and Political Rights in 1947, for example, a representative of the United Kingdom on the Working Group on the Convention on Human Rights proposed a draft Article 4 in the following terms: "[U]nder the general principles of international law, in time of war States were not strictly bound by conventional obligations unless the conventions contained provisions to the contrary. In order to prevent States from arbitrarily derogating from their obligations in respect of human rights in time of war, the United Kingdom proposed the text of Article 4." U.N. Doc. E/CN.4/AC.3/SR.8, at 10 (1947).

These restrictions were expected to go further than those permitted under ordinary circumstances for purposes such as the maintenance of public order. Much of the work of treaty-based human rights monitors with respect to states of emergency has involved setting the contours for emergency derogations from such rights.

In a United Nations survey of governments the rights most often mentioned as having been the subject of derogations during emergencies were liberty and security of the person, liberty of movement, protection of privacy, freedom of expression and opinion, and the right of peaceful assembly.[37] Many monitors have noted that excessive invasions of these and other rights have occurred during many emergencies, often in association with deprivations of non-derogable rights, such as the right to life and the prohibition on torture. But, as the International Commission of Jurists observed:

Some writers have emphasized the effects of states of emergency on individual rights, particularly the right to be free from arbitrary deprivation of freedom and the right to a fair trial. This tends to create a somewhat false image of states of emergency, for one of their most fundamental characteristics is precisely the breadth of their impact on a society. They typically affect trade union rights, freedom of opinion, freedom of expression, freedom of association, the right of access to information and ideas, the right to an education, the right to participate in public affairs . . . not only individual rights but also collective rights and rights of peoples, such as the right to development and the right to self-determination.[38]

The scope of these effects[39] naturally results in a potential concern with states of emergency by all the monitoring bodies with an interest in any of this wide range of rights. These potentially extensive effects have also influenced the debate over the drafting of non-treaty-

37. L. Despouy, *First Annual Report and List of States which, since 1 January 1985, have Proclaimed, Extended or Terminated a State of Emergency*, U.N. Doc. E/CN.4/Sub.2/1987/19/Rev.1, at para. 54 (1988) [hereinafter Despouy Report].

38. STATES OF EMERGENCY, *supra* note 3, at 417 (footnote omitted).

39. The state of siege in Argentina, for example, helped the military regime pursue economic policies that temporarily benefited the middle classes but that ultimately, because of heavy reliance on foreign debt, created a severe economic crisis for the nation. *See* I. GUEST, *supra* note 19, at 27–30. As the representative of Argentina noted at the Human Rights Committee's review of Argentina's initial report in 1990, "The economic crisis in Argentina made it difficult to protect and promote economic, social and cultural rights. . . . [T]he full implementation of the Declaration on the Right to Development was still remote, since there were other, much more urgent needs to be handled. In their consideration of Argentina's compliance with the International Covenant on Civil and Political Rights, the experts should bear in mind the prevailing social and economic situation in the country." U.N. Doc. CCPR/C/SR.952, at para. 4 (1990) (remarks of Mrs. Regazzoli).

based substantive standards for government behavior during states of emergency.[40]

## E. Administrative Detention

Despite the cautionary note sounded by the International Commission of Jurists that states of emergency have a profound and troubling impact upon rights other than the liberty of the person,[41] the special connection between states of emergency and the practice of administrative detention merits extended discussion. It was in the course of its annual review of the human rights of persons subjected to detention or imprisonment that the Sub-Commission developed its specific interest in the human rights implications of states of emergency.[42] While the Sub-Commission's work on states of emergency has become delinked from the specific issue of administrative detention,[43] cogent reasons exist for devoting special attention to this aspect of government behavior during emergencies.

First, one of the most serious defects in existing international standards governing states of emergency is the absence of precise and agreed limits on the derogability of the right of personal liberty. Second, international norms are equally ambiguous on the question whether administrative detention is ever permissible in a non-emergency context. While the next chapter will be devoted to the general question of standard-setting for emergencies by human rights monitors, a brief digression into the lack of clarity surrounding the issue of administrative detention may help to set the stage for that discussion, as well as to illuminate some general flaws in the monitoring system.

The practice of administrative detention examined here can be defined as detention ordered by the executive, without charge and without intention to place the detainee on trial, of persons suspected of threatening public order or state security.[44] One thing is clear: such

40. *See* Chapter III *infra* (noting the differences in defining the list of rights that should be non-derogable, in whole or in part).

41. *See supra* note 38.

42. Questiaux Report, *supra* note 5, at paras. 7–11.

43. The Sub-Commission's Special Rapporteur in his fourth annual report on states of emergency discusses the specific phenomenon of administrative detention. U.N. Doc. E/CN.4/Sub.2/1991/28, at paras. 26–42 (1991). The Sub-Commission undertook a study of administrative detention that considered but was not limited to states of emergency, and ultimately created a Working Group on Arbitrary Detention, not limited to emergency detentions nor administrative detention. *See* Chapter V *infra*.

44. Louis Joinet's report on administrative detention for the Sub-Commission adopted the following definition: "[D]etention is considered 'administrative detention' if, *de jure* and/or *de facto*, it has been ordered by the executive alone and the power of decision

practices are not categorically prohibited under the key human rights treaties that specify permissible derogations from human rights during states of emergency.[45] Yet the treaty drafters left their job unfinished by simply deciding to make the relevant rights derogable without precisely specifying the circumstances under which administrative detention would be tolerated. They identified neither the nature of an emergency justifying the practice (and, indeed, whether it would be tolerable only under a genuine emergency), nor mandatory safeguards to prevent abusive application of detention measures.

This lack of clarity in treaty standards has contributed to a widespread laxness of practice:

Contrary to what one might suppose, administrative detention is not banned on principle under international rules. . . . Virtually all countries, including those which regard themselves as being among the most democratic, provide in their legislation for detention where the power of decisions lies with the administrative authority alone. . . .

---

rests solely with the administrative authority, even if a remedy *a posteriori* does exist in the courts." U.N. Doc. E/CN.4/Sub.2/1990/29, at para. 22 (1990) [hereinafter Joinet Report].

Joinet's report addressed detentions for security reasons, but also considered detention of refugees and asylum seekers, reeducation camps, disciplinary measures such as solitary confinement for convicted prisoners and "measures to combat social maladjustment" including detention of vagrants and juveniles. *Id.* at para. 24. Joinet's study emerged from a concern by the Sub-Commission in 1985 that information made available to it from non-governmental organizations in consultative status with the Economic and Social Council had revealed that "hundreds and, in some cases, thousands of persons and their families were being subjected to detention as an administrative measure, without any arrest warrant, charge or trial by an independent judicial body, and these persons were, often during states of emergency, being held incommunicado for several months, or years, or even indefinitely, without the services of a lawyer or the possibility of exercising their right of defence." *Id.* at para. 2. *See* D. Prémont, *United Nations Procedures for the Protection of All Persons Subjected to Any Form of Detention or Imprisonment*, 20 Santa Clara L. Rev. 603 (1980) (discussing the origins of the Sub-Commission's concern with the rights of detainees).

45. Proposed drafts of Article 4 of the Covenant on Civil and Political Rights submitted by French and U.S. representatives, for example, would have made the prohibition on arbitrary arrest, the right to prompt notice of charges, and the right to fair and prompt trial non-derogable. Both proposals, however, would have made derogable the right to take prompt judicial proceedings to challenge the lawfulness of detention. U.N. Doc. E/CN.4/324 (1949) (French draft); U.N. Doc. E/CN.4/325 (1949) (U.S. draft). The representative of the U.K. objected that the prohibition against arbitrary arrest and the right of fair and public trial might be impossible to respect during wartime. U.N. Doc. E/CN.4/SR.126, at 4–5 (1949) (remarks of Miss Bowie). The U.K. view prevailed when the list of non-derogable rights was agreed to provisionally in 1950. *See* J. Hartman, *Working Paper for the Committee of Experts on the Article 4 Derogation Provision*, 7 Hum. Rts. Q. 89, 115–18 (1985).

Governments might at the very least be expected to use it only in truly exceptional cases, while judicial detention remained the rule. In all too many countries, on the contrary, the exception is tending to become the rule, not only when states of emergency are declared but also under "internal security" or "State security" laws which remain permanently in force.[46]

The dangers of administrative detention, as well as a perceived need for its availability during times of extreme crisis, affected the drafting of the derogation articles in each of the three major human rights treaties. The earliest to be completed was the European Convention,[47] whose drafters were nevertheless able to draw on the models of the Universal Declaration of Human Rights, as well as the embryonic United Nations covenant, when they began their work in 1949.[48] During the early debates, an Irish delegate raised the issue of protecting minorities from deprivations of liberty under emergency laws as a matter of urgency requiring protection in the draft.[49] Although a specific derogation article was inserted in the Convention, the prohibition on arbitrary detention did not figure among the non-derogable

46. Joinet Report, *supra* note 44, U.N. Doc. E/CN.4/Sub.2/1990/29, at paras. 17, 19.

47. European Convention for the Protection of Human Rights and Fundamental Freedoms, *opened for signature* Apr. 11, 1950, *entered into force* Nov. 4, 1950, 213 U.N.T.S. 222, [hereinafter European Convention].

48. An initial draft prepared by members of the European Movement, strongly influenced by the Universal Declaration and the early drafts of the Covenant, was considered by the Consultative Assembly in August 1949. 1 COLLECTED EDITION OF THE TRAVAUX PREPARATOIRES OF THE EUROPEAN CONVENTION ON HUMAN RIGHTS 166 (1975) [hereinafter COLLECTED EDITION OF THE TRAVAUX].

49. The Irish delegate stressed the need to protect minorities from provisions such as the Special Powers Act for Northern Ireland. 1 *id.* at 104. A delegate from the United Kingdom rejoined that "[i]t is defined in every declaration of human rights that in times of emergency the safety of the community is of first concern." *Id.* at 152. Thereafter, the U.K. led the move to insert a specific derogation article in the draft treaty. The draft initially adopted by the Consultative Assembly had included only a general limitation clause based on Article 29 of the Universal Declaration, which permitted limitations "with the sole aim of ensuring recognition and respect for the rights and freedoms of others, and in order to meet the proper requirements of morality, order, public safety and the general well-being in a democratic society." *Id.* at 178. A committee of experts had the Secretary-General of the Council of Europe undertake a comparative study of the European draft and the U.N. draft covenant; this study concluded that the general limitations article made a specific derogation clause superfluous. 3 COLLECTED EDITION OF THE TRAVAUX, *supra* note 48, at 28.

The U.K. delegation persisted, however, and in March 1950 submitted a draft derogation article. *Id.* at 280–82. The experts also included a nearly identical derogation article in a March 1950 draft submitted to the Ministers. 4 COLLECTED EDITION OF THE TRAVAUX, *supra* note 48, at 56. Neither version made the rights of personal liberty or fair trial non-derogable, although the article's inclusion of a list of non-derogable rights was seen by the drafters as its most desirable feature. *Id.* at 30.

provisions. On the other hand, Article 5 of the Convention, concerning liberty of the person, contains no clause permitting limitations for reasons of public order or national security,[50] suggesting that only in times of emergency meeting the requirements of Article 15 could the provisions of Article 5 be compromised.[51]

At the time of the drafting of the European Convention and in the early stages of drafting the Covenant on Civil and Political Rights, the experiences of democratic governments during the Second World War were fresh in memory. These experiences included widespread use of administrative detention, against both enemy aliens and citizens whose loyalty was questioned.[52] While early proposals for derogation articles in the Covenant, submitted by the United States and France, would have made the provisions on arbitrary detention and fair trial non-derogable, objection was raised by the United Kingdom that the exigencies of war might require suspension of such rights.[53]

As in the case of the European Convention, the drafters did not include the provisions on arbitrary detention and fair trial within the list of non-derogable rights in Article 4(2) of the Covenant, but, at the same time, they inserted no limitations clauses in Article 9 on detention and Article 14 on fair trial, other than a clause permitting the closure of all or part of a trial to the public under certain circumstances.[54]

---

50. Article 5(1)(c) of the European Convention permits detention of a person "for the purpose of bringing him before the competent legal authority on reasonable suspicion of having committed an offence *or when it is reasonably considered necessary to prevent his committing an offence* or fleeing after having done so" (emphasis added). European Convention, *supra* note 47. However, Article 5(3) requires that all persons detained under Article 5(1)(c) be brought promptly before a judge or other officer authorized to exercise judicial power, and that all such persons "shall be entitled to trial within a reasonable time or to release pending trial." Article 5(2) requires prompt notice of the reasons for the arrest and of "any charge"; Article 5(4) mandates that all detained persons may take proceedings to have the lawfulness of their detention "decided speedily by a court."

Article 6 on fair trial contains a limitations clause only to the provision on public trial, permitting exclusion of the press and public "in the interests of morals, public order or national security in a democratic society. . . ."

51. *See infra* notes 77–90 (discussing the *Brogan* case).

52. Both the United Kingdom and the United States made extensive use of administrative detention during the war. *See* A.W. Brian Simpson, *Detention without Trial in the Second World War: Comparing the British and American Experiences,* 34 LAW QUADRANGLE NOTES 48 (1990) (published by the University of Michigan) (offering a brief comparison between American and British experiences).

53. *See supra* note 45.

54. Article 14(1) of the International Covenant on Civil and Political Rights, *adopted* Dec. 19, 1966, *entered into force* Mar. 23, 1976, G.A. Res. 2200 (XXI), 21 U.N. GAOR Supp. (No. 16) 52, U.N. Doc. A/6316 (1966), provides, in part, that the "[p]ress and the public may be excluded from all or part of a trial for reasons of morals, public order (*ordre public*) or national security in a democratic society."

During the drafting of the American Convention on Human Rights, the suspendability of the provisions on arbitrary detention and fair trial also became a matter of debate, eventually leading to the insertion of a phrase that marks an advance over the earlier two treaties. A draft convention prepared by the Inter-American Commission on Human Rights (IACHR) in 1968, at the request of the Council of the OAS, included "protection against arbitrary detention" and "due process of law" among the rights from which no derogation was permitted.[55] Two objections were raised by delegates attending the Conference of San José in 1969: (1) Mexico argued that there should be no list of non-derogable rights at all, because its constitution "establishes the possibility of suspending all those rights that may be an obstacle to dealing rapidly and effectively with an emergency situation";[56] and (2) the United States objected that the IACHR draft was vague in its definition of the non-derogable rights.[57]

A small drafting committee[58] was appointed to revise the derogation article, and its recommendation was substantially different from the IACHR proposal. It added provisions such as protection of the family while deleting the references to arbitrary detention and fair trial.[59] The

---

55. *Draft Inter-American Convention on Protection of Human Rights*, OEA/Ser.L/II.19, doc. 48, rev. 1 (1968), *reprinted in* 2 HUMAN RIGHTS: THE INTER-AMERICAN SYSTEM, pt. 2, Booklet No. 13, at art. 24 (Thomas Buergenthal and Robert Norris eds. 1982) [hereinafter HUMAN RIGHTS: THE INTER-AMERICAN SYSTEM].

56. Preliminary Draft of Observations by the Government of Mexico on the Draft Inter-American Convention on Protection of Human Rights, submitted 3 July 1969, to the Conference of San José, *reprinted in* HUMAN RIGHTS: THE INTER-AMERICAN SYSTEM, *supra* note 55, at 138. In a submission dated 5 November 1969, however, Ecuador indicated that it was also concerned with the disparity between IACHR draft Article 24 and the terms of its own constitution, and suggested that the article be rephrased to forbid the suspension of "the rights to life and to the integrity of one's person." The submission also indicated that "Mexico shares that desire." *Id.* at 117. During the discussion of the IACHR draft on 17 November 1969, however, Mexico proposed the deletion of the entire list of non-derogable rights. This motion was defeated. *Id.* at 134–36.

57. The U.S. delegate stated that he considered "paragraph 2 of Article 24[27] essential but warns that, in order to ensure its adequate functioning, the specific human rights that cannot be derogated from at any time must be cited in detail." *Id.* at 136. In written comments submitted to the Conference of San José on 2 July 1969, the United States had proposed a list of non-derogable rights, based primarily on Article 4(2) of the Covenant on Civil and Political Rights. The United States list did not include provisions against either arbitrary detention or fair trial. *Id.* at 164.

58. The drafting committee included members who were delegates for the United States, Brazil, Chile, El Salvador, and Ecuador. *Id.*, Booklet No. 12, at 136.

59. The revised Article 24(2) prohibited the suspension of the right to judicial personality, the right to life, integrity of the person, freedom of conscience and religion, right to matrimony and protection of the family, right to a name, right to nationality and right to

U.S. delegate objected that the provisions on "the protection of an individual arrested without being informed on the cause or charges, and his right to have a hearing to respond to the accusations that are brought against him" should also have been included.[60] This proposal was defeated,[61] but three days later the United States successfully proposed the addition of "the judicial guarantees essential for the protection of such rights" to the list of non-derogable rights.[62]

Where these formulations leave the permissibility of administrative detention under the three treaties is not entirely clear. Under both the European Convention and the Covenant, it appears that administrative detention is permissible during emergencies if "strictly required by the exigencies of the situation."[63] The implementation bodies created by these two treaties have devoted substantial attention to applying this rule of proportionality to derogating states resorting to administrative detention.[64] While the Inter-American Court of Human Rights has clarified that access to *habeas corpus* must remain available even during emergencies by virtue of the "essential judicial guarantees" language of Article 27(2) of the American Convention,[65] its opinion does not categorically exclude the possibility of administrative detention.[66] Within

---

participate in government. Slavery and *ex post facto* laws were also prohibited. All rights referred to the draft Convention articles defining these rights. *Id.* at 137.

60. *Id.*

61. *Id.*

62. *Id.* at 254.

63. All measures taken in derogation of rights under the treaties are subject to this overarching principle of proportionality, by virtue of Article 15(1) of the European Convention and Article 4(1) of the Covenant. *See supra* note 47, at art. 15(1); *see also* Chapter III *infra* note 11.

64. *See* Chapter VI *infra* (discussing the European Commission on Human Rights and the European Court of Human Rights); Chapter IV *infra* (discussing the Human Rights Committee).

65. *Habeas Corpus in Emergency Situations (Arts. 27(2), 25(1) and 7(6) of the American Convention on Human Rights)*, Inter-Am. Ct. H.R. (Advisory Opinion OC-8/87 of January 30, 1987), O.A.S. Doc. OC-8/87 (ser. A) No. 8 (1987) [hereinafter *Habeas Corpus in Emergency Situations*]. *See* American Convention on Human Rights, Nov. 22, 1969, OEA/Ser. K/XV.1.1, doc. 65, rev. 1, corr. 1 (1970) [hereinafter American Convention].

66. In its request for an advisory opinion, the IACHR acknowledged that "the right to personal liberty may be temporarily suspended in time of war, public danger or other emergency that threatens the independence or security of the State, and that the authority vested in the executive branch permits the temporary detention of a person solely on the basis of information that he or she endangers the independence or security of the State." *Habeas Corpus in Emergency Situations, supra* note 65, at 15.

The Court emphasized that *habeas corpus* plays an essential role in ensuring not only that non-derogable rights such as the right to life are protected, but also that emer-

some systems of administrative detention, *habeas corpus* jurisdiction is preserved, but the courts examine the subjective good faith of the official ordering the detention and do not inquire whether objective reasons exist to suspect that the detainee poses a public danger, nor do they insist that recognizable criminal charges be filed and fair trial be provided to detained individuals.[67]

The suspendability of the rights of personal liberty and fair trial has become a central focus of efforts to draft non-treaty-specific guidelines for protection of human rights during emergencies, with a number of efforts being made to identify a core of irreducible procedural guaran-

---

gency measures meet the strict requirements of Article 27(1), such as the principle of proportionality:

> A further question that needs to be asked, and which goes beyond the consideration of habeas corpus as a judicial remedy designed to safeguard the non-derogable rights set out in Article 27(2), is whether the writ may remain in effect as a means of ensuring individual liberty even during states of emergency, despite the fact that Article 7 is not listed among the provisions that may not be suspended in exceptional circumstances.
>
> . . . .
>
> [A] violation would occur, for example, if the measures taken infringed the legal regime of the state of emergency, if they lasted longer than the time limit specified, if they were manifestly irrational, unnecessary or disproportionate, or if, in adopting them, there was a misuse or abuse of power.
>
> If this is so, it follows that in a system governed by the rule of law it is entirely in order for an autonomous and independent judicial order to exercise control over the lawfulness of such measures by verifying, for example, whether a detention based on the suspension of personal freedom complies with the legislation authorized by the state of emergency. In this context, habeas corpus acquires a new dimension of fundamental importance.

*Id.* at 28.

67. *See, e.g.,* Liversidge v. Anderson, [1941] 3 All E.R. 338, 348 (H.L.) (in which the House of Lords held, over a passionate dissent by Lord Atkin, that persons detained under Defence (General) Regulations, reg. 18B, during the Second World War for "hostile associations" could take "no appeal from the decision of the Secretary of State in these matters, provided only that he acts in good faith"). While *Liversidge* was brought as an action for false imprisonment, the companion case of *R. v. Home Secretary, Ex parte Greene,* was brought as an action in *habeas corpus,* and a similar result obtained. R. v. Home Secretary, *Ex parte* Green, [1941] 3 All E.R. 104. Even for Lord Atkin, the issue was not whether Parliament could create a system of administrative detention not subject to effective judicial control, but merely whether Parliament had in fact authorized such a system through adoption of the Emergency Power (Defence) Act, 1939, 2 & 3 Geo. 6, ch. 62: "In England amidst the clash of arms the laws are not silent. They may be changed, but they speak the same language in war as in peace. . . . In this case, I have listened to arguments which might have been addressed acceptably to the Court of King's Bench in the time of Charles I." *Id.* at 361.

tees.[68] In addition, the Body of Principles for the Protection of All Persons Under Any Form of Detention or Imprisonment,[69] though not intended specifically as guidelines for administrative detention[70] or for detention during emergencies, provides important procedural guarantees for all detainees, regardless of emergency context.[71]

The three major human rights treaties not only leave lingering ambiguities concerning the constraints under which governments must operate in instituting administrative detention during emergencies, they also do not make it entirely clear whether administrative detention is ever allowed outside the context of a genuine public emergency. The typology of emergencies presented in Chapter I indicated that many states have permanent internal security laws that permit the executive to detain suspected opponents without charge or trial and without the formal imposition of a state of emergency.[72] The Joinet study of administrative detention also noted this fact.[73]

Yet the Special Rapporteur on States of Emergency has indicated a belief that administrative detention is permissible only pursuant to a valid declared emergency.[74] Non-governmental organizations such

68. *See* Chapter III *infra.*

69. G.A. Res. 43/173 of Dec. 9, 1988, 43 U.N. GAOR Supp. (No. 49) at 297, U.N. Doc. A/43/49 (1989).

70. The Body of Principles applies to regimes of administrative detention, as the Commission on Human Rights recently observed. Commission Res. 1991/42 of Mar. 5, 1991, U.N. ESCOR Supp. (No. 2) at 105, U.N. Doc. E/1991/22, E/CN.4/1991/91 (1991).

71. The Body of Principles does not exclude the possibility of administrative detention without charge or trial, but it does require, *inter alia,* supervision of detention by a judicial or other authority with competence, impartiality, and independence (Principle 4); prompt disclosure of the reasons for the arrest and any charges (Principle 10); an effective opportunity to be heard by a judicial or other authority (Principle 11(1)); prompt and full communication of any detention order and review of continuance of detention by a judicial or other authority (Principles 11(2) and (3)); information to the detainee on how to exercise his or her rights (Principle 13); provision for notice to family and counsel (Principles 15–17); the right to communicate with counsel (Principle 18); and the right to take proceedings before a judicial or other authority to challenge the lawfulness of detention (Principle 32). *See* AMNESTY INTERNATIONAL, A GUIDE TO THE UNITED NATIONS BODY OF PRINCIPLES FOR THE PROTECTION OF ALL PERSONS UNDER ANY FORM OF DETENTION OR IMPRISONMENT, AI Index: IOR 52/04/89 (1989).

72. *See* Chapter I *supra* text accompanying note 49 (noting the factors involved with the Type 4 or the "ambiguous or potential" *de facto* emergency. *See also* Chapter I *supra* text accompanying notes 27–28).

73. *See supra* note 44.

74. "Note should also be taken of another serious problem, which the Special Rapporteur proposes to analyze in depth, that exists in some countries, where persons can be arrested and detained, sometimes for very long periods, without a state of emergency have been proclaimed." *Third annual report and list of States which, since 1 January 1985, have*

as the International Commission of Jurists also have supported this view.[75] The absence of limitations clauses in the treaty articles on arbitrary detention and fair trial (aside from the narrow issue of public trial) can be read in either of two ways: that denial of due process rights is permissible only where governments enter a valid derogation in time of emergency; or, conversely, that governments have essentially carte blanche discretion to intern their political opponents administratively during ordinary non-emergency times, rather than placing them on trial for specific charges, at least as long as the detainee is informed of the reasons for the detention, can take proceedings (*e.g.*, by *habeas corpus*) to question the lawfulness of the detention and can receive compensation for unlawful detention.[76]

---

*proclaimed, extended or terminated a state of emergency*, U.N. Doc. E/CN.4/Sub.2/1989/30/ Rev.1, at para. 33(d) (1990). In presenting his report to the Sub-Commission in 1989, the Special Rapporteur stated: "Administrative detention was the only possibility of holding people for any length of time without a charge being made against them, but a state of emergency had to have been publicly proclaimed in such cases. However, there were countries where it was possible to hold persons under administrative detention without the need to declare any state of emergency. He invited members to give thought to the question of how to restrict such arbitrary administrative detention without prior declaration of a state of emergency." U.N. Doc. E/CN.4/Sub.2/1989/SR.32, at para. 26 (1989).

75. The Oral Intervention of the International Commission of Jurists on Administrative Detention to the Forty-first session of the United Nations Sub-Commission on Prevention of Discrimination and Protection of Minorities stated: "[T]he I.C.J. has, ever since its congress in Lagos in 1952, recommended: that it only be adopted during an officially declared state of emergency which threatens the life of the nation, forthwith reported to, and subject to ratification by, a democratically elected legislature; and that the detention be for a specified and limited period of time not exceeding six months." U.N. Doc. E/CN.4/Sub.2/1989/SR.32, at para. 66 (1989).

76. *See, e.g.*, The Covenant on Civil and Political Rights, 21 U.N. GAOR Supp. (No. 16), U.N. Doc. A/6316 (1966), at arts. 9(1), 9(2), 9(4) and 9(5). The Human Rights Committee's "general comment" on Article 9 simply states that "if so-called preventive detention is used, for reasons of public security, it must be controlled by . . . provisions, *i.e.*, it must not be arbitrary, and must be based on grounds and procedures established by law (paragraph 1), information available (paragraph 4) as well as compensation in the case of breach (paragraph 5)," without indicating whether "preventive detention" is limited to public emergencies. *Report of the Human Rights Committee*, 37 U.N. GAOR Supp. (No. 40), U.N. Doc. A/37/40, at 96 (1982).

In a case concerning the "prompt security measures" applied principally during the period of military rule in Uruguay (involving a ten-year pre-trial detention prior to conviction by a military tribunal), the Human Rights Committee indicated that "administrative detention may not be objectionable in circumstances where the person concerned constitutes a clear and serious threat to society which cannot be contained in any other manner. . . ." Cámpora Schweizer v. Uruguay, Comm. No. 66/1980, decided October 12, 1982, *in* 2 SELECTED DECISIONS OF THE HUMAN RIGHTS COMMITTEE UNDER THE OPTIONAL PROTOCOL, U.N. Doc. CCPR/C/OP/2, at 90 (1990). The *Cámpora Schweizer* decision is inconclusive on the issue whether administrative detention is permissible

The European Court of Human Rights in its decision in the *Brogan* case[77] grapples with this issue in an interesting way, but does not entirely eliminate the ambiguities. After terminating its emergency derogation from the European Convention with respect to events in Northern Ireland in 1984, the United Kingdom invoked the provisions of the Prevention of Terrorism (Temporary Provisions) Act 1984 (PTA)[78] to arrest persons suspected of commission or involvement in acts of terrorism and to hold them for up to seven days without access to judicial authority.[79] Brogan and three other persons were arrested in their homes in Northern Ireland in 1984 on suspicion of involvement in terrorism and held for periods ranging from four days and six hours to six days and sixteen hours, before being released without charge and without having had an opportunity to challenge their detentions before a judicial authority.[80]

The PTA was adopted as part of the U.K.'s "criminalisation" policy in Northern Ireland, which replaced internment with a program of prosecution on terrorism charges under modified rules of criminal process.[81] However, as the ratio of those charged to those arrested began to fall (from 90% in 1978 to 27% in 1986),[82] the impression grew that the PTA was being used primarily for intelligence gathering, rather than as a prelude for prosecution. As such, detention for up to seven days under the PTA would in essence be a form of short-term administrative detention for purposes of interrogation, rather than a type of pre-trial detention.[83] Since the United Kingdom no longer purported to be

---

under the Covenant in non-emergency contexts, for several reasons: the Uruguayan regime of prompt security measures, as used by the *de facto* military government, always entailed the prospect of trial on criminal charges (albeit before an inadequate military tribunal) and did not really involve administrative detention of the type mentioned by the Committee; the issue of derogation was not raised by the state party (which participated only to the extent of filing a preliminary objection to admissibility on grounds of non-exhaustion of domestic remedies) though the events occurred during a *de facto* state of siege; and the Human Rights Committee correctly found that violations of Article 9(3) and (4) had occurred in that Cámpora Schweizer was denied an opportunity for judicial challenge to his lengthy pre-trial detention.

77. Brogan v. United Kingdom, 145 Eur. Ct. H.R. (ser. A) (1988) (judgment).

78. PUBLIC GENERAL ACTS & MEASURES OF 1984 (pt. I), ch. 8, § 12, at 34–35.

79. After an initial forty-eight-hour period, the suspect's detention could be extended by up to another five days by an order of the Secretary of State. *Id.* § 12(4), 12(5).

80. *Brogan, supra* note 77, at 19–21.

81. S. Livingstone, *A Week Is a Long Time in Detention: Brogan and Others v. United Kingdom,* 40 N. IR. L.Q. 288 (1989).

82. *Id.* at 289.

83. In *Ex parte Lynch,* Lord Lowry LCJ had held that a detention under section 12 of the PTA "is not necessarily . . . the first step in a criminal proceeding against a suspected

derogating from its obligations under the European Convention, the *Brogan* case theoretically presented the European Commission and Court with an opportunity to consider whether non-emergency regimes of administrative detention were permissible under Article 5 of the Convention.

This opportunity was not really seized by either body. Both the Commission and the Court accepted the government's argument that the applicants' detention might have led to the filing of criminal charges against them, had sufficient evidence been obtained during their interrogations, and that a reasonable suspicion of involvement in terrorism had existed in each case.[84] Thus, the applicants' characterization of their detentions as being purely for purposes of interrogation about the activities of others was simply not accepted, and the cases were seen to resemble an ordinary criminal case in which the state's evidence is not sufficiently strengthened following arrest to justify further proceedings against the arrestee, who is then released without charge.

However, the "administrative detention" aspect of *Brogan* was explored in relation to the exclusion of judicial involvement in detention beyond the initial forty-eight-hour period. The reasoning of the Commission majority is particularly interesting, citing the "struggle against terrorism" as justifying more extensive isolation from judicial supervision than in "ordinary criminal cases."[85] This might be taken to suggest that there are some implicit limitations permitted under Article 5 even outside the context of an emergency derogation.[86]

The Court's rejection of this reasoning is thus equally noteworthy.[87] While noting the government's concerns that judicial supervision of detentions under the PTA would present difficulties in the context of a continuing terrorist threat, the Court simply found that Article 5(3)'s requirement that suspects be brought "promptly" before a judicial authority had very little scope for flexibility and had been breached with respect to all four applicants.[88]

---

person on a charge which was intended to be judicially investigated." *Ex parte* Lynch, [1980] N. Ir. 126, 131.

84. *Brogan, supra* note 77, at 28–30. The relevant portions of the Commission's decision are reprinted in the same document. *Id.* at 59–62.

85. *Id.* at 63. The Commission majority found that detention for up to four days eleven hours was compatible with Article 5(3).

86. The Commission majority notes that "the background of a continuing terrorist threat in Northern Ireland" must be taken into account, and cites a previous decision (in the *Klass* case of 1981) to the effect that organized terrorism has emerged as an important issue in Europe after the drafting of the Convention, and must be taken into account in balancing individual rights against the interests of the society. *Id.* at 59.

87. *Brogan, supra* note 77, at 30–34.

88. *Id.* at 33.

Events subsequent to the *Brogan* judgment invite further reflection on the question whether administrative detention can be justified in non-emergency contexts. Having determined that the seven-day period of non-judicial detention was indispensable to its antiterrorism strategy, the U.K. government reenacted the PTA in 1989,[89] after filing a new notice of derogation from the European Convention on 23 December 1988.[90] This sequence of events appears to suggest that non-judicial detention can only be justified under the Convention as a formal emergency measure. This appearance is a bit deceiving, however, since it is possible to devise a system of administrative detention that involves prompt recourse to limited judicial supervision and which nevertheless entirely dispenses with the possibility of trial on criminal charges.

89. When the PTA was enacted in 1984, it was presented as temporary and non-renewable. Comment, *The United Kingdom's Obligation to Balance Human Rights and Its Anti-Terrorism Legislation: The Case of Brogan and Others,* 13 FORDHAM INT'L L.J. 328, 350 (1989–90).

90. *Id.* at 353.

# Chapter III
## Setting Standards

### A. Introduction

A logical precursor to monitoring human rights abuses during states of emergency is setting reasonable standards for government behavior during such crises, in order to create a benchmark against which actual events can be measured. In part, this standard-setting process has occurred in the context of treaty drafting and interpretation, and at least four major treaties (or sets of treaties) merit close examination.[1] These treaty provisions possess interesting similarities and differences, thereby complicating the process of monitoring emergencies. The effectiveness of various treaty implementation bodies in monitoring states of emergency will be examined closely in subsequent chapters. At this point, the treaties will be analyzed for purposes of comparing the substantive standards that they impose on the states parties.

Because of divergences among treaty standards, inherent flaws in the treaty texts, and less than universal ratification of these instruments, various groups have attempted to articulate non-treaty-based standards for protection of human rights during states of emergency. Twin aims seem to dominate this continuing articulation of norms: (1) the creation of universal standards binding outside any treaty process, and thus applicable without regard to specific acceptance by states and capable of invocation by any human rights monitor; and (2) the creation of model legislation that could be voluntarily adopted by states as a preventive measure against future abuse of human rights during emergencies, particularly by states undergoing a process of democratization after a long period of repression. Several of these sets of

---

1. These four treaties include the Covenant on Civil and Political Rights (*see infra* note 11); the European Convention on Human Rights (*see infra* note 6); the American Convention on Human Rights (*see infra* note 15); and the four Geneva Conventions of 1949 in their Common Article 3 (*see infra* note 2).

standards will be examined in this chapter, both to explore the impulses behind this ongoing norm-creating process and also to set the stage for examining the monitoring roles for the various non-treaty-based organs that are also the subject of this study.

## B. Treaty Standards

Approaching this question chronologically, the first legally significant standard is Article 3 common to the four Geneva Conventions of 1949, also known as "Common Article 3."[2] Applicable during periods of internal armed conflict, a frequent setting for the invocation of emergency powers in the past several decades, Common Article 3 prescribes a set of minimal protections[3] that must be afforded even under these dire circumstances. The guarantees of Common Article 3 are further elaborated in Articles 4 to 6 of Protocol II of 1977, particularly with respect to non-derogable fair trial standards.[4] Indeed, the entire body

2. *See* Convention for the Amelioration of the Condition of the Wounded and Sick in Armed Forces in the Field, Aug. 12, 1949, 6 U.S.T. 3114, T.I.A.S. No. 3362, 75 U.N.T.S. 31; Convention for the Amelioration of the Condition of the Wounded Sick and Shipwrecked Members of Armed Forces at Sea, Aug. 12, 1949, 6 U.S.T. 3217, T.I.A.S. No. 3363, 75 U.N.T.S. 85; Geneva Convention Relative to the Treatment of Prisoners of War, Aug. 12, 1949, 6 U.S.T. 3316, T.I.A.S. No. 3364, 75 U.N.T.S. 135; Convention Relative to the Protection of Civilian Persons in Time of War, Aug. 12, 1949, 6 U.S.T. 3516, T.I.A.S. No. 3365, 75 U.N.T.S. 287.

3. Common Article 3 of the Geneva Conventions of 1949 states: "In the case of armed conflict not of an international character occurring in the territory of one of the High Contracting Parties, each Party to the conflict shall be bound to apply, as a minimum, the following provisions: (1) Persons taking no active part in the hostilities, including members of armed forces who have laid down their arms and those placed *hors de combat* by sickness, wounds, detention, or any other cause, shall in all circumstances be treated humanely, without adverse distinction founded on race, colour, religion or faith, sex, birth or wealth, or any other similar criteria.

"To this end, the following acts are and shall remain prohibited at any time and in any place whatsoever with respect to the above-mentioned persons: (a) violence to life and person, in particular murder of all kinds, mutilation, cruel treatment and torture; (b) taking of hostages; (c) outrages upon personal dignity, in particular humiliating and degrading treatment; (d) the passing of sentences and the carrying out of executions without previous judgment pronounced by a regularly constituted court, affording all the judicial guarantees which are recognized as indispensable by civilized peoples. (2) The wounded and sick shall be collected and cared for.

"An impartial humanitarian body, such as the International Committee of the Red Cross, may offer its services to the Parties to the conflict.

"The parties to the conflict should further endeavor to bring into force, by means of special agreements, all or part of the other provisions of the present Convention.

"The application of the preceding provisions shall not affect the legal status of the Parties to the conflict."

4. Protocol Additional to the Geneva Conventions of August 12, 1949 and Relating to

of international humanitarian law, both customary and codified, is highly relevant to protection of human rights during states of emergency, especially in defining non-derogable rights. International humanitarian law by nature is designed to apply in full force during the subset of emergencies involving armed conflict,[5] so in a sense it is all emergency law. And because situations of armed conflict tend to be among the direst of emergencies, protections available then should logically be available in any other emergency context.

Two crucial sets of treaty standards were also drafted at approximately the same time as Common Article 3. Article 15 of the European Convention[6] was drafted primarily during early 1950 with the benefit of almost three years of discussion by drafters of the Covenant on Civil and Political Rights within the United Nations.[7] The derogation article of the European Convention served as a focal point for the debate between two alternate approaches to treaty drafting, which might be called "general enumeration" and "precise definition." The proponents of general enumeration favored drafting a document with positive definitions of rights and no exceptions or restrictions other than a single general limitations clause, similar to Article 29 of the Universal Declaration.[8] The proponents of precise definition, on the other hand, wanted not only specific limitations clauses in many provisions defining particular rights but also a derogation article for emergencies,

---

the Protection of Victims of Non-International Armed Conflicts, done at Geneva June 8, 1977, *entered into force* Dec. 7, 1978, *reprinted in* 1977 U.N. Jurid. Y.B. 135 [hereinafter Additional Protocol II].

5. *See generally*, T. MERON, HUMAN RIGHTS IN INTERNAL STRIFE: THEIR INTERNATIONAL PROTECTION (1987) (functioning to catalogue, analyze, and compare not only the relevant provisions of Common Article 3 but also other portions of the Geneva Conventions of 1949 and the two Additional Protocols of 1977 to human rights treaties).

6. European Convention for the Protection of Human Rights and Fundamental Freedoms, *signed* Nov. 4, 1950, *entered into force* Sept. 3, 1953, 213 U.N.T.S. 222 [hereinafter European Convention].

7. The Committee of Ministers, for example, ordered its appointed group of drafting experts to pay "[d]ue attention . . . to the progress which has been achieved in this matter by the competent organs of the United Nations." 2 COLLECTED EDITION OF THE TRAVAUX PRÉPARATOIRES OF THE EUROPEAN CONVENTION ON HUMAN RIGHTS 290 (1975). The Secretary-General of the Council of Europe thereafter made a comparative study of the Consultative Assembly and UN drafts, which concluded that a derogation article would be unnecessary if the European Convention included a general limitations article. 3 *id.* at 28.

8. An initial draft of the European Convention prepared by the Rapporteur of the Consultative Assembly of the Council of Europe contained simply a collective guarantee of existing rights under the national laws of the member states and a general limitations clause similar to Article 29 of the Universal Declaration. 1 *id.* at 178.

arguing that these clauses would actually prevent abusive suspension or denial of rights.[9] During the final stages of the drafting process, the attraction of entrenching a list of non-derogable rights swayed a majority to favor inclusion of the derogation article.[10]

Whereas the drafting of the Covenant on Civil and Political Rights dragged on until 1966,[11] debate on the advisability and specific terms of a derogation article occurred during the relatively compressed period between 1947 and 1952.[12] Article 4 became the focus of the division of opinion between the general-enumeration and precise-definition camps, as had Article 15 in the case of the European Convention.[13] Another key division, leading to an awkward compromise,

9. In March 1950, for example, the United Kingdom submitted a proposal containing both a derogation article (based on draft Article 4 of the Covenant) and exceptions clauses to the articles concerning public trial, religion, expression, assembly, and association. 3 *id.* at 280–82, 284–88.

10. The French and Italian experts on a committee appointed by the Committee of Ministers protested that a derogation clause was inconsistent with the general enumeration approach. However, the majority favored the derogation article, especially because of its absolute protection for certain rights. 4 *id.* at 30. A Conference of Senior Officials in June 1950 included the derogation article in the final draft, and presented the draft for signature in November 1950. 4 *id.* at 92, 280.

11. The Covenant was adopted by the General Assembly and opened for signature on December 16, 1966, and entered into force three months after the thirty-fifth ratification. G.A. Res. 2200 A (XXI), 21 U.N. GAOR Supp. (No. 16), U.N. Doc. A/6316 (1966), *entered into force* Mar. 23, 1976 [hereinafter Covenant].

12. The United Kingdom submitted a draft derogation article in 1947 to the Drafting Committee of the Commission on Human Rights, which was working on both the Universal Declaration of Human Rights as well as the draft covenant. U.N. Docs. E/CN.4/AC.1/4, E/CN.4/21 Annex B (1947). The last significant amendments to Article 4 were made in 1952 by the Commission on Human Rights when the non-discrimination clause was added to Article 4(1). *Summary Record of the Commission on Human Rights,* U.N. Doc. E/CN.4/SR.331 (1952). Only minor revisions were made by the Third Committee of the General Assembly in 1963 (clarifying that two notices must be provided by derogating states, once when the emergency is notified and later when it is terminated). *Report of the Third Committee,* U.N. Doc. A/5655 (1963).

13. As in the Council of Europe, the United Kingdom was the primary proponent of the precise definition approach during the early drafting stages. *See supra* note 8 and accompanying text. The United States favored a general limitations clause. *See* U.N. Doc. E/CN.4/AC.1/SR.22 (1948). The derogation clause was rejected by the Drafting Committee in 1947 (U.N. Doc. E/CN.4/AC.3/SR.8 (1947)), but sent forward as an alternative to the Commission in 1948. *Report of the Commission on Human Rights,* 4th Sess., U.N. Doc. E/600 (1948). After specific limits had been attached to various substantive articles, support for a general limitations clause eroded. U.N. Doc. E/CN.4/SR.126 (1949). Support then built for a derogation clause, but delegates disagreed on the details. When the Commission provisionally adopted a version of Article 4 in 1949, for example, the organization left a blank space in place of the list of non-derogable rights. U.N. Doc. E/CN.4/SR.127 (1949).

developed on the question whether the clause on non-derogable rights should include only those rights most important and central to human dignity and most at risk during typical emergencies, or should be expanded to include all rights that no reasonable government would need to limit substantially in any conceivable emergency.[14]

The drafters of the American Convention on Human Rights, who began work in earnest in the 1960s, had the benefit of earlier-drafted human rights treaties as a model and began with an apparent consensus on the precise-definition approach.[15] Moreover, the OAS had the benefit of a specific study of the problem of the protection of human rights during states of emergency, conducted by the Inter-

14. The initial United Kingdom proposal of 1947 did not contain a non-derogable rights clause, although this omission was rectified in an amended proposal of 1949 by the insertion of absolute protections for the right to life; protection against torture, cruel treatment, and unconsented medical experimentation; prohibition on slavery; and ban on retroactive criminal penalties. U.N. Docs. E/CN.4/AC.1/4 (1947); E/CN.4/188 (1949). These rights are essentially the same as those made non-derogable by the European Convention in its Article 15(2).

France, on the other hand, suggested several additional non-derogable rights in a proposal made in 1949 including bans on arbitrary arrest, imprisonment for contractual obligations, right of emigration, fair trial, and the right to juridical personality. U.N. Doc. E/CN.4/324 (1949). As noted in Chapter II, the arbitrary arrest and fair trial provisions were eventually made derogable, along with the right of emigration. Ultimately, however, Article 4(2) did include the ban on imprisonment for contractual obligations and the right to juridical personality, as well as freedom of thought, conscience, and religion. *See Report of the Commission on Human Rights,* 6th Sess., U.N. Doc. E/1681 (1950).

15. In May 1966, the Council of the Organization of American States sent draft conventions prepared by the Inter-American Council of Jurists (IACJ) and the governments of Chile and Uruguay to the Inter-American Commission on Human Rights for its recommendations. Then the IACHR prepared a draft treaty, after undertaking a comparative study of the drafts it had received, as well as the International Covenant on Civil and Political Rights and the International Covenant on Economic, Social, and Cultural Rights. The IACHR draft treaty was transmitted to the Council of the OAS in July 1968. The Council resolved to use this draft as a working document for the Conference of San José in 1969, at which the American Convention was completed. INTER-AM. C.H.R., HANDBOOK OF EXISTING RULES PERTAINING TO HUMAN RIGHTS, OEA/Ser.L/V/II.23 doc. 21, rev. 6 (1979). The IACHR draft treaty included not only a derogation clause (as had the earlier drafts by the IACJ, Chile, and Uruguay) but specific limitations clauses in a number of treaty provisions. Annotations on the Draft Inter-American Convention on Protection of Human Rights, prepared by the Secretariat of the IACHR, *reprinted in* 2 HUMAN RIGHTS: THE INTER-AMERICAN SYSTEM 27–31 (Thomas Buergenthal & Robert Norris eds., booklet 13, 1982).

At a symposium in 1959, discussing the possibility of an Inter-American human rights treaty, the suggestion was made by one participant (Dr. Alfonsin) that there be no derogation clause, but that states be permitted flexibility for dealing with emergencies through reservations to the treaty. Martins study, *infra* note 16, at 39. *See* American Convention on Human Rights, Nov. 22, 1969, OEA/Ser. K/XV/1.1, doc. 65, rev. 1, corr. 2 (1970) [hereinafter American Convention].

American Commission on Human Rights.[16] This study was undertaken with three aims, which sound rather familiar to anyone who has worked in this field: (1) to examine the history of states of siege in the Americas to see how human rights had been violated; (2) to determine if it would be possible to articulate general principles that could be binding on all countries in the region and that might be incorporated into the internal laws of those countries; and (3) to determine if there might be international organs that could control the juridical and practical regimes of states of siege.[17] The special interest developed within the OAS on protecting human rights during states of emergency may help explain the rather different form the derogation article takes in the American Convention, as compared to those in the European Convention and the Covenant.

A brief comparison of the three derogation articles in the human rights treaties to the relevant portions of the major humanitarian law instruments reveals some interesting similarities and differences, as well as "lacunae,"[18] that have attracted ongoing efforts to formulate additional, more complete standards. Discussion will be limited to the substantive aspects of these emergency provisions, since the ensuing chapters will focus upon measures for their implementation. Certain basic principles are embodied in each of the three derogation articles: a threshold of severity of cause, requirements of notification and/or proclamation, good faith motivation, consistency with other international obligations of the derogating state, proportionality between cause and measures taken, non-discrimination in the application of emergency measures, and entrenchment of a core of non-derogable rights.

## 1. Severity

While the threshold for a legitimate derogation under the three human rights treaties is largely similar, there are interesting variations in terminology. The Covenant offers the simplest formulation: a public emergency threatening the life of the nation. The European Convention in addition makes explicit reference to "war," but the inclusion of

16. Inter-Am. C.H.R., La Protección de los Derechos Humanos frente a la Suspensión de las Garantías Constitucionales o "Estado de Sitio," 39 OEA/Ser.L/ V/II.15, doc. 12 (1966) (prepared by IACHR member Daniel Hugo Martins) [hereinafter Martins study].

17. *Id.* at iv.

18. *See* T. Meron, *On the Inadequate Reach of Humanitarian and Human Rights Law and the Need for a New Instrument*, 77 Am. J. Int'l L. 589 (1983) (noting the inadequate reach of human rights law in situations short of armed conflict).

war as a ground for derogation is implicit in the Covenant.[19] The text of Article 27 of the American Convention differs strikingly: "war, public danger, or other emergency that threatens the independence or security of a State Party." On the surface, the American Convention might appear to set a lower threshold than the two earlier treaties, but the drafting history of the provision suggests the contrary.[20]

While "the life of the nation" is clearly intended to have a restrictive meaning, its scope is not self-evident. An emergency that threatens the life of the nation must imperil some fundamental element of statehood or survival of the population—for example, the functioning of a major constitutional organ, such as the judiciary or legislature, or the flow of vital supplies.[21] Threats to a discrete segment of the national territory are particularly problematic, although a risk of detachment or loss of control over an important region, which would have a significant impact on central institutions and the general population, would appear to be sufficient.[22] Though not arising out of political causes, certain natural disasters might meet the criteria for derogation.[23]

19. Explicit reference to "war" in Article 4 of the Covenant was deleted in 1952 out of a sentiment that an organization such as the United Nations, devoted to peace, should avoid mentioning the possibility of war, even though there was no indication of an intention to prohibit derogation in wartime should the life of the nation be threatened. *Summary Records of the Commission on Human Rights*, 5th Sess., U.N. Doc. E/CN.4/SR.127 (1949); *Summary Records of the Commission on Human Rights*, 8th Sess., U.N. Doc. E/CN.4/SR.330 (1952). At one point the phrase "threatening the life of the nation" was replaced by "threatening the interests of the people," in order to stress that derogation should not be made to protect a regime against the interests of its people. However, this decision was reversed out of concern that the latter phrase was too vague. *Summary Records of the Commission on Human Rights*, 5th Sess., U.N. Doc. E/CN.4/SR.127 (1949); *Summary Records of the Commission on Human Rights*, 6th Sess., U.N. Doc. E/CN.4/SR.195 (1950); *Summary Records of the Commission on Human Rights*, 8th Sess., U.N. Doc. E/CN.4/SR.330 (1952).

20. The drafting history of the threshold for derogation under Article 27 is lucidly described in R. Norris & P. Reiton, *The Suspension of Guarantees: A Comparative Analysis of the American Convention on Human Rights and the Constitutions of the States Parties*, 30 AM. U. L. REV. 189, 191–99 (1981) [hereinafter Norris & Reiton].

21. J. Hartman, *Derogation from Human Rights Treaties in Public Emergencies*, 22 HARV. INT'L. L.J. 1, 16 (1981). A study conducted by Daniel Hugo Martins for the IACHR identified the three constituent elements of the state as the people, the national territory, and the legal order. Only if the integrity or existence of the state were threatened would an emergency be legitimate. *See supra* note 16, at 31. The commentary to the draft Guidelines for the Development of Legislation on States of Emergency suggests that "even serious disruption of the organized life of the community . . . would not constitute sufficient grounds for a state of emergency if the disruption would not present a serious danger to the life, physical security, or other vital interests of the population." *Draft Guidelines for the Development of Legislation on States of Emergency*, U.N. Doc. E/CN.4/Sub.2/1991/28 Annex I (1991).

22. Hartman, *supra* note 21, at 16.

War presents its own special problems. As a textual matter, it has been suggested that a reference to "war" in a derogation clause encompasses only external war and not internal armed conflict, though the latter would fit under the general term "emergency."[24] Satisfaction of technical criteria for the existence of a state of war is neither necessary nor sufficient for derogation from human rights treaties, though it bears obvious importance with respect to the applicability of international humanitarian law.[25] Derogation would not be permissible in the case of a war that did not threaten the "life of the nation" or "the independence or security" of the derogating state. For example, involvement in foreign hostilities that did not threaten attack or have a significant impact on domestic institutions,[26] or the mere existence of a state of war without active hostilities,[27] would not meet the threshold of severity to justify substantial restrictions on the domestic enjoyment of fundamental rights.

Despite the benefit of the high threshold set in the earlier two human

---

23. *Id.*; S. Marks, *Principles and Norms of Human Rights Applicable in Emergency Situations: Underdevelopment, Catastrophes and Armed Conflicts, in* THE INTERNATIONAL DIMENSIONS OF HUMAN RIGHTS at 175 (Karel Vasak and Philip Alston eds., 1982). At one point, draft Article 4 of the Covenant made specific mention of natural disaster, but later this phrasing was replaced by the phrase "life of the nation." *Summary Records of the Commission on Human Rights,* 6th Sess., U.N. Doc. E/CN.4/SR.195, at 18 (1950). The consequences of natural disasters may have a political dimension, through public dissatisfaction with governmental responses to the crisis. The appropriateness of derogating from human rights obligations because of a natural disaster was questioned by one member of the Human Rights Committee, owing to little linkage between natural disasters and political rights. *See Summary Records of the Human Rights Committee,* U.N. Doc. CCPR/C/SR.430, at para. 32 (1983) (detailing Peru's extension of a state of emergency). Norris and Reiton explained the insertion of the phrase "public danger" in Article 27 of the American Convention as motivated by a desire to have the article conform as closely as possible to the constitutions of OAS states. Many of these constitutions contained provisions allowing "for the declaration of a state of exception as a means of responding to a 'public disaster,' 'calamity,' or 'catastrophe.' " *See supra* note 20, at 199.

24. *See* Norris & Reiton, *supra* note 20, at 195 (using Oppenheim's definition that "war" is a contention between two or more states and thus "would not include civil wars").

25. While satisfaction of some definition of armed conflict is necessary for the application of humanitarian law, the precise rules that apply are determined by the specific nature of the conflict. "Although Protocol II has expanded and improved the content of human rights applicable under the provisions of common Article 3 in armed conflicts not of an international character, it raises the threshold of applicability to an exceedingly high level." Meron, *supra* note 5, at 46. The scope of armed conflict ranges from an essentially undefined "armed conflict not of an international character" to an armed conflict between the armed forces of a state and dissident armed groups "which, under responsible command, exercise such control over a part of its territory as to enable them to carry out sustained and concerted military operations and to implement this Protocol."

26. Hartman, *supra* note 21, at 16 n.86.

27. Norris & Reiton, *supra* note 20, at 195.

rights treaties and significant experience within the region of problems arising out of states of emergency, initial proposed drafts of the American Convention would have set a very low threshold of severity for derogation. The version prepared by the Inter-American Council of Jurists (IACJ) permitted derogation in undefined "exceptional situations"; the proposals of Chile and Uruguay also adopted this formula, while making it explicit that each state could define such "exceptional situations" for itself.[28] The IACHR, with the benefit of the Martins study, criticized this terminology and adopted a resolution in 1968 stating that suspension of guarantees should be permissible only "when adopted in case of war or other serious public emergency threatening the life of the nation or the security of the State."[29] The IACHR draft submitted to the Conference of San José offered the formula "[i]n time of war or other emergency which threatens the independence or security of a State Party or Parties."[30]

During the Conference, the term "public danger" was inserted. Norris and Reiton explain that while this phrase may seem "strikingly broad,"[31] it was intended to cover "public calamity" that was "not necessarily a threat to internal or external security."[32] They question the need for this provision, suggesting that the limitations clauses in particular treaty articles would be adequate to permit governments to deal with such natural disasters.[33]

## 2. Notification and Proclamation

Because the notification requirements are basically procedural in nature and implicate the competence of the treaty organs, they will be discussed in greater detail in connection with the performance by those bodies of their monitoring roles.[34] For the present, it is sufficient to note that all three treaties require formal notification, though the

28. *Id.* at 191–92.

29. *Id.* at 192 (quoting the 1968 IACHR resolution).

30. 2 HUMAN RIGHTS: THE INTER-AMERICAN SYSTEM, *supra* note 15, at 11 (booklet 13, draft article 24). Norris and Reiton found no explanation for the IACHR's failure to use precise language in its 1968 resolution as shown by including the "life of the nation" phrase in the draft convention. *See supra* note 20, at 192.

31. *Id.* at 198 (Norris and Reiton observed that "public danger" "might mean almost anything").

32. Proposal by an El Salvador delegate, *quoted and translated in* Norris & Reiton, *supra* note 20, at 198.

33. *Id.* at 199.

34. *See generally* Human Rights Committee, Chapter IV *infra* text accompanying notes 52–75; the European Commission and Court, Chapter VI *infra* text accompanying notes 98–100, 105; and the IACHR, Chapter VI *infra* text accompanying notes 4, 10.

details vary in three respects: (1) while the Covenant and the American Convention require that the other states parties be notified through the intermediary of the secretaries-general of the United Nations and Organization of the American States, respectively, the European Convention simply requires notification to the Secretary-General of the Council of Europe, without mentioning the states parties; (2) the Covenant and the American Convention require that this notice be supplied "immediately," while the European Convention is silent as to timing; and (3) the Covenant requires information concerning the provisions from which the state has derogated, the European Convention demands an explanation of the "measures which it has taken," and the American Convention requires information concerning "the provisions the application of which it has suspended, the reasons that gave rise to the suspension, and the date set for the termination of such suspension."[35]

The Covenant is unique among the three in also requiring proclamation of a public emergency. The aim of this provision was to ensure that derogating states also complied with domestic legal requirements for states of emergency.[36]

### 3. Good Faith Motivation

This requirement is merely implicit in the derogation articles themselves, though it is express in certain other clauses of the three treaties, which provide that no state party may perform any act aimed at the destruction or undue limitation of rights and freedoms protected by the treaties.[37] Thus, a state of emergency declared in order to destroy a democratic system of government would arguably be invalid.

### 4. Other International Obligations

Each of the three human rights treaties specifically forbids derogations that are inconsistent with the state's other obligations under international law.[38] Chief among these obligations in relevance would be nonderogable rights in customary and conventional international human-

---

35. *See* Hartman, *supra* note 21, at 18–21 (citing specifically Article 4(3) of the Covenant, Article 15(3) of the European Convention, and Article 27(3) of the American Convention).

36. *Id.* at 18; U.N. Doc. A/2929, at 23 (1955).

37. Covenant, *supra* note 11, at Article 5; European Convention, *supra* note 6, at Article 17; American Convention, *supra* note 15, at Article 29(a).

38. Covenant, *supra* note 11, at Article 4(1); European Convention, *supra* note 6, at Article 15(1); American Convention, *supra* note 15, at Article 27(1).

itarian law,[39] as well as the more restrictive or demanding provisions of other human rights treaties and customary human rights law (*e.g.*, any human rights that are *jus cogens* and thus not subject to suspension or denial under any circumstances). An intriguing question is whether these other international obligations are thereby substantively incorporated into the derogation articles and thus subject to the treaty-based monitoring mechanisms.

## 5. Proportionality

Along with the threshold of severity, the principle of proportionality is the most important and yet most elusive of the substantive limits imposed on the privilege of derogation. The three treaties impose a similar standard—measures in derogation of treaty rights are permitted only to the extent "strictly required by the exigencies of the situation,"[40] although the American Convention also makes explicit the preeminently important requirement that such measures may be imposed only "for the period of time strictly required."[41] The principle of proportionality embodied in the derogation clauses has its roots in the principle of necessity, which also forms one of the key pillars of international humanitarian law.[42] The existence of competent, active, and informed organs of supervision, both at the national as well as at the international level, is vital if the proportionality principle is to have meaning in practice. As the ensuing chapters will demonstrate, both

39. Commission on Human Rights Chairman Eleanor Roosevelt specifically mentioned the Geneva Convention of 1949 when she suggested that the provision meet other international obligations through Article 4 of the Covenant. *Summary Records of the Commission on Human Rights*, 6th Sess., U.N. Doc. E/CN.4/SR.195, at para. 45 (1950).

40. Covenant, *supra* note 11, at Article 4(1); European Convention, *supra* note 6, at Article 15(1).

41. American Convention, *supra* note 15, at Article 27(1).

42. As Meron describes it: "Although humanitarian considerations are also a powerful motivating force behind the law of armed conflict, these considerations blend with others . . . to create a counterforce to military necessity. The tension between military necessity and restraint on the conduct of belligerents is the hallmark of humanitarian law. The weight assigned to these two conflicting factors has changed greatly in the course of history. Originally, military necessity was dominant. The principle of humanitarian restraints, once of limited force, is of growing importance, particularly in the elaboration of new instruments, although, regrettably, not necessarily in actual practice." T. Meron, *supra* note 5, at 10–11.

Meron notes several provisions of Geneva Convention IV of 1949 that explicitly permit certain conduct by governments with respect to protected persons for "imperative military reasons." Examples of "imperative military reasons" include the evacuation of the civilian population (Article 49(2)), the replacement of the penal laws of occupied territory (Article 64(1)), and the internment of civilians (Article 78(1)). *Id.* at 15.

logistical (access to information and ability to act promptly) and at-titudinal (deference to national authorities, *e.g.,* by extension of a "margin of appreciation") factors affect the functioning of the various treaty implementation organs.

## 6. Non-Discrimination

The Covenant and the American Convention include clauses specify-ing that derogation measures may not be imposed in a manner that discriminates on the grounds of race, color, sex, language, religion, or social origin.[43] Three interesting issues are raised by these clauses: (1) why no similar provision exists in the European Convention, and whether its absence denotes a real substantive difference among the treaties; (2) what the term "discrimination" is intended to mean; and (3) whether this meaning is affected by the further inclusion of the qualifying term "solely" in the Covenant.

Article 15 of the European Convention is silent on the issue of discrimination in the application of emergency measures. Of course the European Convention, like the other two treaties, elsewhere pro-hibits discrimination on the grounds listed.[44] But these various non-discrimination provisions outside the derogation articles are generally subject to derogation.[45] The issue of discriminatory treatment of mi-norities in the application of emergency measures was touched on dur-ing the drafting of the European Convention,[46] but it never achieved prominence in the discussions, and no concrete proposals for a non-discrimination clause were made. Nevertheless, arbitrary discrimina-

43. Covenant, *supra* note 11, at Article 4(1); American Convention, *supra* note 15, at Article 27(1).

44. The European Convention includes a general non-discrimination clause in Article 14, which also extends to classifications based on political or other opinion, national origin, association with a national minority, property, birth, or other status. The Cove-nant also contains a general non-discrimination clause in Article 2(1), as well as provi-sions on the equal rights of men and women in Article 3, equality in marriage in Article 23(4), non-discrimination among children in Article 24, and equality before the law in Article 26. The American Convention contains a general non-discrimination clause (including classifications on the basis of economic status) in Article 1(1), as well as provisions on equality in marriage in Article 17(2) and (4), equal rights between children born within and outside wedlock (Article 17(5)), and equal protection of the law (Article 24).

45. Article 17 of the American Convention, which concerns the rights of the family, is made non-derogable by Article 27(2).

46. An Irish delegate to the Consultative Assembly of the Council of Europe stressed the need to protect minorities from deprivations of liberty as had occurred under the Special Powers Act in Northern Ireland. 1 Collected Edition of the Travaux Pre-paratoires, *supra* note 8, at 104.

tion against disfavored groups of various types would be difficult to justify as being "strictly required."[47] Thus, there may be no substantive difference between the silence of the European Convention and the explicit non-discrimination clauses of the other two treaties, if only arbitrary distinctions are outlawed by the latter.

Draft non-discrimination provisos to the Covenant's derogation article were proposed by the United States (in 1948)[48] and by France (in 1949),[49] but adding the element of non-discrimination was not easily accomplished. The Commission on Human Rights voted in May 1950, on the basis of an oral amendment during debate, to add Article 20, the non-discrimination article, to the list of non-derogable rights in Article 4.[50] Objections were immediately raised that disparate treatment of enemy aliens would be necessary during wartime, and the decision was reversed the following day.[51] A way around this impasse was found in 1952 when a non-discrimination clause, not including the classification of national origin, was added to the draft derogation article.[52]

47. The non-discrimination aspect of Article 15 was a prominent part of the case of Ireland v. United Kingdom, 25 Eur. Ct. H.R. (ser. A) (1978). The European Court of Human Rights did not distinguish itself in its discussion of the non-discrimination aspect. *See* Chapter VI *infra.*

48. In 1948, the United States opposed the inclusion of a derogation article and favored instead a general limitations clause. In May of that year, the United States suggested that the then draft derogation article be replaced with a limitations clause that would permit "action reasonably necessary for the preservation of peace, order or security or the promotion of the general welfare . . . taken only pursuant to law, in conformity with Article 20 [the draft non-discrimination article] hereof." U.N. Doc. E/CN.4/AC.1/19, at 4 (1948). This suggestion was renewed by the United States in May 1949, U.N. Doc. E/CN.4/170, at 5 (1949), although U.S. resistance to a derogation article began to wane at that time. *See* U.N. Doc. E/CN.4/170/Add. 1 (1949) (noting the U.S. suggestion for adding a clause on non-derogable rights to draft Article 4).

49. France appeared to abandon its support for the general limitations approach and submitted a comprehensive derogation article in May 1949, which provided that emergency measures may not "be applied in a manner to imply discrimination in respect of race, religion, sex, language or origin." U.N. Doc. E/CN.4/187 (1949); U.N. Doc. E/CN.4/SR.89, at 9 (1949) (remarks of Mr. Cassin). However, this proposal was withdrawn in favor of an amendment to insert a clause on non-derogable rights into the draft derogation article proposed by the United Kingdom. U.N. Doc. E/CN.4/SR.126, at 4 (1949) (remarks of Mr. Cassin). The non-discrimination aspect of the French proposal was thus lost.

50. *Summary Records of the Sixth Session,* U.N. Doc. E/CN.4/SR.195, at paras. 142–43 (1950) (proposal of Mr. Malik of Lebanon, vote of 8–4–1).

51. U.N. Doc. E/CN.4/SR.196, at paras. 1–19 (1950) (vote of 8–2–3).

52. The government of Israel, in comments on the draft Covenant made at the Fifth Session of the General Assembly, argued that derogation from the non-discrimination principle would violate the UN Charter, at least if it involved discrimination on the grounds of race, sex, religion, or language, as opposed to political opinion or national origin. U.N. Doc. E/CN.4/528, at para. 53 (1951). At the Eighth Session of the Commis-

The idea that only arbitrary discrimination is outlawed by Article 4(1) is underlined by the deliberate inclusion of the word "solely" in its text.[53] Even without this term, however, the reference to discrimination in Article 4 conveys the implication that only arbitrary and unjustifiable distinctions in the application of emergency measures would be outlawed.[54] Thus, where an identifiable racial or religious group poses a distinct security threat not posed by other members of the community, presumably, emergency measures could be deliberately targeted against the group, despite the non-discrimination clause.

The absence of the word "solely" from the non-discrimination clause in Article 27(1) of the American Convention on Human Rights apparently has no intended significance. The word was included in the draft prepared by the IACHR but "disappeared from the final text, and the records of the conference provide no clue as to the reason."[55] Thus, the three treaties would seem to impose a virtually identical non-discrimination obligation, despite disparate phraseology.

## 7. Non-Derogable Rights

The three treaties diverge dramatically with respect to defining absolute rights never subject to suspension. The process of defining non-derogable rights has been a markedly progressive one, with each later-drafted instrument expanding the core of non-derogable rights. The European Convention begins with just four, sparely defined: the right to life, excepting deaths resulting from lawful acts of war (Article 2); the ban on torture or inhuman or degrading treatment or punishment (Article 3); the prohibition on slavery or servitude (Article 4(1)); and the prohibition on retroactive criminal penalties (Article 7).[56]

---

sion on Human Rights, the delegate from the United Kingdom successfully offered an amendment to add a non-discrimination clause to the derogation article. The United Kingdom's proposal was altered by a friendly amendment to add the notion of "social origin." U.N. Docs. E/CN.4/SR.330, at 4, 10; E/CN.4/SR.331, at 6 (1952).

53. A separate vote was taken on the U.K. proposal to frame the clause in terms of discrimination "solely" on one of the forbidden grounds. U.N. Doc. E/CN.4/SR.331, at 6 (1952) (vote of 9–7–2). Support for inclusion of "solely" was premised on the notion that wartime measures aimed at a particular nationality, for example, might predominantly affect persons of a particular race without being race-based. U.N. Doc. E/CN.4/SR.330, at 10 (1952) (remarks of Mr. Hoare of the U.K.).

54. Norris and Reiton suggest that discrimination in international human rights law encompasses "'only arbitrary, invidious or unjustified distinctions, unwanted by those made subject to them.'" Norris & Reiton, *supra* note 20, at 204 n.105 (quoting W.A. McKean).

55. *See id.* at 205 (referring to the 1969 Conference of San José).

56. European Convention, *supra* note 6, at Article 15(2).

The United Kingdom's initial proposal for a clause on non-derogable rights in the Covenant tracked this list closely,[57] but suggestions were immediately made for extensive expansion of the catalogue of non-derogable rights.[58] When the blank space for the list of non-derogable rights was filled in by the United Nations Commission on Human Rights in 1950, the additional provisions included the ban on imprisonment for failure to fulfill a contractual obligation, right to juridical personality, and freedom of thought, conscience and religion.[59]

The drafters of the Covenant touched on the basic issue whether defining non-derogable rights should proceed from the perspective of identifying those rights most vital to human integrity and most likely at risk during abusive emergencies, or whether those rights should include all provisions whose suspension could not conceivably be necessary during times of public emergency.[60] Article 4(2) appears to be an uneasy compromise between these two camps, especially with respect to the anomalous inclusion of the ban on imprisonment for contractual debt and the provision on freedom of religion, which has the distinction of being non-derogable, yet subject to limitation at all times.[61]

The American Convention is somewhat more consistent in its approach and includes many rights that are not as central as the right to life or the protection against torture, but whose suspension would not be justifiable in an imaginable emergency. The 1966 study by IACHR member Martins favored the approach of listing rights subject to derogation and suggested making suspendable only the provisions on arbitrary detention and prompt notice of charges, interference with

57. Whereas the article on torture in the Covenant bars unconsented medical experimentation, the U.K. proposed to make such medical practices non-derogable. U.N. Doc. E/CN.4/188 (1949).

58. France simultaneously submitted a draft derogation article that included, in addition to the rights contained in the U.K. proposal, the protections against arbitrary arrest and imprisonment for contractual obligations, along with guarantees allowing the right to emigrate, the right to a fair trial and the right to juridical personality. U.N. Doc. E/CN.4/187 (1949).

59. *Summary Records of the Human Rights Committee*, 6th Sess., U.N. Doc. E/CN.4/SR.195, at paras. 113–146 (1950).

60. At one point, the Philippines made the radically different proposal that Article 4 should permit derogation only from a specific list of *suspendable rights*, including the provisions against arbitrary arrest and detention, liberty of movement, expulsion of aliens, freedom of speech and freedom of association. U.N. Doc. E/CN.4/365, at 19 (1950).

61. Covenant, *supra* note 11, at Article 18(3). Article 18(3) permits limitations on the *manifestation* of religious belief for purposes of public safety, order, health, morals, or the fundamental rights and freedoms of others. *Id.*

private life and correspondence, and prior restraint on publication; the rights of assembly, association, and movement would not need to be included because they would be subject to limitation even under ordinary circumstances.[62] The IACHR draft presented to the Conference of San José did not follow this recommendation, but offered instead a list of non-derogable rights only slightly more expansive than that of the Covenant.[63]

During Conference debate, the suggestion was made that the IACHR draft was too vague, and a working group was appointed to redraft the clause.[64] Their product was a major transformation of the IACHR draft, adding not just numerical references to particular treaty articles that would be non-derogable, but deleting three rights[65] and including five new rights.[66] The handiwork of the working group was later modified by the addition to Article 27(2) of the key phrase "the judicial guarantees essential for the protection of such rights," which

62. Martins study, *supra* note 16, at 30, 37–44. Martins recommended that national constitutions take the same approach, with economic, social and cultural rights being non-derogable because their continued enjoyment poses no obstacle to the re-establishment of public order. *Id.* at 30, 41.

63. The significant additions were "protection against arbitrary detention" and "due process of law." HUMAN RIGHTS: THE INTER-AMERICAN SYSTEM, *supra* note 15, at 56 (booklet 13, draft Article 24(2)).

64. The suggestion came from the United States delegate, whose primary concern seemed to be, not that the IACHR list was incomplete, but that the non-derogable rights "must be cited in detail." Summary Minutes of the Conference of San José, *in* HUMAN RIGHTS: THE INTER-AMERICAN SYSTEM, *supra* note 15, at 136 (booklet 12) (remarks of Mr. Kearney). The delegates appointed by the President of the Conference to serve on the working group were from the United States, Brazil, Chile, El Salvador, and Ecuador. *Id.*

65. The deleted rights were protection against arbitrary detention and due process of law, and against imprisonment for contractual debt. *Id.* at 137. The IACHR had included the first two as a result of its 1968 resolution on states of siege, which identified the rights to life, liberty, security of the person, protection against arbitrary detention, to due process of law, and to freedom of thought, conscience, and religion as the key non-derogable rights. INTER-AM. C.H.R., ANNOTATIONS OF THE DRAFT INTER-AMERICAN CONVENTION ON PROTECTION OF HUMAN RIGHTS, *reprinted in* HUMAN RIGHTS: THE INTER-AMERICAN SYSTEM, *supra* note 15, at 57 (booklet 13). The rights to juridical personality and against imprisonment for contractual debt were included in the IACHR draft specifically in order "to coordinate the Preliminary Draft with paragraph 2 of Article 4 of the United Nations International Covenant on Civil and Political Rights." *Id.* at 59.

66. The five new non-derogable provisions included the rights not to be subject to *ex post facto* laws, to contract matrimony and to protection of the family, to a name, to nationality, and to participate in government. Later, the five non-derogable provisions became six Convention articles when draft Article 18 was subdivided into two provisions, concerning the rights of children and the right to nationality. These two provisions are now contained in Articles 19 and 20 of the Convention.

includes at least some aspects of the protections against arbitrary detention and for due process of law that would have been nonsuspendable under the original IACHR proposal.[67]

The gradual expansion of the list of non-derogable rights in the three major human rights treaties and, particularly, the recognition of a core of fundamental process rights for detainees in the American Convention have stimulated non-treaty-based efforts to articulate standards for protection of human rights during states of emergency. Efforts to refine and perfect these standards continue to the present. An awareness that, in some respects, the principles of international humanitarian law are more advanced than those of the human rights treaties has been an especially important factor in stimulating some of these standard-drafting efforts.

## C. The Search for General Standards

As indicated, the treaty texts are imperfect documents. And, as will be discussed, the implementation of the treaties has been basically weak. This dual sense—that the obligations themselves, as well as the system for securing conformance to them, are deeply flawed—has fed the ongoing search for more effective standards attracting a higher rate of compliance. These efforts have been various and have involved inter-governmental bodies (IGOs), non-governmental organizations (NGOs), scholars, activists, and national officials.

These standard-setting exercises can be grouped under four basic headings, with some overlap among the categories: (1) efforts to define binding obligations under existing customary international law; (2) attempts by entities other than the treaty implementation bodies to interpret the terms of the treaty texts and to make recommendations for more effective implementation; (3) conclusions drawn from comparative studies of states of emergency by human rights groups or IGO experts, and efforts by scholars and NGOs to articulate comprehensive standards without particular concern that the standards be demonstrably part of the existing body of customary law; and (4) creation of model emergency laws, sometimes as an abstract exercise, but frequently in the context of offering expert advice to the constituent organs of a specific state, often upon emerging from a lengthy period of repression.

---

67. *See* Norris & Reiton, *supra* note 20, at 211–13.

## 1. Efforts to Identify *Lex Lata*

Rigorous attempts to identify actual norms of customary law have not dominated this standard-setting. Relevant principles of customary international humanitarian law do exist,[68] but the scope of these norms remains a subject of debate.[69] Some of these norms may even merit designation as *jus cogens*,[70] but the restricted scope of international humanitarian law *ratione materiae* limits the usefulness of customary humanitarian law as a source of comprehensive norms for protecting human rights during all types of emergencies.

While proof that certain norms governing human rights during states of emergency have achieved the status of customary law "would strengthen the moral claim of the international community for their observance,"[71] the technical legal nature of these norms is, at best, moderately significant. One might assert, for example, that the four non-derogable rights common to the three major human rights treaties merit recognition as customary norms, perhaps even norms of *jus*

---

68. Hans Peter Gasser has found that "[i]t has been generally recognized that the substance of Article 3, based on customary law, is part of *jus cogens,* and therefore binding on all states. Consequently, the obligations stated in Article 3 transcend that article's field of application; they are valid for all forms of armed conflict. The International Court of Justice recently confirmed this in its judgment in the case of Nicaragua versus the United States [footnote omitted]. The Court reached the conclusion that Article 3, as part of customary law, constitutes a 'minimum yardstick' applicable to all armed conflicts." H. Gasser, *A Measure of Humanity in Internal Disturbances and Tensions: Proposal for a Code of Conduct,* 28 INT'L REV. RED CROSS, Jan.–Feb. 1988, at 38, 44–45.

69. Theodor Meron, unlike Hans-Peter Gasser, sharply criticizes at least the methodology by which the International Court of Justice in the Nicaragua Case concluded that Common Article 3 formed a part of the corpus of customary law. Meron has stated [footnotes omitted]: "The Court's discussion of the Geneva Conventions is remarkable, indeed, for its total failure to inquire whether *opinio juris* and practice support the crystallization of Articles 1 and 3 into customary law. . . . [T]he parties to the Geneva Conventions have built a poor record of compliance with the norms stated in Article 3 and evidence of practice by nonparties is lacking. Nevertheless, it is not so much the Court's attribution of customary law character to both Articles 1 and 3 of the Geneva Conventions that merits criticism; rather, the Court should be reproached for the virtual absence of discussion of the evidence and reasons supporting this conclusion." T. Meron, *The Geneva Conventions as Customary Law,* 81 AM. J. INT'L L. 348, 357–58 (1987).

70. Meron observes that "the Geneva Conventions, and especially common Article 3, state a great number of basic rights of the human person, some that may have attained the status of *jus cogens." Id.* at 355. Meron also notes the conclusion of the International Law Commission that some of the rules of humanitarian law impose obligations of *jus cogens. Reports of the International Law Commission on the Work of its Thirty-Second Session,* 35 U.N. GAOR Supp. (No. 10) at 98, U.N. Doc. A/35/10 (1980).

71. Meron, *supra* note 69, at 350.

*cogens.*[72] But only in the context of actual adjudication, before either an international or domestic court in a case where the treaty itself could not be invoked,[73] is the outcome likely to turn on this question.

## 2. Treaty Interpretation

The primary vehicles for interpreting the derogation articles of the three human rights treaties are the bodies specifically charged by the treaties with monitoring their implementation.[74] These bodies discharge their interpretive roles in a variety of ways, ranging from application of treaty articles to specific facts presented in individual applications[75] to the issuance of "general comments."[76] The effectiveness with which these organs have fulfilled their interpretive roles will be

72. The four common non-derogable rights are the right to life, the prohibition on torture and cruel and degrading treatment or punishment, the prohibition on slavery, and the prohibition on *ex post facto* criminal laws. However, these rights are not identically defined in the three treaties. For example, the prohibition on torture and cruel treatment extends to unconsented medical experimentation in Covenant Article 7, but the American and European Conventions make no explicit mention of this practice.

The Siracusa Principles on the Limitation and Derogation Provisions in the International Covenant on Civil and Political Rights, adopted by a group of experts at a conference convened in 1984 by several non-governmental organizations, assert that the right to life, the freedom from torture, inhuman or degrading treatment or punishment and unconsented medical or scientific experimentation, the right not to be held in slavery or involuntary servitude, and the right not to be subjected to retroactive criminal penalties may not be denied under any circumstances, as a matter of customary international law. The Siracusa Principles on the Limitation and Derogation Provisions in the International Covenant on Civil and Political Rights, *reprinted in* 7 HUM. RTS. Q. 3 (1985) [hereinafter Siracusa Principles]; 36 REV. INT'L COMM'N JURISTS 47 (1986); U.N. Doc. E/CN.4/1985/4, at principle 69.

73. In Military and Paramilitary Activities (Nicar. v. U.S.), 1986 I.C.J. 14 (June 27), the issue was important because of questions concerning the Court's jurisdiction to enforce the Geneva Conventions in the circumstances of the case. As Meron notes, states that have failed to implement their treaty obligations in domestic law may nevertheless permit domestic enforcement of customary law on the same subject. Meron, *supra* note 69, at 348.

74. These bodies include the Human Rights Committee under the Covenant, the European Commission and Court of Human Rights under the European Convention, and the Inter-American Commission and Court of Human Rights under the American Convention.

75. The mechanisms for hearing individual applications are largely optional, with the exception of the authority of the IACHR to receive individual communications. *See* Chapters IV and VI *infra.*

76. The Human Rights Committee possesses rather abstract authority by virtue of Article 40(4) of the Covenant.

examined as part of the critique of their performance in the ensuing chapters and, accordingly, will not be addressed here.

However, other groups have sometimes attempted to assist these bodies by tackling the interpretive task. For example, a conference of experts organized by several non-governmental organizations in 1984 promulgated the Siracusa Principles on the Limitation and Derogation Provisions in the International Covenant on Civil and Political Rights.[77] The Siracusa Principles address both the substantive limits and the procedural requirements of Article 4 of the Covenant. Specific substantive issues addressed by the Principles include the permissibility of emergencies premised on economic causes,[78] the presumption that measures in derogation of the Covenant cannot be "strictly required" if ordinary measures permissible under the specific limitations clauses of the Covenant would have been adequate to deal with the threat,[79] and the elaboration of a core of procedural rights for detainees whose suspension "can never be strictly necessary in any conceivable emergency" and whose respect "is essential in order to ensure enjoyment of non-derogable rights and to provide an effective remedy against their violation."[80] This latter standard imports a notion of "essential judicial guarantees" into Article 4 of the Covenant, analogous to that of Article 27(2) of the American Convention.

Large portions of the Siracusa Principles are addressed to procedural aspects of Article 4, many of which had not been comprehen-

77. *See supra* note 72 (stating the basic standards of the Siracusa Principles).

78. Principle 41 provides that economic difficulties *per se* cannot justify derogation from the Covenant's obligations. *Id.*

79. *Id.* at principle 53.

80. *Id.* at principle 70. These rights, drawn from the theoretically derogable provisions of Articles 9 and 14 of the Covenant, include the recording of arrests and places of detention, the right not to be detained indefinitely, a ban on incommunicado detention beyond three to seven days, the right to periodic review of administrative detention by an "independent review tribunal," the right to a fair trial by a competent and impartial court for persons charged with criminal offenses, the close control on use of military courts to try civilians, the presumption of innocence, the right to be informed promptly and intelligibly of any criminal charge, the right to adequate time and facilities for preparing a defense, the right to a lawyer of one's choice and free legal counsel if necessary, the right to be present at one's trial, the right not to testify against oneself and protection against coerced confession, the right to attendance of witnesses, the right to trial in public unless security reasons prevent, the right to appeal, the right to a record of the proceedings and the protection against double jeopardy. The drafters of the Siracusa Principles assumed that although these rights are derogable under Article 4(2), their denial is often not justified under the principle of proportionality contained in Article 4(1). Accordingly, except in the most unusual emergencies, these rights are functionally non-derogable.

sively addressed by the Human Rights Committee. The recommendations made to the Human Rights Committee include more detailed guidelines for the contents of an adequate notion of derogation[81] and the suggestion that the Committee develop a procedure for requesting additional reports under Article 40(1)(b) from those states giving notice of derogations or reasonably believed to have imposed emergency measures subject to the constraints of Article 4.[82] The Siracusa Principles also venture into the territory covered by non-treaty-based studies, with recommendations addressed to national authorities, such as involvement of the legislature in the review of the necessity for specific derogation measures[83] and maintenance of the jurisdiction of the ordinary courts to adjudicate complaints that non-derogable rights have been violated.[84]

## 3. Conclusions to General Studies and Comprehensive Standards

A great variety of efforts both by inter-governmental and non-governmental organizations fits under this category. The Martins study for the IACHR[85] and the Questiaux Report for the United Nations Sub-Commission on Prevention of Discrimination and Protection of Minorities,[86] for example, canvass available information about the behavior of states during emergencies, categorize the types of human rights abuses that appear to be associated with emergencies and offer a set of recommendations directed to national authorities and to the IGOs sponsoring the studies on preventive measures to reduce the level of abuse. Though not cast in formal terms as sets of principles, nor even as conscious efforts to interpret specific treaty texts,[87] the conclusions

81. *Id.* at principle 45.
82. *Id.* at principle 73.
83. *Id.* at principle 55.
84. *Id.* at principle 60.
85. *See supra* note 16 and accompanying text.
86. *Study on the Implications for Human Rights of Recent Developments Concerning Situations Known as States of Siege or Emergency,* U.N. Doc. E/CN.4/Sub.2/1982/15 (1982) [hereinafter Questiaux Report].
87. The Martins study predated the drafting of the American Convention. While this is not true of the Questiaux Report and the Covenant, Questiaux's recommendations are addressed only in part to the Human Rights Committee and in Article 4 of the Covenant. For example, she suggests that regional human rights bodies might serve as more effective monitors because "they are in a position to take action that is more acceptable to Member States." The list of non-derogable rights "should be extended by reference to the instrument which specifically confers the most liberal guarantees." The American Convention is less liberal than the other human rights treaties because it excludes the

of these IGO studies are important referents for more conscious efforts to elaborate guidelines on states of emergency. Equally relevant are the conclusions and recommendations contained in comparative studies undertaken by academics or non-governmental organizations, such as the 1983 study by the International Commission of Jurists.[88]

In addition, NGOs and academics in recent years have elaborated several sets of general guidelines for controlling human rights abuse during states of emergency, which are designed to apply to all types of emergencies[89] without being grounded in the text of a single specific treaty. These guidelines are the 1984 Paris Minimum Standards of Human Rights Norms in a State of Emergency adopted by the International Law Association,[90] the 1987 Oslo Statement on Norms and Procedures in Times of Public Emergency or Internal Violence,[91] and the 1990 Turku/Åbo Declaration of Minimum Humanitarian Standards.[92] The Paris Minimum Standards include a number of procedural and structural recommendations to national authorities and international monitoring bodies, and the thrust of the Oslo Statement is essentially structural; these recommendations can usefully be compared to those of the Questiaux Report, the ICJ study, and the Siracusa Principles. But the most intriguing aspect of these standards is their attempt to expand and to refine the core of absolute rights never

---

right not to be imprisoned for contractual debt from its provisions. U.N. Doc. E/CN.4/Sub.2/1982/15, at 44–45 (1982).

88. INTERNATIONAL COMMISSION OF JURISTS, STATES OF EMERGENCY: THEIR IMPACT ON HUMAN RIGHTS 459–64 (1983) [hereinafter STATES OF EMERGENCY].

89. The draft code of conduct applicable in internal disturbances and tensions, prepared by Hans-Peter Gasser of the International Committee of the Red Cross, merits discussion although the provisions were never formally adopted by that body. Although similar to those standards discussed, the proposed set of guidelines would have had a more restrictive scope of application than the other standards. Gasser, *supra* note 68, at 49–50.

90. 1984 Paris Minimum Standards of Human Rights Norms in a State of Emergency, *reprinted in* 79 AM. J. INT'L L. 1072 (1985).

91. NORWEGIAN INSTITUTE OF HUMAN RIGHTS, 1987 OSLO STATEMENT ON NORMS AND PROCEDURES IN TIMES OF PUBLIC EMERGENCY ON INTERNAL VIOLENCE, *reprinted in* U.N. Doc. E/CN.4/Sub.2/1987/31 (1987); 5 MENNESKER OG RETTIGHETER—NORDIC J. HUM. RTS. 2 (1984) (adopted at a meeting of experts convened by the Norwegian Institute of Human Rights in June 1987).

92. THE ÅBO AKADEMI UNIVERSITY INSTITUTE FOR HUMAN RIGHTS IN TURKU/ÅBO, FINLAND, THE 1990 TURKU/ÅBO DECLARATION OF MINIMUM HUMANITARIAN STANDARDS, *reprinted in* 85 AM. J. INT'L L. 375 (1991) [hereinafter Turku/Åbo Declaration]. Also noteworthy is a code of minimum combatant duties adopted in Manila in 1988 with the involvement of Eduardo Marino. *See* HUMAN RIGHTS READER: TOWARDS A JUST AND HUMANE SOCIETY 162–66 (Ed Garcia ed., 1990).

subject to suspension. This element of the standard-setting impulse merits close attention.

As previously noted, the Questiaux Report and the Siracusa Principles, though basically focused on Article 4 of the Covenant, both recommended that an irreducible core of procedural rights for detainees be recognized. An awareness that international humanitarian law provides many such guarantees in the context of armed conflict affected the formulation of the Siracusa Principles[93] and the Paris Minimum Standards.[94] The most groundbreaking aspect of the Paris Minimum Standards is its dramatic expansion and precise elaboration of a broad range of non-derogable rights, including certain social and economic rights.[95] The apparent deficiencies of human rights law applicable in situations short of armed conflict, especially in relation to non-derogable rights, attracted the interest of Hans-Peter Gasser of the International Committee of the Red Cross (ICRC) and academics such as Theodor Meron, who began to propose a synthesis of norms and the possible elaboration of a new instrument that either would guide the ICRC's activities in situations of internal strife[96] or could be promulgated as a set of general standards applicable in all emergencies without regard to treaty ratification.[97]

A comparison of these various documents reveals a diversity of views concerning the rights that should be recognized as absolute. The continuing articulation of comprehensive sets of norms may promote greater respect for human rights during emergencies simply by draw-

93. Siracusa Principles, *supra* note 72, at principle 67.

94. INTERNATIONAL LAW ASSOCIATION, REPORT OF THE COMMITTEE ON THE ENFORCEMENT OF HUMAN RIGHTS LAW, SIXTY-FIRST CONFERENCE OF THE INTERNATIONAL LAW ASSOCIATION, THE PARIS MINIMUM STANDARDS 84–85 (1984) (fair trial rights). *See* S.R. CHOWDHURY, RULE OF LAW IN A STATE OF EMERGENCY: THE PARIS MINIMUM STANDARDS OF HUMAN RIGHTS NORMS IN A STATE OF EMERGENCY 145, 209–15 (1989).

95. Paris Minimum Standards, § C, arts. 1–16, *reprinted in* 79 AM. J. INT'L L. 1072, 1075–81 (1985) [hereinafter PARIS MINIMUM STANDARDS].

96. *See supra* note 68 (noting the thrust of the Code of Conduct floated by Gasser in 1988); *see also ICRC Protection and Assistance Activities in Situations Not Covered by International Humanitarian Law,* INT'L REV. RED CROSS 9 (Jan.–Feb. 1988) (describing the ICRC's competence in situations short of armed conflict and the historical roots of its involvement in such activities).

97. Meron's original focus was on the declaration of norms applicable in situations of internal strife. *See* T. Meron, *Towards a Humanitarian Decision on Internal Strife,* 78 AM. J. INT'L L. 859 (1984); T. Meron, *Draft Model Declaration on Internal Strife,* 28 INT'L REV. RED CROSS 59 (Jan.–Feb. 1988); *see also infra* note 18. However, the focus of the Turku/Åbo Declaration of December 1990 "shifted from exclusive applicability in internal strife to applicability in all situations, including internal violence, disturbances, tensions and public emergency." *See supra* note 92, at 376.

ing public and governmental attention to the fact that despite earlier efforts to set standards, "the abuses continue unabated."[98] Also, ideas can be refined with each new elaboration of norms.

Yet, after a certain point, a proliferation of instruments may become counterproductive by creating confusion concerning applicable standards, particularly where no precise effort is made to distinguish norms that could reasonably be said to be part of customary law and those that may be at most *de lege ferenda*. By comparing definitions of non-derogable rights in these various documents, a judgment might be made whether the human rights community has passed the threshold of counterproductivity or whether continuing the effort to define new standards is justified as a legitimate component in the monitoring of emergency-specific human rights abuses.

An examination of the treatment of several clusters of rights in these instruments helps to illuminate their differences in focus and origin. For comparison purposes, these rights include the right to life, non-discrimination, the rights of the child and of the family, and fair trial rights.

The right to life, without doubt, is the most basic of all rights, and its fundamental nature is recognized in the three major human rights treaties as well as in international humanitarian law. But the right to life is a limited one, subject to certain exceptions even under ordinary circumstances, for instance, with respect to the death penalty or deaths resulting from lawful acts of war. The scope of those exceptions varies among the treaties, and these variations carry over into the non-treaty standards examined here.

For example, the Paris Minimum Standards of the ILA would exempt from the death penalty persons over seventy or under eighteen years of age, pregnant women, and mothers of young children.[99] The draft Code of Conduct and the Turku/Åbo Declaration would exempt some of these groups, but not persons over seventy.[100] The Paris Minimum Standards thus draw from and combine the most protective provisions in all the international human rights and humanitarian law instruments.[101] In the two other documents the approach appears to have been to adopt the most advanced standards from international

---

98. Turku/Åbo Declaration, *supra* note 92, at 376.

99. Paris Minimum Standards, *supra* note 95, Section c, at art. 4(5).

100. Gasser, *supra* note 68, at 53 (Rule 9); Turku/Åbo Declaration, *supra* note 92, at 379–80 (Article 8).

101. Thus, the American Convention contributes the protection for those over seventy, while mothers of young children are specifically protected only in Article 6 of Additional Protocol II of 1977.

humanitarian law.[102] With respect to persons under eighteen and pregnant women, an argument could be made that their execution violates customary international law[103] in light of state practice and widespread ratification of instruments containing such prohibitions.[104] However, exemption of the elderly and of new mothers from the death penalty is found only in instruments that have not been universally ratified, and state practice in this regard is unclear.[105] Why the later two sets of standards should mark a step back from the Paris Minimum Standards is not easily explained, unless execution of the elderly was simply not regarded as an important issue.[106]

The Paris Minimum Standards adopt Questiaux's suggestion, also reflected in the American Convention,[107] that the death penalty should not be adopted as an emergency measure and should not be imposed

102. Gasser specifically identifies Protocol II as the source of his standard. *See supra* note 68, at 57.

103. *See* J. Hartman, *"Unusual" Punishment: The Domestic Effects of International Norms Restricting the Application of the Death Penalty*, 52 Cinn. L. Rev. 655 (1983); *Safeguards Guaranteeing Protection of the Rights of Those Facing the Death Penalty*, E.S.C. Res. 1984/50, U.N. ESCOR, 1st Sess., Supp. (No. 1) at 33, U.N. Doc. E/1984/84 (1985); G.A. Res. 39/118, 39 U.N. GAOR, Supp. (No. 51) at 211, U.N. Doc. A/39/51 (1985), *reprinted in* Amnesty International, When the State Kills . . . The Death Penalty: A Human Rights Issue 245 (1989) (endorsing the Economic and Social Council's decisions by providing that persons under age eighteen at the time of the crime, pregnant women, new mothers, and insane persons may not be executed).

104. Article 68 of Geneva Convention IV of 1949 prohibits the execution of persons under age eighteen during international armed conflicts. Article 6(5) of the Covenant prohibits such executions at any time, as does the American Convention but not the European Convention. However, Protocol No. 6 to the European Convention would abolish the death penalty entirely during peacetime, and as of January 1993 it had been ratified by eighteen states of the Council of Europe. J.B. Marie, *International Instruments Relating to Human Rights: Classification and status of ratifications as of 1 January 1993*, 14 Hum. Rts. L.J. 57, 63 (1993). *See supra* notes 2, 6, 11.

105. As of 29 February 1992, there were ninety-eight states parties to Protocol II. *Ratifications and Accessions to the Geneva Conventions and/or the Additional Protocols Between 1.5.1991 and 29.2.1992,* Dissemination, Apr. 22, 1992, at 5. The American Convention had been ratified by twenty-two of the thirty-four members of the Organization of American States by February 1991. Inter-Am. C.H.R., Annual Report of the Inter-American Commission on Human Rights 1990–1991, OEA/Ser.L/V/II.79 doc. 12, Annex "A" (1991). Note, however, that mothers of young children are included in ECOSOC resolution 1984/50. *See supra* note 103.

106. According to Meron and Rosas, the Turku/Åbo Declaration draws on both human rights and humanitarian sources. "Many," but presumably not all, of the Declaration's provisions "codify minimum standards already recognized by extant human rights or humanitarian law." *See supra* note 92, at 377.

107. Articles 4(3) and 4(4) prohibit the reintroduction of the death penalty in states that have abolished it and its imposition for political crimes. *See* American Convention, *supra* note 15, at Articles 4(3), 4(4).

for political crimes.[108] The Code of Conduct and the Turku/Abo Declaration are silent on these questions, which are not a codified part of international humanitarian law.[109] Unlike execution of the elderly, these concerns seem highly relevant in many emergencies, and their absence in the later-drafted sets of standards is noteworthy.

Some commonality can be found in the documents' assertion that emergency measures may not be applied in a discriminatory manner[110] and in entrenching certain rights of minorities, which are not included in any of the treaty clauses on non-derogable rights.[111] But the Paris Minimum Standards go further in adopting the suggestion of the International Commission of Jurists that prohibitions on hate speech should also be non-derogable.[112] This suggestion is anomalous in the sense that it requires permanent restrictions on the right of free expression (rather than preserving enjoyment of that right, as is the case with other non-derogable rights), but the offered justification is the heightened danger of violence resulting from hate speech during times of crisis.[113] The reasons for the absence of this provision from the later-drafted standards are unclear, but international humanitarian law is silent on this issue.

Differences in treatment of the rights of the child and the rights of

108. Paris Minimum Standards, *supra* note 95, section c, at arts. 4(2), 4(4) (finding that the death penalty should not be adopted as an emergency measure in countries that have abolished it and should not be imposed for political crimes). *See* Questiaux Report, *supra* note 86, at 36, 45 (noting that the application of the death penalty often increases dramatically during emergencies and should either be abolished or, at a minimum, be prohibited in circumstances involving political offenses). Guideline 7(d)(vii) of the Draft Guidelines for the Development of Legislation on States of Emergency tracks this recommendation. *See infra* note 125.

109. Indeed, Article 68 of Geneva Convention IV provides that protected persons should be executed only for espionage or serious acts of sabotage against the occupying power's military installations, as well as other intentional homicides.

110. While the Paris Minimum Standards (in Article 3(2) of Section (C)) list the grounds on which discrimination may not be based (including the factor of nationality that was excluded from Article 4(1) of the Covenant), the Turku/Åbo Declaration more generally forbids "any adverse discrimination" (in Article 2). The Code of Conduct addresses discrimination only in regard to the care of the wounded (Rule 10), though Article 2 of Additional Protocol II contains a broad non-discrimination clause (defining "adverse distinction").

111. The phrasing of the Paris Minimum Standards and the Turku/Åbo Declaration is quite different. Article 10 of the Paris Standards guarantees to "ethnic, religious or linguistic minorities" the rights to enjoy their culture, practice their religion, and use their language. Article 16 of the Turku/Åbo Declaration requires protection of the "dignity and identity" of "groups, minorities and peoples." *See supra* notes 92–95.

112. Paris Minimum Standards, *supra* note 95, section C, at art. 10(2). *See* STATES OF EMERGENCY, *supra* note 88, at 440.

113. *Id.;* Chowdhury, *supra* note 94, at 238.

the family in the three sets of standards also seem to derive primarily from the relative influence of international humanitarian law versus human rights law in their drafting. The Code of Conduct and the Turku/Åbo Declaration both prohibit the participation of children under age fifteen in the armed forces,[114] and the Turku/Åbo Declaration further provides that displaced children should be kept with their families.[115] The rights of the child and the family are given only general protection in the Paris Minimum Standards.[116]

Though children have been victimized in emergencies, especially by the practice of disappearances, the non-derogability of their rights as a matter of law is addressed only in the American Convention[117] and in certain respects by international humanitarian law. The United Nations Convention on the Rights of the Child does not contain a derogation clause that would identify which of its wide-ranging rights (which include such provisions as a ban on execution or life imprisonment for those under eighteen) are to be regarded as absolute.[118]

Of more central importance is the treatment of fair trial rights in the three documents under discussion. The deficiencies of the human rights treaties are especially great in this area, leaving much room for improvement in standards, particularly if those standards could be incorporated back into the treaties by interpretation of the principle of proportionality. A high degree of consensus among these NGO documents might be of great value in promoting this progressive development, but unfortunately the overlap among them is far from complete. For example, while the Code of Conduct and the Turku/Åbo Declaration insist on "necessary right and means of defence,"[119] it is not clear if

---

114. Turku/Åbo Declaration, *supra* note 92, at Article 10. *See supra* note 92 (noting Rule 12 of Gasser's Code of Conduct).

115. Turku/Åbo Declaration, *supra* note 92, at Article 7(1).

116. Article 11 protects the right to marry and calls for protection of the family; Article 13 assures minor children the "protection required by his condition." Paris Minimum Standards, *supra* note 95, section C, at arts. 11, 13. A similar provision is included in Article 10 of the Turku/Åbo Declaration. *See supra* note 92. A controversial suggestion in the draft of the Paris Minimum Standards that governments could limit the size of families to one child (draft Article 11(4)) was deleted. INTERNATIONAL LAW ASS'N, REPORT OF THE COMM. ON ENFORCEMENT OF HUMAN RIGHTS LAW, SIXTY-FIRST CONFERENCE IN PARIS 89 (1984).

117. American Convention, *supra* note 15, at Article 27(2).

118. *Convention on the Rights of the Child*, G.A. Res. 44/25, Nov. 20, 1989, 44 U.N. GAOR Supp. (No. 49) at 166, U.N. Doc. A/44/49 (1990).

119. Turku/Åbo Declaration, *supra* note 92, at Article 9(a); Gasser, *supra* note 68, at 52 (stating Rule 8(c) of the Code of Conduct). Article 75 of Additional Protocol I and Article 6 of Additional Protocol II adopt similar terminology. *See* Protocol Additional to the Geneva Conventions of August 12, 1949 and Relating to the Protection of Victims of

this includes a right to counsel (guaranteed by Article 7(2) of the Paris Minimum Standards), or the right to present defense witnesses and to cross-examine or test the veracity of non-appearing prosecution witnesses (guaranteed by Article 7(13) of the Paris Minimum Standards).[120] Nor do the latter two documents adopt the suggestion of the Questiaux Report and the Paris Minimum Standards that if the right to public trial is suspended, at least the family of the accused should be permitted to attend.[121] They are also silent on the right to appeal (Paris Minimum Standards Article 7(12)).

Conversely, both the Turku/Åbo Declaration and the Code of Conduct take from international humanitarian law the requirement that trial be provided within a reasonable time,[122] which is not guaranteed by the Paris Minimum Standards. Ironically, the International Commission of Jurists' study concluded that only three fair trial rights should ever be subject to suspension in emergencies, among them the right to prompt trial.[123] Perhaps there is no contradiction here in that a trial whose delayed start was compelled by the exigencies might nevertheless be held within a "reasonable" time. But a greater degree of consistency, both in substance and in style, among these various efforts to articulate an agreed set of non-derogable fair trial rights would enhance their rhetorical force and offer a greater likelihood of positive influence on the thinking of treaty implementation bodies and also of governments.

## 4. Model Emergency Laws

Given the weakness of the treaty-based and other international monitoring systems, the implementation of international standards in do-

---

Non-International Armed Conflicts, *reprinted in* 16 I.L.M. 1391, 1423; *see also* Additional Protocol II, *supra* note 4, at Article 6.

120. Article 75(4)(g) of Additional Protocol I insures similar rights. Additional Protocol I, *supra* note 119, at Article 75(4)(g).

121. Questiaux Report, *supra* note 86, at 45; Paris Minimum Standards, *supra* note 90, at Article 7(4). Article 6(3) of Additional Protocol II provides that convicted persons shall be advised of the availability and time-limits of judicial or other remedies. Additional Protocol II, *supra* note 4, at Article 6(3).

122. Turku/Åbo Declaration, *supra* note 92, at Article 9(a); Gasser, *supra* note 68, at 52 (stating Rule 8(d) of the Code of Conduct).

123. STATES OF EMERGENCY, *supra* note 88, at 429. The ICJ suggested that "[p]ermitting larger delay than normal in proceeding to trial" might be permissible if strictly required by the exigencies, along with suspending the right to public trial and permitting testimony by non-appearing prosecution witnesses if means are available to test the veracity of their evidence.

mestic law is vital, especially in the basic or constitutional law of each state. The creation of effective legal and institutional infrastructures at the national level for the control of abuses of emergency powers has received growing attention.[124] The Special Rapporteur on states of emergency has devoted increasing attention to this matter, and the Sub-Commission in 1990 directed him to draft standard emergency provisions that could be adopted into national law.[125]

Model emergency laws must not just define and entrench non-derogable rights but also create structures of national government that reduce the potential for abuse, such as preserving the integrity and authority of the legislature and of the judiciary, setting time limits upon states of emergency, and the like. Many of these concerns were addressed generally in the Questiaux Report and in Martins' study for the IACHR,[126] and more specifically in the recommendations of the International Commission of Jurists[127] and in the International Law Association's Paris Minimum Standards.[128]

An attempt to assist the Sub-Commission's Special Rapporteur in drafting a model code of emergency law was made by a group of experts in 1991 at a meeting convened in Geneva by the Association of International Consultants on Human Rights.[129] The terms of this model code track many of the substantive recommendations made in the sets of standards discussed above, such as defining an irreducible core of fair trial rights and protections for detainees, particularly those

124. The Oslo Statement on Norms and Procedures in Times of Public Emergency or Internal Violence, for example, concentrates upon creation of adequate control mechanisms at the national level as well as improvement of international supervision. *See supra* note 91.

125. The Special Rapporteur indicated an intent to undertake the task of drafting model legal provisions in his second annual report. U.N. Doc. E/CN.4/Sub.2/1988/18, at 7 (1988). The Sub-Commission in resolution 1990/19 of August 30, 1990 invited "[g]overnments which have not yet done so to consider the adoption of internal legislation consistent with the requirements of international instruments concerning states of emergency and request[ed] the Special Rapporteur to continue his work with the aim of submitting to the Sub-Commission draft standard provisions on emergency situations, including situations of internal unrest." U.N. Doc. E/CN.4/1991/2, at 42–44 (1990). The Special Rapporteur's fourth annual report was dominated by a set of draft guidelines for the development of legislation on states of emergency, prepared at a meeting of experts in March 1991 in Geneva. *See supra* note 21; *see also infra* notes 129–32.

126. Martins examined the texts of the constitutions and other emergency laws of the OAS states and made a series of recommendations, including the adoption of specific emergency measures by the legislature rather than by executive decree and the preservation of the immunities of legislators. *See* Martins study, *supra* note 16, at 33–35.

127. STATES OF EMERGENCY, *supra* note 88, at 432–38, 459–63.

128. Paris Minimum Standards, *supra* note 90, §§ A, B.

129. U.N. Doc. E/CN.4/Sub.2/1991/28 Annex I (1991).

subject to administrative detention.[130] Specific proposals for creating adequate national institutions to control abuse of emergency powers are also included, such as protection of the tenure and immunities of the judiciary,[131] a prohibition on dissolving the legislature during an emergency, and the exclusive retention of legislative functions by that body during the emergency.[132]

While the idea of promulgating model laws suitable for adoption by a variety of states[133] has attracted attention by IGOs and NGOs concerned with human rights abuse during emergencies, various efforts also have been made to provide advice tailored to the needs of specific states. In recent years, a number of countries have undergone a process of democratization, with varying degrees of success. Many of these transformations have involved the drafting of new or substantially revised constitutions and other basic laws. In many cases the constituent assemblies or other authorities charged with this responsibility have sought the assistance of human rights and comparative constitutional law experts, creating an opening for the implementation in national law of the derogation clauses of human rights treaties or other sets of standards.

For many countries emerging from a period of severe repression, adequate control over states of emergency is a subject deserving careful treatment in the new national legal order. Nations that have given close attention to states of emergency in recently drafted constitutions include the Philippines,[134] Nicaragua,[135] Haiti,[136] and Namibia,[137] whose

130. *Id.* at guidelines 7(d), 8.

131. *Id.* at guideline 9(b).

132. *Id.* at guideline 10.

133. A certain level of generality is necessary in devising such instruments. The Guidelines drafted at the 1991 meeting organized by the Association of International Consultants on Human Rights, for example, refers only vaguely to the "competent authority" empowered to declare the emergency (Guideline 2(a)). As Chapter I explained, the civil law and common law traditions differ substantially in their treatment of the relative roles of the executive and legislative branches of government during times of emergency.

134. Section 18 of the Constitution of the Republic of the Philippines provides that the President may suspend the privilege of habeas corpus for a period of sixty days and place the nation under martial law in case of insurrection or rebellion. Within forty-eight hours, however, the President must make a report to Congress and the Congress may by majority vote revoke or extend the proclamation. The Supreme Court, upon the petition of any citizen, may review the sufficiency of the factual basis for the President's proclamation. The Constitution also provides that civilians may not be tried by military courts during martial law "where civil courts are able to function." Any person detained under martial law must be charged or released within three days. 14 A. BLAUSTEIN & G. FLANZ, CONSTITUTIONS OF THE COUNTRIES OF THE WORLD 185–86 (1986).

135. Article 185 of the 1987 Constitution provides that the President may suspend

various treatments of the subject indicate some indebtedness to international standards, as well as a large indigenous element reflecting differing legal traditions and priorities.[138]

Persons involved in monitoring human rights abuse during emergencies, such as representatives of NGOs or IGOs, may assist in this drafting process in a variety of ways. More formal approaches can be initiated under the rubric of the advisory services program of the United Nations Centre for Human Rights. One portion of the advisory services program is devoted to assisting governments in revising their national laws to bring them into conformity with international human rights standards.[139] For example, in January 1991 the UN Centre for

---

the Constitution in case of war or when demanded by the security of the nation, economic conditions, or natural catastrophe. Article 186, however, makes many rights non-suspendable, including the right to life, access to legal redress, non-discrimination, the prohibition on torture, freedom of thought and religion, and fair trial rights except for provisions on prompt trial and sentence. 12 BLAUSTEIN & FLANZ, *supra* note 134, at 33–34.

136. Article 278 of the 1987 Constitution of Haiti, adopted by plebiscite with a vote of 99.8% in favor, provides that a state of siege can be declared only in cases of civil war or foreign invasion by an act of the President that has been countersigned by all the Ministers. The National Assembly must be immediately convoked, and the state of siege will lapse unless it is renewed by the legislature every fifteen days. INTER-AM. C.H.R., REPORT OF THE SITUATION OF HUMAN RIGHTS IN HAITI, OEA/Ser.L/V/II.74, doc. 9, rev. 1, at 39, 48–49 (1988).

137. Article 26 of the 1990 Constitution provides that the President may declare a state of emergency "[a]t a time of national disaster or during a state of national defence or public emergency threatening the life of the nation or the constitutional order." The state of emergency will lapse within seven days, if the National Assembly is in session, or otherwise within thirty days, unless the Assembly approves it by a vote of two-thirds of all its members. The emergency can be extended by a two-thirds vote for periods of no more than six months. Article 24 provides basic protections for persons subject to administrative detention under the state of emergency, and makes non-derogable the rights to life, the prohibition on torture and cruel treatment, the ban on slavery, fair trial rights, the rights of the child, cultural rights, freedom of thought, and freedom of association, among others. *Further Report of the Secretary-General Concerning the Implementation of Security Council Resolution 435 (1978), Concerning the Question of Namibia*, U.N. Doc. S/20967/Add.2 (1990), *reprinted in* 11 BLAUSTEIN & FLANZ, *supra* note 134, at 24–26. Special Rapporteur Leandro Despouy of the Sub-Commission refers to these provisions as "a veritable model constitution in this respect." U.N. Doc. E/CN.4/Sub.2/1991/28, at para. 50 (1991).

138. Efforts to craft constitutional provisions that might reduce the incidence of human rights abuse during emergencies are not a twentieth-century phenomenon. Martins, for example, discusses Article 29 of the 1853 Argentine Constitution, which forbade the legislature from granting extraordinary powers to the executive, a provision described by one commentator as having been "escrito con la sangre de nuestros hermanos" (written with the blood of our brothers). Martins study, *supra* note 16, at 24.

139. *Advisory Services in the Field of Human Rights, Report of the Secretary-General*, U.N. Doc. E/CN.4/1990/43 (1990). Much of the advisory services program is devoted to

Human Rights co-sponsored a conference on human rights in constitutional and statutory development in Bulgaria in cooperation with the Bulgarian Grand National Assembly, which had begun revising the Bulgarian constitution as part of the democratization process. The topics included minority rights, due process, freedom of speech and press, as well as emergency powers.[140]

Academic institutions may also sponsor conferences that focus upon providing assistance in drafting new constitutions for particular states. For example, such efforts have been undertaken at universities in the United States with such states as South Africa[141] and Nicaragua.[142]

Thus, human rights monitors concerned with states of emergency perform a portion of their monitoring task through the creation or restatement of standards, in treaty texts, in customary law, in proposed codes of conduct that invite progressive development of the law, and by assisting in the revision of national laws. But the heart of the monitoring process occurs when these benchmarks are applied to concrete situations. The effectiveness of this monitoring system in practice is the focus of the remainder of this study.

---

training programs for national officials rather than to assistance in drafting national law. Of the forty-three additional requests for advisory services listed in a chart in this report, only eleven requested expert advice in the drafting of legal texts. The others concerned library resources or training programs. *Id.* at Annex III. The training programs may address the issue of human rights abuse during states of emergency, as was the case with the Andean Workshop on Human Rights held in Quito in May 1989. *Id.* at 24–25.

The more elaborate programs of advisory services, to states such as Guatemala, may contain a substantial concentration upon ameliorating human rights abuse during emergencies. *See, e.g., Assistance to the Government of Guatemala in the Field of Human Rights,* U.N. Doc. E/CN.4/1990/45/Add.1 (1989) (stating the findings of Hector Gros Espiell). In 1990, Guatemala was made the subject of *ad hoc* fact-finding by the Commission on Human Rights, and the advisory services role was combined with this. *See Report on the Situation of Human Rights in Guatemala,* U.N. Doc. E/CN.4/1991/5 (1991).

140. Bulgaria Grand National Assembly, International Human Rights Law Group and United Nations Centre for Human Rights, Conference on Human Rights in Constitutional and Statutory Development in Bulgaria, January 21–23, 1991, Sofia, Bulgaria (mimeo 1991).

141. S. Ellmann, *A Constitution for All Seasons: Providing Against Emergencies in a Post-Apartheid Constitution,* 21 Col. Hum. Rts. L. Rev. 163 (1989); N. Haysom, *States of Emergency in a Post-Apartheid South Africa,* 21 Col. Hum. Rts. L. Rev. 139 (1989) (papers presented at a Columbia University conference on "Human Rights in the Post-Apartheid South African Constitution"). *See* J. Dugard, *A Bill of Rights for South Africa?* 23 Cornell Int'l L.J. 441, 457–59 (1990) (discussing the draft bill of rights prepared in 1989 by the South African Law Commission and its relevance to emergency powers); W. Nagan, *Law and Post-Apartheid South Africa,* 12 Fordham Int'l L.J. 399 (1989) (analyzing texts prepared by South African liberation groups).

142. Conference on the Nicaraguan Constitutional Process, at New York University (Apr. 18–20, 1986).

# Chapter IV
# The United Nations System: Treaty Organs

## A. Introduction

A dazzling variety of political and expert bodies within the United Nations and its specialized agencies possesses competence to address the protection of human rights in states experiencing various types of emergencies. Few of the United Nations mechanisms that will be examined in this and the next chapter involve the formal consideration of states of emergency *per se,* and even fewer have involved the precise application of international legal standards governing emergency measures. Nevertheless, each is relevant because of its potential effect upon shaping government behavior and because of the complex interrelationships among the various UN organs and their interactions with bodies outside the UN. This chapter examines those bodies whose competence relates to the implementation of specific treaty provisions concerning human rights and emergencies, with greatest prominence given to the Human Rights Committee's effort to secure compliance with Article 4 of the International Covenant on Civil and Political Rights.[1]

## B. The Human Rights Committee

The drafters of the Covenant devoted at least as much attention to the instrument's measures of implementation as to its substantive provisions.[2] The measures that emerged are far from ideal, or even ade-

1. G.A. Res. 2200A (XXI), 21 U.N. GAOR Supp. (No. 16) at 52, Dec. 16, 1966, U.N. Doc. A/6316 (1966), *entered into force* Mar. 23, 1976, 999 U.N.T.S. 171 [hereinafter Covenant].
2. *See* A. H. Robertson, *The Implementation System: International Measures, in* THE INTERNATIONAL BILL OF RIGHTS: THE COVENANT ON CIVIL AND POLITICAL RIGHTS 332, 333–37 (Louis Henkin ed., 1981).

quate.[3] These include the report review process under Article 40 of the Covenant, the Human Rights Committee's authority to make "general comments" on state reports under Article 40(4), the so-far unused optional mechanism for inter-state complaints under Articles 41 and 42, and consideration of communications from individuals alleging violations of the Covenant by states that have ratified the Optional Protocol.[4] The Human Rights Committee, a body of eighteen experts elected periodically by the states parties to the Covenant, has consistently enjoyed the services of many qualified and dedicated members, but, as with all United Nations human rights bodies, it suffers from meagerness of resources.[5] This underfunding affects its ability to promote implementation of Article 4, along with the rest of the Covenant.

3. The process leading up to the Covenant's implementation provisions is unencouraging. In 1950, the General Assembly instructed the Commission on Human Rights to combine civil, political, economic, social, and cultural rights into one draft treaty. G.A. Res. 421, 5 U.N. GAOR Supp. (No. 20) at 43, U.N. Doc. A/Res/421 (1950). The Commission prepared the combined draft but expressed reservations as to whether reporting was an appropriate implementation mechanism for civil and political rights. *See* U.N. Doc. E/CN.4/530/Add.1, at 8 (1952). The General Assembly authorized the drafting of two separate covenants in 1951 but urged that they contain as many articles in common as possible. G.A. Res. 543, 6 U.N. GAOR Supp. (No. 20) at 36, U.N. Doc. A/Res/543 (1951).

In its 1954 draft covenant, the Commission proposed periodic reports to the Economic and Social Council (ECOSOC). *See* U.N. Doc. A/2929, at 274 (1955). While some Commission members thought the reports would be valuable to the Human Rights Committee, which was expected to possess quasi-judicial powers and implement a mandatory inter-state complaint procedure, others thought reporting to the Committee would be inappropriate because of the risk of prejudgment of issues that would arise in contentious procedures. *See* U.N. Docs. E/CN.4/SR.427 (1954), E/CN.4/SR.428. In revising the draft covenant in 1963, the Third Committee of the General Assembly made both the inter-state complaint procedure and individual communication procedure optional. Accordingly, the Human Rights Committee was left in danger of losing any significant function. Advocates of implementation then pressed "to ensure the efficacy of the only other means of implementation, namely, the reporting system," by transferring authority over it from ECOSOC to the Human Rights Committee. U.N. Doc. A/6546, at 87 (1966).

4. Covenant, *supra* note 1, at 59.

5. The Human Rights Committee's comments on the "Study on possible long-term approaches to enhancing the effective operation of existing and prospective bodies established under United Nations human rights instruments," U.N. Doc. A/44/668 (1989), pointedly noted that "staffing levels as well as financial resources to support the activities of the treaty bodies are grossly inadequate. . . . If the treaty bodies are to be able to cope successfully with their growing work-loads, such support must clearly be increased. . . . [T]he human rights sector was receiving less than 1 per cent of the regular budget of the United Nations." *Report of the Human Rights Committee*, 45 U.N. GAOR Supp. (No. 40), U.N. Doc. A/45/40 Annex VIII (1990) [hereinafter *1990 Human Rights Committee Report*]. In 1986, the Committee was forced to cancel one of its three annual sessions because of the financial crisis within the United Nations. *Report of the Human*

The primary authority of the Human Rights Committee and its main tool for securing compliance with Article 4 is the review of reports filed by the states parties on the progress of their implementation of the Covenant.[6] While the Committee over time has adjusted the report review process in order to enhance its effectiveness,[7] this author finds still accurate an evaluation she made a decade ago: "The article 40 report process fails as a device for fact-finding in derogation situations because it is unfocused, subject to substantial delays, and unequipped either to produce or to test the veracity of relevant information."[8]

While a working group of the Committee now prepares concise questions to guide consideration of second and subsequent periodic reports[9] (these are to focus upon gaps in earlier reporting and events subsequent to the last review of that state's compliance), review of initial reports still takes the form of questioning of state representatives by individual members of the Committee. This questioning can be

---

*Rights Committee*, 42 U.N. GAOR Supp. (No. 40), U.N. Doc. A/42/40, at para. 4 (1987) [hereinafter *1987 Human Rights Committee Report*].

6. Covenant, *supra* note 1, Article 40. Reports must be filed within one year of ratification or accession, and thereafter every five years. *Report of the Human Rights Committee*, 37 U.N. GAOR Supp. (No. 40), U.N. Doc. A/37/40 Annex IV (1982). *See generally* D. Fischer, *Reporting under the Covenant on Civil and Political Rights*, 76 Am. J. Int'l L. 142 (1982); P.R. Ghandhi, *The Human Rights Committee and Derogation in Public Emergencies*, 32 Germ. Y.B. Int'l. L. 321 (1990); F. Jhabvala, *The Practice of the Covenant's Human Rights Committee, 1976–82: Review of State Party Reports*, 6 Hum. Rts. Q. 81 (1984); J. Hartman, *Working Paper for the Committee of Experts on the Article 4 Derogation Provision*, 7 Hum. Rts. Q. 89, 122–30 (1985); D. McGoldrick, The Human Rights Committee (1991); Robertson, *supra* note 2, at 347–49.

7. One key development was the creation of a working group under rule 62 of its rules of procedure to prepare concise lists of issues concerning second and third periodic reports, to guide the states' preparation of the periodic reports and the Committee's questioning of state representatives at the public sessions during which such reports would be discussed. *See Report of the Human Rights Committee*, 44 U.N. GAOR Supp. (No. 40), U.N. Doc. A/44/40 Annex VII (1989) [hereinafter *1989 Human Rights Committee Report*]. Two recent developments of relevance to this study are the Committee's decision at its forty-fourth session in March–April 1992 to append "comments of the Committee as a whole" to the summaries of its reviews of state reports in the Committee's annual reports, and the Committee's "special decisions" to request reports from two states undergoing emergencies (a request for the belated submission of Yugoslavia's third periodic report in November 1991 and a supplemental report from Peru in April 1992 shortly after completion of the review of its second periodic report). *Report of the Human Rights Committee*, 47 U.N. GAOR Supp. (No. 40), U.N. Doc. A/47/40 para. 18 and Annex VII (1992) [hereinafter *1992 Human Rights Committee Report*].

8. J. Hartman, *Derogation from Human Rights Treaties in Public Emergencies*, 22 Harv. Int'l L.J. 1, 41 (1981).

9. *See supra* note 7.

disjointed since it depends on the varying interests and knowledge of the members, the degree to which they are prepared to probe, and the ability and willingness of the state's representative to respond orally or to provide supplementary information. Because the entire scope of the Covenant is under consideration, the level of attention to Article 4 varies widely and not necessarily because of its actual relevance to the human rights situation in the country under scrutiny.

Much seems to depend on the general notoriety of the state's experience with emergencies and human rights abuse. When the initial report of Argentina was discussed in 1990, for example, many Committee members raised pertinent questions concerning that country's recent experience with states of siege, probing such issues as the ability of the judiciary to review emergency measures,[10] whether a state of siege could be declared on the mere possibility of internal disturbance,[11] why the constitution did not make inviolable the non-derogable rights in Article 4(2),[12] what control the legislature could exercise over the state of siege,[13] and whether it had been constitutional for the President to impose a state of siege after the return to civilian rule.[14] When Zambia's initial report was reviewed in 1987, in contrast, several members asked in passing[15] whether Zambia had ever invoked the emergency powers in its constitution, which were briefly described in the state's report.[16] In a somewhat startling reply, the state representative responded that Zambia was at that time under a state of emergency for vaguely described reasons.[17] Since Zambia had not given notice of this emergency pursuant to Article 4(3),[18] the review produced the bare fact of an existing emergency, but the Committee's questions were not adequate to establish whether the substantive limits of Article 4 were being respected by Zambia.

While the Committee in its early years had sometimes seemed timid

10. U.N. Doc. CCPR/C/SR.952, at para. 16 (remarks of Ms. Chanet), 22 (remarks of Mr. Fodor) (1990).

11. *Id.* at para. 11 (remarks of Mr. Aguilar Urbina).

12. *Id.* at para. 13 (remarks of Mr. Prado Vallejo), 22 (remarks of Mr. Fodor).

13. *Id.* at para. 31 (remarks of Mr. Cooray).

14. *Id.* at para. 36 (remarks of Mrs. Higgins).

15. *See, e.g.,* U.N. Doc. CCPR/C/SR.771, at para. 33 (1987) (remarks of Mr. Cooray); U.N. Doc. CCPR/C/SR.771, at para. 44 (1987) (remarks of Ms. Chanet).

16. U.N. Doc. CCPR/C/36/Add.3 (1987).

17. The reasons included Zambia's involvement in liberation struggles in South Africa, refugee problems, tribal divisions, and economic stress. U.N. Doc. CCPR/C/SR.776, at paras. 4–7 (1987).

18. As drawn up by the Sub-Commission's Special Rapporteur, Zambia was not on the list of states that had declared a state of emergency. U.N. Doc. E/CN.4/Sub.2/1987/19/Rev.1 (1988).

in its questioning of non-Western states concerning their derogations from the Covenant,[19] the Committee now appears to treat these states with equal candor. For example, members of the Committee questioned Togo's representative as to why there had been no notice of that state's 1986 emergency, what controls and remedies existed over emergency measures, and what were the powers of the State Security Court.[20] A number of questions were addressed to the representative from Cameroon concerning compliance with Article 4, with one Committee member remarking that flagrant banditry and high crime rates could not meet the standard under Article 4(1) as the basis for a permissible derogation.[21] Trinidad and Tobago's reservation to Article 4(2) was sharply questioned by Committee member Rosalyn Higgins.[22]

19. In 1978, for example, Madagascar's representative justified the application of exceptional measures even after the end of the "state of national necessity" in 1975 on the grounds that "retention of the full range of fundamental freedoms would constitute an obstacle to the country's evolution." U.N. Docs. CCPR/C/SR.83, at 3 (1978), CCPR/C/SR.87, at 10. One member of the Committee remarked that extraordinary measures should not be premised on persistent economic problems and that notice under Article 4(3) should be given for any emergency measures. U.N. Doc. CCPR/C/SR.84, at para. 11 (1978) (remarks of Mr. Uribe Vargas). The member from Iran cautioned his fellow Committee members to adopt a "realistic approach" toward Third World countries. U.N. Doc. CCPR/C/SR.67, at para. 15 (1978).

20. The representative informed the Committee that the President of Togo had merely ordered a curfew in 1986, which did not require notification under Article 4(3). The representative also stated that the President had the sole authority to impose an emergency, and that the provisions authorizing administrative detention of up to three years for persons suspected of endangering public order or state security lacked "a sufficient legal foundation . . . [and were] to have disappeared in 1977 but that had not yet happened." *1989 Human Rights Committee Report, supra* note 7, at paras. 258, 261.

21. *Id.* at para. 461. In reviewing Yemen's report, the Committee Chairman remarked that "the problem of underdevelopment could not be advanced as an excuse for inadequate enjoyment of human rights." *1990 Human Rights Committee Report, supra* note 5, at para. 70.

22. Professor Higgins noted that the Netherlands had taken the unusual step of objecting to Trinidad and Tobago's reservation as being contrary to the objectives and purposes of the Covenant, and stressed that certain rights were not subject to any derogation. During its 1970 emergency, for example, she noted that the state had not allowed arbitrary deprivation of life or retroactive crimes. "[S]he considered that the reservation was an empty and unusable weapon in the armoury developed by the Government of Trinidad and Tobago against any possible future disorders and that it was incompatible with the objectives of the Covenant." She urged that the constitution be revised and the reservation withdrawn. U.N. Doc. CCPR/C/SR.765, at paras. 16–18 (1987). Dominick McGoldrick suggests that reservations to Article 4 may be inconsistent with the objectives and purposes of the Covenant, and that the Committee should, as a body, pronounce on the validity of such reservations. McGoldrick, *supra* note 6, at 305–7. *See also* JAIME ORAA, HUMAN RIGHTS IN STATES OF EMERGENCY IN INTERNATIONAL LAW (1992).

Nevertheless, states that have not been the focus of NGO activism, that have not been the subject of other international procedures, that file a brief and abstract report and/or that send a low-level representative to the Committee's meetings may escape from the report review essentially unscathed, without the true picture of their human rights situation emerging.[23] On the other hand, states that file an abstract, unreal report may sometimes force the Committee to rely primarily upon critical data from other sources, making the questioning more heated.[24]

But some states that persist in a facade of normality may stymie the Committee's ability to examine their situation in light of Article 4. For example, Iraq insisted that despite its being engaged in a major war with Iran and later in the Gulf war, it was in full compliance with its obligations under the Covenant, had not found it necessary to declare a state of emergency, and indeed had found it possible to expand the enjoyment of human rights.[25] Committee members were able to elicit only the admission that certain "administrative measures" differing from ordinary law were in effect in the conflict zones.[26] Vietnam made no mention of Article 4 in its report and did not respond to Committee members' questions as to whether an emergency still existed.[27]

In general, reviews of supplemental and second (or subsequent) periodic reports tend to be more focused and probing, especially if issues under Article 4 surfaced during earlier reviews. When the initial report of Chile was reviewed in 1979, members of the Committee sharply criticized the idealized and abstract picture of the legal system and requested additional information on the practical enforcement of the Covenant's provisions.[28] Members inquired whether all the measures taken under the state of siege notified in 1976 were still being applied, or whether measures "intended to be limited in space and

23. The Committee confessed hopelessness with respect to the situation in Lebanon, even though that country had never even filed a notice of derogation. U.N. Doc. CCPR/C/SR., at 442–43, 446 (1983).

24. A good example is the review of Afghanistan. U.N. Doc. CCPR/C/SR.604, at para. 68 (1985) (remarks of Mr. Dimitrijevic).

25. *1987 Human Rights Committee Report, supra* note 5, at para. 355; *1992 Human Rights Committee Report, supra* note 7, at para. 197.

26. *Id.* The representative of Panama indicated that no emergency had been declared at the time of the United States invasion in 1989, since such an action "would have increased the danger of human rights violations." *Report of the Human Rights Committee*, 46 U.N. GAOR Supp. (No. 40), U.N. Doc. A/46/40, at para. 425 (1991) [hereinafter *1991 Human Rights Committee Report*].

27. *1990 Human Rights Committee Report, supra* note 5, at paras. 458, 463.

28. *Report of the Human Rights Committee*, 38 U.N. GAOR Supp. (No. 40), U.N. Doc. A/38/40, at para. 73 (1983).

time . . . had been transformed into institutional restrictions in force throughout the country for an indefinite period," noting that each restriction "required convincing proof of the existence of a danger which could not be overcome in any other way."[29] During this initial review, the Committee had access to extensive information from sources other than the state report itself.[30] In an unusual move, the Committee termed the report "insufficient" and demanded a new report,[31] but the new report was not filed until five years later under the ordinary rules on periodicity.[32] This second periodic report was closely scrutinized during eight meetings by the Committee, which extended over two sessions.[33] The review of the third periodic report took place in November 1989, after the lifting of the state of emergency but before the democratic election of a new president.[34] This review revealed that military courts retained jurisdiction to try civilians under the Anti-Terrorism Act if the target was military or police,[35] a situation described by Committee members as "an anomaly and something utterly negative."[36]

Apparent entrenchment of emergency provisions into ordinary law also emerged during the careful review of Poland's second periodic report in 1987.[37] The Polish report was thorough and its representative well informed, which permitted the Committee to learn that after

29. *Id.* at paras. 78, 87.

30. Most notably, the Committee referred to the reports of the Ad Hoc Working Group on the Situation of Human Rights in Chile, which was appointed by the United Nations Commission on Human Rights. *See* U.N. Doc. CCPR/C/SR.128 (1979).

31. *Report of the Human Rights Committee*, 34 U.N. GAOR Supp. (No. 40), U.N. Doc. A/34/40, at para. 108 (1979).

32. U.N. Docs. CCPR/C/32/Add.1 (1984); CCPR/C/32/Add.2. The Committee Chairman noted that the "information received . . . was, however, insufficient. The Committee deeply deplored that fact but wished to pursue the dialogue with the Chilean Government and to examine with it the reports it had submitted." U.N. Doc. CCPR/C/SR.527, at para. 1 (1984).

33. U.N. Doc. CCPR/C/SR.527 (1984), CCPR/C/SR.528, CCPR/C/SR.529, CCPR/C/SR.530, CCPR/C/SR.531, CCPR/C/SR.546, CCPR/C/SR.547, CCPR/C/SR.548. During these sessions, the Committee referred to a prepared list of follow-up questions (U.N. Doc. M/CCPR/84/6) as well as to General Assembly resolutions on the Chilean human rights situation. *See, e.g.,* U.N. Docs. CCPR/C/SR.527, at para. 25 (1984), CCPR/C/SR.528, at para. 22. Various reports by the Special Rapporteur on the Chilean human rights situation were also utilized. *See, e.g.,* U.N. Doc. CCPR/C/SR.529, at paras. 2, 12, 29, 34–35, 37 (1984).

34. Review of this report consumed four meetings of the Committee. *1990 Human Rights Committee Report, supra* note 5, at paras. 170–211.

35. *Id.* at para. 193.

36. *Id.* at para. 209.

37. *1987 Human Rights Committee Report, supra* note 5, at paras. 55–104.

the lifting of martial law in 1983 censorship actually may have been increased.[38]

The review of Nicaragua's second periodic report likewise met the Committee's standard for a constructive dialogue.[39] Occurring after the elections of February 1990 but prior to the transfer of power, the review revealed that Nicaragua had "decided to lift the state of emergency prevailing in the country even though its cause had not been removed" for the sake of "the overall peace of Central America."[40] Other specific improvements in the human rights situation included a revised Amparo Act and abolition of the Anti-Somocista People's Tribunals.[41] Committee members praised the "excellent report," but noted continuing concerns "that there had been derogations from a whole range of rights during several very long states of emergencies and that certain specific questions . . . had not been satisfactorily answered."[42]

However, Committee members do not always ask very probing questions concerning even current or recent emergencies. One example is the review of Tunisia's second periodic report in 1987.[43] While the Committee was able to engage in a substantive review of the relatively detailed report, little attention was paid to the emergency proclaimed in January 1984. Although members were startled by the report's assertion that the emergency measures were "more symbolic than real," and some raised questions as to whether food riots had really constituted a threat to the life of the nation,[44] the Committee seemed reassured by the fact that the emergency had been of limited duration and had involved limited measures.[45] The 1984 Tunisian emergency

---

38. *Id.* at para. 98. Dominick McGoldrick notes that the five-year cycle for periodic reporting meant that the Committee never reviewed the Polish situation during the period of martial law. *See supra* note 6, at 316. In general, however, he concludes that review of the second periodic reports has been much more focused and critical with respect to Article 4 than the comparatively disjointed review of the initial reports. *Id.* at 311, 315.

39. *1990 Human Rights Committee Report, supra* note 5, at paras. 388–427.

40. *Id.* at para. 398. Great stress is placed on a state choosing to lift a state of emergency in Central America under the Esquipulas peace plan. *International Law Ass'n, The Second Interim Report of the Comm. on the Enforcement of Human Rights Law, Sixty-Third Conference in Warsaw* 142–43 (1988).

41. *Id.* at paras. 389, 391, 394, 409.

42. *Id.* at para. 425.

43. *1987 Human Rights Committee Report, supra* note 5, at paras. 105–148.

44. U.N. Doc. CCPR/C/SR.713, at para. 11 (1987) (remarks of Prof. Higgins).

45. *Id.* at paras. 12–14. The measures included a curfew, prohibition on public demonstrations, and searches for pillaged goods. *1987 Human Rights Committee Report, supra* note 5, at para. 115.

may simply not have appeared to the Committee to be central to the human rights problems faced by the country.

More recently, during the review of the Soviet Union's third periodic report,[46] members touched on the states of emergency in Nagorno-Karabakh and Azerbaijan that had been notified in 1988, seeking information on the impact of the emergency on the enjoyments of rights guaranteed by the Covenant.[47] The state representative expressed hope that the emergency would soon be lifted and indicated that further review of the legal provisions for the emergency might be undertaken by the Supreme Soviet, "[s]ince the state of emergency was a new phenomenon and lacked legal definition in certain respects."[48] Again, the emergency appeared peripheral to the Committee's primary concerns.

The Article 40 report review process suffers from certain drawbacks as a method for reaching definitive conclusions concerning a state's compliance with Article 4, although the Committee has made recent improvements. The Committee applied its newly assumed authority to make "comments of the Committee" at the conclusion of state reviews by, *inter alia,* expressing doubt about respect for due process by military tribunals in Algeria and noting that any violations of non-derogable rights during the Algerian emergency "should not be allowed to continue"; finding "no evidence" that the April 1992 imposition of the Government of Emergency and National Reconstruction in Peru would assist in the restoration of internal law and order and that the concentration of power in the executive had "impeded the application of the Covenant in Peru"; asserting that detention of women and children during the Peruvian emergency was "not compatible with the rights guaranteed under article 9"; and regretting the "many cases" of violation of non-derogable rights by the Yugoslav federal army.[49] Nevertheless, the Committee's corporate comments on the existence of emergency conditions and the permissibility of emergency measures tend to be rather superficial, possibly reflecting the continuing limits on the Committee's fact-finding capacities.

46. Questioning during review of third periodic reports might be expected to be a bit more cursory since the Committee has decided to limit its review to no more than three meetings, but at the same time these reviews are expected to be focused upon special problem areas that have been identified in earlier sessions. *1989 Human Rights Committee Report, supra* note 7, at Annex VII.

47. *1990 Human Rights Committee Report, supra* note 5, at para. 88.

48. *Id.* at para. 89.

49. *1992 Human Rights Commission Report, supra* note 7, at paras. 297, 299, 342, 347, and 466. McGoldrick had noted that "[h]owever harsh and critical the comments of individual members they could not compare with a determination by the HRC as a body that article 4 was not being complied with." McGoldrick, *supra* note 6, at 316.

Even before the Committee began drafting comments on state reports as a body, comments made by individual Committee members in the course of asking questions of the state representative were sometimes quite critical. For example, Mr. Prado Vallejo indicated during the review of Chile's second periodic report that a continued emergency since 1973 could not be justified by the exigencies and noted that "various members of the Committee had already had occasion to denounce measures enacted in Chile which were contrary to the provisions of the Covenant."[50] Similarly trenchant comments have been made even by Committee members whose general approach to Article 4 is highly deferential to state discretion.[51] It is difficult for the Committee to develop a coherent jurisprudence on emergency powers through the occasional comments and questions of individual members, especially if it is unclear that other members share such views.

The effectiveness, as well as the coherence, of the Committee's implementation of Article 4 is affected by substantial delays in the receipt of necessary information. The Committee's review of state reports has revealed widespread nonfeasance with the notification requirement of Article 4(3).[52] Total failure to file reports[53] or timing of report due

50. U.N. Doc. CCPR/C/SR.528, at para. 18 (1984).

51. Sir Vincent Evans, for example, observed in 1984 that there was no apparent justification for the continued suspension of free elections in Chile. U.N. Doc. CCPR/C/SR.528, at para. 11 (1984). Evans also requested that the Nicaraguan representative provide more information concerning each right that had been suspended. U.N. Doc. CCPR/C/SR.420, at para. 37 (1983). On other occasions, however, he asserted that "[n]either article 4 nor the Covenant in general gave the Committee any special role as far as monitoring emergency situations was concerned. . . . Obviously Governments must not abuse the right of derogation, but they had to use their judgement in deciding what measures should be taken under the circumstances." U.N. Doc. CCPR/C/SR.351, at para. 31 (1982). With respect to notification under Article 4(3), Evans believed that a state could formally declare an emergency, suspend rights such as freedom of assembly and expression, and yet not provide notification, if the actions taken might also be justified under the limitations clauses of the suspended articles. U.N. Doc. CCPR/C/SR.520, at para. 37 (1984).

52. *E.g., Report of the Human Rights Committee*, 34 U.N. GAOR Supp. (No. 40), U.N. Doc. A/34/40, at para. 293 (1979) (noting the case of Syria); *Report of the Human Rights Committee*, 35 U.N. GAOR Supp. (No. 40), U.N. Doc. A/35/40, at para. 297 (1980) (noting the case of Suriname); *Report of the Human Rights Committee*, 37 U.N. GAOR Supp. (No. 40), U.N. Doc. A/37/40, at para. 306 (1982) (noting the case of Iran); U.N. Doc. CCPR/C/SR.475 (1983) (noting the case of Guinea); U.N. Doc. CCPR/C/SR.477 (1983) (noting the case of Sri Lanka); U.N. Doc. CCPR/C/SR.442 (1983) (noting the case of Lebanon); U.N. Doc. CCPR/C/SR.468 (1983) (noting the case of El Salvador); U.N. Doc. CCPR/C/SR.499 (1984) (noting the case of Egypt); U.N. Doc. CCPR/C/SR.528 (1984) (noting the case of Chile); U.N. Doc. CCPR/C/SR.604 (1985) (noting the case of Afghanistan); U.N. Doc. CCPR/C/SR.776 (1987) (noting the case of Zambia). Jordan's representative defended his country's failure to comply with Article 4(3) on grounds that "the

dates that are remote from periods when emergencies are imposed also diminish the ability of the Committee to determine in a timely fashion if compliance with Article 4 is seriously in question within a particular state. Many notices that are filed are so vague as to provide little guidance as to whether the situation meets the threshold of severity,[54] whether non-derogable rights are being suspended,[55] and exactly how derogable rights are affected in practice by emergency measures.[56]

This lack of timely and comprehensive information about derogations has not escaped the Committee's notice. For a decade the Committee discussed the possibility of creating a special obligation on derogating states to file a timely supplemental report with the Committee.[57] One model of such a procedure would have coordinated the Secretary-General's functions as depositary of derogation notices with the Committee's power to request supplemental reports under Article 40(1)(b); it provides:

> Furthermore, the Committee instructs the Secretariat, whenever a notification under Article 4(3) has been made, to transmit it to the members of the Committee, and to draw the attention of the State party concerned to general comment 5/13, informing it that the Committee will decide in due course whether to request a report under Article 40(1)(b) outside the time indicated

---

Secretary-General and the United Nations as a whole were aware of the situation." *1991 Human Rights Committee Report, supra* note 26, at para. 578.

53. The Sudan's initial report was due in June 1987, yet not until January 1991 was a "brief and incomplete" report filed, which "had not been prepared in accordance with the Committee's reporting guidelines." *1991 Human Rights Committee Report, supra* note 26, at paras. 493–94. The second periodic reports of Libya and Iran, due in 1983, had not been received by October 1991. *Id.* at Annex IV.

54. *See, e.g., Report of the Human Rights Committee,* 38 U.N. GAOR Supp. (No. 40), U.N. Doc. A/38/40, at para. 263 (1983) (citing the notice from Peru noting "perverse delinquency" as a justification for emergency measures).

55. *See, e.g., Report of the Human Rights Committee,* 37 U.N. GAOR Supp. (No. 40), U.N. Doc. A/37/40, at para. 270 (1982) (finding that the vague notice filed by Uruguay gave the disturbing impression that all of the Covenant's rights had been suspended).

56. The derogation notice filed by the United Kingdom with respect to Northern Ireland in 1977, after briefly explaining the nature of the emergency, simply stated: "The Government of the United Kingdom have found it necessary (and in some cases continue to find it necessary) to take powers, to the extent strictly required by the exigencies of the situation, for the protection of life, for the protection of property and the prevention of outbreak of public disorder, including the exercise of powers of arrest and detention and exclusion. In so far as any of these measures is inconsistent with the provisions of Articles 9, 10.2, 10.3, 12.1, 14, 17, 19.2, 21 or 22 of the Covenant, the United Kingdom hereby derogates from its obligations under those provisions." U.N. Doc. CCPR/C/2, at 11–12 (1977).

57. *See, e.g.,* U.N. Doc. CCPR/C/SR.349, at 4–5 (1982) (stating the proposal by Mr. Opsahl) [hereinafter 1982 Human Rights Committee meeting].

above, and that meanwhile the Committee in any event will appreciate being kept currently informed about the development of the emergency insofar as it affects the implementation of the Covenant.[58]

A number of different proposals surfaced, each appearing to have broad support but achieving no consensus. In 1981 Mr. Tarnopolsky proposed that guidelines for state reports require a precise description of the nature and extent of each derogated right.[59] In 1982 Mr. Opsahl made a specific proposal similar to that quoted above, but unfortunately this proposal coincided with Poland's notice of derogation and it was effectively opposed by Committee members from the eastern bloc.[60] Mr. Tarnopolsky submitted a new proposal in 1982 that special reports be requested not upon receipt of notices of derogation, but based on reliable information that the state was experiencing a "significant new development."[61] This suggestion was not considered for lack of time.[62] Mr. Opsahl's renewed proposal, quoted above, was also shelved for the same reason.[63]

Attention shifted in 1984 to the newly established working group on Article 40, which was assigned the task of preparing lists of questions for the review of second periodic reports and which also occasionally toyed with the idea of creating some standards or mechanisms for requesting additional information about emergencies.[64] This working group, under the chairmanship of Mr. Opsahl, proposed in 1985 a new general comment on the reporting requirement under Article 4, but this proposal was not discussed and is not even mentioned in the annual report of the Committee.[65] In 1989 the Committee heard the suggestion that "it would be of great benefit if . . . Committee members had the opportunity to exchange ideas on the Committee's role between periodic reports in respect of states of emergency."[66] Further inconclusive discussion ensued during the Committee's thirty-eighth session in 1990, when Professor Higgins suggested that "the Commit-

58. U.N. Doc. CCPR/C/SR.463, at 3 (1983) (proposal by Mr. Opsahl).

59. U.N. Doc. CCPR/C/SR.308, at paras. 58–59 (1981). McGoldrick notes that the Committee decided not to mention derogations in its general guidelines on reporting, for fear of confusing the states' obligation of notification under Article 4(3). McGoldrick, *supra* note 6, at 302. The Committee failed to cure this lapse in its revised guidelines for state reports. *1991 Human Rights Committee Report, supra* note 26, at Annex VII.

60. U.N. Docs. CCPR/C/SR.334 (1982); CCPR/C/SR.349; CCPR/C/SR.351.

61. U.N. Doc. CCPR/C/SR.404 (1982).

62. U.N. Doc. CCPR/C/SR.414 (1982).

63. U.N. Doc. CCPR/C/SR.463 (1983).

64. *See* U.N. Docs. CCPR/C/SR.513 (1984); CCPR/C/SR.520; CCPR/C/SR.541.

65. U.N. Doc. CCPR/C/SR.575, at para. 10 (1985); U.N. Doc. A/40/40, at 138 (1985).

66. *1989 Human Rights Committee Report, supra* note 7, at para. 24.

tee needed to consider at length how to monitor compliance with human rights instruments during states of emergency," and that it was "obviously not satisfactory to deal with such situations solely in the context of the periodic reports submitted to the Committee."[67] The Chairman agreed that substantive discussion should be scheduled, especially in light of General Assembly resolution 44/129, "which had emphasized the need for States parties to provide the fullest possible information during states of emergency."[68]

A breakthrough appears to have occurred when the Committee took the unusual decision to demand submission of Iraq's overdue third periodic report on April 1991, in light of "the recent and current trends in Iraq that have affected human rights."[69] The Committee requested that the report focus on Articles 6, 7, 9, and 27 (right to life; prohibition on torture; detention; and minority rights), rather than Article 4, however.[70]

The significance of this development is highlighted by the Committee's "special decisions" to request in November 1991 that Yugoslavia submit its overdue third periodic report[71] and that Peru file a supplemental report concerning its April 1992 emergency.[72] The Committee expressed concern at the successive states of emergency in Kosovo under which "excessive steps have been taken to limit the rights and freedoms guaranteed in the Covenant."[73] The Committee expressed its "gravest concern" with regard to atrocities being committed during the armed conflicts, including violation of non-derogable rights.[74] The Committee regretted the failure of the federal government to investi-

67. U.N. Doc. CCPR/C/SR.973, at para. 33 (1990).

68. *Id.* at para. 43.

69. *1991 Human Rights Committee Report, supra* note 26, Annex VI. The report was due in April 1990. In suggesting this action, Mr. Prado Vallejo noted that Article 40(1)(b) "had been included in the Covenant to cover cases in which extreme circumstances were seriously affecting human rights; to date, the Committee had never felt it necessary to exercise its authority under that provision." U.N. Doc. CCPR/C/SR.1062/Add.1, at para. 13 (1991).

70. *Id.* A rather contentious review session was held in July 1991, with members of the Committee observing that hopes for a constructive dialogue had not been realized. *Id.* at para. 651. In the continuation of this review in October 1991, Iraq continued to assert that it had made no derogations under Article 4. *See supra* note 25.

71. The report had been due in 1988. *Report of the Human Rights Committee,* 46 U.N. GAOR Supp. (No. 40), U.N. Doc. A/46/40 Annex IV (1991). *See supra* note 7.

72. *See supra* note 7.

73. *Comments on the Human Rights Committee on the third periodic report of Yugoslavia,* U.N. Doc. M/CCPR/92/16 at 2 (1992).

74. *Id.*

gate these violations and to punish the guilty.[75] The Committee expressed concern that Peru's emergency would impede rather than promote respect for the Covenant, and objected to violations of both non-derogable as well as derogable rights.[76] Moreover, the Committee pointedly criticized Peru's failure to file a notice of derogation.[77]

The Committee thus seems to have overcome objections concerning the lack of a legal basis for any special reporting procedure in emergency situations,[78] the necessity for intersessional structures for the Committee,[79] or the lack of any authority by the Committee to exercise a supervisory function over derogations made by states parties.[80] Under Article 4(3) derogating states are technically required to give immediate notice to the Secretary-General, who must then convey the information to the other states parties. The Committee is not a formal part of this process, though nothing prevents the Secretary-General from also conveying the information in a timely fashion to the Committee. The Committee possesses flexible authority under Article 40(1)(b) to request additional information from any state party "whenever the Committee so requests."

At the early stages of its existence, the Committee was sometimes divided on the legitimacy of referring to information outside the states' reports themselves.[81] While the Committee now widely uses such information, it tends not to identify the sources when the information emanates from a non-governmental organization.[82] Although the quality of state reports overall has improved since the Committee's early years, inadequate reports continue to be filed, and the oral presentation by the state representative often does little to fill the gaps.[83]

---

75. *Id.* The Committee also noted that the inability of the federal government to exercise control over the entire territory of the former Yugoslavia prevented it from receiving adequate information about respect for the Covenant within those areas. *Id.* at 1.

76. *See supra* note 49.

77. *1992 Human Rights Committee Report, supra* note 7, at para. 345.

78. 1982 Human Rights Committee meeting, *supra* note 57, at 6 (remarks of Mr. Hanga).

79. *Id.* at 6 (1982) (remarks of Mr. Dieye).

80. *Id.* at 9–10 (1982) (remarks of Mr. Graefrath); U.N. Doc. CCPR/C/SR.492, at 5 (1984) (remarks of Mr. Graefrath).

81. *See, e.g.,* U.N. Doc. CCPR/C/SR.65, at 6 (1978) (noting the critical comments by Mr. Graefrath); U.N. Doc. CCPR/C/SR.82, at 6 (1978) (noting the findings Mr. Hanga); U.N. Doc. CCPR/C/SR.181, at 4 (1979) (noting the comments of Mr. Lallah).

82. The Committee had worked out an informal compromise to operate in this manner. *See* Fischer, *supra* note 6, at 146.

83. At the conclusion of the March 1990 review of the second periodic report of the

Thus, access to reliable, timely, and complete information from other inter-governmental and non-governmental bodies remains crucial to the Committee's reviews. The Committee's success in determining the level of compliance with Article 4 depends heavily on the effectiveness and comprehensiveness of the other components of the international monitoring system that are the subject of this study.[84]

The Committee's authority to make "general comments" on state reports under Article 40(4) has played a fairly minor role in the implementation of Article 4. In 1980 the Committee members resolved an internal dispute over whether Article 40(4) permitted them to comment on a particular state's breach of Covenant obligations by deciding to issue general interpretive guidelines that would be addressed to all states parties.[85] Finally in 1992 the Committee, in concluding comments on reviews of state reports, began to suggest the existence of violations in certain countries.[86]

The Committee directed its newly defined authority to issue general comments rather quickly toward Article 4, which "posed a number of problems for the Committee when considering reports from some States parties."[87] General comment 5/13 provides little in the way of detailed and nuanced substantive interpretation of Article 4,[88] although it does restate the principles of severity, proportionality, and non-derogability of certain rights.[89] The comment identifies recurring

Dominican Republic, Committee members stated that neither of that state's reports had met the Committee's guidelines, that specifics on the actual implementation of Dominican law were lacking, and that unless more information were provided then a useful dialogue would not be possible. *1990 Human Rights Committee Report, supra* note 5, at para. 385.

84. In making her comment on the desirability of new discussions on the question of special reporting by derogating states, Professor Higgins mentioned the possibility of a university (presumably Queen's University in Belfast) setting up a data center on states of emergency. U.N. Doc. CCPR/C/SR.973, at para. 33 (1990).

85. U.N. Doc. CCPR/C/SR.260, at 2 (1980) (noting that the Committee's authority was to be "without prejudice to the further consideration of the Committee's duties under article 40, paragraph 4 of the Covenant").

86. *See supra* notes 7, 49.

87. *Report of the Human Rights Committee, General Comment 5/13,* 36 U.N. GAOR Supp. (No. 40), U.N. Doc. A/36/40 Annex VII (1981) [hereinafter *General Comment 5/13*].

88. One commentator has found General Comment 5/13 "profoundly illuminating," although he refers primarily to its identification of deficiencies in state reports. Ghandhi, *supra* note 6, at 332.

89. General Comment 5/13 states: "(1) Article 4 of the Covenant has posed a number of problems for the Committee when considering reports from some States parties. When a public emergency which threatens the life of a nation arises and it is officially proclaimed, a State party may derogate from a number of rights to the extent strictly required by the situation. The State party, however, may not derogate from certain

deficiencies in state reports and notices of derogation, particularly the tendency to provide at most a bare legal description of the emergency regime, without indicating "the nature and extent of each right derogated from together with the relevant documentation."[90] Other general comments by the Committee occasionally have touched on emergency-related issues.[91]

Of even less impact has been the optional mechanism for interstate complaints under Article 41 and 42 of the Covenant. While a sizable number of states have made the declaration under Article 41,[92] no communications have been filed. In any such case parties would be obliged to provide the Committee with "any relevant information," and the Committee could make an authoritative finding of facts but could not express its views as to breach.[93] Because the parties enjoy multiple opportunities to bring the entire proceedings to a halt, one commenta-

---

specific rights and may not take discriminatory measures on a number of grounds. The State party is also under an obligation to inform the other State parties immediately, through the Secretary-General, of the derogations it has made including the reasons therefor and the date on which the derogations are terminated.

"(2) States parties have generally indicated the mechanism provided in their legal systems for the declaration of a state of emergency and the applicable provisions of the law governing derogations. However, in the case of a few States which had apparently derogated from Covenant rights, it was unclear not only whether a state of emergency had been officially declared but also whether rights from which the Covenant allows no derogation had in fact not been derogated from and further whether the other States parties had been informed of the derogations and of the reasons for the derogations.

"(3) The Committee holds the view that measures taken under article 4 are of an exceptional and temporary nature and may only last as long as the life of the nation concerned is threatened and that in times of emergency, the protection of human rights becomes all the more important, particularly those rights from which no derogations can be made. The Committee also considers that it is equally important for States parties, in times of public emergency, to inform the other States parties of the nature and extent of the derogation they have made and of the reasons therefor and, further, to fulfil their reporting obligations under article 40 of the Covenant by indicating the nature and extent of each right derogated from together with the relevant documentation." *See supra* note 82.

90. *Id.*

91. General comment 13(21), for example, addresses the issue of military courts trying civilians and notes that such measures are sometimes taken during emergencies. The Committee states that while such courts are not absolutely barred, they must meet the basic standards of fairness set out in Article 14 and must be tailored to the "exigencies of the actual situation." *Report of the Human Rights Committee,* 39 U.N. GAOR Supp. (No. 40), U.N. Doc. A/39/40, at 144 (1984).

92. As of October 1992, thirty-six of the one-hundred-twelve states parties to the Covenant had made the Article 41 declaration. *1992 Human Rights Committee Report, supra* note 7, at Annex I.

93. *See* Hartman, *supra* note 8, at 41–42.

tor concludes that it is "hard to imagine a more toothless procedure."[94] While the experience of the Council of Europe human rights bodies has been that states of emergency are a prime subject for overcoming the inertia against invocation of such interstate complaint mechanisms, the greater diversity and ideological division among states parties to the Covenant appear to act as a continuing powerful deterrent to interstate complaints.

The increasing rate of ratification of the Optional Protocol[95] and its growing visibility have resulted in a virtual explosion in the adjudicatory workload of the Committee.[96] The Committee has created a special working group to increase its efficiency in handling these communications, delegating it the authority to declare communications admissible if all five members agree.[97] Furthermore, a special rapporteur on communications has been designated to maintain the ongoing process of transmitting communications to the respondent government for its views,[98] and another special rapporteur is assigned to track follow-up by states to the Committee's suggested remedies in cases where violations have been found.[99]

While dozens of communications have been filed against derogating states, particularly Uruguay, the Committee has only rarely been required to grapple with a respondent state's assertion that its challenged actions were taken in legitimate derogation from the Covenant. As a result, the derogation jurisprudence of the Committee lacks detailed texture and clarity and sometimes appears erratic.

In no case has the Committee explicitly found that a derogating state had exceeded the principle of severity in declaring an emergency without adequate basis. But, in its views in the *Landinelli Silva* case,[100] the Committee asserted the "principle of objective reviewability"[101]— that the Committee possesses authority to determine whether a public

94. Ghandhi, *supra* note 6, at 357.

95. As of October 1992, sixty-six of the one-hundred-twelve states that were party to the Covenant had ratified the Optional Protocol. *1992 Human Rights Committee Report, supra* note 7, at Annex I.

96. As of October 1992, the Committee had adopted views as to 138 individual communications. *Id.* at para. 609. At the Committee's forty-fifth session, 153 cases were pending. *Id.* at para. 615.

97. *1991 Human Rights Commission Report, supra* note 26, at para. 670.

98. *Id.* at para. 669. *See id.* at Annex X.

99. *Id.* at paras. 701–704; *1990 Human Rights Committee Report, supra* note 5, at Annex XI.

100. Silva v. Uruguay, Comm. No. 34/1978 (decided Apr. 8, 1981), *in Selected Decisions under the Optional Protocol,* U.N. Doc. CCPR/C/OP/1, at 65 (1985) [hereinafter *Selected Decisions*].

101. Ghandhi, *supra* note 6, at 336.

emergency actually exists in a state attempting to justify certain denials of protected rights under Article 4. *Landinelli Silva* involved a challenge by five Uruguayan exiles to Institutional Act No. 4 of 1 September 1976 which barred all persons who had been candidates of certain political parties in the 1966 and 1971 elections from engaging in any political activity (including voting) for a period of fifteen years.[102] When Uruguay chose to invoke Article 4 to justify this restriction on political rights (protected by Article 25 of the Covenant, which Uruguay pointed out is not included among the non-derogable rights in Article 4(2)),[103] the issue of the legitimacy of Uruguay's emergency measures was clearly joined.

The Committee reacted by noting that Uruguay's 1979 notice of derogation under Article 4(3) lacked factual detail and made no attempt "to indicate the nature and scope of the derogations actually resorted to . . . or to show that such derogations were strictly necessary."[104] Uruguay's promise to provide more information in its Article 40 report had not been kept, as no report had been filed.[105] The Committee asserted that "a State, by merely invoking the existence of exceptional circumstances, cannot evade the obligations which it has undertaken by ratifying the Covenant,"[106] but is "duty-bound to give a sufficiently detailed account of the relevant facts when it invokes article 4(1) of the Covenant in proceedings under the Optional Protocol."[107] The Committee added:

It is the function of the Human Rights Committee, acting under the Optional Protocol, to see to it that States parties live up to their commitments under the Covenant. In order to discharge this function and to assess whether a situation of the kind described in article 4(1) of the Covenant exists in the country concerned, it needs full and comprehensive information. If the respondent Government does not furnish the required justification itself . . . the Human Rights Committee cannot conclude that valid reasons exist to legitimize a departure from the normal legal regime prescribed by the Covenant.[108]

While these are bold and significant words, their emphasis upon the essentially procedural question of the sufficiency of the government's factual submission on the principle of severity enabled the Committee to avoid elaborating a clear standard by which to judge the factual

102. Silva v. Uruguay, *supra* note 100, at para. 2.
103. *Id.* at para. 6.
104. *Id.* at para. 8.2.
105. *Id.*
106. *Id.*
107. *Id.* at para. 8.3.
108. *Id.*

bases for declared emergencies. In a large number of other Uruguayan cases involving detainees, the Committee similarly avoided determining whether the crisis had ever amounted to an emergency within the meaning of Article 4(1) by the recitation of what became a boilerplate paragraph concerning the government's failure to supply adequate information:

> The Human Rights Committee has considered whether acts and treatment, which are *prima facie* not in conformity with the Covenant, could for any reasons be justified under the Covenant in the circumstances. The Government has referred to provisions of Uruguayan law, in particular the "prompt security measures." However, the Covenant (art. 4) does not allow national measures derogating from any of its provisions except in strictly defined circumstances, and the Government has not made any submissions of fact or law to justify such derogation. Moreover, some of the facts referred to above raise issues under provisions from which the Covenant does not allow any derogation under any circumstances.[109]

Eventually, the Uruguayan government apparently stopped relying on Article 4 at all to justify its regime of "prompt security measures." When victims of these measures attempted to establish that Uruguay had violated Article 4, the Committee found it "inappropriate to make a finding in respect of this article" since "the State party has not purported to rely on any derogation from provisions of the Covenant pursuant to article 4."[110] Thus, the dozens of Uruguayan communications under the Optional Protocol provide no real guidance to the Committee's interpretation of the concept of a "public emergency threatening the life of the nation."

Another missed opportunity to advance understanding of the principle of severity was presented in two cases challenging a prolonged state of siege in Colombia that had originated in a quickly terminated

109. Weismann v. Uruguay, Comm. No. 8/1977 (decided Apr. 3, 1980), *in Selected Decisions, supra* note 100, at 48, para. 15. Identical or nearly identical language appears in such decisions as Weinberger v. Uruguay, Comm. No. 28/1978 (decided Oct. 29, 1980), *id.* at 60, para. 14; Tourón v. Uruguay, Comm. No. 32/1978 (decided Mar. 31, 1981), *id.* at 62, para. 10; Buffo Carballal v. Uruguay, Comm. No. 33/1978 (decided Mar. 27, 1981), *id.* at 64, para. 11; Millán Sequeira v. Uruguay, Comm. No. 6/1977, *id.* at 54, para. 14; Grille Motta v. Uruguay, Comm. No. 11/1977 (decided July 29, 1980), *id.* at 57, para. 15; López Burgos v. Uruguay, Comm. No. 52/1979 (decided July 29, 1981), *id.* at 91, para. 11.6; Pietraroia v. Uruguay, Comm. No. 44/1979 (decided Mar. 27, 1981), *id.* at 79, para. 14; Soriano de Bouton v. Uruguay, Comm. No. 37/1978 (decided Mar. 27, 1981), *id.* at 73, para. 12.

110. Conteris v. Uruguay, Comm. No. 139/1983 (decided July 17, 1985), 2 *Selected Decisions of the Human Rights Committee under the Optional Protocol*, U.N. Doc. CCPR/C/OP/2, at 171, para. 7.5 (1990) [hereinafter 2 *Selected Decisions*].

strike among public health employees.[111] As in the Uruguayan cases, the Committee saw no necessity to evaluate whether the situation in Colombia remained grave enough to justify derogation, since Colombia had not provided "a sufficiently detailed account of the relevant facts to show that situation of the kind described in article 4(1) of the Covenant exists."[112]

Rather than grapple with the overall existence of an emergency, the Committee considered in these cases whether specific rights, both derogable and non-derogable, had been violated. The arguable emergency context for these violations had only slight relevance. In *Landinelli Silva*, the Committee invoked the principle of proportionality in finding that a fifteen-year ban on political activity had not been justified as necessary "to deal with the alleged emergency situation and pave the way back to political freedom."[113]

Obviously, the existence of a *bona fide* emergency has no bearing on whether violations of non-derogable rights have been committed. Since no emergency can justify such actions, the Committee need only determine the fact of the violations themselves. In *Suarez de Guerrero v. Colombia*,[114] which involved the killing of seven persons in a raid by police acting with impunity pursuant to a Colombian decree issued during the state of siege, the Committee noted that Colombia's derogation could not extend to arbitrary deprivation of life under Article 6. Numerous Uruguayan cases similarly involved violations of other non-derogable provisions, such as the ban on torture or retroactive criminal penalities.[115]

But many communications also or exclusively concern violations of derogable rights, which presumably would require the Committee to assess the existence of the emergency and to apply of the principle of proportionality. Yet, aside from *Landinelli Silva*, the Committee essentially never undertakes this analysis.[116] The reason is that the state's

---

111. Salgar de Montejo v. Colombia, Comm. No. 64/1979 (decided Mar. 24, 1982), *Selected Decisions, supra* note 100, at 129, paras. 8.2, 10.2, 10.3; Fals Borda v. Colombia, Comm. No. 46/1979 (decided July 27, 1982), *id.* at 144, para. 13.2.

112. *Salgar de Montejo, id.* at 129, para. 10.3.

113. *Silva v. Uruguay, supra* note 100, at para. 8.4.

114. Suarez de Guerrero v. Colombia, Comm. No. 45/1979 (decided Mar. 31, 1982), *id.* at 117, para. 12.2.

115. *See, e.g., Grille Motta, id.* at 57, para. 15; *Buffo Carballal, id.* at 64, para. 11; *Pietraroia, id.* at 80, para. 17.

116. The only reference to the "principle of proportionality" with respect to Article 25 and the fifteen-year ban on political activity is found in *Pietraroia v. Uruguay. Pietraroia, id.* at 79, para. 16. The "principle of proportionality" refers to the limitations clause of that article and not to Article 4.

claim of derogation is either inadequately supported, as in *Landinelli Silva,* or irrelevant to the issues raised. For example, Colombia's notified derogation to Articles 19 and 21 was found to be irrelevant to alleged violations of Articles 9 and 14 in the *Fals Borda* case.[117]

The Committee's determination not to consider these cases in terms of Article 4 seems to weaken the clarity and force of its analysis and to contribute to inconsistencies in approach, especially with respect to issues arising under Articles 9 (detention), 14 (fair trial) and 19 (freedom of expression). For example, several communications challenged the permissibility of subjecting civilians to trial by military courts. The Committee in its "general comment" on Article 14 had rather reluctantly recognized that such trials might be permissible in an emergency.[118] These cases presented the Committee with a potential opportunity to explore the factors that would render military courts a proportionate response to a threat to public order or security.

But rather than confronting this interesting interpretive issue, the Committee devoted primary attention to assessing whether the author of the communication had shown that certain guaranteed elements of fair process were denied.[119] The Committee did not acknowledge any inherent unfairness in military trial of civilians, even in the absence of a genuine emergency. No violation was found with respect to two of the alleged victims in the *Fals Borda* case, for example, who were given terms of rigorous imprisonment by military tribunals for "rebellion":

The allegations . . . seem to be based on the premise that civilians may not be subject to military penal procedures and that when civilians are nevertheless subjected to such procedures, they are in effect deprived of basic judicial guarantees aimed at ensuring fair trial, which guarantees would be afforded to them under the normal court system, because military courts are neither competent, independent and [sic] impartial. The arguments of the author in substantiating these allegations are set out in general terms and principally linked with the question of constitutionality. . . . [H]e does not, however, cite any specific incidents or facts in support of his allegations of disregard for the

117. *Fals Borda, id.* at 144, para. 13.2. As in *Silva v. Uruguay, supra* note 100, however, the Committee did not decide whether a valid derogation is contingent upon proper notification under Article 4(3).

118. *See supra* note 91.

119. In *Campora Schweizer v. Uruguay,* the Committee announced that it "does not feel that it is in a position to pronounce itself on the general compatibility of the regime of prompt security measures under Uruguayan law with the Covenant. . . . Although administrative detention may not be objectionable in circumstances where the person concerned constitutes a clear and serious threat to society which cannot be contained in any other manner, the Committee emphasizes that the guarantees enshrined in the following paragraphs of article 9 fully apply in such instances." Campora Schweizer v. Uruguay, Comm. No. 66/1980 (decided Oct. 12, 1982), 2 *Selected Decisions, supra* note 110, at 93, para. 18.1.

judicial guarantees provided for by article 14. . . . Since the Committee does not deal with questions of constitutionality, but with the question of whether a law is in conformity with the Covenant, as applied in the circumstances of the case, the Committee cannot make any finding of breaches of article 14 of the Covenant.[120]

The Committee's insistence on specific detailing of violations appears to waver inexplicably at times. For instance, civilians represented by appointed military counsel before Uruguayan military tribunals were sometimes found to have suffered deprivation of rights under Article 14(3)(b),[121] and sometimes not.[122] Allegations that detention or prosecution for subversive activities constituted impermissible persecution for political beliefs in violation of Article 19 sometimes resulted in a finding of violation;[123] a finding of violation, but with dissenting views by some Committee members;[124] or rejection of the claim, sometimes on grounds that the victim had not sufficiently detailed the nature of his or her beliefs.[125]

With respect to important procedural issues in handling Optional Protocol communications, the Committee devised effective methods of rendering defensible views within the constraints of its attenuated fact-finding capacities. The Committee takes evidence only in written form[126] from both the author and the respondent state. Uruguay

120. *Selected Decisions, supra* note 100, at 144, para. 13.3.

121. *See, e.g.,* Oxandabarat Scarrone v. Uruguay, Comm. No. 103/1981 (decided Nov. 4, 1983), in 2 *Selected Decisions, supra* note 110, at 130, para. 11; Vasilskis v. Uruguay, Comm. No. 80/1980 (decided Mar. 31, 1983), *id.* at 108, paras. 9.3, 11; Viana Acosta v. Uruguay, Comm. No. 110/1981 (decided Mar. 29, 1984), *id.* at 148, para. 15.

122. In *Martínez Machado v. Uruguay,* the claim is made that appointed military counsel, subject to superior orders, could not be adequate. Martínez Machado v. Uruguay, Comm. No. 83/1981 (decided Nov. 4, 1983), *id.* at 110, para. 4.2. In its findings, however, the Committee found a violation of Article 14(3)(b) only in respect to the seven-month period of incommunicado detention when the victim was not permitted any access to counsel. *Id.* at 111, para. 13.

123. *See, e.g., Pietraroia, Selected Decisions, supra* note 100, at 79, para. 15, at 80, para. 17; Weismann, *id.* at 49, para. 16.

124. *See, e.g.,* Muteba v. Zaire, Comm. No. 124/1982 (decided July 24, 1984), 2 *Selected Decisions, supra* note 110, at 160, para. 12 (dissenting views by Messrs. Aguilar, Cooray, Ermacora, Errera, Mavrommatis); *Grille Motta, Selected Decisions, supra* note 100, at 57, para. 17 (dissenting views of Mr. Tomuschat).

125. *See, e.g.,* Gómez de Voituret v. Uruguay, Comm. No. 109/1981 (decided Apr. 10, 1984), *in* 2 *Selected Decisions, supra* note 110, at 146, at paras. 2.5, 2.6; Conteris, *id.* at 170, para. 7.4.

126. *See Amended Rules of Procedure, Report of the Human Rights Committee,* 44 U.N. GAOR Supp. (No. 40), U.N. Doc. A/44/40 Annex IX (1989) (noting the contents of Rule 94).

The Committee uses reports of on-site visits made by other bodies, including the report of one of its own members in the case of Suriname as the Special Rapporteur on

presented the Committee with vague and general denials of the victims' allegations, often in situations where the state had better access to the most precise relevant information. The response of the Committee was to establish that refutations in general terms were not sufficient to block a finding of a violation[127] and that a state party has a duty to investigate allegations under the Optional Protocol in good faith and to report the results of its investigation.[128] Especially where the victim can support the allegations with statements of witnesses to the events, the Committee is inclined to find a violation where the respondent state does not address the claims in specific detail.[129] The Committee sees the burden of proof as shared, rather than resting exclusively on the victim.[130] But in some cases the Committee seems inclined to make findings only with respect to matters that are relatively easy to assess objectively and from a distance, for instance, by finding denials of the right to trial within a reasonable time and avoiding decisions on allegations that the tribunal or appointed counsel lacked independence.[131]

The failure of Uruguayan authorities to supply requested copies of court records contributed to many findings by the Committee of violations of fair trial rights.[132] The Committee noted during its review of

---

Summary and Arbitrary Executions for the Commission on Human Rights. Baboeram v. Suriname, Comms. Nos. 146/1983 & 148–154/1983, 40 U.N. GAOR Supp. (No. 40), U.N. Doc. A/40/40 Annex X, at paras. 9.1, n. a (1985). Mr. Wako excused himself from decision in the case to avoid the appearance of prejudgment.

Mr. Tomuschat of the Committee once suggested that an on-site visit to Afghanistan might assist the Committee in its review of that state's report. However, this unprecedented step was never taken. U.N. Doc. CCPR/C/SR.608, at para. 52 (1985). The Committee noted with approval the suggestion in the Third Committee of the General Assembly that members of human rights treaty bodies participate in fact-finding missions during humanitarian emergencies. *1992 Human Rights Committee Report, supra* note 7, at para. 28.

127. *See, e.g.,* Valcada v. Uruguay, Comm. No. 9/1977 (decided Oct. 26, 1979), *Selected Decisions, supra* note 100, at 44, para. 11.

128. *See, e.g., Martínez Machado,* 2 *Selected Decisions, supra* note 110, at 108, para. 12.2; *Oxandabarat Scarrone, id.* at 130, para. 10.2.

129. *E.g., Conteris, id.* at 170, para. 7.2: "In cases where the author has submitted to the Committee allegations supported by witness testimony, as in this case, and where further clarification of the case depends on information exclusively in the hands of the State party, the Committee may consider such allegations as substantiated in the absence of satisfactory evidence and explanations to the contrary submitted by the State party."

130. *See, e.g.,* Bleier v. Uruguay, Comm. No. 30/1978, *Selected Decisions, supra* note 100, at 112, para. 13.3.

131. *Machado,* 2 *Selected Decisions, supra* note 110, at 111, paras. 8, 9, 13.

132. *See, e.g.,* Romero v. Uruguay, Comm. No. 85/1981 (decided Mar. 29, 1984), *id.* at 118, para. 12.2.

Uruguay's report under Article 40 that the Uruguayan representative had stated that these documents could easily be supplied.[133] The persistent non-appearance of these records led the Committee to speculate that perhaps military proceedings were not even recorded.[134] The Committee also asserted its right to communicate directly with detained victims.[135] The proliferation of emergency-related Uruguayan cases enabled the Committee to simplify its admissibility decisions through the accumulation of knowledge on subjects such as the availability of unexhausted effective domestic remedies[136] and the significance of pending proceedings before such bodies as the IACHR.[137]

With ratifications of the Optional Protocol now increasing and greater follow-up by the Committee on compliance with its views in such cases, the Optional Protocol procedure offers promise as an effective monitoring mechanism. The Committee at its twenty-fourth session in 1985 was heartened by praise from the newly elected Uruguayan government, which thanked the Committee for persisting in its consideration of the many communications from victims of the military government.[138] However, the Committee's heavier caseload and continued restriction to written evidence suggest that substantial delays will persist, and perhaps even increase,[139] thereby limiting the Optional Protocol's effectiveness in coping with transient crises. Nonetheless, the Committee has demonstrated an increasing sophistication in the development of its jurisprudence,[140] which may promise greater depth in its consideration of Article 4 in future communications.

133. Oxandabarat Scarrone, *id.* at 130, para. 10.2.

134. Tourón v. Uruguay, Comm. No. 32/1978, *Selected Decisions, supra* note 100, at 62, para. 11.

135. Antonaccio v. Uruguay, Comm. No. 63/1979 (decided Oct. 28, 1981), *id.* at 104, para. 18.

136. In *Ramírez v. Uruguay,* the Committee noted from a previous case that habeas corpus is not available to persons subject to "prompt security measures." Ramírez v. Uruguay, Comm. No. 4/1977 (decided July 23, 1980), *id.* at 51, para. 14.

137. In *Estrella v. Uruguay,* the Committee noted that in a previous case it had learned of a petition concerning hundreds of persons that had been filed with the IACHR without the authorization of the victims. The Committee found that this still-pending mass petition was not "the same matter" so as to bar its consideration of Estrella's individual communication under Optional Protocol Article 5(2)(a). Estrella v. Uruguay, Comm. No. 74/1980 (decided July 17, 1980), 2 *Selected Decisions,* at 93, paras. 4.2, 4.3.

138. U.N. Doc. CCPR/C/SR.599, at para. 15 (1985).

139. The Committee itself warns that it "will not be able to examine communications at the same speed or to maintain the same level of quality unless the Secretariat staff is reinforced." *1990 Human Rights Committee Report, supra* note 5, at para. 595.

140. The Committee, for example, offers a useful digest of significant aspects of its latest decisions in its 1990 Report. *Id.* at paras. 604–628.

## C. The International Labour Organisation

Many states of emergency imposed on the basis of internal tension or disturbances include sharp restrictions on freedoms of association and assembly, with trade unionists as frequent targets of harsh measures. The International Labour Organisation (ILO) has a specialized mandate in the field of human rights and it has evolved an unusually complex battery of procedures of supervision, investigation, and conciliation. Its monitoring processes are more continuous and interactive with governments than are the procedures of similar bodies; private groups such as labor unions have a direct participatory role in its processes; and a very large number of states are included within the ILO system. This continuous involvement places the ILO in a position to respond rapidly to new emergencies, although the form and intensity of the response vary over time and among situations.

The ILO procedures take three main forms. First, there is a convention-based system of regular reports by states parties thereto, which are examined first by the Committee of Experts on the Application of Conventions and Recommendations; the Committee of Experts, in turn, reports to the International Labour Conference, which sets up a Committee to examine this report each year. Second, the ILO Constitution creates constitutional procedures of complaint under Article 26 and procedures of representation under Article 24, both of which are available only in respect of ratified conventions. Third, a special complaints procedure in respect of freedom of association may be invoked by governments or by employers' or workers' organizations regardless of whether a state has ratified the conventions. This procedure normally will lead to examination by the Governing Body's Committee on Freedom of Association and, in exceptional cases, with the consent of the state concerned, can lead to referral to the Fact-Finding and Conciliation Commission on Freedom of Association.

Several case studies help illustrate the complexity of this implementation scheme. Prior to the declaration of emergencies in both Greece and Poland, the ILO was actively involved in attempting either to investigate allegations of violations of trade union rights under the special freedom of association procedure[141] or to secure reform of

---

141. In March 1965, the ILO Governing Body followed the recommendations of the Committee on Freedom of Association in deciding to set up a three-person Fact-Finding and Conciliation Commission to investigate charges by the General Greek Confederation of Labour (GGCL) that amendments to labor legislation violated trade union rights. The elected Centre Union government suggested the establishment of the Commission as well as visiting Greece. In July 1966, the Commission permitted the new leadership of the GGCL to withdraw the complaint, but only after a careful review to determine that

labor legislation under both the freedom of association procedure and the regular supervision procedure.[142] When the emergencies were declared, reaction was swift. International unions rapidly filed complaints against both Greece and Poland with the Governing Body's Committee on Freedom of Association, which led to sustained contacts between the ILO and these governments. In both instances some time elapsed before a formal complaint seeking the creation of a Commission of Inquiry was filed under Article 26 of the Constitution, and additional time was spent seeking conciliation before such commissions were actually set up.[143]

Whenever a special fact-finding body has not been created, the ILO can seek to influence governments through a variety of means. For example, the Committee of Experts on the Application of Conventions and Recommendations regularly evaluates domestic labor legislation and practice.[144] The Conference Committee on the Application of

---

the withdrawal was voluntary. 49 ILO OFFICIAL BULLETIN No. (SPECIAL SUPPLEMENT) 79, para. 716 (1966). In April 1967, the Centre Union government was overthrown by military coup.

142. The International Confederation of Free Trade Unions (ICFTU) filed a complaint against Poland in July 1978 with the Governing Body's Committee on Freedom of Association and sought a referral to a Fact-Finding and Conciliation Commission, which alleged that the lack of independence mandated by the 1949 Trade Unions Act violated Poland's obligations under the Freedom of Association and Protection of the Right to Organize Convention (No. 87) and the Right to Organize and Collective Bargaining Convention (No. 98). The ILO's regular supervisory bodies had expressed concern for many years about the content of this legislation. The complaint led to exchanges and direct contacts missions in May and October 1980 and May 1981 as well as consultations between high-ranking labor ministry officials and the Committee on Freedom of Association in June and November 1980. Changes in the Trade Unions Act in October 1980 and greater freedom for independent unions also resulted from the complaint. In December 1981, martial law was declared. 62 ILO OFFICIAL BULLETIN (SPECIAL SUPPLEMENT), SERIES B 10–15 (1984).

143. A formal complaint against Greece was filed in June 1968 by four delegates to the 52nd International Labour Conference under Article 26 of the ILO Constitution, alleging violations of Convention No. 87. The Governing Body, after communications with the Greek government, chose in March 1969 to create a Commission of Inquiry. 54 ILO OFFICIAL BULLETIN (SPECIAL SUPPLEMENT), No. 2, 1–7 (1971).

A formal complaint under Article 26 was filed against Poland in June 1982 by two delegates alleging violations of Conventions No. 87 and No. 98. After a number of contacts with the Polish Government, the Governing Body decided in May 1983 to set up a Commission of Inquiry. 67 ILO OFFICIAL BULLETIN (SPECIAL SUPPLEMENT), 1984 SERIES B 5–8 (1984). *See* T. Franck & H.S. Fairley, *Procedural Due Process in Human Rights Fact-Finding by International Agencies,* 74 AM. J. INT'L. L. 308, 332–44 (1980).

144. The Committee of Experts commented on Poland's application of Convention No. 87 in March 1983. At the same time, the Committee on Freedom of Association was seeking Poland's approval for a direct contacts mission.

Conventions and Recommendations may hold discussions with representatives of the government and, if the situation is considered sufficiently serious, may mention the situation in a "special paragraph" of the Committee's report or include it in the list of "cases of continued failure over several years to eliminate serious deficiencies in the application of ratified Conventions."[145] The Governing Body's Committee on Freedom of Association may publish evaluations of the situation.[146] Direct contacts missions[147] or technical assistance missions[148] may be initiated. The Director General of the ILO may also approach a government on his own initiative, although such an approach does not trigger any formal procedure.

Evaluations performed with or without the creation of a special *ad hoc* investigatory body may cover both legal questions of the conformity of domestic legislation to the applicable conventions and defects in the state's actual practice. ILO bodies have sometimes addressed the impact of emergencies as an abstract question. For example, in 1945 the Governing Body had before it a report on the effects of war upon obligations under ILO conventions in which it essentially concluded that belligerent states would be excused from such of their obligations as they were prevented from performing by *force majeure,* whether or not the conventions contained an explicit suspension clause.[149] One treaty that does contain an explicit suspension clause is the Forced Labour Convention (No. 29), which excludes from the definition of

145. At the 71st Session of the International Labour Conference in June 1985, the special paragraphs covered Guatemala, Haiti, Iran, and Yemen.

146. The Committee's 224th Report in February 1983, which reviewed events in Turkey, expressed "profound concern" over the gravity of the trade union situation, criticized the 1982 Constitution, expressed regret at the refusal of Turkey to permit interviews of detainees during direct contacts missions, and urged the lifting of martial law. 66 ILO OFFICIAL BULLETIN, SERIES B 102–115 (1983).

147. Turkey, which has not become the subject of a special Fact-Finding and Conciliation Commission or Commission of Inquiry, has nevertheless received three direct contacts missions since 1982 within the framework of complaints being examined by the Committee on Freedom of Association. 66 ILO OFFICIAL BULLETIN, SERIES B, No. 3, 240, 242 (1983); 67 OFFICIAL BULLETIN, SERIES B, No. 3, 256 (1984).

148. During the period of the direct contacts missions to Turkey, a technical assistance mission also visited in May 1983. The Greek government made requests for a technical assistance mission in 1968 to forestall a Commission of Inquiry, although this suggestion was rejected by the Governing Body.

149. ILO, REPORT OF THE ACTING DIRECTOR, MINUTES OF THE 95TH SESSION OF THE GOVERNING BODY, app. XI, Annex A (1945). *See* REPORT OF THE COMMITTEE OF EXPERTS ON THE APPLICATION OF CONVENTIONS AND RECOMMENDATIONS, 69TH SESSION OF THE INTERNATIONAL LABOUR CONFERENCE, Vol. B., Report III (Part 4B), paras. 71–73 (1983) (noting the contents of Articles 19, 22, and 35 of the Constitution) [hereinafter REPORT OF THE COMMITTEE OF EXPERTS].

forced labor services exacted in case of specified emergencies. In 1968, the Committee of Experts on the Application of Conventions and Recommendations identified as a problem an "unduly wide recourse to emergency powers" and urged that call-ups for emergency service "should be confined to circumstances in which the existence or well-being of the whole or part of the population is endangered, and the duration, extent and nature of the compulsory service should be limited to what is strictly required by the exigencies of this situation."[150] This standard is closely in line with general human rights standards governing states of emergency.

Yet forced labor often is not the issue. Many governments imposing emergency measures will suspend trade union rights and arrest and subject trade union leaders to torture, arbitrary execution, or exile. The Greek Government argued in 1969 that its obligations under Conventions No. 87 and No. 98 must give way to emergency measures permitted under the Greek Constitution.[151] The Commission of Inquiry flatly rejected this notion (footnotes omitted):

The Commission takes the view that it is an accepted principle of international law that a State cannot rely on the terms of its national law, or otherwise involve the concept of national sovereignty, to justify non-performance of an international obligation. Any doubt concerning the extent of such obligation must be determined by exclusive reference to the relevant principles of international law. . . .

The relevant provisions of international law applicable in the present case are contained in Conventions Nos. 87 and 98. . . . In neither . . . is there any provision allowing the possibility of basing a plea of emergency, as an exception to the obligations arising under the Conventions, on the terms thereof.

. . . If a plea of emergency is to be treated in international law as a legal concept there . . . has to be appraisal by an impartial authority at the international level. It is for this reason that international tribunals and supervisory organs, when seized of such a plea, have invariably made an independent determination of whether the circumstances justified the claim, and have not allowed the state concerned to be the sole judge of the issue.

With regard to the whole question of the circumstances said to constitute a state of emergency, the Commission received insufficient information from the

---

150. Report of the Committee of Experts on the Application of Conventions and Recommendations, 52nd Session of the International Labour Conference, Report III (Part 4), para. 136 (1968).

151. The Greek Government, referring to Conventions No. 87 and No. 98, which do not contain suspension clauses, stated: "Greece had not undertaken to repeal Article 91 of the 1952 Constitution relating to the state of emergency. . . . Granted that the law must conform to the Constitution and the Government was the sole judge of the need to proclaim the state of emergency, the safeguards required by the Convention were clearly not inviolate and their suspension, however regrettable had been in no way arbitrary." 54 ILO Official Bulletin, No. 2, 24–25 (1971).

Greek Government, which took the attitude that it was a matter to be decided solely by the Government and not by any tribunal. . . . Accordingly, the Commission rejects the plea of the Government that it was entitled to derogate from the Conventions in the circumstances which prevailed in Greece in April 1967.[152]

The Commission of Inquiry into the Polish labor situation took a similar approach.[153]

In 1983, the Committee of Experts on the Application of Conventions and Recommendations referred to the Greek case in restating the limited basis for restricting labor rights in times of emergency:

[T]he freedom of association Conventions do not contain any provision permitting derogation . . . or any suspension of their application, based on a plea that an emergency exists. The Committee considers that, as regards the enjoyment of civil liberties which are essential for the effective exercise of trade union rights, the plea of a state of emergency to justify the restriction of these liberties should only be invoked in circumstances of extreme gravity constituting a case of *force majeure* and subject to the condition that any measures affecting in any way the guarantees established in the Conventions should be limited both in extent and in time to what is strictly necessary to deal with the particular situation. The Committee considers that, while it is conceivable that in such situations some civil liberties such as the right of public assembly or the right to hold street demonstrations might be prohibited, it is not permissible, however, that, in the field of trade union activities, the guarantees relating to the security of the person should be abolished, suspended or even limited.[154]

The ILO generally succeeds in gaining access to necessary information. Its established relationship with trade unions, especially international ones, places it in a direct line for the receipt of timely communications. With respect to Chile, Greece, Poland, and Turkey, ILO bodies also have been largely successful in conducting on-site visits, although not without some difficulties. Poland adamantly refused to permit entry to the Commission of Inquiry. That refusal did not prevent the

152. *Id.* at paras. 108–109, 111–112. *But see* 62 ILO OFFICIAL BULLETIN, No. 3, at 152 (noting the qualified statement of the Committee on Freedom of Association with respect to Turkey). The statement notes: "In cases where it has considered complaints concerning alleged infringements of trade union rights committed under a state of emergency or siege, the Committee has always expressed the opinion that it was not competent to come to a decision on the needs or advisability of such legislation, which is a question purely political in character, but it has taken the view that it should consider the repercussions which such legislation might have on the free exercise of trade union rights." *Id.*

153. 68 ILO OFFICIAL BULLETIN (SPECIAL SUPPLEMENT), SERIES B, paras. 479–481 (1984).

154. REPORT OF THE COMMITTEE OF EXPERTS, *supra* note 149, at para. 72 (noting Articles 19, 22, and 35 of the Constitution).

Commission from writing a thorough and critical report that led to Poland's decision in 1984 to withdraw from the ILO.[155] When an on-site visit is refused, the ILO body in question may rely on evidence from past direct contacts missions, reports by other ILO bodies, and information not supplied by the government or parties to the complaint.[156] In the Polish case, the Commission heard ten of twenty proposed witnesses, persons who had been able to leave Poland.[157]

ILO on-site visits may be subject to delay or to government refusals to conform to the organization's conditions for visits. Poland, for example, in April 1983 insisted that a direct contacts mission could confer only with government officials; the Director General responded that ILO practice requires access to trade union representatives as well. After an extensive on-site visit by a Fact-Finding and Conciliation Commission to Chile in November–December 1974, there were allegations of government reprisals against witnesses.[158] During direct contacts missions to Turkey, access to detainees at first was denied, then permitted, but only with a small number of detainees and only in the presence of a guard.[159]

Although ILO bodies need not rely on party-supplied information, reference to data from non-ILO sources is not common. NGOs that are not labor unions have difficulty in providing information directly to the Committee on Freedom of Association, but Commissions of Inquiry decide on their own procedure and generally have been willing to receive reliable and relevant information. The levels of contact and supervision in the ILO are multiple and continuous, so there is generally a wealth of available information. Sometimes there is reliance on legal standards derived from the Universal Declaration of Human Rights or the International Covenants.[160] The various ILO reports

155. *Id.* at para. 472. The notice of withdrawal expires in November 1986.

156. *Id.* at para. 476.

157. *Id.* at para. 97.

158. INTERNATIONAL LABOR OFFICE, THE TRADE UNION SITUATION IN CHILE: REPORT OF THE FACT-FINDING AND CONCILIATION COMMISSION ON FREEDOM OF ASSOCIATION, paras. 435–443 (provisional ed. 1975).

159. Access to detainees was initially denied in July 1982, but later permitted in September 1983 under seemingly objectionable conditions. 66 ILO OFFICIAL BULLETIN, SERIES B, 102, 110–115 (1983); 66 ILO OFFICIAL BULLETIN, SERIES B, No. 2, 240–255 (1984).

160. *See, e.g.,* 68 ILO OFFICIAL BULLETIN (SPECIAL SUPPLEMENT), SERIES B, para. 589 (1984) (noting the report of the Commission of Inquiry into the Polish labor situation). With respect to Chile, which had not ratified Conventions No. 87 and 98, the Fact-Finding and Conciliation Commission asserted that freedom of association had become a customary rule of law aside from the Conventions. *See supra* note 155, at para. 466.

generally make specific findings of facts as to abuses, criticize particular practices and contain precise recommendations for reform in domestic labor legislation and its application.[161]

Of particular note is the restatement by the Committee of Experts on the Application of Conventions and Recommendations of its standards for assessing emergency measures, made in the course of its review of trade union rights in Nicaragua:

> [T]he pleas of a state of emergency to justify restrictions on civil liberties, and above all on trade union rights, should be invoked only in circumstances of extreme gravity, constituting a case of *force majeure* and subject to the condition that any measures affecting the guarantees . . . should be limited both in extent and in time to what is strictly necessary to deal with the particular situation. . . .[162]

The Committee of Experts expressed concern about restrictions on labor rights in emergency decrees of October 1985 and made specific recommendations for bringing Nicaraguan practice into conformity with standards subject to ILO supervision.[163]

## D. The Committee Against Torture

The Convention Against Torture and Other Cruel, Inhuman, or Degrading Treatment or Punishment[164] is distinguished by having what might be called a non-derogation clause: "No exceptional circumstances whatsoever, whether a state of war or a threat of war, internal political instability or any other public emergency, may be invoked as a

---

161. With respect to Turkey, for example, the Committee on Freedom of Association, relying *inter alia* upon the report of a direct contacts mission, noted the release from detention of many trade union leaders and the fact that the assets of the Trade Union Confederation (DISK) appeared to be intact. The Committee renewed its criticism of the prolonged and unfair trials of some labor leaders on capital charges relating to union activity, and noted the incompatibility of the martial law regime with major trade union rights. 67 ILO OFFICIAL BULLETIN, SERIES B, No. 3, 211 (1984). The report of the Fact-Finding and Conciliation Commission created to investigate Chile made eleven specific recommendations and noted that previous ILO comments on the draft labor code had been ignored. *See supra* note 157, at para. 527.

162. COMMITTEE OF EXPERTS ON THE APPLICATION OF CONVENTIONS AND RECOMMENDATIONS, INTERNATIONAL LABOR ORGANIZATION, REPORT OF THE COMMITTEE OF EXPERTS ON THE APPLICATION OF CONVENTIONS AND RECOMMENDATIONS, 72ND SESSION OF THE INTERNATIONAL LABOR CONFERENCE, REPORT III (PART 4A) 169 (1986) (noting Articles 19, 22, and 35 of the Constitution).

163. *Id.* at 170.

164. G.A. Res. 39/46, 39 U.N. GAOR Supp. (No. 51) 197, U.N. Doc. A/RES/39/46 (1984), *adopted* Dec. 10, 1984, *entered into force* June 26, 1987.

justification of torture."[165] Like the Human Rights Committee, the ten-member Committee Against Torture (CAT) seeks compliance primarily through the review of periodic state reports under Article 19 of the treaty, although it has already begun to consider confidential allegations of systematic torture practices under Article 20[166] and individual communications under Article 22.[167]

CAT's approach to report reviews is generally similar to that of the Human Rights Committee, but its authority under Article 19 to make "general comments" on state reports is less ambiguous than Article 40 of the Covenant. It thus includes evaluative and frank general conclusions in the summaries of the review of each state report. For example, CAT noted that certain aspects of Colombian legislation "still needed to be improved,"[168] and that the antitorture training of Chilean public officials "was still unsatisfactory."[169] It also requested additional reports from Cameroon[170] and China[171] because of deficiencies in their initial reports. CAT relies on information from non-state sources, for example, the reports of the Special Rapporteur on Torture of the United Nations Commission on Human Rights.[172]

Many of the Torture Convention's provisions are preventive in nature, and the focus of CAT's reviews is dual—to consider any actual practices of torture or cruel treatment and to examine the adequacy of the state's legal system and training practices in light of the Convention's requirements. The state's experience of an emergency is logically irrelevant by virtue of the non-derogability of the prohibition on torture, but CAT's reviews are likely to be influenced by the frequent association of widespread torture practices with public emergencies.[173]

---

165. *Id.* at art. 2(2).

166. *Report of the Committee Against Torture*, 45 U.N. GAOR Supp. (No. 44), U.N. Doc. A/45/44, at paras. 533–537 (1990) [hereinafter REPORT AGAINST TORTURE]. The Committee held four closed meetings at its fourth session to consider such allegations. An additional twelve closed meetings were held during the fifth through eighth sessions of the Committee. *Report of the Committee Against Torture*, 47 U.N. GAOR Supp. (No. 44), U.N. Doc. A/47/44, at paras. 365–369 (1992).

167. *Id.* at paras. 370–381, Annex V; REPORT AGAINST TORTURE, *supra* note 166, at 538–551, Annexes V & VI.

168. *Id.* at para. 340.

169. *Id.* at para. 375.

170. *Id.* at para. 279.

171. *Id.* at para. 501. The state representative informed CAT that he would transmit its request to his government, but he could not promise the report would be filed.

172. *Id.* at para. 500.

173. Amnesty International reports that the United Kingdom was reminded of the non-derogability of its obligations under the Convention by CAT in the review of its initial report in November 1991. CAT noted that the denial of lawyers during interroga-

CAT also may contribute to the development of more general legal norms. For example, while compelled to declare three Argentinean communications challenging the Punto Final law inadmissible *ratione temporis*, CAT stated in self-described *obiter dictum* that the remedy depriving law was "incompatible with the spirit and purpose of the Convention" and urged the state to provide alternative remedies for torture victims of the state-of-siege era.[174]

---

tion sessions under emergency legislation denied basic protections and was "enormously unpersuaded" that those sessions could not be videotaped. AMNESTY INTERNATIONAL, 15 November 1991 (press release).

174. REPORT AGAINST TORTURE, *supra* note 166, at Annex V, paras. 549–550.

# Chapter V
# The United Nations System: Non-Treaty Mechanisms

## A. Introduction

Within the United Nations, all of the structures and mechanisms with any competency in human rights matters have undertaken some activity related to monitoring human rights abuse during states of emergency. Although a thorough canvass of all these activities is impossible, it is important at least to examine a selection of mechanisms that only touch on emergencies, as well as to scrutinize those with a conscious focus upon states of emergency.

This chapter will concentrate upon two bodies, the Commission on Human Rights and its Sub-Commission on the Prevention of Discrimination and Protection of Minorities, and the following four areas of their work in the past two decades: (1) the confidential procedure under Resolution 1503[1] of the Economic and Social Council (ECOSOC); (2) *ad hoc* studies of the human rights situation in particular countries and the advisory services program; (3) theme mechanisms established to examine worldwide certain types of human rights violations; and (4) the Sub-Commission's Special Rapporteur on States of Emergency. Only the last process consciously focuses upon states of emergency as a discrete phenomenon, but all are important components in the monitoring system with complex links to each other, as well as to the treaty-based mechanisms discussed in the previous chapter and the regional bodies that will be analyzed in the next.

---

1. E.S.C. Res. 1503 (XLVIII) of May 27, 1970, 48 U.N. ESCOR, Supp. (No. 1A) at 8, U.N. Doc. E/4832/Add.1 (1970).

## B. The Commission on Human Rights

### 1. The Resolution 1503 Procedure

Originally intended to be the United Nations body primarily charged with competence in human rights outside the implementation regime of any particular treaty, the Commission on Human Rights has dealt only tangentially with states of emergency as a separate question. However, through the confidential procedure established by ECOSOC Resolution 1503, *ad hoc* studies of various country situations, thematic mechanisms, general debate on human rights conditions, and the adoption of resolutions concerning the human rights situation in certain states, the Commission has made itself one of the most important international bodies currently monitoring human rights abuses under states of emergency. A high percentage of the matters discussed by the Commission relates to the protection of human rights during formal and *de facto* emergency situations. In its various tasks, the Commission has been substantially handicapped by politicization, deep splits over the value of innovation in monitoring mechanisms, recurrent debate over duplication or preemption of various procedures, and unevenness in treatment of equally grave situations.[2]

For much of its early existence, the Commission devoted itself primarily to drafting substantive standards on human rights, including the Universal Declaration of Human Rights and, of primary relevance to states of emergency, the International Covenant on Civil and Political Rights. The Commission continues to play a key role in substantive standard-setting relevant to emergencies, for example, in reviewing the Declaration on the Protection of All Persons from Enforced Disappearances, which was adopted by the General Assembly in 1992.[3]

---

2. *See* H. TOLLEY, THE U.N. COMMISSION ON HUMAN RIGHTS (1987) (for a thorough exposition of the Commission's evolving authority and performance). I. GUEST, BEHIND THE DISAPPEARANCES: ARGENTINA'S DIRTY WAR AGAINST HUMAN RIGHTS AND THE UNITED NATIONS (1990) (giving additional insights into the political intrigues that hamper the Commission's effectiveness, especially with respect to grave emergencies).

3. G.A. Res. 47/133 of Dec. 18, 1992, U.N. Doc. A/RES/47/133 (1992); *Report of the Sub-Commission on Prevention of Discrimination and Protection of Minorities on its Forty-Second Session*, U.N. ESCOR, HUM. RTS. COMM., U.N. Doc. E/CN.4/1991/2, E/CN.4/Sub.2/ 1990/59, at 63 (1990) (Draft Declaration on the Protection of all Persons from Enforced or Involuntary Disappearances); U.N. Doc. E/CN.4/Sub.2/1990/32 Annex (1990); *Report of the Working Group on the Declaration on the protection of all persons from enforced disappearances*, U.N. Doc. E/CN.4/1992/19/Rev. 1 (1992). The Declaration would, *inter alia*, label the systematized practice of disappearances a "crime against humanity," emphasize the non-derogable nature of the rights imperiled by the practice of disappearances, provide that *habeas corpus* as a means to locate detainees may not be sus-

Despite the fact that the Commission remains actively involved in the elaboration of further substantive human rights standards,[4] a new era of implementation of human rights norms by the Commission dawned with the adoption in 1970 of ECOSOC Resolution 1503, which has profoundly affected the Commission's role, especially with respect to abuses associated with states of emergency.

At its first session in 1947, the Commission "made a critical declaration of impotence . . . beginning a twenty year period of self-denial," when it resolved that "it had no power to take any action in regard to any complaints concerning human rights."[5] Because petitions alleging violations of human rights continued to pour in from around the world, the Secretariat was directed to prepare lists of petitions, which would then be perfunctorily reviewed by a working group of the Commission.[6] Under ECOSOC Resolution 728F, adopted in 1959, the Secretariat was to prepare a non-confidential list that briefly indicated the substance of communications concerning human rights principles and a confidential list of other communications, and to provide these lists to the Commission and Sub-Commission.[7] Communications referring to a specific state were sent to that state, keeping the author's identity confidential unless he or she wished to divulge it, and any reply from the state could be supplied to the Commission.

The Commission in 1967 requested authority for itself and the Sub-Commission to examine the individual communications as among the

---

pended, that persons accused of committing forced disappearances must be tried or extradited, and that amnesty may not be extended to them.

4. Howard Tolley notes: "Despite the priority given to protection activities, between 1980 and 1986 the Commission worked on two conventions and four declarations, more norms than had been considered in any previous period. In addition, the Commission either approved or requested work by the Sub-Commission on six other norms." Tolley, *supra* note 2, at 134.

5. *Id.* at 16–17 (*quoting Report of the First Session of the Commission on Human Rights*, U.N. Doc. E/259, at para. 22 (1947)).

6. E.S.C. Res. 75(V) of August 5, 1947, U.N. Doc. E/573, at 20 (1947); E.S.C. Res. 116(VI) of March 1 & 2, 1948, U.N. Doc. E/777, at 16 (1948). *See* H. Tolley, *supra* note 2, at 17–18. According to John Humphrey, then Director of the Division on Human Rights: "At every session the Commission went through the farce of clearing the conference room for a secret meeting which lasted only a few minutes, time enough for the Commission to adopt a resolution taking note of the list." J. HUMPHREY, HUMAN RIGHTS AND THE UNITED NATIONS: A GREAT ADVENTURE 28 (1984). Humphrey concludes that this process constituted "probably the most elaborate wastepaper basket ever invented." *Id.*

7. E.S.C. Res. 728F (XXVIII), 28 U.N. ESCOR Supp. (No. 1) at 19, U.N. Doc. E/3290 (1959).

available sources documenting consistent patterns of violations of human rights.[8] The emergency stemming from the Greek coup d'etat of that year was a major catalyzing event in pushing the Commission into a more active monitoring role.[9] ECOSOC granted its approval in Resolution 1235 (XLII), which authorized the Commission to make a "thorough study" and to report on situations of violations of human rights.[10] Pursuant to Resolution 1235, the Commission and Sub-Commission added an agenda item on the question of violations of human rights, which served as the vehicle for public discussion of gross abuses, including many occurring in the context of states of emergency.

As Frank Newman and David Weissbrodt explain:

These debates began as rather reserved discussions in which governments claimed that they could not be criticized by name. By the late 1970's, however, governments and nongovernmental organizations (NGOs) accepted this agenda item as the occasion for lively public discussion of violations committed by named governments. Based on those debates, the Commission and Sub-Commission began to adopt resolutions expressing concern about human rights violations in particular countries.[11]

These public discussions began to lead to the undertaking of in-depth *ad hoc* studies of the human rights situation in particular states.

But the Resolution 1235 procedure did not provide a mechanism for resolving the issues raised in the confidential communications and did not even provide any formal role for the communications to play in the public debate.[12] In 1968 the Sub-Commission proposed a three-step procedure under which confidential communications would be reviewed first by a working group of the Sub-Commission, then by the Sub-Commission as a whole, and finally by the Commission.[13] Despite opposition from the eastern bloc and many third world countries, ECOSOC in 1970 approved this multistage procedure with the condi-

---

8. *Commission Res. 8 (XXIII) of Mar. 16, 1967*, 42 U.N. ESCOR Supp. (No. 6) at 131, U.N. Doc. E/4322, E/CN.4/940 (1967).

9. R. LILLICH, INTERNATIONAL HUMAN RIGHTS: PROBLEMS OF LAW, POLICY AND PRACTICE 372–441 (2d ed. 1991).

10. E.S.C. Res. 1235 (XLII), 42 U.N. ESCOR Supp. (No. 1) at 17, U.N. Doc. E/4393 (1967).

11. F. NEWMAN & D. WEISSBRODT, INTERNATIONAL HUMAN RIGHTS 113 (1990).

12. Tolley describes several abortive efforts by Sub-Commission members to cite communications by code numbers in resolutions proposing study of the human rights situation in states such as Haiti and Greece. *See supra* note 2, at 59.

13. *See id.* at 59 (citing *Sub-Commission Res. 2 (XXI) of 1968* and the *Report of the Twenty-fifth Session of the Commission*, U.N. Doc. E/4621, at paras. 407–35 (1969)).

tion that all proceedings would remain confidential until the point at which the Commission made recommendations to ECOSOC.[14]

The Sub-Commission and its working group in confidential session examine the communications to determine if they appear to reveal, in the words of Resolution 1503, "a consistent pattern of gross and reliably attested violations of human rights" in a particular country. The Sub-Commission's evaluation is reported to the Commission, which invites the government in question to send a representative to address a confidential session of the Commission and answer questions put by its members. The author of the communication is not entitled to participate and indeed is never notified that his communication has been referred to the Commission or informed of the government's response. Thereafter, the Commission decides whether to drop the country from the confidential procedure, to keep it under review for further consideration the subsequent year, or to take further steps to deal with the situation. Such further steps in the past have included asking the Secretary-General to establish direct contacts with the government, undertaking a "thorough study," or making the file public.

As Howard Tolley notes, early enthusiasm for the Resolution 1503 mechanism quickly became tarnished with disillusionment:

> Western activists hailed the passage of Resolution 1503 as a major initiative creating an individual right of petition to the United Nations. Petitioners could attack human rights violations by any government, even states which did not belong to the United Nations. The procedure encompassed all human rights and fundamental freedoms, political and civil as well as economic and social. . . . In order to maximize Resolution 1503's potential impact, nongovernmental organizations published directions on how to file admissible communications. In practice, the activists soon criticized the Resolution 1503 procedures as so politicized, secretive, and slow that offending governments escaped meaningful scrutiny.[15]

Shortly before Resolution 1503 was adopted, the Secretary-General of the United Nations directed all United Nations Centers located in member states not to receive or forward communications concerning human rights after Soviet protest over an incident in Moscow and out of fear that the information centers might otherwise be closed.[16]

---

14. E.S.C. Res. 1503, 48 U.N. ESCOR, Supp. (No. 1A) 8, U.N. Doc. E/4832/Add.1, at para. 8 (1970) [hereinafter Resolution 1503]. *See* H. Tolley, *supra* note 2, at 60 (describing Tanzanian amendment on confidentiality).

15. *Id.* at 71 (footnotes omitted).

16. *Id.* at 73 (*citing* Press Release SG/SM/1200 of December 22, 1969, at 5–7); R. Lillich, *The U.N. and Human Rights Complaints: U Thant as Strict Constructionist,* 64 Am. J. Int'l L. 610 (1970). One indication of changing attitudes in the post–Cold War era is the

The picture that emerges after two decades of experience with Resolution 1503 is decidedly mixed. Precise evaluation of its merits and demerits is hampered by its confidentiality,[17] though it is now possible at least to learn the names of the states whose situations were discussed by the Commission.[18] The list of states that have been subject to consideration by the Commission under Resolution 1503 indicates a substantial degree of correlation between being credibly accused of a consistent pattern of gross violations and being under a *de jure* or *de facto* emergency.[19] Resolution 1503 provides unusual access to UN procedures on behalf of victims, although it treats communications only as establishing patterns and is not designed to provide individual redress.[20]

It is interesting to note that the communications most likely to pro-

---

suggestion by the Special Rapporteur on Extrajudicial, Summary or Arbitrary Executions that these information centers become a central vehicle for dissemination concerning reports and complaint processes of the Commission's theme mechanisms. *Report of the Special Rapporteur on Extrajudicial, Summary or Arbitrary Executions*, U.N. Doc. E/CN.4/1993/46, at para. 703 (1992).

17. Howard Tolley in particular has attempted to overcome the barrier of confidentiality and to make a systematic evaluation of Commission action under Resolution 1503. *See supra* note 2; *The Concealed Crack in the Citadel: The United Nations Commission on Human Rights' Response to Confidential Communications*, 6 HUM. RTS. Q. 420 (1984) [hereinafter *Concealed Crack*].

18. Parker and Weissbrodt cite Chad, Myanmar, Somalia, the Sudan, and Zaire as being the subjects of Resolution 1503 discussion by the Commission at its forty-seventh session in 1991. *See supra* note 3, at 26. Of this group Zaire was dropped "despite evidence of continuing human rights violations." Chad, Somalia, and the Sudan were presumably kept under review, and the Commission determined to dispatch an independent expert to assess the situation in Myanmar through direct contacts. An earlier visit to Myanmar had been hampered by restricted access. *Id.* at 25, 26.

19. In 1985, for example, the Commission considered the status of the following countries' situations under Resolution 1503: Albania, Benin, Haiti, Indonesia/East Timor, Pakistan, Paraguay, the Philippines, Turkey, Uruguay, and Zaire. U.N. Doc. E/CN.4/1985/SR.41 (1985). Consideration of Uruguay was terminated explicitly because of its return to democracy. U.N. Doc. E/CN.4/1985/SR.48 Add.1 (1985).

Howard Tolley has compiled information on states subject to Commission review under Resolution 1503. For the period 1973–79, he lists twenty states referred by the Sub-Commission, including six from Africa, six from Asia, six from Latin America, two from Western Europe (including Northern Ireland in 1973), and none from Eastern Europe. *See supra* note 2, at 77 tbl. 4.2. From 1978 to 1986, he counts thirty states as subject to Commission review under Resolution 1503, including nine from Africa, eight from Asia, ten from Latin America, two from Eastern Europe, and one from Western Europe (Turkey). *Id.* at 128 tbl. 6.4.

20. Tolley cites a few instances of symbolic releases of prisoners that can be linked to consideration of certain states under the 1503 procedure. *Concealed Crack, supra* note 17, at 457.

ceed to serious consideration are the ones carefully prepared by the major non-governmental organizations that also have consultative status and the consequent ability to participate in the public sessions of the Commission and Sub-Commission. Tolley notes the advantages of NGO-prepared communications:

NGOs have an advantage over individual petitioners in the Resolution 1503 procedure, since their staff can document enough different violations by a government to establish a consistent pattern or situation. NGOs simplify the Sub-Commission's task by aggregating individual cases, and help the Secretariat by identifying which international instruments apply, by submitting twelve copies of their work, and by preparing brief summaries suitable for referral to Commission members.[21]

While the objective value of the Resolution 1503 mechanism as a means of monitoring human rights abuse during states of emergency is difficult to assess, many sophisticated NGOs continue to devote substantial resources to filing communications and appear to have faith that the process is a useful avenue of approach to the Commission on particular country situations. Whether this faith indicates that Resolution 1503 is effective in exposing or moderating emergency-related abuses (for instance, by inducing governments to provide specific information or to take concrete remedial steps that would not have emerged in response to public debate), or simply that NGOs have no more faith in the alternatives, or lack a realistic perspective on the process, is impossible to determine. Accurate assessment, even by participating NGOs, is hampered also by confidentiality, as apparently cooperative state representatives can easily take a different tack in the closed sessions. Iain Guest states that it is hard to tell whether the participating NGOs love or loathe Resolution 1503, but that "[l]ife without 1503 would be drab and lifeless, mainly because no other procedure so richly sums up their frustration with the U.N."[22]

Events do not always follow the scenario set out in the literal terms of Resolution 1503: confidential review within the Sub-Commission and Commission, followed either by a "thorough study" by the Commission and a report to ECOSOC under the terms of Resolution 1235, or an investigation by an *ad hoc* committee upon the express consent of the subject state.[23] Of the thirty states examined by the Commission from 1978 to 1986, the situations in seven were transferred to public procedures, but not necessarily as a result of the Commission's consider-

21. Tolley, *supra* note 2, at 72 (footnotes omitted).
22. GUEST, *supra* note 2, at 117.
23. Resolution 1503, *supra* note 14, at para. 6.

ation of the confidential communication.[24] Not a single one of the thirty states was made subject to a "confidential ad hoc committee investigation subject to approval,"[25] as envisioned in para. 6(b) of Resolution 1503, although five became the subject of direct contacts by a designee of the Secretary-General.[26]

Most often, the Commission will either terminate consideration of a situation or decide simply to keep it under consideration for another year. Occasionally, the termination of consideration under Resolution 1503 appears directly linked to a dramatic improvement in the human rights situation, including the lifting of a state of siege. For example, consideration of Argentina in 1984 and Uruguay in 1985 was terminated when each country returned to democratic government and reported substantial improvements in human rights practices to the Commission.[27] Both governments also requested ECOSOC to release the confidential materials gathered under the 1503 procedure during the respective five- and seven-year periods each was under Commission review.[28] On the other hand, consideration is sometimes terminated without any obvious improvement in the situation, and the Commission never publicly explains its reasons for such dispositions.[29]

---

24. Tolley, *supra* note 2, at 130–31. Consideration of Afghanistan, for example, was terminated in 1984 because the Commission had decided to initiate an *ad hoc* study of its human rights situation. U.N. Doc. E/CN.4/SR.63, at para. 1 (1984). But Tolley notes that both the Commission and Sub-Commission "had adopted public resolutions on self-determination in Afghanistan unrelated to the confidential situation" prior to the decision to initiate an *ad hoc* study. *Id.* at 268 n.130. Five years of frustration in considering Albania under the 1503 procedure led to the transfer of discussion of Albania's human rights situation to public procedures in 1988 and resolutions critical of Albania's human rights practices in 1990 and 1991. P. Parker & D. Weissbrodt, *Major Developments at the UN Commission on Human Rights in 1991,* 13 Hum. Rts. Q. 573 (1991).

25. Tolley, *supra* note 2, at 131.

26. *Id.* The five direct contacts missions concerned Equatorial Guinea, Ethiopia, Haiti, Paraguay, and Uruguay. Several of these missions appear to have been distinctly ineffectual. Tolley notes that Jonas K.D. Foli found the Haitian Tontons Macoutes to have become a "constructive forestry group," in sharp contrast to a recent highly critical report by the IACHR. *Id.* at 129 & n.125. Iain Guest trenchantly describes the whitewash attempted by Javier Pérez de Cuellar (then Under-Secretary General) in his "majestically misleading report" to the Commission in 1980 following his direct contacts mission to Uruguay during the period of military rule. Guest, *supra* note 2, at 142–45.

27. Tolley, *supra* note 2, at 132.

28. *Id.* at 128, 132.

29. Discussion of Paraguay, for example, was terminated two times, but renewed with the submission of new communications by the Sub-Commission. *Id.* at 130. Paraguay was monitored for nine years "without a thorough study, investigation, or public disclosure of the evidence presented." *Id.*

Likewise hard to predict is the Commission's determination that a communication does not reveal a consistent pattern of gross violations.[30] The quality of government responses to 1503 communications is difficult to evaluate due to confidentiality, but only a fairly small minority fail to respond at all, particularly if the situation is kept under review for more than one year.[31] Exasperation over government intransigence can lead the Commission to "go public" or, conversely, to keep a state on the list even though the abuses may have abated.[32] One of the most troubling aspects of the Resolution 1503 procedure is the participation by government officials who are Commission members in the consideration of communications against their own government.[33] This striking ethical lapse achieves an even more aggravated form when Sub-Commission "independent experts" who are in fact officials of their government participate in screening communications concerning their state.[34]

30. Examining seven such dispositions from 1978 to 1986, Tolley speculates that these situations "appear to have attracted less press and NGO attention than the cases kept under review," as an explanation for the Commission's action. *Id.* at 129. The seven were Burma in 1979, Mozambique in 1981, Gabon in 1986, Japan in 1981, Malaysia in 1984, Pakistan in 1984 and 1985, and Venezuela in 1982.

31. Tolley's information indicates that only eight of twenty-nine states he studied failed to respond to communications the Commission had decided to review. *Id.* at 127, 129 tbl. 6.5.

32. A Special Rapporteur on Equatorial Guinea was appointed in 1979, after the government merely responded by objecting to the 1503 procedure as an interference in its internal affairs. U.N. Doc. E/CN.4/SR.1515/Add.1 (1979). *See* M.E. Tardu, *United Nations Response to Gross Violations of Human Rights: The 1503 Procedure*, 20 SANTA CLARA L. REV. 559, 563 n.18 (Equatorial Guinea), 580 (public recommendation to ECOSOC in 1980 with respect to abuses in Malawi between 1972 and 1975, to which the Malawi government had never responded) (1980). While Equatorial Guinea sent observers to the Commission sessions in two of the four years it was under review, Malawi never sent observers during any of the three years it was under review. Tolley, *supra* note 2, at 128 tbl. 6.4.

At its 1976 session, the Commission found no consistent pattern of gross violations in Equatorial Guinea, after hearing an extensive submission by the state's representatives. The Commission acted without the benefit of additional information from NGOs considered by the Sub-Commission in August 1975 but not provided to the Commission under the then applied rule of treating supplemental information as a new communication. Tolley reports the Commission did find a consistent pattern in 1977, with the benefit of this updated material. *Id.* at 78. The Commission also recommended that ECOSOC disclose the confidential 1503 materials when Equatorial Guinea was transferred to the public procedures. *Id.* at 81.

33. *See id.* at 79 (citing instances involving Ethiopia, Uganda, and Uruguay).

34. *See id.* at 75 (citing instances involving experts from Morocco, Sri Lanka, Argentina, and the United States). A proposal by Sub-Commission expert Benjamin Whitaker

The combined effect of high politicization and confidentiality make the Resolution 1503 procedure an especially weak vehicle for enhancing understanding of international norms relating to states of emergency. So far as can be determined, such norms do not play a significant role in the Commission's confidential deliberations. The procedure, to the extent it is effective at all, serves as a prelude to more active fact-finding, as by the appointment of a Special Rapporteur, or by multilateral diplomatic "humanitarian intervention" in particularly grave situations. Standing alone, consideration under Resolution 1503 does not serve as a comprehensive fact-finding mechanism or as an opportunity for precise evaluation of the legitimacy of an emergency or the legality of particular emergency measures.

One important aspect in evaluating Resolution 1503 that should not be ignored is the danger that the procedure might be manipulated to foreclose consideration of emergency situations under other monitoring mechanisms. The Human Rights Committee does not regard Resolution 1503 as a procedure of international investigation and settlement that would block its own consideration of an individual communication under the Optional Protocol.[35] But at one point the Commission imposed a proviso that when a country is the subject of a Resolution 1503 communication, its human rights situation could not be publicly debated in the Commission.[36] NGOs who attempted to evade this ban by refraining from naming the states whose practices they were criticizing were forced to reveal the name and then ordered to cease speaking.[37] The ban ironically created an incentive for countries to come under Resolution 1503 in order to foreclose public debate or *ad hoc* investigative procedures.

The prize for mastery of this form of manipulation undoubtedly should go to Argentina, which escaped censure and public fact-finding during five years of ineffectual Commission review under Resolution 1503 through extremely diligent and heavy-handed lobbying.[38] Argen-

---

that government employees not be permitted to cast votes on 1503 communications concerning their countries was ignored. *Id.* at 74.

35. *Report of the Human Rights Committee*, 33 U.N. GAOR Supp. (No. 40), U.N. Doc. A/33/40, at paras. 580–586 (1978). Similarly, the Human Rights Committee firmly rejected suggestions by Iraq that its scope of inquiry in the report review process was limited by the simultaneous involvement of the Security Council in matters relating to the Gulf War in 1991. *Report of the Human Rights Committee*, 46 U.N. GAOR Supp. (No. 40), U.N. Doc. A/46/40, at paras. 622–623, 651–652 (1991).

36. U.N. Doc. E/CN.4/SR.1466 (1978).

37. U.N. Doc. E/CN.4/SR.1440 (1978).

38. Iain Guest's study provides a lively account of this distressing tale, rich with detail and vivid characterization. *See supra* note 2. Among the tactics used by Argentina to

tina was assisted by surprising friends, including a so-called "unholy alliance"[39] of Soviet and Pakistani experts on the Sub-Commission, who came from countries that either historically opposed effective monitoring mechanisms or were themselves in danger of being included in the 1503 blacklist.[40] But some Commission members always insisted that consideration of a communication under Resolution 1503 did not make the entire human rights situation confidential, foreclose public debate on the country, or block other monitoring mechanisms available to the Commission.[41] Some efforts to foreclose public debate because of simultaneous review under Resolution 1503 have failed.[42]

---

intimidate its opponents was the initiation of a review of the credentials of NGOs with consultative status that had criticized Argentina's abuses. *Id.* at 111–15.

39. T. Gardeniers et al., *The U.N. Sub-Commission on Prevention of Discrimination and Protection of Minorities: Recent Developments,* 4 HUM. RTS. Q. 353 (1982).

40. Tolley, *supra* note 2, at 75; GUEST, *supra* note 2, at 118–21 (describing the unauthorized disclosure in *Le Monde* about the voting in the Sub-Commission on Argentina in 1978).

41. Mr. Kooijmans of the Netherlands, who was later designated as the Special Rapporteur on Torture, summarized the debate over the effects of Resolution 1503 confidentiality in 1985, noting the inconsistency of some other members as follows: "[I]n 1977, 1978 and 1984, the Commission had attempted to resolve the discrepancy between the public and confidential procedures available for examining allegations of human rights violations. In 1984, a number of delegations had asserted that it should refrain from adopting public resolutions on situations already being dealt with under the confidential procedure, but the majority had seen no impediment to its doing so. . . . A similar question had arisen in respect of Uganda in 1977, but the majority of delegations had then opposed undertaking a public inquiry because the situation was already being considered under the confidential procedure. The complexity of the problem was further illustrated by the fact that one delegation which had vigorously argued against public action had co-operated two years earlier in the establishment of the *ad hoc* Working Group on the Situation of Human Rights in Chile even though Chile, like Uganda, was being considered under the confidential procedure. . . . A special problem arose in respect of information received from private sources: in 1967, the Council had authorized the Commission to examine such information and had reinforced that authorization in resolution 1503 (XLVIII) of 1970. Those directives had been intended to enlarge the Commission's sphere of action, and not to restrict its competence to deal with human rights violations wherever they occurred. . . . [T]hey did not, however, preclude members from discussing in public sessions, on the basis of information other than communications received from private sources, particular problems relating to human rights in a specific country. Any other interpretation would unacceptably curtail the Commission's and Sub-Commission's competence. By way of illustration, he recalled that at the Commission's fortieth session, it had before it a draft resolution on the state of siege in Paraguay. The existence of that state of siege had been common knowledge and the Commission had been entirely justified in adopting a resolution on that aspect of the situation, notwithstanding the confidential consideration of private communications relating to the same country." U.N. Doc. E/CN.4/1985/SR.45, at paras. 35–39 (1985). Tolley notes that the communication concerning Paraguay, referred to by Kooijmans,

Certainly no one could claim that the heavily politicized consideration of consistent patterns of gross violations under Resolution 1503 has served as an effective screening mechanism to identify and to redress the most egregious instances of emergency-related human rights abuse. On the other hand, the availability of Resolution 1503 permits NGOs and concerned Commission and Sub-Commission members to place pressure on at least some governments abusing emergency powers or engaging in patterns of gross violations in the context of *de facto* emergencies. More even-handed treatment of situations under Resolution 1503 may result as Sub-Commission experts vote by secret ballot on confidential communications, insulating them from lobbying pressure.[43] On the other hand, the increase in the size of the Commission to fifty-three members, with the addition of many seats for the developing world, may aggravate the problem of regional blocs coalescing to prevent review of situations within their region.[44]

## 2. Ad Hoc Investigations and Advisory Services

On a selective basis, when political coalitions can be forged, the Commission has taken quite vigorous action to investigate and even condemn abuses in emergencies. By now, a fairly wide spectrum of countries has been made the subject of special *ad hoc* investigatory

---

concerned the treatment of indigenous peoples rather than the state of siege *per se.* Tolley, *supra* note 2, at 132.

42. In 1984, for example, the Commission refrained from taking any decision on Afghanistan under 1503 on the grounds that there would be subsequent discussion of a draft Sub-Commission resolution on the Afghan situation during the public procedures. When the draft resolution came up, however, efforts were made to foreclose discussion because the situation was already the subject of Resolution 1503. These efforts failed, and eventually a Special Rapporteur was appointed pursuant to Commission Res. 1984/ 55. U.N. ESCOR Supp. (No. 4) at 105, U.N. Doc. E/1984/14, E/CN.4/1984/77 (1984). *See* U.N. Docs. E/CN.4/1984/SR.59 (1984); E/CN.4/1985/21 (1985).

43. *See Report of the Subcommission, supra* note 3, at 68. The Sub-Commission also requested ECOSOC and Commission approval to vote by secret ballot on resolutions under agenda item 6, the public consideration of human rights situations. *See id.* at 67 (noting Sub-Commission Decision 1990/105 of August 23, 1990). The Commission approved these procedural changes. Parker & Weissbrodt, *supra* note 3, at 26.

44. Parker and Weissbrodt assert that the Latin American group on the Commission in recent years has been able to control the terms of the resolutions on El Salvador and Guatemala and to block active consideration of Colombia and Peru, while the African group has managed to block action against countries in its region. *See supra* note 3, at 20. However, the perceived cohesion of the Asian bloc did not prevent a condemnatory resolution against the military regime in Myanmar from being adopted by the General Assembly in 1991. P. Lewis, *U.N. Rebukes Burma Military for Refusing to Yield Power,* N.Y. TIMES, Nov. 30, 1991, at 1, col. 3.

mechanisms with Commission approval.[45] The quality, thoroughness and candor of these reports vary widely in part due to the relative resourcefulness and interest of the investigators appointed and the different mandates issued to them. In this section, a profile will be offered of the unusual features of each *ad hoc* investigation, any innovations it may have signaled, and its usefulness as a device for monitoring states of emergency. A brief indication also will be given of any controversy it generated at the Commission. The ongoing debate over the suitability of the "advisory services" approach, as an alternative to *ad hoc* fact-finding, will be examined. Finally, noteworthy instances of failure to take action will be discussed.

### a. Chile

Chile has been the subject of the most path-breaking *ad hoc* measures related to states of emergency. Chile was entrenched as a separate agenda item for public discussion from 1974 until 1990,[46] but at the Commission's thirtieth session in 1974 several delegations voiced substantial opposition to a special fact-finding mechanism.[47] Starting in 1975, five different *ad hoc* mechanisms[48] were employed at various times: the Special Rapporteur on the Impact of Foreign Economic Aid and Assistance on Respect for Human Rights in Chile;[49] the Ad Hoc

---

45. For many years, the pariah regimes of South Africa, Israel in the Occupied Territories, and Chile were the only ones under special investigation. The list was expanded to include Afghanistan, Bolivia, Cuba, El Salvador, Equatorial Guinea, Guatemala, Haiti, Iran, Iraq, Myanmar, Poland, and Romania, though the form of this special monitoring varies considerably depending on the politics of the Commission.

46. At its forty-sixth session in 1990 the Commission decided to consider Chile under agenda item 12 (general item on human rights violations) and to eliminate agenda item 5 concerning the situation in Chile. R. Brody et al., *Major Developments in 1990 at the UN Commission on Human Rights*, 12 HUM. RTS. Q. 559, 567 (1990).

47. Some initial opponents, who gradually came to support special fact-finding concerning Chile, premised their resistance on a concern for shielding domestic matters from international scrutiny. *See, e.g.,* U.N. Doc. E/CN.4/SR.1287 (1974) (remarks by Mr. Chernichenko of the USSR finding that an *ad hoc* investigatory mechanism for Chile would be a "breach of the principle of non-intervention" under Article 2(7) of the Charter, although the body on which it would be modeled, then studying Southern Africa, was not in breach of Article 2(7) since South Africa was a threat to peace).

48. The Commission also sent a cable in 1974 expressing concern for the fate of certain named prisoners. U.N. Docs. E/CN.4/SR.1272 (1974); E/CN.4/SR.1279.

49. This study was initiated by Sub-Commission Res. 3A (XXIX) of August 31, 1976. U.N. Doc. E/CN.4/1218, E/CN.4/Sub.2/378, at 46 (1976). The Special Rapporteur on the Impact of Foreign Aid and Assistance on Respect for Human Rights in Chile was authorized by Commission Res. 9 (XXXIII) March 9, 1977. 62 U.N. ESCOR Supp. (No. 6) at 8, U.N. Doc. E/5927, E/CN.4/1257 (1977). *See Sub-Commission Res. 11 (XXX) of*

Working Group on the Situation of Human Rights in Chile;[50] replaced in 1979 by the Special Rapporteur on the Situation of Human Rights in Chile;[51] the Expert on the Question of the Fate of Missing and Disappeared Persons;[52] and the special trust fund for victims of human rights abuses in Chile.[53]

Each of these mechanisms broke new ground in Commission practice, and the last four have served as models for studying country situations or as means for dealing worldwide with a particular phenomenon of human rights abuse. Now that the chapter on special investigation of Chile has been closed,[54] it is particularly interesting to assess the effectiveness of these *ad hoc* measures.

The government of Chile consistently and strongly protested the *ad hoc* measures on essentially two grounds: that they were discriminatory, and that by questioning measures chosen to deal with an emergency situation, they imposed impermissible international supervision over matters of exclusively domestic concern. Especially after the Covenant on Civil and Political Rights entered into force, Chile made the added argument that the Covenant's procedures superseded the Commission's competence.[55] As late as November 1989, the representative

---

*August 31, 1977*, U.N. Doc. E/CN.4/1261, E/CN.4/Sub.2/399, at 49 (1977). *See also* U.N. Doc. E/CN.4/Sub.2/412, at vols. I–IV (1978).

50. 58 U.N. ESCOR Supp. (No. 4) at 66, U.N. Doc. E/5635, E/CN.4/1179 (1975) (established by Commission Res. 8 (XXXI) in 1975). The Working Group was extraordinary by including no members from the eastern bloc, at the insistence of the government of Chile. The Working Group issued a series of reports. *See* U.N. Docs. E/CN.4/1188 (1976); E/CN.4/1221 (1977); E/CN.4/1266 (1978).

51. *See* G.A. Res. 33/175, 33 U.N. GAOR Supp. (No. 45) at 159, U.N. Doc. A/33/45 (1978); *Commission Res. 11 (XXXV)*, 33 U.N. ESCOR Supp. (No. 6) at 115, U.N. Doc. E/1979/36, E/CN.4/1347 (1979). Three persons have successively served as Special Rapporteur, including Judge Abdoulaye Dieye of Senegal, Judge Rajsoomer Lallah of Mauritius, and Professor Fernando Volio Jiménez of Costa Rica. U.N. Doc. A/44/635, at para. 3 (1989).

52. *See* G.A. Res. 33/175 (1978), 33 U.N. GAOR Supp. (No. 43) at 159, U.N. Doc. A/33/43 (1979); U.N. Doc. A/34/583/Add.1 (1979). The Special Rapporteur was asked to take over the problem of missing persons in Chile by *Commission Res. 21 (XXXVI) of February 29, 1980*, U.N. ESCOR Supp. (No. 3) at 181, U.N. Doc. E/1980/13, E/CN.4/1408 (1980).

53. The United Nations Trust Fund for Chile was established by G.A. Res. 33/174, 33 U.N. GAOR Supp. (No. 45) at 158, U.N. Doc. A/33/45 (1978).

54. In 1990, the Commission adopted by consensus a resolution terminating the mandate of the Special Rapporteur. *Commission Res. 1990/78*, U.N. ESCOR Supp. (No. 2) at 160, U.N. Doc. E/1990/22, E/CN.4/1990/94 (1990).

55. One early example of these Chilean objections was the statement by Mr. Bazan Davila at the Commission's Thirtieth session: "The possibility of suspending temporarily

presenting Chile's report to the Committee Against Torture lamented his country's disfavored status within the Commission:

[D]espite the many problems it faced, his Government had never ceased to co-operate with international human rights bodies on condition that Chile should be considered under established procedures and not as a special case. He regretted that the General Assembly and the Commission on Human Rights had not yet accepted that condition.[56]

This sense of persecution resulted in a wavering pattern of cooperation and non-cooperation with the Commission's *ad hoc* investigators.[57]

As fact-finding mechanisms the reports comprehensively collected and analyzed data obtained from a wide variety of appropriate sources, including NGOs, the International Committee of the Red Cross, and the IACHR. The Working Group made a successful on-site visit in 1978, after a planned visit in 1975 was canceled.[58] Special Rapporteur Volio Jiménez, perhaps because he was viewed initially by the Chilean government as more sympathetic to its concerns than were his pre-

---

the exercise of certain individual rights was recognized in all international conventions on human rights. . . . The act whereby a State defined the circumstances and temporarily suspended the exercise of certain rights was an internal act of that State. The . . . conventions . . . obliged the State which temporarily suspended certain rights to inform the other States parties, but those parties were not entitled to change, object to, or derogate from what the State concerned had decided. That would be tantamount to intervening in its domestic affairs, which was contrary to Article 2 of the United Nations Charter." U.N. Doc. E/CN.4/SR.1272, at 76 (1974).

56. *Report of the Committee Against Torture*, 45 U.N. GAOR Supp. (No. 44), U.N. Doc. A/45/44, at para. 343 (1990).

57. Special Rapporteur Volio Jiménez made four visits to Chile during which he received varying degrees of cooperation from government officials. On his third visit, in December 1987, he had productive discussions with some officials but encountered during a meeting with the Minister of Justice a "hostile, discourteous and uncooperative attitude of the Minister, who gave him warnings that were clearly out of place." U.N. Doc. E/CN.4/1988/7, at para. 7 (1988). In 1989, when Professor Volio Jiménez agreed to continue his mandate as Special Rapporteur, after initially indicating a desire to resign for health reasons, the Chilean government announced its intransigent refusal to coop-erate with any further *ad hoc* procedures. "[Chile] would not be prepared to accept, in future, an *ad hoc* approach to the situation of human rights in Chile, experience having shown that co-operation in such an approach was pointless and unproductive for Chile. The Minister [for Foreign Affairs] said that his Government's cooperation had not been appreciated by the United Nations bodies entrusted with the protection of human rights, which had persisted in taking a discriminatory, selective and unfair approach which contrasted not only with the Special Rapporteur's reports but also with the objective reality of the progress made in Chile." U.N. Doc. A/44/635, at para. 13 (1989).

58. A description of this visit is contained in the Working Group's report. U.N. Doc. E/CN.4/1310 (1979).

decessors,[59] was permitted to make a series of four visits beginning in 1985.[60]

However, obtaining otherwise unavailable information was never the primary reason for the Commission's *ad hoc* studies of the Chilean situation. Even before the Working Group planned a visit for 1975, on-site visits had been made in 1974 and reported by such bodies as the IACHR, an ILO Fact-Finding and Conciliation Commission, Amnesty International, the International Commission of Jurists, and the Chicago Commission of Inquiry into the Status of Human Rights in Chile. The Commission's aim was, by exposing information obtained directly or indirectly by its investigators, to encourage the Chilean government to alter its human rights practices and accelerate or complete its return to democracy. How much credit the Commission deserves for its persistence in monitoring the human rights situation in Chile through the democratic elections in December 1989 is difficult to calculate, but as the Special Rapporteur noted in his final report:

[M]uch remains to be done to ensure that Chilean society enjoys a reliable system of legal protection for freedom. The representative democracy that will take its place in March 1990 is without doubt an extraordinarily important starting-point from which to pursue the combat to ensure that freedom prevails. . . . [T]he new regime will face [major obstacles] . . . as a result of the very nature of the system of Government and of democratic life, and on account of the deep rifts created within Chilean society over many years of acute political conflict, exacerbated by violence.[61]

In contrast to the reticence of the Human Rights Committee as a body, the *ad hoc* studies of Chile have tended to contain evaluative statements concerning the legitimacy of various aspects of the state of emergency. For example, the Working Group found in 1979 that the "continued application in Chile of the state of siege was not justified"[62] and that Decree Law No. 2191 providing amnesty to torturers was

59. "President Augusto Pinochet authorized Mr. Volio's 10-day visit after his preliminary report was considered too lenient by groups such as the Vicariate [of Solidarity] and the Chilean Human Rights Commission." *Chilean Police Use Force On Human Rights Rally*, N.Y. TIMES, Dec. 11, 1985, at 5, col. 1 (national edition).

60. *See* U.N. Docs. E/CN.4/1986/2 (1986); A/42/556 (1987); E/CN.4/1988/7 (1988); E/CN.4/1989/7 (1989) (noting reports on these visits).

61. U.N. Doc. E/CN.4/1990/5, at para. 28 (1990). Upon terminating the Special Rapporteur's mandate in 1990, the Commission specified that the new Chilean government should report on its progress at a special meeting during the next session. The progress report was made through an appearance of the Vice-Minister of Foreign Affairs before the Commission on 26 February 1991, but was done without debate and without a special meeting. Parker & Weissbrodt, *supra* note 3, at 22.

62 U.N. Doc. E/CN.4/1310, at 103 (1979).

"legally ineffective [because] contrary to the generally accepted princi-ples of law."[63] Special Rapporteur Volio Jiménez criticized the lack of democracy, the entrenchment of the state of emergency, systematic torture, the practice of administrative banishment, the passive attitude of the civil judiciary and serious flaws in the system of military justice.[64] In his report preceding the holding of the 1988 plebiscite on the Chilean presidency, he urged as a "basic prerequisite" for a fair election the lifting of the two states of emergency then in force.[65] He added: "The states of emergency make things easier for those who, in exercis-ing political power, have a tendency to commit acts contrary to human rights, under the protection of the states of emergency and with the excuse of protecting national security, which is not always borne out by the facts."[66]

The Commission as a body passed a series of highly condemnatory resolutions following review of the *ad hoc* reports.[67] Similar resolutions were also repeatedly adopted by the General Assembly.[68] Though the *ad hoc* mechanisms appeared for many years to be having little if any effect in inducing Chile to abandon exceptional regimes and return to democracy, a softening of the condemnatory language was strongly resisted by many Commission members.[69] Chile achieved pariah status in the Commission along with South Africa and Israel, but the tech-niques of *ad hoc* investigation applied to its situation served as a model

63. *Id.* at 104.

64. *See, e.g.*, U.N. Doc. E/CN.4/1986/2, at paras. 155–185 (1986); U.N. Doc. E/CN.4/1988/7, at paras. 105–116 (1988). In the latter report, Professor Volio Jiménez singled out Colonel Fernando Torres, the Special Military Prosecutor, as personally "reprehensi-ble" and responsible for actions that "have violated the inalienable rights of the persons within his jurisdiction." *Id.* at para. 105.

65. U.N. Doc. E/CN.4/1988/7, at para. 128 (1988).

66. *Id.* at para. 90.

67. *See, e.g., Commission Res. 1985/47*, U.N. ESCOR Supp. (No. 2) at 93, U.N. Doc. E/CN.4/1985/66 (1985). The Commission's Resolution *inter alia* expresses "dismay" at the "institutionalization and consolidation of states of emergency and the extension of the jurisdiction of the military tribunals, all of which amounts to an integrated system negating civil and political rights and freedoms," and calls upon the Chilean government to "put an end to the regime of exception and especially the practice of declaring states of emergency, under which serious and continuing violations of human rights are committed."

68. *See, e.g.*, G.A. Res. 39/121, 39 U.N. GAOR Supp. (No. 51) at 214, U.N. Doc. A/39/51 (1984). In 1987, however, the Special Rapporteur on Chile protested that a critical resolution adopted by the Sub-Commission (Sub-Commission Res. 1987/20) had interfered with his relations with the Chilean government. U.N. Doc. E/CN.4/1988/37, E/CN.4/Sub.2/1987/42, at 32 (1987). *See* U.N. Doc. A/42/556, at para. 72 (1987).

69. *See, e.g.*, U.N. Docs. E/CN.4/SR.1616, E/CN.4/SR.1617 (1981) (debate at the Commission's thirty-seventh session).

for additional studies of other states. Several of these subsequent investigations will be described, in the order of their initiation by the Commission, to provide a more complete picture of *ad hoc* investigation as a method of monitoring human rights abuse during emergencies. In addition, several notable instances of nonaction will be contrasted with the Commission's apparent successes.

### b. Equatorial Guinea

Equatorial Guinea embodies one of the key dilemmas in human rights implementation by the United Nations—the handicap of an inadequate national infrastructure to secure fully either political or economic rights in tension with the danger of implying hardship exemptions either to universally applicable standards or to norms voluntarily adhered to through treaty ratification. Recognition and resolution of this tension are especially important in the context of monitoring states of emergency because many underdeveloped countries experience *de facto* or declared emergencies.

The Special Rapporteur on Equatorial Guinea was appointed in 1979 in response to that country's failure to achieve any improvement in its very grave human rights record through the Resolution 1503 process.[70] Unlike the studies on Chile, the reports on Equatorial Guinea do not explicitly discuss its situation as a state of emergency, though they do emphasize the importance of a return to democracy and the rule of law.[71] When a change of government occurred with the overthrow of the Macias Nguema regime, the work of the Special Rapporteur was transformed from that of fact-finding to technical assistance or "advisory services" for the improvement of human rights conditions.[72] A "plan of action" was prepared with the cooperation of the government and missions were conducted in an attempt to implement this plan.[73] The Expert reported in 1985 that significant progress had been made in legal development, but that an "enormous gap" remained in actual observance of human rights and that further UN cooperation was contingent upon the government's good faith efforts.[74] Scant results from this infusion of advisory services have not

70. *See Commission Res. 15 (XXXV)*, U.N. ESCOR Supp. (No. 6) at 122, U.N. Doc. E/1979/36, E/CN.4/1347 (1979); U.N. Doc. E/CN.4/1371, at para. 1 (1980).

71. *See, e.g.,* U.N. Doc. E/CN.4/1371, at paras. 239–249 (1980).

72. *See Commission Res. 33 (XXXVI)*, U.N. ESCOR Supp. (No. 3) at 194, U.N. Doc. E/1980/13, E/CN.4/1408 (1980); U.N. Doc. E/CN.4/1439 (1980).

73. *See* U.N. Doc. E/CN.4/1985/9, at para. 3 (1985); U.N. Doc. E/CN.4/1990/42 (1990) (visit by consultant in place of the ill expert).

74. *Id.* at paras. 49–75.

prevented the Commission from repeatedly extending the mandate of the Expert.[75]

### c. Guatemala

The battle over whether to keep Guatemala under *ad hoc* fact-finding or to place it in advisory services was resolved by the Commission in 1990 by the creation of a "new hybrid . . . an independent expert . . . to examine the human rights situation in that country and, at the same time, to supervise the provision of advisory services."[76] Before examining the feasibility of this dual role, it is useful to trace the history of the Commission's concern with Guatemala and the degree of its focus upon the emergency there.

Guatemala only gradually became the subject of study by a Special Rapporteur, although reports of extensive human rights abuses under declared emergencies persisted under several different regimes. The Commission's first action was a telegram expressing concern over an assassination in 1979, followed by Resolution 32 (XXXVI) of 1980, which noted with approval a planned visit by the IACHR and requested the Secretariat to review information from all relevant sources.[77] The government declined a request to receive a Special Representative of the Secretary-General,[78] so Commission fact-finding was limited to two notes by the Secretariat collecting less-than-comprehensive information supplied by governments and NGOs.[79]

The Commission determined to appoint a Special Rapporteur in

---

75. *Commission Res. 1992/79*, U.N. ESCOR Supp. (No. 2) at 195, U.N. Doc. E/CN.4/1992/84 (1992); *Commission Res. 1990/57*, U.N. ESCOR Supp. (No. 2) at 124, U.N. Doc. E/1990/22, E/CN.4/1990/94 (1990); Parker & Weissbrodt, *supra* note 3, at 23 (1991 extension of mandate "[d]espite serious questions about the effectiveness of advisory services tendered to the government"). Despite the infusion of advisory services, Equatorial Guinea is one of the worst offenders in terms of overdue initial reports under the Covenant on Civil and Political Rights. Its initial report, due in December 1988, had not been filed by October 1992. Only Gabon had been more tardy. *Report of the Human Rights Committee*, 47 U.N. GAOR Supp. (No. 40), U.N. Doc. A/47/40, at Annex IV (1992).

76. *Id.* at 23. The Independent Expert was instructed to examine the human rights situation and to provide assistance to the Government in the field of human rights. U.N. Doc. E/CN.4/1992/5, at para. 7 (1992).

77. U.N. ESCOR Supp. (No. 3) at 193, U.N. Doc. E/1980/13, E/CN.4/1408 (1980); U.N. Doc. E/CN.4/1438, at paras. 1–2 (1981). The Chairman of the Commission in September 1980 addressed a letter at the request of the governments of Austria, Denmark, and the Netherlands to the Guatemalan government expressing concern at the level of violence. *Id.* at para. 5.

78. *Id.* at para. 6.

79. U.N. Docs. E/CN.4/1438 (1981); E/CN.4/1501.

1983.[80] His first two reports were subjected to extensive criticism for being too conciliatory toward the Guatemalan government and for painting an inaccurate picture of conditions following government-controlled fact-finding visits in August 1984 and January 1985.[81] While the Special Rapporteur acknowledged these criticisms in an interim report to the General Assembly in 1985, the tone and conclusions of his report did not alter appreciably.[82] The Special Rapporteur apparently envisaged his role as one of literally studying the situation of human rights[83] and offered little in the way of analysis of the situation as a state of emergency or discussion of applicable standards.

After the election of a civilian government in January 1986, the Special Rapporteur indicated his belief that the new government was in control of the security forces and was implementing the recommendations he had made; the Commission in response decided to terminate his mandate as Special Rapporteur and transform him into a Special Representative to provide advisory services and make a report on implementation of the new legal order for the protection of human rights.[84] Following receipt of the Special Representative's report in 1987,[85] the Commission decided to terminate his mandate and to appoint an Expert to make recommendations for the further restoration of human rights.[86]

But while elaborate assistance was provided to Guatemala through the United Nations to improve its laws and institutions,[87] the expert glumly noted that there remained "an apparently insurmountable gulf between law and reality, between what should be and what is and between the rule and what is actually done."[88] As human rights condi-

80. *Commission Res. 1983/37*, 38 U.N. ESCOR Supp. (No. 3) at 168, U.N. Doc. E/1983/13, E/CN.4/1983/60 (1983).

81. *See* U.N. Doc. E/CN.4/1985/19, at paras. 17–18 (1985). Iain Guest is harshly critical of the Special Rapporteur, Viscount Colville of Culross: "He went to the country with preconceived, highly political ideas: the guerrillas were subversive terrorists, while the military regime was battling manfully to introduce democracy. Colville's report on his visit makes it absolutely clear than [sic] he had decided to take the government's side and play a political role in supporting multiparty elections." GUEST, *supra* note 2, at 371.

82. U.N. Doc. A/40/865, at paras. 9–31 (1985).

83. *See* U.N. Docs. E/CN.4/1984/30, at paras. 3.1–3.18 (1984); E/CN.4/1985/19, at paras. 20–188 (1985); A/40/865, at paras. 86–217 (1985).

84. U.N. Doc. E/CN.4/1986/23, at paras. 67–71 (1986); *Commission Res. 1986/62*, U.N. ESCOR Supp. (No. 2) at 138, U.N. Doc. E/1986/22, E/CN.4/1986/65 (1986).

85. U.N. Doc. E/CN.4/1987/24 (1986).

86. *Commission Res. 1987/53*, U.N. ESCOR Supp. (No. 5) at 118, U.N. Doc. E/1987/18, E/CN.4/1987/60 (1987). *See* U.N. Doc. E/CN.4/1988/42, at para. 11 (1987).

87. *See, e.g.*, U.N. Doc. E/CN.4/1990/45/Add.1 (1989) (describing the efforts of the Expert and six additional advisors operating through the advisory services program).

88. U.N. Doc. E/CN.4/1990/45, at para. 76 (1989).

tions in Guatemala worsened and NGOs urged a return to monitoring under the Commission's violations agenda item,[89] the Commission crafted the compromise of appointing an Independent Expert (avoiding the "Special Rapporteur" appellation) who would examine the human rights situation as well as supervise advisory services, thus "raising the level of scrutiny one-half notch."[90]

The Independent Expert[91] emphasized his fact-finding role,[92] drawing sometimes harsh conclusions[93] based in part on personal observations made during on-site visits. But the expert took care to make specific recommendations for advisory services, such as continued support from UN and other sources for the innovative and courageous work of the Procurator for Human Rights, an office attached to the Congress that can investigate and initiate judicial and administrative action concerning human rights violations.[94] Interestingly, the facts found by the new "hybrid" expert are frequently more condemnatory of the government than were those of Special Rapporteur Colville.[95]

However, none of the reports produced by any of the rapporteurs or experts appointed at the behest of the Commission have focused upon Guatemala as a *de facto* emergency or placed any emphasis upon analyzing the situation there under international norms governing emergencies.[96] There is some discussion of norms of international human-

---

89. *See, e.g.,* U.N. Doc. E/CN.4/1990/NGO/53 (1990) (statement by Amnesty International to the forty-sixth session of the Commission); Lawyers Committee for Human Rights, Abandoning the Victims—the U.N. Advisory Services Program in Guatemala 95–96 (1990).

90. R. Brody et al., *supra* note 46, at 572.

91. Christian Tomuschat of Germany later replaced Hector Gros Espiell, who had become Uruguay's foreign minister. U.N. Doc. E/CN.4/1991/5, at para. 5 (1991).

92. Of the five major sections of his report to the Commission's forty-seventh session, four concern fact-finding on the human rights situation and one is devoted to advisory services. U.N. Doc. E/CN.4/1991/5 (1991).

93. In one striking passage, the expert notes that "almost everyone in Guatemala who takes part in the social and political life of the nation lives in a state of fear of becoming a victim of a murderous attack." U.N. Doc. E/CN.4/1991/5, at para. 48 (1991). He adds that he "considers it inconceivable that the armed forces should not be able to gather the necessary intelligence to identify those paramilitary groups and to put an end to their criminal activities." *Id.* Independent Expert Christian Tomuschat urged the abolition of the civilian self-defense patrols as inimical to the rule of law. U.N. Doc. E/CN.4/1992/5, at paras. 46–49, 193 (1992).

94. U.N. Doc. E/CN.4/1991/5, at paras. 26, 146–147 (1991).

95. Mr. Tomuschat, for instance, investigated a massacre at Santiago Atitlán "for which, clearly, military authorities must bear responsibility." *Id.* at para. 45. One basis for criticism of Viscount Colville had been his eagerness to excuse the Guatemalan military of responsibility for similar massacres. *See* Guest, *supra* note 2, at 370–371.

96. Guatemala has deflected suggestions that it ratify the Covenant on Civil and

itarian law that are frequently violated during the armed conflict.[97] As a device to reduce the extent of violations of non-derogable rights, the Commission's attention to the Guatemalan situation cannot be counted a dramatic success, but it has at least exposed the roots of the apparently intractable violence that plagues the country.[98]

### d. Bolivia

The Sub-Commission took the initiative in 1980 of appointing one of its members to make an analysis of information on Bolivia received by the Secretary-General from various sources.[99] In apparent response, the government of Bolivia indicated its readiness to permit a delegation from the Commission to visit Bolivia to dispel the "distorted picture of its human rights practices."[100] International concern was prompted by a coup d'etat of 17 July 1980, when a military junta prevented an elected government from taking office and imposed martial law. Following the coup, allegations were made of massacres and assassinations, especially of miners and labor leaders.[101] The Sub-Commission's action was thus very timely and was followed in December 1980 by the General Assembly's direction to the Commission to accept Bolivia's invitation to visit.[102]

The Commission's reaction was to chastise the Sub-Commission for exceeding its mandate and to refuse to consider the Sub-Commission's informational report.[103] Bolivia had complained that the Sub-Commission could not act while Bolivia remained under consideration

---

Political Rights, though it is a party to the American Convention on Human Rights. *See* U.N. Doc. E/CN.4/1991/5/Add.1, at para. 17 (1991).

97. *See, e.g.,* U.N. Doc. E/CN.4/1991/5, at paras. 83–93 (1991).

98. The United States State Department's 1991 country report on Guatemala sarcastically notes that "the President's Advisory Commission on Human Rights engaged in little activity and seemed more interested in efforts to defend the official record at the United Nations than in carrying out work in Guatemala," suggesting some possible downside to the Commission's scrutiny. COUNTRY REPORTS ON HUMAN RIGHTS PRACTICES FOR 1990, U.S. DEP'T OF STATE REPORT SUBMITTED TO THE SENATE COMM. ON FOREIGN RELATIONS AND THE HOUSE COMM. ON FOREIGN AFFAIRS, 102d Cong., 1st Sess. 816 (Joint Comm. Print 1991) [hereinafter COUNTRY REPORTS FOR 1990].

99. *Sub-Commission Res. 23 (XXXIII),* U.N. Doc. E/CN.4/1413, E/CN.4/Sub.2/459, at 79 (1980).

100. U.N. Doc. E/CN.4/1441, at para. 3 (1980).

101. *Id.* at paras. 13–20.

102. G.A. Res. 35/185, 35 U.N. GAOR Supp. (No. 48) at 202, U.N. Doc. A/35/48 (1981).

103. U.N. Doc. E/CN.4/1500, at para. 6 (1981).

in the Commission pursuant to Resolution 1503.[104] Political allies of Bolivia, as well as governments generally hostile to innovations in human rights implementation, made numerous comments in the Commission condemning the Sub-Commission's mistaken impression of its independence and postulating the superiority of the Commission, as a political body, for approaching governments.[105]

The Commission adopted a non-judgmental resolution appointing a "Special Envoy" whose aim would be to respond to the General Assembly's request and approach the Bolivian government.[106] The two reports submitted by the Special Envoy were couched in careful language with respect to factual allegations of human rights violations,[107] but were, nevertheless, quite comprehensive and included detailed information on the legal system, political developments, evidence of violations, and the results of two substantial on-site visits.[108] The Special Envoy drew some fairly harsh conclusions about the military regime in his first report, finding "grave, massive and persistent violations of human rights," which were either inexcusable because they abused non-derogable rights or were not justified by any "serious or intensive terrorist activity," which was found not to exist.[109] Thus, international standards relating to states of emergency seem to have informed the Special Envoy's task. The Special Envoy also reacted critically to the military government's announced philosophy of "total national security."[110]

The second report noted with satisfaction the return to democratic government in October 1982 and found "an auspicious and positive situation of full respect for human rights."[111] The Special Envoy em-

---

104. U.N. Doc. E/CN.4/SR.1592 (1981).

105. *See, e.g.,* U.N. Docs. E/CN.4/SR.1592 (remarks of delegate from Brazil); E/CN.4/SR.1593 (remarks of delegate from USSR); E/CN.4/SR.1594 (remarks of delegate from Bulgaria) (1981).

106. *Commission Res. 34 (XXXVII),* U.N. ESCOR Supp. (No. 5) at 235, U.N. Doc. E/1981/25, E/CN.4/1475 (1981).

107. In compiling information on human rights abuses, the Special Envoy stated: "[T]hese allegations are cited for information purposes only; reference to them in no way implies that the facts contained in the above-mentioned information and communications are accepted or, on the other hand, rejected." U.N. Doc. E/CN.4/1500, at para. 57 (1981).

108. *Id.*; U.N. Doc. E/CN.4/1983/22 (1983). The Special Envoy was Hector Gros Espiell of Uruguay.

109. U.N. Doc. E/CN.4/1500, at paras. 121–122 (1981).

110. *Id.* at para. 45 n.13. This doctrine was also explicitly repudiated by the Special Rapporteur on Chile. *See* U.N. Doc. E/CN.4/1986/2, at paras. 144, 147 (1986).

111. U.N. Doc. E/CN.4/1983/22, at para. 103 (1983). On 19 September 1985, the government of Bolivia declared a state of siege to suppress a general strike and report-

phasized the need to bring the perpetrators of human rights violations to justice to maintain the credibility of the new government, although the choice of sanctions would be within the "exclusive competence of the Government."[112] The Special Envoy found that the cooperative approach taken by the UN toward Bolivia had been "extremely positive and most exemplary," achieving real progress through grassroots contacts "without intervention in matters which are not of the United Nations competence."[113] This approach indicates a preference for flexible fact-finding, good-offices initiatives, and an aversion to more rigorous, evaluative techniques.[114]

*e. El Salvador*

Special investigation of El Salvador began with General Assembly Resolution 35/192 of 15 December 1980, which requested the Commission to examine the human rights situation in that country. From the outset, events connected with the armed conflict, prospects for peaceful settlement with rival forces, and the greater democratization of the government have been at the forefront of concern by the Commission, along with the more common urging that specific abuses cease and that security forces be brought under control.[115] As in the cases of Afghanistan and Iran, the Commission's involvement in monitoring the human rights situation in El Salvador operates parallel to the Secretary-General's good offices in mediating an end to the conflict. The Special Representative's mandate persisted, even after the precedent-setting creation of the United Nations Observer Mission in El Salvador (ONUSAL), which set up regional offices for active monitoring of human rights violations in El Salvador, and the appointment of a Truth Commission to document human rights abuses since 1980.[116]

---

edly arrested 150 labor leaders and sent them into internal exile. *Bolivia Declares a State of Siege*, N.Y. TIMES, Sept. 20, 1985, at 8, col. 6. This emergency was terminated on 19 December 1985. A second emergency, imposed in response to a later general strike, was proclaimed on 27 August 1986 and terminated on 27 November 1986. U.N. Doc. E/CN.4/Sub.2/1987/19, at 18 (1987).

112. U.N. Doc. E/CN.4/1983/22, at para. 106 (1983).

113. *Id.* at para. 113.

114. Bolivia eventually became the recipient of United Nations Advisory Services. *See Commission Res. 1984/43*, U.N. ESCOR Supp. (No. 4) at 79, U.N. Doc. E/1984/14, E/CN.4/1984/77 (1984). *See also* U.N. Doc. E/CN.4/1984/46 (1984).

115. *See Commission Res. 32 (XXXVII)*, U.N. ESCOR Supp. (No. 5) at 233, U.N. Doc. E/1981/25, E/CN.4/1475 (1981).

116. During July 1990, the government and the guerrillas negotiated an Agreement

The debate over El Salvador has sometimes been politically charged. For example, the Special Representative declined an invitation from the Third Committee of the General Assembly to present his initial report orally, for fear of prejudicing his contacts with the government of El Salvador.[117] El Salvador occasionally sought to terminate the Commission's special investigation on grounds that it interfered with the Contadora process by which the Central American states were attempting to resolve regional conflicts.[118] The Special Representative's response was to urge peaceful settlement while trying to avoid "the slightest indication in his report concerning the venue, public or confidential nature and conditions of the talks."[119] Both the Special Representative[120] and the Commission[121] have given special emphasis to the necessity to resolve the conflict through negotiations.

The Special Representative followed the usual approaches in preparing his reports, including a number of on-site visits.[122] The scale of human rights violations in El Salvador often exceeded the Special Representative's fact-finding capabilities,[123] but his conclusions consis-

---

on Human Rights, under which both sides acknowledged their obligation to respect basic rights, undertook "to respect the most elementary rights of the individual," and called for the establishment of a United Nations Mission upon the cessation of the armed conflict for purposes of "international verification," but without prejudice to the application of other international procedures for the promotion and respect of human rights. U.N. Doc. A/45/630, at para. 92 (1990); U.N. Doc. A/44/971, S/21541 (1990). The framework for ONUSAL's activities was set out by the Secretary-General in U.N. Doc. S/22494 (1991). ONUSAL established its presence in July 1991. *U.N. Opens Observer Office to Monitor Salvador Rights*, N.Y. TIMES, July 27, 1991, at A4, col. 6. ONUSAL reports through the Secretary-General to the Security Council and the General Assembly, U.N. Doc. S/22494, at para. 8 (1991). In September 1991, under the auspices of the Secretary-General, the New York Agreement was signed by the government and the guerrillas, calling *inter alia* for the reduction and purging of the armed forces. In December 1991 the Secretary-General appointed a three-member Truth Commission to investigate and publish findings on serious acts of violence since 1980. U.N. Doc. E/CN.4/1992/32, at paras. 11–31 (1992). The Truth Commission published its report in March 1993. *Truth Will Out*, THE ECONOMIST, Mar. 20, 1993, at 47 (NEXIS).

117. U.N. Doc. E/CN.4/1502, at para. 5 (1982).

118. *See* U.N. Doc. E/CN.4/1984/SR.32 (1984).

119. U.N. Doc. A/40/818, at para. 35 (1985).

120. *See, e.g.*, U.N. Doc. A/45/630, at paras. 4–16, 117, 119 (1990).

121. *See, e.g., Commission Res. 1985/35*, U.N. ESCOR Supp. (No. 2) at 74, U.N. Doc. E/CN.4/1985/66 (1985).

122. The second through fifth visits were made "in his personal capacity and not as representative of the Commission on Human Rights, since the Government still had reservations of a legal nature concerning his mandate." U.N. Doc. A/40/818, at para. 13 (1985). Later visits were performed in a more official capacity. *See* U.N. Docs. A/42/641, at para. 2 (1987); A/45/630, at para. 2 (1990); E/CN.4/1992/32, at paras. 2, 32 (1992).

123. *See* U.N. Doc. E/CN.4/1983/20, at para. 116 (1983) (finding that "the massive

tently found violations that were not excusable as emergency measures.[124] The existence of a formal emergency was at least noted, if not
closely analyzed.[125] At times, the Special Representative undertook a
detailed analysis in light of international standards of emergency measures such as Decree No. 618, the "law of criminal procedures applicable when constitutional guarantees have been suspended."[126] While
praising the government for its cooperative attitude, he stressed the
gap between intentions and actual progress in bringing the security
forces and "death squads" under control.[127] He has paid special attention to the passivity of the judiciary and the persistence of international
humanitarian law violations, commending the work of the International Committee of the Red Cross.[128]

*f. Poland*

El Salvador was the fourth Latin American country in the throes of
an emergency to be made the subject of special investigation by the
Commission. When attention turned to Poland in 1982, however, politicization of Commission discussion took a quantum leap. Poland's
political allies on the Commission were among the members who most
consistently opposed innovative implementation mechanisms, and
they often resorted to skillful manipulation of procedure to stifle action
or debate. The effects on the Commission's ability to investigate the

---

character of violations of human rights in El Salvador prevents him from undertaking
the necessary investigation to ascertain the facts of each of the cases about which he has
received information"). The Special Representative found that the nature of the information he received made it "difficult to subject it to a detailed, critical review in the light
of the international instruments which are binding on the Republic of El Salvador." U.N.
Doc. E/CN.4/1986/22, at para. 72 (1986).

124. *See* U.N. Doc. A/40/818, at paras. 118, 121 (1985).

125. *See* U.N. Doc. E/CN.4/1987/21, at para. 3 (1987); U.N. Doc. A/45/630, at para.
17 (1990). The non-renewal of the state of siege imposed in November 1989 was
favorably noted by the Special Representative. U.N. Doc. E/CN.4/1991/34, at para. 19
(1991).

126. U.N. Doc. A/42/641, at paras. 43–46 (1987).

127. *See* U.N. Doc. E/CN.4/1984/25, at paras. 173, 178 (1984); U.N. Doc. E/CN.4/
1986/22, at para. 199(b),(c) (1986); U.N. Doc. A/45/630, at para. 115 (1990). "There can
be no doubt as to the determination of the President of the Republic . . . to improve the
human rights situation. Although this has occasioned a decrease in the number of
serious violations of human rights . . . it is a nevertheless indisputable fact that such
violations continue." *Id.*

128. U.N. Docs. E/CN.4/1984/25, at paras. 171, 172 (1984); A/40/818, at para. 170
(1985); A/45/630, at paras. 96, 112, 120 (1990); E/CN.4/1992/32; at paras. 96–117
(1992).

situation in Poland were dramatic: no on-site visit was permitted;[129] public debate was shut off;[130] two brief, apologetic, legalistic, but not entirely laudatory reports were prepared by an Under-Secretary-General;[131] and a procedural vote was taken in 1984 to take no decision on the second report,[132] thus terminating the possibility of obtaining the thorough study requested in 1982. Poland attracted attention among the socialist bloc states because it was undergoing a state of emergency (martial law lasted from December 1981 to December 1982) in a region where such changes in the formal legal circumstances were relatively unusual at the time.[133] But the short-lived nature of the

129. The Polish government rejected Commission Res. 1982/26 of 10 March 1982, which requested the Secretary-General to undertake a thorough study of human rights in Poland, as "illegal, null and void, politically harmful and morally hypocritical." U.N. Doc. E/CN.4/1983/18, at para. 3 (1983). The government did permit officials of the Secretariat to visit on official business in 1982 and 1983. U.N. Doc. E/CN.4/1984/26, at para. 14 (1984).

130. Public debate was terminated, apparently due to the pending Resolution 1503 consideration. See U.N. Doc. E/CN.4/1982/SR.3 (1982).

131. As the second report stated: "Objections to the validity of the resolutions of the Commission on Human Rights on the situation of human rights in Poland are matters to be considered primarily by the Commission itself. As for the Secretary-General, inasmuch as he has received a mandate from the Commission, he is required to take action on it." U.N. Doc. E/CN.4/1984/26, at para. 6 (1984). The reports contain brief summaries of factual allegations of human rights violations, descriptions of international norms, appendices of legal texts, and praise for government progress. However, the reports also conclude that certain aspects of domestic law both during and after the period of martial law were not in complete conformity with the Covenant. U.N. Docs. E/CN.4/1983/18, at para. 57 (1983); E/CN.4/1984/26, at paras. 38, 40 (1984).

132. Proposed by Cuba and adopted 17–14–12. U.N. Doc. E/CN.4/1984/SR.57 (1984). No resolution was introduced in 1985 on Poland, although theoretically the 1984 decision was simply to defer consideration for one year.

133. Later, the Commission would turn its attention to Romania primarily because of the repressive policy of "rural systematization" and oppression of minorities under the Ceausescu regime. However, the Commission found itself studying an emergency developing in a revolutionary context. See U.N. Docs. E/CN.4/1990/28 (1989); E/CN.4/1990/28/Add.1 (1990). After the situation stabilized, the mandate of the Special Rapporteur was terminated. Commission Res. 1992/64, U.N. ESCOR Supp. (No. 2) at 150, U.N. Doc. E/CN.4/1992/89 (1992).

Commission attention to the situation in Cuba did not arise out of events occurring during an emergency but out of long-standing repression through, inter alia, lengthy detention of political prisoners. The Commission in 1988 decided to send a mission to Cuba, on the invitation of the Cuban government, after steady pressure by the United States for the invocation of more formal investigative procedures. See U.N. Doc. E/CN.4/1989/46 (1989). Reports of reprisals against persons who spoke to members of the mission and the increasing isolation of Cuba on the Commission eventually resulted in redesignating discussion of Cuba as a "violations" agenda item and the appointment of a special representative to maintain direct contacts with the Cuban government and

martial law regime may have been in part due to the pressure of international concern that it attracted.

### g. Afghanistan

Hostile Commission members were unable to block *ad hoc* fact-finding with respect to the situation in Afghanistan in 1984, setting the stage for what may have been the most contentious investigation yet. The situation of Afghanistan had been under consideration by the Security Council, the General Assembly, the Commission, and the Sub-Commission since 1980. The internationalized non-international armed conflict which underlay Afghanistan's emergency gave it unusual prominence because of the threat to peace and the grievous nature of reported abuses. The Commission adopted resolutions calling for withdrawal of foreign troops and peaceful settlement in 1981, 1982, and 1983,[134] despite Afghan protests that such measures interfered with the Secretary-General's efforts to effect a peaceful solution.[135] It was only in 1984, however, upon the suggestion of the Sub-Commission, that the Commission appointed a Special Rapporteur to study the human rights situation.[136]

The integrity of the Special Rapporteur was sharply challenged in the Commission, and he was accused of being a neo-Nazi by Afghanistan's political allies.[137] The familiar arguments were made that other procedures, such as review by the Human Rights Committee,[138] pre-

---

people. Parker & Weissbrodt, *supra* note 3, at 23. In 1992 the Commission responded to Cuba's intransigence by replacing the Special Representative with a Special Rapporteur. *Commission Res. 1992/61*, U.N. ESCOR Supp. (No. 2) at 141, U.N. Doc. E/CN.4/1992/84 (1992).

134. *Commission Res. 13 (XXXVII)*, U.N. ESCOR Supp. (No. 5) at 213, U.N. Doc. E/1981/25, E/CN.4/1475 (1981); *Commission Res. 1982/14*, U.N. ESCOR Supp. (No. 2) at 123, U.N. Doc. E/1982//12, E/CN.4/1982/30 (1982); *Commission Res. 1983/7*, U.N. ESCOR Supp. (No. 3) at 127, U.N. Doc. E/1983/13, E/CN.4/1983/60 (1983).

135. *See* U.N. Doc. E/CN.4/1982/SR.27 (1982).

136. *Sub-Commission Res. 1983/20*, U.N. Doc. E/CN.4/1984/3, E/CN.4/Sub.2/1983/43, at 87 (1983); *Commission Res. 1984/55*, U.N. ESCOR Supp. (No. 4) at 94, U.N. Doc. E/1984/14, E/CN.4/1984/77 (1984). Objections were raised because Afghanistan was being considered under Resolution 1503, and it was argued that no resolution could be adopted. However, this view was not accepted. *See* U.N. Doc. E/CN.4/1984/SR.59 (1984).

137. U.N. Doc. E/CN.4/1985/SR.46/Add.1 (remarks of delegate from Czechoslovakia).

138. U.N. Doc. E/CN.4/SR.48/Add.1 (1985) (remarks of delegate from German Democratic Republic).

empted Commission action; that *ad hoc* investigation would interfere with the Secretary-General's efforts at peaceful settlement;[139] and that Afghanistan was free to select any measures it chose to deal with its internal emergency.[140]

The Special Rapporteur initially was denied access to Afghanistan and, instead, traveled to Pakistan to interview refugees and relied in the usual fashion on NGO and government sources.[141] Afghanistan finally granted him access in 1987.[142] The Special Rapporteur has specifically addressed the situation as a state of emergency, measuring Afghan practice against the standards of the Covenant, the Universal Declaration, and international humanitarian law, and pointing out Afghanistan's failure to comply with the notification requirement of Article 4(3) of the Covenant.[143] He made special note of human rights violations associated with states of emergency, such as the "massive arrests" that took place during the state of emergency declared in February 1989.[144] The first report contains a section arguing that Article 2(7) of the Charter is no bar to human rights fact-finding in situations of grave violations.[145]

The Special Rapporteur's findings encompassed torture practices, large-scale detentions without trial, disappearances, indiscriminate bombardment, degrading treatment of civilians, mistreatment of prisoners of war, and the use of "toy bombs" targeted at the civilian population.[146] He also expressed concern for economic and cultural rights, especially the "traditional" life-style of certain elements of the

---

139. *Id.*

140. U.N. Doc. E/CN.4/SR.46 (1985) (remarks of delegate from Bulgaria).

141. *See* U.N. Docs. E/CN.4/1985/21, at paras. 62, 66 (1985); A/40/843, at paras. 36–37.

142. U.N. Doc. A/42/667, at paras. 3–7 (1987). The Special Rapporteur did not gain access to areas in Afghanistan not under government control until his visit of September 1990. During these later visits, the Special Rapporteur also continued his consultations with refugee populations in Pakistan. U.N. Doc. A/45/664, at para. 5 (1990).

143. U.N. Doc. A/40/843, at paras. 150, 182 (1985). However, the Special Rapporteur regarded the task of comparing the Revolutionary Council's Statement on Fundamental Principles to the Covenant's provisions to be "a task which should be entrusted to the Human Rights Committee." *Id.* at para. 154. *See, e.g.,* U.N. Doc. E/CN.4/1986/24, at paras. 70, 100, 119 (1986) (referring to humanitarian law).

144. The state of emergency was imposed on the withdrawal of Soviet troops and lifted on 28 May 1990 when a Loya Jirgah (a form of legislative body) was convened. The Special Rapporteur noted that this emergency was officially notified under Covenant Article 4(3). U.N. Doc. A/45/664, at para. 36 (1990).

145. U.N. Doc. E/CN.4/1985/21, at paras. 33–35 (1985).

146. *Id.* at paras. 66–119; U.N. Doc. A/40/843, at paras. 41–116 (1985).

populace.[147] While the Special Rapporteur called for respect for the right of self-government, he cautioned that the United Nations should study the prospect for general elections "in the light of the political history of Afghanistan and the traditions and customs of Afghan society."[148]

While the Afghan situation is not unique among those studied by the Commission for its link with an ongoing armed conflict and its coincidence with other United Nations efforts to mediate that conflict,[149] it is unusual in the degree of confusion concerning legal responsibility for human rights violations. The Special Rapporteur has stressed that the insurgent groups "are equally bound by international human rights standards and the principles of human rights enshrined in the various international instruments," but he also discouragingly notes that "there are almost 140 'governments' in Afghanistan."[150] The effectiveness of monitoring addressed to such shadowy authorities might be doubted, but the Special Rapporteur stressed that despite the anarchic situation in 1992, Afghanistan remained bound by its international obligations, including the strict terms of Article 4 of the Covenant.[151]

147. The Special Rapporteur found in his first report that the rapid political changes imposed by the government produced an antagonistic response in parts of the population, and indeed seemed to imply that any reforms in land tenure or the status of women (including literacy programs) would somehow constitute a violation of a fundamental right to a traditional life-style. *See* U.N. Doc. E/CN.4/1985/21, at paras. 41–55, 67–69, 120–134, 173–174 (1985). Later, these comments were toned down to emphasize coercive measures for implementing reforms as the spark to revolt. U.N. Doc. A/40/843, at paras. 41–49 (1985).

In reports on conditions following the withdrawal of Soviet troops, as the armed conflict dragged on despite mediating efforts by the United Nations, the Special Rapporteur became more critical of the human rights practices of the insurgent forces, noting the absence of orderly civil administration in areas under their control, denial of access to prisons under their control, and acts of terrorism against the civilian population in Kabul. U.N. Doc. A/45/664, at paras. 72, 75, 86–88 (1990).

148. *Id.* at para. 130. The Special Rapporteur gave heightened emphasis to self-determination in his 1992 report, in light of fierce factional fighting among opposition groups, the tenuous situation of the government, and ensuing delays in the return of refugees. U.N. Doc. E/CN.4/1992/33, at paras. 28–35, 89–92, 93–96, 112 (1992).

149. The parallel United Nations initiatives seem, as in the case of El Salvador, to enhance the Commission's work rather than impede it. The Special Rapporteur, for example, gained access to the areas not under Afghan government control, owing to the efforts of the Office of the Coordinator for United Nations Humanitarian and Economic Assistance Programmes Relating to Afghanistan. U.N. Doc. A/45/664, at para. 13.

150. *Id.* at para. 20, 21. Following the resignation of President Najibullah in March 1992, the Special Rapporteur noted that law and order in Kabul had broken down and that "there was a different Government on every street corner." U.N. Doc. A/47/656, at para. 35 (1992).

151. *Id.* at paras. 55–57, 131.

*h. Iran*

Although Iran, like Afghanistan, was involved in a major war that brought in the good offices of the Secretary-General during at least the initial stages of the Commission's *ad hoc* investigation, the war has hardly figured in the reports of the Special Representative. The focus of the Special Representative has been on massive and persistent abuses of fundamental rights instituted by the revolutionary government, purportedly to promote and institutionalize its religious values. Although the Special Representative has suggested occasionally that the Iranian situation might be analyzed as a state of emergency, he has noted that the Iranian government has not properly exercised any privilege of derogation:

Termination and suspension of international obligations are ruled out with respect to human rights. Nonetheless there are a few ways open to countries which encounter difficulties of application of or are displeased with existing norms.

. . . The International Covenant on Civil and Political Rights permits that in case of public emergency which threatens the national life, a State party may take measures derogating from its obligations regarding a number of provisions, "to the extent strictly required by the exigences [sic] of the situation." Though the Iranian situation appears to meet the condition indicated in that provision, the Iranian Government has not taken advantage of the authorization under the Covenant.[152]

The "novel views"[153] of the Iranian government often forced the Special Representative to dwell upon the problem of cultural relativity in defining human rights norms,[154] or to assert that Iran, at least until new norms had evolved, would be bound by existing customary and conventional norms.[155] The Iranian government provided only limited cooperation in the Special Representative's study, at first supplying only abstract information on legal provisions[156] while criticizing the

152. U.N. Doc. E/CN.4/1988/24, at paras. 56–57 (1988).

153. *Id.* at para. 26.

154. U.N. Doc. E/CN.4/1985/20, at paras. 12–21 (1985). "[N]o state can claim to be allowed to disrespect basic, entrenched rights such as the right to life, freedom from torture, freedom of thought, conscience and religion, and the right to a fair trial which are provided for under the Universal Declaration and the International Covenants on Human Rights, on the ground that departure from these standards might be permitted under national or religious law." *Id.* at para. 18.

155. U.N. Doc. E/CN.4/1988/24, at para. 58 (1988). "Claims and criticisms against existing norms may constitute the first stage of a process leading to the establishment of new norms. In principle all norms of international law are susceptible to change, even those of *jus cogens* . . . and no rule or human institution is immune to change." *Id.*

156. U.N. Doc. A/40/874 Annex IV (1985).

legitimacy of the Special Representative's mandate,[157] and later agreeing to brief meetings with the Special Representative.[158] Although Iranian government intransigence resulted in reports that were cursory and non-judgmental,[159] the Special Representative did begin to gather evidence of human rights abuse firsthand by holding a series of informal hearings with exiles in Geneva,[160] as well as through receipt of written information from NGOs.

Finally, in January 1990 Iran consented to a visit by the Special Representative. While the resulting report contains synopses of the testimony of numerous persons who sought to meet with the Special Representative, the report's tone remained non-judgmental. It included without evaluation much contradictory information from pro-government sources and rationalizations by government officials, who cited the war and terrorism.[161] This cautious approach was rewarded with a second visit in 1991, producing an equally tepid report and an ambiguous Commission resolution that Iran interpreted as providing for the termination of the Special Representative's mandate in 1992 if similar "progress" was made.[162] However, the increasingly critical Special Representative challenged this interpretation, found that "no appreciable progress" had been made, and had his mandate renewed by the Commission in 1992 and 1993.[163]

---

157. *See* U.N. Doc. A/42/648, at para. 3 (1987).

158. *See* U.N. Doc. E/CN.4/1987/23, at para. 5 (1987) (informal meeting with Iranian ambassador to the UN); U.N. Doc. A/42/648, at para. 10 (1987) (meeting in Geneva with an official of the Ministry of Foreign Affairs, who informed the Special Representative that his government would not respond to the detailed allegations of human rights abuse transmitted by the Special Representative since Iran regarded the Commission's resolutions on human rights in Iran to be "politically biased and, therefore, totally unacceptable").

159. *See* U.N. Doc. E/CN.4/1986/25 (1986). In introducing his interim report to the General Assembly in November 1985, the Special Representative described the task of dealing with the Iranian government as "difficult and thankless." The Special Representative cautioned that the publication of a critical report should be the final stage, since the procedure is the only sanction available to inter-governmental bodies and should not be reached precipitously before all avenues of securing government cooperation were pursued. *Id.* at Annex II.

160. *See* U.N. Doc. E/CN.4/1987/23, at para. 13 (1987).

161. *See* U.N. Doc. E/CN.4/1990/24 (1990). *See* Brody et al., *supra* note 46, at 574. "Several observers believed the restraint manifested in the report was in exchange for permission to conduct a second visit." *Id.*

162. Parker & Weissbrodt, *supra* note 3, at 24.

163. U.N. Doc. E/CN.4/1992/34, at para. 474 (1992); *Commission Res. 1992/67,* U.N. ESCOR Supp. (No. 2) at 156, U.N. Doc. E/CN.4/1992/84 (1992); R. Evans, *U.N. Rights Body Condemns Iraq, Iran, Cuba, Spares China,* Reuter Lib. Rpt., Mar. 10, 1993 (NEXIS).

*i. Haiti*

The Haitian situation offers yet another new paradigm: termination of consideration under Resolution 1503 following a change in government, the appointment of an Independent Expert to offer advisory services, and the gradual evolution of the expert's role into that of a Special Rapporteur under the Commission's "violations" agenda, followed by a premature return to advisory services, and eventually the reinstitution of a Special Rapporteur.[164] The expert was initially unable to discharge his mandate because the government insisted on delaying a planned visit until after the completion of the violence-plagued elections.[165] As it became more and more apparent that the military governments of Haiti had no genuine interest in receiving advisory services,[166] except as a means to deflect more stringent review by the Commission, the reports of the expert[167] became increasingly critical. In fact, some delegations to the Commission criticized the 1990 report for its harshly critical tone, but the expert's mandate was extended to encompass both advisory services and examination of the human rights situation, and discussion of his next report was transferred to the "violations" agenda item.[168]

The expert's reports on Haiti are particularly interesting for purposes of this study, since he took the unusual step of filing an addendum devoted to discussion of the state of siege imposed by General

164. Brody et al., *supra* note 46, at 573. The premature return to advisory services occurred at the Commission's session in 1991, prior to the September 1991 military coup, when the democratically elected government of Jean-Bertrand Aristide was in power. Parker & Weissbrodt, *supra* note 24, at 587. The Independent Expert was replaced by a Special Rapporteur in 1992. Commission Res. 1992/77, U.N. ESCOR Supp. (No. 2) at 190, U.N. Doc. E/CN.4/1992/84 (1992).

165. U.N. Doc. E/CN.4/1988/38 (1988) (report analyzing the 1987 Constitution).

166. As the expert asked in 1990, "Is it possible to go on offering advisory services to people who do not want them?" U.N. Doc. E/CN.4/1990/44, at para. 102 (1990).

167. Three persons served as Expert: Andre Braunschweig, U.N. Doc. E/CN.4/1988/38 (1988); Philippe Texier, U.N. Docs. E/CN.4/1989/40 (1989), E/CN.4/1990/44, E/CN.4/1990/44/Add.1 (1990); and Marco Tulio Bruni Celli, U.N. Docs. E/CN.4/1992/50 and Add.1 (1992); A/47/621 (1992). The first report of Bruni Celli adopted a strikingly unbalanced tone of harsh criticism for the "direct democracy" approach of elected President Aristide (*see, e.g.*, U.N. Doc. E/CN.4/1992/50, at paras 66–79, 136–138, 148–150), compared to an almost indifferent recitation of gross human rights violations by forces of the coup leaders, including an estimated 1,500 civilian deaths (*id.* at paras. 93–98). A far more critical report on the practices of the *de facto* government was filed by Special Rapporteur Bruni Celli in November 1992. U.N. Doc. A/47/621 (1992).

168. Brody et al., *supra* note 46, at 573.

Avril on 20 January 1990, and a series of "unlawful arrests, whose clear objective was to terrorize the country's democratic forces."[169] The expert noted the suspension of the 1987 Constitution in March 1989 and the subsequent revival of various provisions, finding that the Avril government was "without legitimate title or a solid legal basis," and, indeed, was a "military dictatorship."[170] He called for total restoration of the Constitution.[171] The Expert expressed skepticism over the government's good faith in announcing an intention, followed by months of inaction, to ratify the Covenant on Civil and Political Rights and several other treaties.[172]

While human rights abuses persisted after the ouster of the Avril government in March 1990, the new government made willing use of assistance from the United Nations and the Organization of American States in organizing free elections in December 1990.[173] Following the September 1991 military coup against the elected president, human rights concerns became a component of the negotiating process to reinstate President Aristide. UN action included a General Assembly resolution calling for Aristide's reinstatement and urging governments to take measures consistent with the embargo ordered by the Organization of American States, and cooperation with the OAS in stationing human rights monitors in Haiti.[174]

### j. Inaction

Given the cost and political controversy of these *ad hoc* mechanisms, it is not surprising that the practice has not become generalized to the dozens of states of emergency occurring in recent years. But it cannot be said confidently that the Commission consciously narrowed its choice of subjects to the worst offenders. Rather, it acted when a political coalition could be built in response to an initiative arising inside or outside the Commission on a truly *ad hoc* basis. Moreover, the disparate approaches of the various persons appointed as investigators

169. U.N. Doc. E/CN.4/1990/44/Add.1, at para. 3 (1990).

170. U.N. Doc. E/CN.4/1990/44, at para. 53, 55 (1990).

171. *Id.* at para. 106(g).

172. *Id.* at paras. 57–59. The expert asked, "Might not the Head of State's aim be, first and foremost, to secure a significant resumption of international assistance so as to enable him to establish his regime on a firm basis?" *Id.* at para. 59.

173. COUNTRY REPORTS FOR 1990, *supra* note 98, at 660.

174. J. Friedman, *Haiti Prime Minister Named As UN Vote Condemns Coup*, NEWSDAY, Oct. 12, 1991, at 83; H. French, *Mediators in Accord Over Haiti*, N.Y. TIMES, Apr. 11, 1993, at A8, col. 1.

or providers of advisory services indicate flaws in the *ad hoc* study technique as a monitoring mechanism for states of emergency.[175]

Noteworthy examples of Commission inaction include the failure of the Commission to launch a public investigation of the human rights abuses committed under Argentina's state of siege. Argentina even managed to precipitate the resignation of the activist Director of the Division on Human Rights.[176] Continual postponement of consideration of Cyprus appeared to be due in part to maneuvering by Turkey, but also to a sense that abuses connected with armed conflict should be handled as part of a larger political settlement under the guidance of the Secretary-General.[177] Similar concerns truncated consideration of Cyprus by the European Commission on Human Rights.[178]

The causes for neglect of the grave situation in Cambodia are complex. During the period of Khmer Rouge control (1975–78), little mention was made of Cambodia in the Commission.[179] In 1978 fierce opposition was raised to the suggestion for the appointment of a Special Rapporteur on the ground that allegations of abuse were based on mass media accounts and that the government of Kampuchea (as it was then called) was not represented.[180] Instead, two brief analyses of information from government and private sources were prepared, under Sub-Commission auspices,[181] but not until after the Vietnamese invasion had created severe political barriers against in-depth fact-finding into Khmer Rouge activities. Commission debates were for a substantial period diverted into discussions of which government was legitimate and whether the Commission and General Assembly could

175. *See* T. Franck & H.S. Fairley, *Procedural Due Process in Human Rights Fact-Finding by International Agencies*, 74 AM. J. INT'L L. 308 (1980).

176. U.N. Docs. E/CN.4/1982/SR.14, E/CN.4/1982/SR.15 (remarks of Mr. Van Boven and of delegate from Argentina); GUEST, *supra* note 2, at 411–18.

177. U.N. Doc. E/CN.4/SR.1449 (1978) (remarks of delegate from Turkey); U.N. Doc. E/CN.4/1510, E/CN.4/1515/Add.1 (1979) (consideration of Cyprus postponed); U.N. Doc. E/CN.4/SR.1635 (1981) (consideration of Cyprus postponed).

178. Cyprus v. Turkey, Apps. No. 6780/74 and 6950/75 2 Eur. Comm'n H.R. Dec. & Rep. 125 (1975); CYPRUS AGAINST TURKEY, REPORT OF THE COMM'N, EUR. COMM'N OF HUM. RTS., (1976); 1979 Y.B. Eur. Conv. on H.R. 440 (Comm. of Ministers Res. DH (79) 1 of Jan. 20).

179. *See* U.N. Doc. E/CN.4/SR.1446 (1978). Mr. Ermacora of Austria remarked that the Commission only acts when humanitarian and political interests coincide. Unfortunately, humanitarianism alone is insufficient to prompt taking up Cambodia.

180. U.N. Docs. E/CN.4/SR.1468, E/CN.4/SR.1469 (1978). *See* Telegram from Minister of Foreign Affairs of Democratic Kampuchea to the Sub-Commission, protesting Sub-Commission Res. 11 (XXXI) of Sept. 15, 1978, U.N. Doc. E/CN.4/1296, E/CN.4/Sub.2/417, at 71 (1978). *See also* U.N. Doc. E/CN.4/Sub.2/414/Add.9 (1978).

181. U.N. Docs. E/CN.4/1437 (1981); E/CN.4/1491.

properly call for the withdrawal of Vietnamese troops.[182] Though Cambodia presented one of the gravest patterns of human rights abuse in recent history, Cold War politics delayed serious scrutiny by the Commission. Finally, in the context of a settlement to the armed conflict brokered by the United Nations, a substantial human rights monitoring presence came to Cambodia under the auspices of the United Nations Transitional Authority in Cambodia (UNTAC) and later through the Commission itself.

Iraq and China present two more recent examples of disillusioning Commission passivity. Only after its invasion of Kuwait was Iraq made the subject of *ad hoc* fact-finding on its human rights practices, including the plight of the Kurds,[183] despite the fact that NGOs for years had pressed for such action.[184] Iraq had cleverly managed to avoid condemnation in both the Commission and Sub-Commission through procedural maneuvers resulting in no action on resolutions condemning its human rights violations.[185] To deflect more orderly scrutiny of its record, Iraq issued an invitation to individual Sub-Commission members to visit Iraq and managed to avoid having this invitation trans-

---

182. U.N. Docs. E/CN.4/SR.1516 (1979); E/CN.4/1985/SR.19 (1985); E/CN.4/1985/32; E/CN.4/1985/34. The United Nations Transitional Authority for Cambodia (UNTAC) has an important human rights monitoring role. Cambodia Documentation Commission, Human Rights, Fundamental Freedoms and the UN Peace Plan for Cambodia (1991). Finally, in 1993 the Commission called for the appointment of a Special Representative (reportedly Corazon Aquino of the Philippines) on the human rights situation in Cambodia. *UN Body Recommends Aquino as Cambodia Investigator*, Reuter Lib. Rpt., Apr. 2, 1993 (NEXIS).

183. *Comm. Res. 1991/74*, U.N. ESCOR Supp. (No. 2) at 167, U.N. Doc. E/1991/22, E/CN.4/1991/91 (1991). A Special Rapporteur was also appointed to examine the situation of human rights in Iraqi-occupied Kuwait (the vote was taken prior to Iraq's withdrawal from Kuwait). *Comm. Res. 1991/67*, U.N. ESCOR Supp. (No. 2) at 154, U.N. Doc. E/1991/22, E/CN.4/1991/91 (1991). *See* U.N. Doc. E/CN.4/1992/26 (1992).

The compelling situation of the Iraqi Kurds also led to extraordinary Security Council action through the adoption of Resolution 688 on 5 April 1991, which insisted that Iraq allow immediate access by humanitarian organizations. *See* 30 I.L.M. 858 (1991). This step toward recognizing a collective right of humanitarian intervention was modestly advanced through adoption of a resolution creating a high-level Emergency Relief Coordinator within the UN. P. Lewis, *U.N. to Centralize Its Humanitarian Relief Efforts*, N.Y. Times, Dec. 18, 1991, at A6, col. 4. But these innovations in humanitarian assistance failed to integrate effectively human rights concerns or United Nations human rights organs. Roberta Cohen, Human Rights and Humanitarian Emergencies: New Rules for U.N. Human Rights Bodies (Refugee Policy Group 1992).

184. R. Brody et al., *The 42nd Session of the Sub-Commission on Prevention of Discrimination and Protection of Minorities*, 13 Hum. Rts. Q. 260, 267–70 (1991).

185. *Id.* at 267; Brody et al., *supra* note 46, at 575.

formed into a more official on-site visit.[186] Meeting shortly after Iraq's invasion of Kuwait and voting by secret ballot, the Sub-Commission finally managed to adopt a resolution critical of Iraq,[187] action that was followed by the Commission's appointing the Special Rapporteur during its session in 1991.

The Special Rapporteur on Iraq carefully addressed and rejected the relevance of exceptional circumstances that might justify Iraq's human rights practices, noting that many violations concerned non-derogable rights and that Iraq had failed to comply with the formal requirements of Article 4 of the Covenant on Civil and Political Rights. He found arguments premised on development, an incomplete revolution, and indigenous values to be legally irrelevant. The Special Rapporteur made the noteworthy recommendation that the exceptional situation in Iraq required the extraordinary measure of sending a team of human rights monitors to investigate abuses, visit places of detention, and observe trials, a recommendation the Commission accepted in 1993.[188] As a result of its international aggressiveness, therefore, Iraq transformed itself from an exemplar of Commission passivity to a major vehicle for innovation in human rights monitoring by the Commission.

The political will to confront the massive violations of human rights occurring during and after the imposition of martial law in China in 1989 continues to elude the Commission. While the Sub-Commission requested in Resolution 1989/5 of 31 August 1989 that the Secretary-General transmit information to the Commission from the government of China and from other sources concerning the "situation in China,"[189] the Commission took no action on a proposed resolution at its 1990 session,[190] and no resolution was even introduced in 1991.[191] A resolution criticizing the situation in Tibet was amended to address the general human rights situation in China, but procedural maneuvers by third world states prevented a vote on the resolution at the sessions in 1992 and 1993.[192]

---

186. *Id.* Four Sub-Commission members from Cuba, Senegal, Somalia, and China accepted the invitation and visited in May 1990. Brody et al., *supra* note 184, at 268.

187. Brody et al., *supra* note 184, at 268.

188. U.N. Doc. E/CN.4/1992/31, at paras. 22–39, 156–157 (1992); *U.N. Rights Panel Accuses Sudan, Iraq of Killings, Terror*, L.A. TIMES, Mar. 11, 1993, at A4, col. 1; U.N. Doc. A/47/367, at para. 17 (1992).

189. U.N. Doc. E/CN.4/1990/2, E/CN.4/Sub.2/1989/58, at 23 (1989). *See* U.N. Doc. E/CN.4/1990/52 (1990).

190. Brody et al., *supra* note 46, at 567–69.

191. Parker & Weissbrodt, *supra* note 3, at 22–23.

192. Reportedly, Pakistan led a move by Third World states to take no action on the

## 3. Theme Mechanisms

One way to decrease politicization of *ad hoc* mechanisms is to create bodies with a worldwide mandate to monitor specific phenomena of human rights abuse. Six "theme" mechanisms[193] created by the Commission on Human Rights since 1980 have marked a dramatic new departure in innovative monitoring and have a high correlation to emergency-related violations. The Working Group on Enforced or Involuntary Disappearances was largely created to break the logjam in the Commission over politically astute major violators, especially Argentina, whose abuses were associated with the state of siege.[194] The five other mechanisms either concern non-derogable rights or abuses strongly associated with states of emergency: they are the Special Rapporteur on Extrajudicial, Summary or Arbitrary Executions, the Special Rapporteur on Torture, the Special Rapporteur on Religious Intolerance, the Special Rapporteur on Mercenaries, and the Working Group on Arbitrary Detention. While these mechanisms may antagonize governments whose practices are investigated or which generally oppose strong monitoring structures,[195] they enjoy increasing cooperation from governments and increasing support within the Commission and ECOSOC.[196]

---

resolution concerning China. *West Fails to Prompt UN Probe of Rights in China*, CHI. TRIB., Mar. 5, 1992, at 12. At the request of the Sub-Commission, the Secretary-General had prepared a note conveying information on the situation in Tibet, supplied by China and various NGOs, to the Commission's 1992 session. U.N. Doc. E/CN.4/1992/37 (1992). Procedural moves and strong Third World backing blocked a vote on a China resolution in 1993 as well. *U.N. Human Rights Commission Steps Lightly around China*, AGENCE FRANCE PRESSE, Mar. 11, 1993 (NEXIS).

193. *See generally,* M. Bossuyt, *The Development of Special Procedures of the United Nations Commission on Human Rights,* 6 HUM. RTS. L.J. 179 (1985); J. Fitzpatrick, *UN Action with Respect to "Disappearances" and Summary or Arbitrary Executions, in* THE UNIVERSAL DECLARATION OF HUMAN RIGHTS 1948–1988: HUMAN RIGHTS, THE UNITED NATIONS AND AMNESTY INTERNATIONAL (Amnesty International USA 1988); M. Kamminga, *The Thematic Procedures of the UN Commission on Human Rights,* 34 NETH. INT'L L.REV. 299 (1987); D. Weissbrodt, *The Three "Theme" Special Rapporteurs of the UN Commission on Human Rights,* 80 AM. J. INT'L L. 685 (1986).

194. *See* GUEST, *supra* note 2, at 190–201.

195. For some years, the former USSR annually attempted to terminate the mandate of the Working Group on Disappearances. *See, e.g.,* U.N. Docs. E/CN.4/1985/SR.28 (1985); E/CN.4/1985/SR.31.

196. In May 1990, as part of the decision to enlarge the Commission to 53 members, ECOSOC recommended that the mandates of the thematic working groups and rapporteurs be extended in three-year increments (as compared to the original one-year tenure and later two-year extensions). *See* Brody et al., *supra* note 46, at 564 (citing U.N. Doc. E/1990/L.26, at 2 (1990)).

*a. Working Group on Enforced or Involuntary Disappearances*

Created in 1980 to deal with the concerns expressed in General Assembly Resolution 33/173 of 20 December 1978,[197] the Working Group on Disappearances can be seen as a kind of specialized Resolution 1503 mechanism in that it functions by receiving communications from individuals about a grave human rights abuse without regard to whether the subject state has ratified a particular treaty or agreed to expose itself to the monitoring system. However, the Working Group's aim is to clarify individual cases and to communicate information to families, while Resolution 1503's exclusive concern is with "patterns." Thus, the Working Group maintains very close relationships with individuals and NGOs that have submitted cases, notifying them when it transmits a case to the government and providing them a copy of any government response. An increasing workload has impaired this contact somewhat, and the Working Group's reports no longer contain the sometimes compelling full text of communications by NGOs and relatives.[198] But the concerns of families and NGOs are carefully summarized, and the Working Group has supported such initiatives as the drafting of a declaration or convention on disappearances.[199]

The Working Group's bywords have been humanitarianism and discretion. By humanitarianism, the Working Group means that its sole concern is to discover the fate of individual victims and to inform the family, without affixing blame on any government or perpetrator.[200] As thoughtfully noted in its 1990 report, the Working Group's handling of individual cases "represents at the same time the strongest and weakest point in its endeavours,"[201] strong because it opened a then unique

197. U.N. GAOR Supp. (No. 43) at 155, U.N. Doc. A/33/43 (1979). These concerns included the need to investigate disappearances, to establish accountability by law enforcement and security forces, the connection between irregular detention practices and grave human rights violations including torture and deprivation of life, and the need for the international community to respond to the anguish and sorrow of the families of the disappeared. *See Commission Res. 20 (XXXVI),* U.N. ESCOR Supp. (No. 3) at 180, U.N. Doc. E/1980/13, E/CN.4/1408 (1980), *approved by* E.S.C. decision 1980/128, U.N. ESCOR Supp. (No. 1) at 42, U.N. Doc. E/1980/80 (1980) (establishing the Working Group).

198. *See* U.N. Docs. E/CN.4/1435 (1981); E/CN.4/1492 (the Working Group's two earliest reports).

199. *See, e.g.,* U.N. Docs. E/CN.4/1990/13, at para. 363 (1990); U.N. Doc. E/CN.4/1991/20, at paras. 28, 414 (1991) (recommending the Commission approve the Sub-Commission's draft Declaration on the Protection of All Persons from Enforced or Involuntary Disappearances, calling it a "major step forward").

200. *See* U.N. Doc. E/CN.4/1988/19, at para. 16 (1988).

201. U.N. Doc. E/CN.4/1990/13, at para. 349 (1990).

"window" into the UN for victims "swiftly and directly"; weak because clarification generally rests in the hands of a probably guilty government that lacks strong incentive to reveal the truth.[202] The Working Group's lack of interest in fixing blame sometimes has frustrated families and NGOs, who have argued that fault should be assigned to governments that have failed to investigate or respond substantially to well-documented cases.[203]

On the other hand, the Working Group's exclusive interest in discovering the precise fate of the individuals brought to its attention insures a certain doggedness that deflects various governments' efforts to exempt their situations from scrutiny. For example, the Chamorro regime in Nicaragua requested that the Working Group delete the outstanding cases there on grounds that a new amnesty law meant that the government would no longer investigate or seek to punish perpetrators of previous disappearances. The Working Group refused, stressing that the consistent principle of its methods of work obliged it not to delete outstanding cases until they are actually clarified by either government or other sources.[204] The Working Group took note of decisions by the Human Rights Committee and the Inter-American Court of Human Rights articulating a governmental duty to investigate abuses of human rights, even after a change in regime, and noted that the advent of democracy is no guarantee that disappearances will not recur.[205]

202. *Id.*

203. *See* U.N. Doc. E/CN.4/1985/15, at paras. 40, 50 (1985). The Working Group has adopted the practice of transferring cases to other thematic procedures when it appears that the missing person has been the victim of a summary execution or arbitrary detention. U.N. Doc. E/CN.4/1992/18, at para. 33 (1992).

204. U.N. Doc. E/CN.4/1991/20, at para. 294 (1991). The Working Group experienced something of a false start in 1982 when it decided to delete seventy-three cases from Mexico upon the government's assurance that it would share whatever information it had with the victims' families. *See* U.N. Doc. E/CN.4/1983/14, at para. 81 (1983). After sustained complaints that only one of the cases had actually been clarified, the Working Group decided to reopen them, serving as a conduit for information between the families and the government. *See* U.N. Doc. E/CN.4/1984/21, at para. 16 (1984). However, the seventy-three cases were not readded to the statistical summaries on Mexico. *See* U.N. Doc. E/CN.4/1988/19, at para. 154 (1988).

205. U.N. Doc. E/CN.4/1990/13, at paras. 360–362 (1990). In an interesting decision on admissibility, however, the Human Rights Committee held that the mother of three disappearance victims in Argentina had no claim under Article 2 of the Covenant even though the government violated her right to a remedy by adopting the Punto Final law (Law No. 23,492) and the Due Obedience Act (Law No. 23,521), which bar the prosecution of her children's killers, because "the Covenant does not provide a right for an

The format of Working Group reports has changed a bit over time, but in general it offers a balance of narrative and statistical information. While the victims remain anonymous, summary information about the context of their disappearances, provided by families or NGOs, is offered in sections organized country-by-country. In 1986 the Working Group launched the "unique"[206] feature of presenting statistical summaries (broken down by cases reported in the last year, outstanding cases, and cases clarified by government or other sources) and graphs indicating year-by-year occurrence of disappearances in countries with more than fifty transmitted cases.[207] In 1991 the Working Group added the innovation of a graph showing worldwide trends in reported disappearances.[208] This highlighting of trends, evocative of Resolution 1503's focus on patterns, slightly obscures the concern for individual victims. But the discovery of individual fates is only one aspect of the Working Group's task, the other two being presentation of situations within countries and a general exploration of the phenomenon, with the ultimate aim being the eradication of disappearances.[209]

Of much greater contribution to monitoring methodology was the Working Group's creation of an "urgent action" mechanism, by which it delegates to its Chairman the authority to send cables to governments concerning disappearances reported to have occurred within three months prior to receipt of the communication. The rate of clarification of the victim's fate has been much higher, about 25%, for cases transmitted by urgent action than it has been for cases transmitted by letter, sometimes occurring many years after the event (for these cases the clarification rate is a discouraging 7%).[210] The Working Group proudly notes that the other theme rapporteurs have emulated this approach. This is an admirable innovation and a testament to the Group members' dedication to their humanitarian task despite potential political fallout in the Commission for having exceeded their man-

---

individual to require that a State party criminally prosecute another person." S.E. v. Argentina, Communication No. 275/1988, decision of Mar. 26, 1990, *in* 2 REPORT OF THE HUMAN RIGHTS COMMITTEE, 45 U.N. GAOR Supp. (No. 40), U.N. Doc. A/45/40, Annex X.J., at para. 5.5 (1990). The Committee noted that Argentina has an obligation to investigate violations occurring after the entry into force of the Covenant and to provide remedies. *Id.* at para. 5.4.

206. U.N. Doc. E/CN.4/1990/13, at para. 355 (1990).
207. U.N. Doc. E/CN.4/1986/18 (1986).
208. U.N. Doc. E/CN.4/1991/20 Annex I (1991).
209. U.N. Doc. E/CN.4/1990/13, at para. 348 (1990).
210. *Id.* at para. 351.

date. The mandate simply authorized the Working Group to develop its methods of work while bearing in mind "the need to be able to respond effectively to information that comes before it and to carry out its work with discretion."[211]

This second byword of discretion marks the Working Group's adherence to anonymity of victims and its steadfast refusal to assign blame to particular perpetrators. It also lies behind the Working Group's establishment of admissibility standards for transmittal of cases to governments. These standards remained murky until they were clearly articulated in 1988,[212] but they have always had a dramatic weeding-out effect. Of approximately fifty thousand reports received by the Working Group by 1990, only nineteen thousand were actually transmitted to governments.[213] While it is hard to fault the Working Group for setting admissibility standards that conform to its parent body's demands and help preempt government excuses for refusing to respond to excessively vague allegations, the barrier of admissibility disadvantages victims from countries where disappearances are particularly surreptitious or where there are no well-organized groups to collect and verify information. The Working Group has expressed the hope that greater publicity for its work will provide improved balance in its coverage of this worldwide phenomenon, especially in countries without a well-developed human rights infrastructure.[214]

The low rate of actual clarification of a particular victim's fate is discouraging[215] in light of the refusal of ever-fewer governments to respond to the transmittals at all.[216] But many governments respond only with general denials, implausible alternate scenarios, expressions

211. *Id.*

212. U.N. Doc. E/CN.4/1988/19, at 6 (1988). The standards require the full name of the missing person, the date of disappearance or last sighting, the place of arrest or abduction or last sighting, the parties presumed to have carried out the abduction, and the steps taken to determine the whereabouts of the missing person or an indication as to why domestic remedies are ineffective. However, the Working Group has emphasized that formal proof of exhaustion of domestic remedies is not required and might impede its humanitarian mission. U.N. Doc. E/CN.4/1991/20, at para. 190 (1991) (response to comments from government of Honduras).

213. U.N. Doc. E/CN.4/1990/13, at para. 356 (1990).

214. *Id.* at para. 359.

215. Of the 3,459 cases transmitted to the Argentine government, for example, forty-three have been clarified by government response and thirty-one by non-government sources. U.N. Doc. E/CN.4/1991/20, at para. 51 (1991).

216. Iran and Lebanon appear to be the worst offenders in this regard, with 451 and 247 cases respectively, to which they have never responded. *Id.* at paras. 212–16, 237–38.

of incapacity to investigate,[217] or, perhaps most difficult for the Working Group, plausible but unprovable alternate explanations.[218]

The Working Group's heavy load of unclarified cases occasionally has induced it to defer to some alternate mechanism. For example, the Working Group encourages the work of the Committee on Missing Persons in Cyprus rather than actively handling the 2,400 reported cases arising from the Turkish invasion.[219] The Working Group generally refuses to take up the cases of persons missing in international armed conflict (*e.g.,* the Iran-Iraq war, the Southern Lebanon conflict zone, or the Falklands war),[220] deferring instead to the tracing activities of the ICRC. It also encourages the development of national commissions on the disappeared, but no longer expects these bodies to be panaceas.[221]

In response to a growing problem, the Working Group created a new "prompt intervention" procedure by which it cables governments when persons who have provided it with information are threatened with reprisal.[222] In one episode, police intercepted a Sri Lankan mem-

217. The Working Group commended the government of Colombia for providing comparatively detailed responses and noted that the governments of states such as Argentina, Mexico, the Philippines, and Sri Lanka tended to stress the general situation or problems in investigation. *Id.* at para. 350.

218. The government of Iraq, for example, claims that 2,280 Kurds from the Barzani clan who disappeared in 1983 collaborated with Iran during the war and fled across the border or were killed in combat. *Id.* at para. 234. Peru argues that many disappearances should be blamed on insurgent groups such as Sendero Luminoso. U.N. Doc. E/CN.4/1991/20, at para. 316 (1991). Peru's concerns have been given new weight by Commission Res. 1990/75, which directed *ad hoc* fact-finding bodies to receive and analyze information about abuses committed by armed groups and drug traffickers. U.N. ESCOR Supp. (No. 2) at 153, U.N. Doc. E/1990/22, E/CN.4/1990/94 (1990). The Working Group's 1991 report scrupulously includes such information, generally provided by governments. *Id.* at para. 18.

219. *See* Fitzpatrick, *supra* note 193, at 44; U.N. Doc. E/CN.4/1991/20, at para. 117.

220. U.N. Docs. E/CN.4/1983/14, at paras. 118–120 (1983); E/CN.4/1984/21, at paras. 20, 79 (1984); E/CN.4/1988/19, at para. 18 (1988).

221. *See* Fitzpatrick, *supra* note 193, at 44–45. The Working Group noted with approval the creation of the National Commission for Truth and Reconciliation in Chile. U.N. Doc. E/CN.4/1991/20, at para. 82 (1991). However, it is unclear whether the report of this commission will clarify any more cases than the analogous National Commission on the Disappearance of Persons (CONADEP) in Argentina. The Chilean Commission reported in March 1991 that 2,279 persons had died under torture, were executed, or disappeared during the military regime. P. Hakim & J. Puryear, *Human Rights Lessons in Chile*, CHRISTIAN SCIENCE MONITOR, May 31, 1991, at 19.

222. *See Commission Res. 1990/76,* U.N. ESCOR Supp. (No. 2) at 155, U.N. Doc. E/1990/22, E/CN.4/1990/94 (1990). *See also* U.N. Doc. E/CN.4/1991/20, at para. 26, 411 (1991).

ber of parliament who was leaving that country to meet the Working Group in Geneva and seized from him five hundred completed Working Group forms. The Sri Lankan government subsequently forwarded the forms to the Working Group.[223]

One other noteworthy methodological innovation of the Working Group is its series of on-site visits to states including Mexico, Cyprus, Bolivia, Guatemala, Peru, Colombia and the Philippines.[224] These visits and reports enable the Working Group to establish ongoing relationships with victims groups and government officials and to identify structural weaknesses that fail to prevent or impede the clarification of disappearances. The Working Group has determined to follow up more systematically on government compliance with its recommendations,[225] which are very precise and concern such subjects as defects in *habeas corpus* systems, lack of control over paramilitary forces, and inadequate military justice.

Although the Working Group does not emphasize abstract analysis of the phenomenon of disappearances or its connection to states of emergency, it has made several observations on the subject. In the Working Group's view, disappearances are associated with emergencies where civil authorities are curtailed and the military is granted "staggering latitude" in coping with a perceived problem.[226] It considers the problem of impunity for perpetrators to be the "single most important factor contributing to the phenomenon of disappearances."[227] While noting that the overall decrease in reported cases may be linked to a decline in authoritarian government, the Working Group believes that militarization of government, judicial reticence, and defective military justice systems contribute to the persistence of disappearances.[228] The Commission on Human Rights similarly has noted the linkage between emergencies and disappearances and called for greater preventive measures in emergency contexts.[229]

223. U.N. Doc. E/CN.4/1991/20, at paras. 340, 363 (1991).

224. *See, e.g., Report of the 1985 visit to Peru,* U.N. Doc. E/CN.4/1986/18/Add.1 (1986); *Report of the 1987 visit to Guatemala,* U.N. Doc. E/CN.4/1988/19/Add.1 (1987); *Report of the 1990 visit to the Philippines,* U.N. Doc. E/CN.4/1991/20/Add.1 (1991).

225. U.N. Doc. E/CN.4/1991/20, at paras. 17, 304 (1991).

226. U.N. Doc. E/CN.4/1990/13, at para. 341 (1990).

227. *Id.* at para. 344. General Pinochet reportedly responded to the report of the Chilean Commission on Truth and Reconciliation by telling military cadets that "the army sees no reason to ask for pardon for its patriotic labor." M. Coad, *Chile to Press Rights Probes Despite Pinochet's Criticism,* WASH. POST, Mar. 29, 1991 at A17, col. 1. *See supra* note 221.

228. U.N. Doc. E/CN.4/1991/20, at paras. 404, 407–408 (1991).

229. *Commission Res. 1990/30,* U.N. ESCOR Supp. (No. 2) at 84, U.N. Doc. E/1990/22, E/CN.4/1990/94, at para. 14 (1990).

*b. Special Rapporteur on Extrajudicial, Summary or Arbitrary Executions*

The Special Rapporteur on Extrajudicial, Summary or Arbitrary Executions has had to pay more attention to abstract issues because of the complexity of his mandate. While disappearances involve a wide range of recognized human rights violations, from arbitrary deprivation of life to denial of the rights of the family, the phenomenon of the forced disappearance is a fairly coherent one. "Extrajudicial, summary or arbitrary executions," are, however, multidimensional and can be subdivided into at least three distinct categories:

1. Summary executions, those carried out in violation of standards set by the Covenant on Civil and Political Rights and norms identified by other UN bodies;
2. arbitrary killings, such as massacres in situations short of armed conflict by security forces; targeted killings of perceived opponents by security forces or death squads, sometimes after disappearance, incommunicado detention, and torture; deaths resulting from excessive use of force by police against criminal suspects or demonstrators, and so on; and
3. deaths in violation of international humanitarian law, such as intentionally killing prisoners of war and other protected persons, executions of civilians without the procedural guarantees of the Geneva Conventions and Protocols, or intentional targeting of civilian populations.[230]

Obviously, many of these practices are closely associated with various types of states of emergency.

The Special Rapporteur has sometimes discussed his mandate in explicit state of emergency terms, noting the distinction between formal and *de facto* emergencies and the relevance of Article 4(2) of the Covenant and the Geneva Conventions.[231] He notes how chaotic emergency situations may impede his mission, as in the case of Liberia where the lack of an organized government deprived him of a recipient for his messages.[232] The Special Rapporteur has drawn on non-treaty standards in developing his methodology, significantly by declaring that he will find governments responsible for killings committed even by non-government actors where the government has failed to meet recognized standards for prevention and investigation.[233]

---

230. *See* Fitzpatrick, *supra* note 193, at 47. The title of the Special Rapporteur was changed in 1992 to add the term "extrajudicial." Special Rapporteur Bacre Waly Ndiaye (replacing Amos Wako) suggests that this expands his mandate to include deprivations of the right to life as defined in numerous international instruments. U.N. Doc. E/CN.4/1993/46, at para. 7 (1992).
231. U.N. Doc. E/CN.4/1986/21, at paras. 160–172 (1986).
232. U.N. Doc. E/CN.4/1991/36, at para. 584.
233. *Id.* at para. 591 (1991) (citing ECOSOC Principles on effective prevention and

The methodology of the Special Rapporteur has varied over time, as he searched for effective techniques and reacted to criticism. The anonymity of his early reports gave way to printing detailed allegations when the government did not respond.[234] Later he included the full text of urgent cables along with any response,[235] and eventually developed his present practice of providing in summary fashion the names of victims, the circumstances, and any response by the government. Both urgent messages and transmittals by letter are summarized.[236]

A noteworthy development of the Special Rapporteur's role in states of emergency was his participation in on-site missions to Bosnia-Herzegovina, Croatia, and Yugoslavia, at the invitation of the Special Rapporteur to investigate the human rights situation in the former Yugoslavia. Also participating in these missions were the Special Rapporteur on Torture, the Chairman of the Working Group on Arbitrary Detention, and the Representative on Internally Displaced Persons. The Special Rapporteur on Extrajudicial, Summary or Arbitrary Executions noted that these missions could mark a new activism in the discharge of his mandate, especially in light of the fact that he had received few allegations from the former Yugoslavia under his normal procedures. Moreover, these missions provided him with exposure to possibilities for establishment of a group of forensic experts to assist in his task and for greater cooperation with other thematic mechanisms.[237]

The Special Rapporteur has considered cases ranging from arbitrary killings (*e.g.*, a woman in East Timor reportedly killed by security forces accusing her of sympathy with the insurgent group Fretilin),[238] to summary executions after unfair trial (*e.g.*, executions of alleged coup leaders in Burkina Faso following martial law trials),[239] to deaths of

---

investigation of extra-legal, arbitrary and summary executions). *See* E.S.C. Res. 1989/65 of May 24, 1989, U.N. ESCOR Supp. (No. 1) at 52, U.N. Doc. E/1989/89 (1990).

234. *See* U.N. Doc. E/CN.4/1984/29, at paras. 31, 78–122 (1984). The Special Rapporteur's report did not identify the involved governments but instead used an awkward type of anonymity ("Situation A," "Situation B") capable of being decoded only by well-informed observers. U.N. Doc. E/CN.4/1985/17, at paras. 15–17 (1985) (naming Iran, Libya, and Malawi).

235. U.N. Doc. E/CN.4/1986/21, at paras. 21–22 (1986) (appeals to fourteen governments, of whom five replied).

236. In his 1991 report, the Special Rapporteur notes sixty-four urgent messages to twenty-five governments, of whom fifteen replied; sixty-one letters were sent to forty-five governments, of whom seventeen replied. U.N. Doc. E/CN.4/1991/36, at paras. 13–19 (1991).

237. U.N. Doc. E/CN.4/1993/46, at paras. 657–672 (1992).

238. U.N. Doc. E/CN.4/1991/36, at para. 220 (1991).

239. *Id.* at paras. 67–70.

demonstrators or civilians living in emergency zones through excessive use of police force (*e.g.*, deaths in the Kashmir region of India; in the Occupied Territories under relaxed rules on deadly force; in Myanmar; and in Nepal),[240] to failure to protect victims of intercommunal violence (*e.g.*, inaction by security forces to protect Armenians in Nagorno-Karabakh in the former USSR),[241] to politically motivated death threats from governmental or death squad sources (*e.g.*, threats by Colombian soldiers to reenact a 1988 massacre against the mayor and townspeople of Segovia if they voted incorrectly in pending elections, and threats by members of military forces against a lawyer in the Philippines).[242]

Governmental replies to the Special Rapporteur's inquiries reinforce the impression that his mandate is closely connected with states of emergency. For example, governments such as that of Colombia have urged that a democratic society should not be judged by the same standards as a dictatorship for security force excesses, and that lawfully constituted states are sometimes compelled to impose a state of emergency in order to preserve law and democracy against groups that combine terrorism and criminality.[243] Despite its reservations, Colombia invited the Special Rapporteur to visit.[244] In contrast, Afghanistan in 1985 simply replied by telephone to the Special Rapporteur's inquiries and insisted that summary and arbitrary executions do not occur there.[245] Pakistan asserted that prosecutions of heinous crimes were transferred to military tribunals "because of the general demand made by the public for the reason that trials in ordinary courts take a longer time to conclude,"[246] but did provide information on the schedule for lifting martial law. Myanmar's reply to the Special Rapporteur about reported deaths of demonstrators simply supplied information on the areas where martial law had been lifted.[247] South Africa provided detailed information concerning its security laws[248] and asserted that the 1986 state of emergency was imposed in order to insure adequate protection of the rights to life and other rights.[249]

---

240. *Id.* at paras. 207–208, 290, 332, 337; U.N. Doc. E/CN.4/1993/46, at paras. 377–379 (1992).

241. U.N. Doc. E/CN.4/1991/36, at para. 505 (1991).

242. *Id.* at paras. 105, 391.

243. U.N. Doc. E/CN.4/1986/21, at para. 108 (1986).

244. *See* U.N. Doc. E/CN.4/1990/22/Add.1 (1990) (for a report of this visit).

245. U.N. Doc. E/CN.4/1986/21, at paras. 65, 102 (1986).

246. *Id.* at para. 84.

247. U.N. Doc. E/CN.4/1991/36, at para. 333–336 (1991).

248. U.N. Doc. E/CN.4/1986/21, at para. 137 (1986).

249. U.N. Doc. E/CN.4/1988/22/Add.1 (1988).

*c. Special Rapporteur on Torture*

The Special Rapporteur on Torture also has demonstrated a thoughtful bent and attention to the linking of his mandate with emergencies.[250] In addition to stressing preventive measures, he highlights the dangers of incommunicado detention[251] and extreme doctrines of national security,[252] as well as the importance of preserving domestic remedies, such as *habeas corpus* and *amparo*.[253] He notes, for example, that since the Body of Principles for the Protection of All Persons under Any Form of Detention or Imprisonment makes no exceptions for times of emergency, detained persons should enjoy the right contained in Principle 32 to take proceedings before a court to challenge the lawfulness of their detention "also under a state of siege or emergency."[254]

The Special Rapporteur initially was cautious about his fact-finding role, identifying only those states to which he had addressed urgent appeals, but without giving a hint of the substance of those cases.[255] His practice evolved from anonymous descriptions of the situations underlying urgent appeals to naming the relevant state,[256] to his present approach of naming the alleged victims and including a brief description of the allegations together with any reply by the state, both with regard to urgent appeals and transmittals by letter.[257] While observing that his caseload has increased, he indicates that this may be attributable not to an increase in torture but rather to his own growing visibility and the fact that "a number of societies have become more transparent in the course of time."[258]

The Special Rapporteur's fact-finding role has inherent difficulties, since torture "can be said to be the most private of human rights violations,"[259] and the truth of allegations often can be established only

---

250. U.N. Doc. E/CN.4/1986/15, at paras. 10, 42–44, 99–100, 112–117 (1986).

251. The Special Rapporteur states that "incommunicado detention might be called the torturer's bosom friend," and recommends that states abolish it. U.N. Doc. E/CN.4/1991/17, at paras. 291, 303(b) (1991).

252. U.N. Doc. E/CN.4/1986/15, at paras. 13, 99, 106–11 (1986).

253. *Id.* at paras. 42–44.

254. U.N. Doc. E/CN.4/1991/17, at para. 303(i) (1991).

255. U.N. Doc. E/CN.4/1986/15, at paras. 18, 62–68 (1986).

256. *See* U.N. Doc. E/CN.4/1988/17, at paras. 17–20 (1988).

257. *See* U.N. Docs. E/CN.4/1990/17 (1990); E/CN.4/1991/17 (1991). In his 1991 report, the Special Rapporteur describes sending seventy urgent appeals to thirty-one governments, of whom fifteen responded. He describes correspondence with fifty-two states. U.N. Doc. E/CN.4/1991/17, at paras. 19–202.

258. *Id.* at para. 5.

259. *Id.* at para. 6.

through prompt medical examination. In response to criticism of his methods within the United Nations Commission on Human Rights, he notes that he does not transmit cases unless they are either sufficiently detailed or consistent with a pattern of allegations concerning the state in question. He observes that an investigation of torture claims at the national level is necessary to verify or disprove such claims and that a government's "flat denial" or mere citation to prohibitions of torture in national law "cannot be seen as satisfactory replies."[260]

The preventive role of the Special Rapporteur on Torture is one he shares with the Working Group on Disappearances and the Special Rapporteur on Extrajudicial, Summary or Arbitrary Executions, but it occupies special prominence in his case because of the often continuing nature of the violations he addresses. He discharges this preventive function by issuing urgent appeals in specific cases and by making general recommendations to governments and more precise recommendations to those governments that have invited him to visit.[261] Like the Working Group, the Special Rapporteur is giving increasing emphasis to follow-up work on his visits.[262]

The issue of redundancy of function is particularly acute for the Special Rapporteur on Torture, in light of the proliferation in recent years of other bodies with somewhat comparable mandates. For example, the Committee Against Torture has been created to implement the Convention Against Torture and Other Cruel, Inhuman and Degrading Treatment or Punishment,[263] and a European Committee has been created under the European Convention for the Prevention of Torture and Inhuman and Degrading Treatment or Punishment.[264] Moreover, the Organization of American States has adopted the Inter-American Convention to Prevent and Punish Torture, which, while not creating

260. *Id.* at paras. 6–11.

261. *See, e.g.,* U.N. Doc. E/CN.4/1988/17/Add.1 (1988) (reports of visits to Argentina, Colombia and Uruguay); U.N. Doc. E/CN.4/1990/17, at paras. 173–254 (1989) (visits to Guatemala and Honduras); U.N. Doc. E/CN.4/1990/17/Add.1 (1990) (visit to Zaire); U.N. Doc. E/CN.4/1991/17, at paras. 203–274 (1991) (visit to the Philippines), U.N. Doc. E/CN.4/1992/17/Add.1, at paras. 66–80 (1992) (visit to Indonesia and East Timor). He notes with regret that he had received no invitations to visit in 1991, although he stressed that an invitation should not be construed as an admission that torture is condoned by the country. U.N. Doc. E/CN.4/1991/17, at paras. 13–14 (1991).

262. *Id.* at paras. 15, 275.

263. *See* REPORT OF THE COMMITTEE AGAINST TORTURE, 45 U.N. GAOR Supp. (No. 44), U.N. Doc. A/45/44 (1990).

264. *See* COUNCIL OF EUROPE, HUMAN RIGHTS INFORMATION SHEET NO. 26, Doc. H/INF (90)2 at 69, 138 (1990) (stating the Rules of Procedure for the European Committee for the Prevention of Torture and Inhuman or Degrading Treatment or Punishment).

any new monitoring body, does confer upon the IACHR a new reporting and analysis role.[265] The Special Rapporteur has responded to the urging of the United Nations Commission on Human Rights to avoid redundancy by meeting with members of the Committee Against Torture and the European Committee to share information about methods of work.[266]

### d. Special Rapporteurs on Religious Intolerance and Mercenaries

The Commission's other two theme rapporteurs, on religious intolerance and mercenaries, also investigate abuses that sometimes correlate to states of emergency. The Special Rapporteur on Religious Intolerance takes an unusual approach in that his focus is specifically on compliance with the terms of the Declaration on the Elimination of All Forms of Intolerance and of Discrimination Based on Religion and Belief. His reports are organized by the various articles of this declaration.[267] He describes allegations of various forms of religious intolerance, some of which occur in the context of extreme civil strife, and provides government responses.[268]

The Special Rapporteur on Mercenaries also plays the unusual role of monitoring adherence to an international instrument, in his case the International Convention against the Recruitment, Use, Financing and Training of Mercenaries, which created no monitoring mechanism.[269] For obvious reasons, many of the events of concern to the Special Rapporteur on Mercenaries arise in emergency contexts, such as the armed conflict in Nicaragua and attempted takeovers in the Maldives and the Comoros.[270]

### e. Working Group on Arbitrary Detention

Of greater relevance to monitoring compliance with international standards governing states of emergency is the creation of a Working Group on Arbitrary Detention at the 1991 session of the Commis-

---

265. *See* The Inter-American Convention to Prevent and Punish Torture, *reprinted in* 25 I.L.M. 519, at art. 17 (1986).

266. U.N. Doc. E/CN.4/1991/17, at paras. 17–18 (1991).

267. *See, e.g.,* U.N. Doc. E/CN.4/1988/45 (1988).

268. *Id.*

269. G.A. Res. 44/34 of Dec. 4, 1989, 44 U.N. GAOR Supp. (No. 49) at 306, U.N. Doc. A/44/49 (1990), and Commission Res. 1990/7, ESCOR Supp. (No. 2) at 27, U.N. Doc. E/1990/22, E/CN.4/1990/94 (1990), *cited in* Brody et al., *supra* note 46, at 584.

270. *See* U.N. Doc. E/CN.4/1990/11 (1990).

sion.[271] This Working Group, like the Special Rapporteur on Extrajudicial, Summary or Arbitrary Executions, devoted serious attention initially to the definition of its mandate, which is potentially diverse and broad. The resolution creating it authorizes the Working Group to investigate "cases of detention imposed arbitrarily or otherwise inconsistently with relevant international standards as set forth in the Universal Declaration of Human Rights or in the relevant international legal instruments accepted by the States concerned."[272] The Working Group chose to divide these cases into three categories: (1) cases where the deprivation of freedom is arbitrary in the sense of lacking a legal basis, as where a person remains detained after the expiration of a sentence; (2) cases where detention is imposed because of the detainee's exercise of rights of belief, expression, association, participation in electoral matters, minority identity, or related rights; and (3) cases where detention is on the basis of a conviction obtained through particularly serious violations of the right to fair trial.[273]

The potential complexity of this task is suggested by the multiple strands of Commission and Sub-Commission concern from which emerged the new Working Group. The Group's immediate genesis was the Commission's consideration of the study on administrative detention undertaken by Louis Joinet for the Sub-Commission.[274] Joinet ultimately recommended that a separate mechanism to monitor administrative detention no longer seemed advisable since the Body of Principles for the Protection of All Persons under Any Form of Detention or Imprisonment did not distinguish among forms of detention.[275] In suggesting a working group, Joinet noted that its members could specialize in certain functional areas (*e.g.,* judicial detention, administrative detention, detention of juveniles or refugees, etc.).[276]

A wholly different influence on the creation of this Working Group

271. *See* Parker & Weissbrodt, *supra* note 3, at 27–28; R. Brody, *The United Nations Creates a Working Group on Arbitrary Detention,* 85 AM. J. INT'L L. 709 (1991).

272. *Id.* at 28.

273. U.N. Doc. E/CN.4/1993/24, at 20 and Annex I (1993). In deciding individual cases, the Working Group makes specific findings whether the case falls into one of these three categories. The Working Group reports that 90% of the cases it receives concern persons alleged to have been detained on the basis of opinion and expression. *Id.* at para. 35.

274. *See* U.N. Doc. E/CN.4/Sub.2/1990/29/Add.1 (1990) (Joinet's recommendations to the Commission); U.N. Doc. E/CN.4/Sub.2/1989/27 (1989) (Joinet's report on administrative detention); U.N. Doc. E/CN.4/Sub.2/1987/16 (1987) (Joinet's explanatory paper).

275. U.N. Doc. E/CN.4/1990/29/Add.1, at para. 89 (1990).

276. *Id.* at para. 90.

may have been several initiatives to create a body to monitor the situation of prisoners of conscience, persons detained for exercising their right to freedom of expression.[277] A Sub-Commission study on freedom of opinion tackles important conceptual issues but does not focus exclusively on detention.[278] The Working Group includes among its concerns prisoners of conscience, as well as persons imprisoned following unfair trial. As with the other theme mechanisms, the Working Group is authorized to receive information from governments, NGOs, and victims or their families and to carry out its work with discretion.

In its first full report, the Working Group specifically noted the linkage between its mandate and the problem of states of emergency, a "fruitful source of arbitrary arrests" and a frequent stimulus for the establishment of special courts that impair judicial independence and lead to serious deprivations of fair trial rights.[279] Because the Working Group has chosen to adopt an adversarial approach, it makes specific findings that the detentions of particular persons are arbitrary within its mandate. Thus the Working Group provides a new venue for challenging detention practices instituted in the context of *de jure* or *de facto* emergencies.

## 4. Special Sessions of the Commission

The Economic and Social Council, in its resolution 1990/48 of 25 May 1990, authorized the Commission to meet exceptionally between its regular sessions if a majority of members agree. The potential relevance of this enhancement in the Commission's flexibility for monitoring states of emergency is obvious, and at the request of the United States[280] the Commission met in its first special session in August 1992 "to discuss the dangerous situation in the former Yugoslavia."[281] While

277. *See* Parker and Weissbrodt, *supra* note 3, at 27 (citing efforts by U.S. Ambassador Moynihan in the 1970s, Canadian-sponsored resolutions since 1984, and unsuccessful British proposals to appoint a special rapporteur on political prisoners).

278. *See* D. Türk & L. Joinet, *Preliminary Report on the Right to Freedom of Opinion and Expression*, U.N. ESCOR, Hum. Rts. Comm., Sub-Commission on Prevention of Discrimination and Protection of Minorities, 41st Sess., Provisional Agenda Item 4, U.N. Doc. E/CN.4/ Sub.2/1990/11 (1990) (the preliminary report on freedom of opinion and expression prepared by Danilo Türk and Louis Joinet).

279. U.N. Doc. E/CN.4/1993/24, at paras. 31–32, 34, 43 (1993). The Working Group noted that states of emergency were being abused to cope with "mere political situations," citing the case of Aung San Suu Kyi of Myanmar (Burma). *Id.* at para. 31.

280. *Letter dated 5 August 1992 from the Permanent Representative of the United States of America to the United Nations Office at Geneva*, U.N. Doc. E/CN.4/1992/S-1/2 (1992).

281. *Id.*

some participants welcomed this opportunity to develop the Commission's capacity to deal effectively with emergency situations,[282] others cautioned that the current crisis revealed how inadequate the Commission's mechanisms remained[283] or expressed fear of dangerous precedents being set by precipitous action.[284]

The Commission appointed a Special Rapporteur who within months made several visits to the territory of the former Yugoslavia and prepared a series of reports.[285] In an interesting innovation, the Special Rapporteur invited the Special Rapporteurs on Torture and on Extrajudicial, Summary or Arbitrary Executions and the Chairman of the Working Group on Arbitrary Detention to accompany him on his fact-finding mission.[286] The Special Rapporteur described the gross violations of human rights and humanitarian law occurring in Bosnia-Herzegovina and Croatia and condemned the practice of "ethnic cleansing."[287] Noting the involvement of a number of international organizations in monitoring the situation in the former Yugoslavia, the

282. *Summary Records of the Commission on Human Rights, First special session*, U.N. Doc. E/CN.4/1992/S-1/SR.2/Add.1 para. 31 (1992) (remarks by observer from Poland that "the international community should try to draw conclusions for the future from the current situation, especially how to prevent gross human rights violations, how to organize enforcement of human rights and what kind of emergency mechanism should be set up to deal with such cases. . . . His country was ready to . . . join in efforts enabling the Commission to react rapidly and effectively in emergencies involving human rights violations").

283. *Id.* at para. 21 (remarks by observer from Finland that "the current crisis . . . demonstrated the inadequacy of the Commission's ability to react to emergency situations of human rights abuse, and the need for a new United Nations mechanism for that purpose. Finland hoped that tangible results could be achieved at the Commission's next session").

284. The member from India emphasized that occasions for convening special sessions should be "rare and exceptional and only for the purpose of dealing with emergency situations involving particularly serious violations of human rights. But such urgent and serious situations should not result in hasty action carrying undesirable implications for the role of the Commission as the primary United Nations body dealing with human rights situations." He also objected to the reports of the Special Rapporteur on the former Yugoslavia being provided to the Security Council in advance of their review by the Commission, as a "precedent that would diminish the importance of the Commission and create a new mandate for the Security Council." *Summary Records of the Commission on Human Rights, First special session*, U.N. Doc. E/CN.4/1992/S-1/SR.3 paras. 71–72 (1992).

285. *Reports on the situation of human rights in the territory of the former Yugoslavia*, U.N. Docs. E/CN.4/1992/S-1/9 and 10 (1992). Tadeusz Mazowiecki of Poland was named Special Rapporteur.

286. *Id.*, U.N. Doc. E/CN.4/1992/S-1/9, at para. 3; U.N. Doc. E/CN.4/1992/S-1/10, at para. 3.

287. *Supra* note 285.

Special Rapporteur cautioned that the "multiplicity of international activities aimed at bringing conflict and human rights violations in the former Yugoslavia to an end limits the efficiency of such efforts."[288]

## C. The Sub-Commission on Prevention of Discrimination and Protection of Minorities

Theoretically distinct from its parent Commission in its character as a body of independent experts, the Sub-Commission on Prevention of Discrimination and Protection of Minorities often becomes mired in the same politicization, especially in discussion of particular country situations and in screening Resolution 1503 communications. The decision to vote by secret ballot on such matters may help reduce the lobbying pressure on the Sub-Commission's experts.[289] In its attention to specific country situations, the Sub-Commission sometimes focuses specifically upon states of emergency, as it did in its 1985 resolution calling for the lifting of the state of emergency in Paraguay.[290] Two distinct functions of the Sub-Commission will be examined here, its Special Rapporteur on States of Emergency and its abstract studies of issues, many of which bear upon the legal norms governing states of emergency.

### 1. Special Rapporteur on States of Emergency

The Sub-Commission has a long-standing interest in states of emergency.[291] The immediate predecessor to the current mandate of the Special Rapporteur was the study and classification of emergencies by Mme. Questiaux, whose final report was issued in 1982.[292] While Sub-Commission Resolution 1983/30 called upon the new Rapporteur to draw up a list of states that had proclaimed or terminated emergencies and their compliance with the internal and international rules governing states of emergency, the process had a slow start, producing an

---

288. *Supra* note 285, U.N. Doc. E/CN.4/1992/S-1/9, at para. 71. The Special Rapporteur noted with approval the creation of a Steering Committee to coordinate efforts by the United Nations and the European Community at the August 1992 London Conference.

289. *See supra* note 43; Brody et al., *supra* note 184, at 265–67.

290. *Sub-Commission Res. 1985/13,* U.N. Doc. E/CN.4/1986/5, E/CN.4/Sub.2/1985/57, at 92 (1985).

291. *See, e.g., Sub-Commission Res. 10 (XXX),* U.N. Doc. E/CN.4/1261, E/CN.4/Sub.2/399, at 48 (1977).

292. *See* Chapter I *supra* (summary of Questiaux's conclusions).

explanatory paper in 1985.[293] This paper explored several troubling definitional issues, as the Special Rapporteur determined not to limit his concern only to states parties to the Covenant, despite the reference in his mandate to "[i]mplementation of the right to derogation provided for under article 4" of the Covenant.[294] He hesitated, however, to include *de facto* emergencies on his list without further guidance from the Sub-Commission.[295]

The Special Rapporteur indicated some awareness of the difficulty of compiling accurate and comprehensive information from the myriad of available sources, none complete in themselves. He ambitiously indicated an intent to cover not just bare notifications of the existence of an emergency, but also its reasons, the nature of the suspensions, the geographical extent, the persons affected, and the duration.[296] Information contained in the reports of the Commission's theme mechanisms and reports prepared by the Secretariat on detention and restraints on use of force were mentioned as useful sources.[297] The Special Rapporteur sounded a note of caution in announcing his intention to seek comment from a government before he would rely on other data that might contradict that government's own view.[298]

But it was not until he had actually drawn up the first list[299] with the assistance of NGOs and the Secretariat that the Special Rapporteur really had to confront the difficulties of his task, which, after substantial delays, has been only partially fulfilled. Even the bare informational

---

293. U.N. Doc. E/CN.4/Sub.2/1985/19 (1985).

294. U.N. Doc. E/CN.4/Sub.2/1985/19, at para. 11 (1985). The Special Rapporteur has relied upon derogation notices to the Secretaries General of the OAS and the Council of Europe in compiling his list. *See, e.g.,* U.N. Doc. E/CN.4/Sub.2/1987/19, at para. 12 (1987). The Special Rapporteur's decision was subject to some criticism within the Sub-Commission. U.N. Doc. E/CN.4/Sub.2/1987/SR.27/Add.1, at 3 (1987) (noting the remarks by Mr. Al-Kasawneh). But the Sub-Commission, rather than restricting the scope of the list, dropped the reference to Article 4 and retitled the agenda item as the "question of human rights and states of emergency." *Sub-Commission Res. 1987/25,* U.N. Doc. E/CN.4/1988/37, E/CN.4/Sub.2/1987/42, at 37–38 (1987).

295. *Id.* at para. 16.

296. U.N. Doc. E/CN.4/Sub.2/1985/19, at paras. 14–15 (1985).

297. *Id.* at para. 41.

298. *Id.* at para. 44. The Special Rapporteur refers to this approach as "the principle of argument and counter-argument." U.N. Doc. E/CN.4/Sub.2/1991/28, at para. 44 (1991).

299. The first list was presented to the Sub-Commission in 1987 because the financial crisis at the UN caused the cancellation of the Sub-Commission's 1986 session. No substantive discussion of the list occurred in 1987, however, because the list was submitted late with few translated copies. *See* U.N. Doc. E/CN.4/Sub.2/1987/19/Rev. 1, at paras. 7–8 (1988).

task of compiling a list of states proclaiming, extending, or terminating an emergency proved problematic. The Special Rapporteur acknowledged that information on the twenty-eight nations on that list was undoubtedly incomplete, and that data on several states undergoing known crises was not available.[300] The list itself, labor-intensive to compile and update, offered often detailed information concerning formal proclamations and terminations, emergency laws, grounds, and geographic scope. Although fifty-two governments replied to his requests for information, their responses were of limited assistance. The Special Rapporteur noted in this regard that many "replies and notifications are highly abstract and legal, saying little about the facts or about the consequences of the measures as far as human rights are concerned."[301]

In his second annual report and list,[302] the Special Rapporteur included updated information on a number of states and expressed an intent, with Sub-Commission approval, to undertake a study of *de facto* emergencies and to prepare model emergency laws that would be consistent with international standards.[303] That the second list remained incomplete was implicit in the Special Rapporteur's plan to forward information to states such as Myanmar which, while reported in the press to be under a state of emergency, were not included in the Sub-Commission's list.[304]

The Special Rapporteur emphasized the substantial resources required for the thorough discharge of his mandate in the truncated version of the third annual list he presented to the Sub-Commission's forty-first session in 1989.[305] As he correctly noted:

Most of this material requires a considerable amount of fact-checking and legal analysis with regard to States' responsibility in respect of their international obligations in this field and regarding compliance with all the inviolable rights . . . in all countries . . . that no organization but the United Nations is in a position to undertake. . . .

However, with the exception of the information on South Africa, which

300. *Id.* at paras. 43–44 (citing a lack of information about Kampuchea, Lebanon, Western Sahara, the Israeli Occupied Territories, and East Timor).

301. *Id.* at para. 50 and Annex II.

302. U.N. Docs. E/CN.4/Sub.2/1988/18 (1988); E/CN.4/Sub.2/1988/Add.1 (1988). A revised and updated version was presented to the Commission's forty-first session. U.N. Doc. E/CN.4/Sub.2/1988/18/Rev.1 (1988).

303. U.N. Doc. E/CN.4/Sub.2/1988/19/Rev.1, at paras. 12, 14, 37, 72–74 (1988).

304. *Id.* at para. 20. Burma (now known as Myanmar) did provide information about martial law in various districts in May 1989. U.N. Doc. E/CN.4/Sub.2/1989/30, at para. 19 (1989).

305. U.N. Doc. E/CN.4/Sub.2/1989/30 (1989).

required two years of study . . . the Special Rapporteur has not been able to provide the Sub-Commission . . . with: (a) a detailed account of the reasons for the establishment, extension and termination of the states of emergency; (b) particulars of the rights affected by the emergency measures; and (c) an assessment of the impact of these measures on human rights.

The Special Rapporteur also began his consideration of uniform criteria that could form the basis for model emergency laws, suggesting such structural protections as preservation of the legislature or judiciary as a monitoring mechanism on executive emergency powers, maintenance of the jurisdiction of non-military courts and judicial guarantees for individuals such as *habeas corpus,* and avoidance of *de facto* emergencies, which "have an extremely adverse effect, not only on the country's internal legal order but also in respect of the most fundamental rights."[306] He also noted as a "serious problem" the practice of administrative detention in non-emergency contexts, and suggested the need for study and restriction.[307]

The third list was not reviewed by the Sub-Commission until 1990, owing to translation problems.[308] The Special Rapporteur noted in it his increased efforts to make specific approaches to governments reportedly undergoing an emergency likely to have an impact on human rights;[309] his reliance on sources in the press and NGOs;[310] and the likely incompleteness of his list of thirty-three states.[311] He took initial steps toward more abstract study of emergency standards with a brief exploration of the principle of non-discrimination in derogation measures,[312] and observations on the principle of proportionality in the context of an analysis of the new constitution of Namibia.[313]

The fourth annual list, presented to the Sub-Commission in 1991, marked a substantial advance. The list includes sixty-one states,[314] including many identified only through press reports[315] and some

306. U.N. Doc. E/CN.4/Sub.2/1989/30/Add.2/Rev.1, at paras. 3, 4 (1989).

307. *Id.* at para. 4(d); U.N. Doc. E/CN.4/Sub.2/1989/SR.32, at para. 26 (1989).

308. U.N. Doc. E/CN.4/Sub.2/1989/30/Rev.2, at para. 4 (1990). The updated version of the third annual list was prepared for the Commission's forty-seventh session in 1991.

309. U.N. Doc. E/CN.4/Sub.2/1989/30/Rev.2, at para. 16 (1990).

310. *Id.* at para. 15.

311. *Id.* at para. 23.

312. U.N. Doc. E/CN.4/Sub.2/1990/33, at paras. 10–18 (1990).

313. He noted that each measure must be scrutinized and justified only if measures admissible in ordinary times would not be adequate. U.N. Doc. E/CN.4/Sub.2/1990/33/Add.1, at paras. 10–13 (1990).

314. U.N. Doc. E/CN.4/Sub.2/1991/28 (1991). Since the list includes all states experiencing emergencies since January 1985, some were no longer in force.

315. *Id.* at para. 11 (*e.g.,* Gabon, Kuwait, Liberia, Mali, Mauritania, Korea, Thailand, Togo).

apparently in the throes of *de facto* rather than formal emergencies.[316] The Special Rapporteur acknowledged that even this list was likely to be incomplete.[317] The report included an extended discussion of arbitrary detention, with the Special Rapporteur noting a "causal link between states of emergency and certain forms of arbitrary detention."[318] The draft Guidelines for the Development of Legislation on States of Emergency, prepared at a March 1991 meeting of experts, were appended to the report[319] in furtherance of the Special Rapporteur's efforts to meet the requests of the Sub-Commission for such model legislation.[320]

The Special Rapporteur's willingness to rely upon press and NGO data for information concerning states of emergency was again evident in his fifth annual report.[321] Even the state of emergency and curfew imposed in Los Angeles and other U.S. cities in April 1992 to cope with the rioting provoked by the verdicts in the Rodney King police brutality case prompted a request by the Special Rapporteur to the United States for detailed information and inclusion on the list of states proclaiming an emergency.[322] Press reports concerning the dissolution of the Peruvian Parliament and suspension of the Peruvian Constitution in April 1992 by President Fujimori impelled similar requests,[323] prompting a telephonic response from the Peruvian mission in Geneva that the Special Rapporteur characterized as a "gesture of cooperation worthy of note."[324] The Special Rapporteur's determination to include *de facto* emergencies was reflected in the presence of Bosnia-Herzegovina and Croatia on his list.[325] But news reports of the at-

316. *Id.* (*e.g.*, Ethiopia, Mauritania).

317. *Id.* at para. 12.

318. *Id.* at para. 28.

319. *Id.* at Annex I.

320. *Id.* at para. 52 (citing *Sub-Commission Res. 1990/19*, U.N. Doc. E/CN.4/1991/2, E/CN.4/Sub.2/1990/59, at 42 (1990); *Commission decision 1991/108*, U.N. ESCOR Supp. (No. 2) at 188, U.N. Doc. E/1991/22, E/CN.4/1991/91 (1991); *E.S.C. decision 1991/262*, U.N. Doc. E/1991/INF/5, at 105 (1991)).

321. *Fifth annual report and list of States which, since 1 January 1985, have proclaimed, extended or terminated a state of emergency*, U.N. Doc. E/CN.4/Sub.2/1992/23 (1992).

322. *Id.* at 25. The United States replied that the civil disturbances were not of the magnitude of public emergencies envisioned in Article 4 and that they did not involve suspensions of non-derogable rights. To the extent the local emergency measures restricted the freedom of movement guaranteed by Article 12 of the ICCPR, the United States asserted that the measures were justified as limitations on grounds of public order. *Id.* at 36.

323. *Id.* at 18.

324. *Id.* at 27.

325. The Special Rapporteur noted in both cases that he awaited more precise information from the governments of these new republics. *Id.* at 6, 8.

tempted coup d'etat in the Soviet Union, during the 1991 session of the Sub-Commission, prompted the most gratifying of the Special Rapporteur's requests for additional information, as the observer for the USSR notified him of the restoration of constitutional power and the termination of the irregular emergency powers invoked by the coup leaders.[326]

The resource demands of seeking out and verifying information on often volatile and complex legal and factual situations, the challenge of even defining the concept once purely formal criteria are recognized as inadequate,[327] and the political delicacy of assessing the legality of the emergency itself, as well as the measures taken, are all serious barriers to the Special Rapporteur's actually fulfilling the task set by the Sub-Commission. Resources at the UN Centre for Human Rights are simply inadequate to meet the needs of all the treaty-based and non-treaty study and monitoring mechanisms. Unless NGOs or academic institutions can themselves secure the resources and make an ongoing commitment,[328] a comprehensive and properly analyzed listing of contemporary emergencies and their various actual effects on enjoyment of human rights is unlikely to come into existence.

## 2. Abstract Studies

The other function that distinguishes the Sub-Commission from its parent Commission is its role as "think tank" on human rights issues.[329] The Questiaux Report[330] on states of emergency is merely one example. Sub-Commission expert Erica-Irene Daes also probed in depth the protection of human rights in time of public emergency in her wide-

326. *Id.* at 31 and Annex II. The subsequent break-up of the Soviet Union and its consequential train of *de facto* emergencies were noted prominently in the Special Rapporteur's list. *Id.* at 4–5 (Armenia); 5 (Azerbaijan); 11 (Georgia); 13 (Kazakhstan); 14 (Kyrgyzstan); 16 (Moldova); 19 (Russian Federation); 23 (Tajikistan); 25 (Uzbekistan).

327. *See* Chapter I *supra* (referring to problems of definition).

328. The Special Rapporteur noted in his fifth report his consultations with academic and other experts who are developing computer-assisted systems for the receipt, storage, and retrieval of information concerning states of emergency, including experts from Queen's University, Belfast. *Id.* at 34. *See* Tom Hadden, Colm Campbell and K.S. Venkateswaran, A Database on States of Emergency: Report of a Feasibility Study (1992). The Special Rapporteur also noted that emphasis must be placed on "the necessity for the development by the Centre for Human Rights of its own general database on human rights, of which states of emergency could be a component." *Id.*

329. The term was used by the Sub-Commission chair, Danilo Türk, at the forty-second session. *UN Sub-Commission on the Prevention of Discrimination and the Protection of Minorities*, 45 The Review (International Commission of Jurists) 15 (1990).

330. *See* Chapter I *supra* (for a detailed description of the Questiaux study).

ranging study of limitations on human rights.[331] Indeed, critics have asserted that the Sub-Commission undertakes too many studies that burden the thin resources of the Secretariat and often overload the agenda of the Sub-Commission's annual meeting.[332] The impact of states of emergency on human rights frequently figures as a component of Sub-Commission studies, particularly those concerned with the rights of detainees, even where emergency powers are not the focus.

For example, a study of fair trial rights that drew upon a comparative analysis of treaty and other norms included a very useful discussion of the arguably non-derogable core of procedural protections that should remain available at all times.[333] The study concluded that "[i]f habeas corpus is going to be an effective remedy to protect other non-derogable rights, not only should habeas corpus itself be non-derogable under all situations, but it should be in practice an efficacious means at all times to challenge the legality of detention."[334] Similarly, the report on administrative detention noted the strong connection between abuse of detainees and states of emergency and suggested further study of the non-derogability of judicial remedies for arbitrary detention, drawing on Inter-American standards.[335] Studies on the independence of the judiciary[336] and on the right to freedom of opinion and expression[337] likewise examined difficulties posed by emergency practices.

---

331. *The Individual's Duties to the Community and the Limitations on Human Rights and Freedoms under Article 29 of the Universal Declaration of Human Rights*, U.N. Doc. E/CN.4/Sub.2/432/Rev.2 (1983) (Part three).

332. *See* Brody et al., *supra* note 46, at 276–90 (noting that the Sub-Commission often commences new studies prior to completing pending ones and sometimes assigns more than one study to a single expert, and that some experts rely entirely on the Secretariat to author their studies).

333. *The Right to a Fair Trial: Brief Report Prepared by Mr. Stanislav Chernichencko and Mr. William Treat in Accordance with Resolution 1989/27 of the Subcommission*, U.N. ESCOR, Hum. Rts. Comm., 42d Sess., Provisional Agenda Item 10(d), U.N. Doc. E/CN.4/Sub.2/1990/34, at paras. 133–145 (1990).

334. *The Right to Fair Trial: Current Recognition and Measures Necessary for its Strengthening, Addendum: Right to Amparo, Habeas Corpus, and Similar Procedures*, U.N. Doc. E/CN.4/Sub.2/1992/24/Add.3 para. 54 (1992).

335. L. Joinet, *Report on the Practice of Administrative Detention*, U.N. Doc. E/CN.4/Sub.2/1990/29, at paras. 28–30, 64–71, 82(d) (1990).

336. L. Joinet, *The Independence and Impartiality of the Judiciary, Jurors and Assessors and the Independence of Lawyers*, U.N. ESCOR, Hum. Rts. Comm., Sub-Commission on Prevention of Discrimination and Protection of Minorities, 42d Sess., Provisional Agenda Item 11, U.N. Doc. E/CN.4/Sub.2/1990/35, at para. 35(f) (1990).

337. D. Türk & L. Joinet, *Preliminary Report on the Right to Freedom of Opinion and Expression*, U.N. Doc. E/CN.4/Sub.2/1990/11, at paras. 37–48, 146–149 (1990).

## D. United Nations Educational, Scientific and Cultural Organization

The United Nations Educational, Scientific and Cultural Organization (UNESCO) created in 1978 its own system for responding to individual communications alleging violation of rights within its sphere of competence.[338] Like Resolution 1503, the UNESCO complaints procedure is confidential and thus makes careful study of its relevance to states of emergency difficult.[339] But, unlike Resolution 1503, the UNESCO process is primarily one of "good offices" dialogue with governments with the aim of ameliorating the individual difficulties of the complainants. While UNESCO has empowered its Committee on Conventions and Recommendations (Committee) to refer to the Executive Board and General Conference "questions" of "massive, systematic and flagrant violations" (which might be expected to coincide with emergencies) for public discussion, this authority has never been exercised.[340] In 1979 the Committee also established a special list for communications concerning disappeared persons, but after the creation of the Working Group on Enforced and Involuntary Disappearances in 1980, it chose to defer to the Working Group in such cases.[341]

338. These rights would include education; the right to share in scientific advancement; the right to participate in cultural life; the right to information, freedom of expression, and religion; the right to protection of interests in scientific or artistic production; and freedom of assembly for related purposes. *See* AMNESTY INTERNATIONAL, PROTECTING HUMAN RIGHTS: INTERNATIONAL PROCEDURES AND HOW TO USE THEM, pt. 3, AI Index: IOR 30/01/89, at 20 (1989). *See also* P. Alston, *UNESCO's Procedures for Dealing with Human Rights Violations*, 20 SANTA CLARA L. REV. 665, 674–75 (1980).

339. The entire published text of the relevant decisions taken at the 110th session of the Executive Board simply stated that "the Board examined the report of the Committee on Conventions and Recommendations concerning this item, *took note* thereof and *endorsed* the Committee's wishes expressed therein." UNESCO Doc. 110 EX/DECISIONS 34 (1980) (emphasis in original). Accordingly, it is difficult to glean information concerning the subject matter of the communications and their possible connection to states of emergency. In June 1990, however, the former Chairman of the Committee on Conventions and Recommendations indicated that 206 cases and 9 general situations had been resolved through intervention by the Committee, with the following relief obtained: 102 persons released or acquitted, 20 permitted to leave the state and 33 permitted to return, 20 returned to jobs or other activities, and 7 able to broadcast or publish after bans lifted. G. DUMONT, UNESCO, DISCREET DIALOGUE, No. 16, at 11 (1990).

340. UNESCO DEC. 3.3, 104 UNESCO EXECUTIVE BOARD, UNESCO Doc. 104 EX/DECISION, paras. 10, 17, 18 (1978). *See* DUMONT, *supra* note 339; S. Marks, *The Complaint Procedure of the United Nations Educational, Scientific and Cultural Organization (UNESCO)*, *in* GUIDE TO INTERNATIONAL HUMAN RIGHTS PRACTICE 104–5 (Hurst Hannum ed., 1984).

341. Marks, *supra* note 340, at 103–4.

The Executive Board of UNESCO in 1978 set admissibility criteria that follow the usual pattern, but with moderate exhaustion barriers.[342] The handling of admissibility issues by the Committee on Conventions and Recommendations has been criticized, however, for being excessively slow, for confusing the issue of admissibility with the finding of a violation and thus contributing to the reluctance to decide admissibility, and for sometimes declaring communications inadmissible on the basis of information provided by governments which the victim was not permitted to challenge.[343] Despite these criticisms, the victim plays a more active role under this procedure than under Resolution 1503, and its slowness has been defended as contributing to the humanitarian aim of securing a friendly settlement.[344]

## E. The Secretary-General and the Security Council

The increasing activism of both the Secretary-General and the Security Council with respect to states of emergency is a factor to which the existing human rights monitoring bodies have not yet adequately adjusted. Security Council Resolution 688 insisting that Iraq provide access to humanitarian assistance for those in the Kurdish "safe zones" arguably provides a precedent for similar action to redress gross human rights violations.[345] The creation by the Security Council of a

342. Decision 3.3, *supra* note 340, at paras. 14(a)(i–x). No anonymous communications, sent either by victim or organization with reliable knowledge, concerning violations within UNESCO competence, compatible with human rights standards, not manifestly ill-founded and containing relevant evidence, not abusive, not based exclusively on mass media, submitted within a reasonable time, indicating any attempts to exhaust domestic remedies, not concerning matters already settled by other international proceedings are permitted.

343. INTERNATIONAL HUMAN RIGHTS LAW GROUP, WORKING SEMINAR ON UNESCO HUMAN RIGHTS PROCEDURES 7–8 (Washington, D.C. 1984); *see UNESCO's Special Committee on Human Rights: An Unfortunate Case,* 29 THE REVIEW (INTERNATIONAL COMMISSION OF JURISTS) 35 (1982) (describing an Argentinian case concerning a university lecturer held in administrative detention under a state of siege, after the completion of a prison sentence, in which the Committee on Conventions and Recommendations declared the case inadmissible on the basis of government claims that the lecturer was a terrorist, without providing an opportunity for refutation).

344. *See* DUMONT, *supra* note 339; Marks, *supra* note 340, at 101–3.

345. Security Council Res. 688 of 5 April 1991, *reprinted in* 30 I.L.M. 858 (1991). Philip Alston suggests that the human rights component of Resolution 688 has been exaggerated, but he agrees that the Security Council and Secretary-General have recently been and are likely to be more active in the human rights field than in the past. P. Alston, *The Security Council and Human Rights: Lessons to Be Learned from the Iraq-Kuwait Crisis and Its Aftermath,* 13 AUST. Y.B. INT'L L. 107 (1992).

Commission of Experts to gather information on war crimes in the former Yugoslavia and plans for the creation of a war crimes tribunal likewise signal a growing visibility of human rights concerns in the work of the Security Council.[346] Far greater resources have been allocated to the monitoring operations of UNTAC or ONUSAL than to the more traditional operations of the Centre for Human Rights.[347]

Greater integration of human rights concerns and institutions into United Nations processes for peace-keeping and political negotiations is required. Secretary-General Boutros Boutros-Ghali called for exploration of means "of empowering the Secretary-General and expert human rights bodies to bring massive violations of human rights to the attention of the Security Council together with recommendations for action."[348] Renewed discussion of a High Commissioner for Human Rights may pave the way for such an entity to play the necessary coordinating role.[349] For the present, the incomplete integration of human rights concerns into the work of the Security Council leads to such anomalies as a pronouncement by the President of the Security Council on the anarchic situation in Afghanistan in April 1992 which makes no reference to respect for human rights.[350]

346. *See* Security Council Res. 780 of 6 October 1992, *reprinted in* 31 I.L.M. 1476 (1992).

347. *See supra* notes 116, 182; I. Guest, *The UN Needs a Stronger Rights Presence Afield,* INT'L HERALD TRIB., Mar. 11, 1993 (NEXIS).

348. *Report of the Secretary-General on the Work of the Organization,* U.N. Doc. A/47/1, at para. 101 (1992).

349. AMNESTY INTERNATIONAL, WORLD CONFERENCE ON HUMAN RIGHTS, AI Index: IOR 41/16/92 (1992).

350. Noted critically by the Special Rapporteur on Afghanistan in U.N. Doc. A/47/656, at para. 46 (1992).

# Chapter VI
## Regional Systems

## A. The Organization of American States

### 1. The Inter-American Commission on Human Rights

In many minds, the popular stereotype of a state of emergency involves a Latin American country. Although this stereotype does not begin to describe the real extent of states of emergency, there have been many members of the Organization of American States (OAS) that fit this picture. The Inter-American Commission on Human Rights (IACHR) has both a flexible array of techniques to investigate emergency situations and a willingness to employ them, making it one of the most active and potentially effective international bodies encompassed by this study. The IACHR, unlike the UN human rights bodies, possesses general authority to monitor all member states under the OAS Charter, as well as supervisory power to assess compliance by states parties to the American Convention on Human Rights. Three mechanisms of the IACHR will be described: (1) special reports on the situation of human rights in particular states; (2) IACHR reports on individual "denunciations" of human rights abuses; and (3) the preparation of annual reports containing brief summaries of country situations as well as comments of a more general nature.

#### a. Special Country Reports

Within a year of its creation in 1959, the IACHR began undertaking special studies of human rights abuses during states of emergency.[1]

---

1. Reports on Paraguay were made in 1961, 1964, and after an on-site visit in 1965. *See* OEA/Ser.L/V/II.10, doc. 2 (1961); OEA/Ser.L/V/II.13, doc. 5 (1964). A report was also prepared in 1978. OEA/Ser.L/V/II.43, doc.13, corr. 1 (1978). Especially noteworthy among IACHR abstract studies of states of emergency is the second report by Daniel Hugo Martins. INTER-AM. C.H.R., LA PROTECCIÓN DE LOS DERECHOS HUMANOS FRENTE A

Major changes in the IACHR's authority occurred in 1965, when it was empowered to receive individual communications, address governments and submit annual reports;[2] in 1967 with the Protocol of Amendment to the Charter of the OAS, which made the IACHR a principal organ of the OAS; and in 1979, when a new Statute of the IACHR was concluded to encompass its added responsibilities under the American Convention on Human Rights, which had entered into force the previous year.[3] The double function of the IACHR as the primary implementation body under the American Convention and as the principal OAS human rights organ does not appear to have substantially affected its method of work.[4]

The IACHR is authorized with regard to any OAS member state "to prepare such studies or reports as it considers advisable for the performance of its duties."[5] The IACHR has demonstrated noteworthy vigor in executing this authority by producing a series of highly detailed, generally candid and evaluative reports on various states' human rights practices. These reports almost always depict some kind of emergency situation, frequently following productive and energetic on-site visits. In contrast to the Human Rights Committee and the European Commission, the IACHR may prepare such reports on its own initiative, although it may also respond to a request from another organ of the OAS,[6] the suggestion of an NGO,[7] or the invitation of a government. A government's invitation to the IACHR to conduct an on-site visit is

---

LA SUSPENSIÓN DE LOS GARANTÍAS CONSTITUCIONALES O "ESTADO DE SITIO," OEA/Ser.L/V/II.15, doc. 12 (1966).

2. Of special importance was Article 9 (bis), added to the IACHR's Statute. Statute of the Inter-American Commission on Human Rights, *reprinted* in HANDBOOK OF EXISTING RULES PERTAINING TO HUMAN RIGHTS IN THE INTER-AMERICAN SYSTEM 24, OEA/Ser.L/V/II.26, doc. 10 (1979) [hereinafter Commission Statute].

3. *See* ANNUAL REPORT OF THE INTER-AMERICAN COMMISSION ON HUMAN RIGHTS 1979–1980, OEA/Ser.L/V/II.50, doc. 13, rev. 1, at 11–13 (1980) (noting articles 18, 19 and 20, which set forth the IACHR's powers).

4. The IACHR does have an important relationship under the Convention to the Inter-American Court of Human Rights from which it can request provisional measures and advisory opinions. American Convention on Human Rights, *adopted* Nov. 22, 1969, arts. 61, 64, OEA/Ser.L/V/II.23 at 1, doc. 21, rev. 2, at 1, *entered into force* July 18, 1978 [hereinafter American Convention].

5. Commission Statute, *supra* note 2, art. 18(c).

6. The OAS Permanent Council requested that the IACHR do a study of Bolivia in 1980 after a military coup displaced the elected government. REPORT ON THE SITUATION OF HUMAN RIGHTS IN BOLIVIA, OEA/Ser.L/V/II.53, doc. 6 (1981).

7. Consideration of Suriname originated due to a 10 December 1982 cable from Amnesty International concerning fifteen reported summary executions. REPORT ON THE SITUATION OF HUMAN RIGHTS IN SURINAME, OEA/Ser.L/V/II.61, doc. 6, rev. 1 (1983).

frequently negotiated behind the scenes.[8] Moreover, unlike the UN Commission on Human Rights and its Sub-Commission, the IACHR appears to be essentially free of political infighting among its members in deciding to undertake new studies.[9] While the IACHR has no special mechanism under the OAS Charter or American Convention to trigger an investigation automatically whenever an OAS state declares an emergency, its experience, reflected in its reports, reveals a high correlation between emergency conditions and grave human rights abuses. For example, the OAS Permanent Council requested the IACHR to examine the situation of human rights in Haiti in June 1988, shortly after the military takeover of the government by General Henri Namphy. With the government's consent, the IACHR visited Haiti and issued several months later a comprehensive and critical report.[10]

*b. On-Site Visits*

The on-site visits conducted by the IACHR deserve special mention. Although the IACHR's capacity to prepare special reports does not hinge upon its success in securing government approval for an on-site visit, its reports prepared without that benefit tend to be more abstract and formulaic.[11] The IACHR has, by far, the greatest experience among international bodies in conducting on-site visits during states of emergency. Before undertaking such visits, the IACHR requires the government to agree to certain conditions designed to secure adequate

8. *E.g.*, Report on the Situation of Human Rights in the Republic of Nicaragua, OEA/Ser.L/V/II.53, doc. 25 (1981); Report on the Situation of Human Rights in El Salvador, OEA/Ser.L/V/II.46, doc. 23, rev. 1 (1978); Report on the Situation of Human Rights in the Republic of Colombia, OEA/Ser.L/V/II.53, doc. 22 (1981).

9. The only note of dissent uncovered in this study respecting a special report was a cryptic annotation to the Second Report on the Situation of Human Rights in Chile, OEA/Ser.L/V/II.37, doc. 19, corr. 1, at 191 (1976). The annotation stated that "Professor Manuel Bianchi, Member of the Commission, presented a reservation which was added to the formal record of the meeting [adopting the report]."

10. Report on the Situation of Human Rights in Haiti, OEA/Ser.L/V/II.74, doc. 9, rev. 1, at 1–2 (1988) (quoting Res. No. 502 by O.A.S. Permanent Council). The IACHR had also visited Haiti on its own initiative in 1979 and in 1987. The killings of twelve persons in San Juan Bosco Church in September 1988, shortly after the issuance of the IACHR's 1988 report on Haiti, led the Permanent Council of the OAS in February 1989 to ask the IACHR to make a further on-site visit. In April 1990, the visit was conducted after the civilian caretaker government of President Ertha Pascal-Trouillot had taken power from General Prosper Avril. Report on the Situation of Human Rights in Haiti, OEA/Ser.L/V/II.77, doc. 18, rev. 1, at 1–4 (1990).

11. Article 18(g) of the Statute of the IACHR requires governmental consent for on-site visits. OEA/Ser.L/V/II.65, doc. 6, at 110 (1985).

facilities for the visit and to protect witnesses against reprisals.[12] The IACHR generally appoints a special commission of some of its members, accompanied by staff, to conduct the visit, though sometimes the entire Commission will participate in the mission. During these on-site investigations, the IACHR typically interviews government officials and hears from complainants and witnesses, whom it assists in completing IACHR forms. Large numbers of new denunciations are sometimes obtained in this manner.[13]

Occasionally an IACHR on-site visit leads to immediate concrete improvements, such as it did in Nicaragua with the release of women prisoners,[14] or by Panama's repeal of certain legal provisions denying fair trial.[15] However, the evidence of IACHR effectiveness in immediately reducing human rights abuses, especially in emergency situations, is quite modest. An investigation can even lead to a crackdown, as in Argentina, when, on the eve of an IACHR visit, the offices of several human rights groups were raided and all their files were seized.[16] Although much of its visit is taken up by interviews with government officials and a wide variety of persons familiar with the particular country's human rights situation, the IACHR can also be adventurous, such as when it located secret cells in El Salvador,[17] examined corpses from clandestine graves in Guatemala,[18] sent staff members to interview Guatemalan refugees in Mexico,[19] and provided safe passage for M-19 guerrillas from Colombia who had been holding hostages at an embassy in Bogotá.[20]

12. Regulations of the Inter-American Commission on Human Rights, arts. 55–59, HANDBOOK OF EXISTING RULES PERTAINING TO HUMAN RIGHTS IN THE INTER-AMERICAN SYSTEM, OEA/Ser.L/V/II.65, doc. 6 (1985) [hereinafter Regulations of the IACHR].

13. *E.g.*, 576 denunciations were received in 1974 at the Hotel Crillon in Santiago, Chile. REPORT ON THE STATUS OF HUMAN RIGHTS IN CHILE, OEA/Ser.L/V/II.34, doc. 21, at 65 (1974).

14. REPORT ON THE SITUATION OF HUMAN RIGHTS IN THE REPUBLIC OF NICARAGUA, OEA/Ser.L/V/II.53, doc. 25, at 14 (1981).

15. REPORT ON THE SITUATION OF HUMAN RIGHTS IN PANAMA, OEA/Ser.L/V/II.44, doc. 38, rev. 1 (1978).

16. The connection between the raid and the IACHR visit was apparent in the warrant's listing of the OAS office in Buenos Aires as a location to be searched. REPORT ON THE SITUATION OF HUMAN RIGHTS IN ARGENTINA, OEA/Ser.L/V/II.49, doc. 19, corr. 1, at 260 (1980).

17. REPORT ON THE SITUATION OF HUMAN RIGHTS IN EL SALVADOR, OEA/Ser.L/V/II.46, doc. 23, rev. 1, at 19–20 (1978).

18. REPORT ON THE SITUATION OF HUMAN RIGHTS IN THE REPUBLIC OF GUATEMALA, OEA/Ser.L/V/II.53, doc. 21, rev. 2, at 37 (1981).

19. *Id.* at 20.

20. REPORT ON THE SITUATION OF HUMAN RIGHTS IN THE REPUBLIC OF COLOMBIA,

Thus, the IACHR should be seen primarily as a fact-finding body with a flexible sense of its own role rather than as a quasi-judicial body. In the case of the Nicaraguan Miskito, the Commission also was able to play a friendly settlement role, after first addressing itself to the abstract legal issue of the permissibility of forced relocation of certain population groups in the context of an emergency and then applying this standard to the particular situation presented.[21] Such consideration of general interpretive questions relating to states of emergency, however, is rather rare in IACHR reports. Each has, instead, a section of conclusions and recommendations listing the particular rights violated by the government in the situation studied, which is also of some jurisprudential or precedential value.

In its discussions with government officials and in government "observations" that are solicited prior to publication of its reports, the IACHR has often been met with the argument that terrorism justifies government action suspending human rights. The IACHR developed for the benefit of the Argentine Government a formal two-part answer to this argument, which it has since used a number of times. First, the IACHR refuses to consider denunciations against non-governmental actors, such as terrorists, because its competence extends only to human rights practices of governments in OAS states. Second, while recognizing that governments have an obligation to maintain order, the Commission notes that they may take emergency measures only in "extremely serious circumstances" and may never suspend certain fundamental rights. In the IACHR's view, only governments lacking broad popular support will resort to state terrorism, while democratic governments will maintain the rule of law when confronting terrorism.[22] This response to the frequently invoked justification of governments, to suspend basic human rights in combating terrorism, forms a significant part of the IACHR's approach to states of emergency.

Increasing pressure from governments and political organs of the OAS has not induced the IACHR to retreat from these principles. Responding to a resolution of the OAS General Assembly requesting it to report on actions of irregular armed groups,[23] the IACHR noted

---

OEA/Ser.L/V/II.53, doc. 22, at 12–15 (1981). This action was taken with the approval of both the Government and the guerrillas.

21. REPORT ON THE SITUATION OF HUMAN RIGHTS OF A SEGMENT OF THE NICARAGUAN POPULATION OF MISKITO ORIGIN, OEA/Ser.L/V/II.62, doc. 10, rev. 3 (1983).

22. REPORT ON THE SITUATION OF HUMAN RIGHTS IN ARGENTINA, OEA/Ser.L/V/II.49, doc. 19, corr. 1, at 25–27 (1980).

23. OAS G.A. Res. AG/RES. 1043 (XX-0/90), *reprinted in* ANNUAL REPORT OF THE

that there was "nothing new" about such acts;[24] that international human rights law imposes obligations on states, but that an atmosphere of violence can be taken into account in addressing human rights violations,[25] in order to "depict the general setting" and, more precisely, "when analyzing the causes invoked as grounds for suspending the exercise of certain rights, in accordance with the provisions of the American Convention on Human Rights."[26] The IACHR cautioned that if it were to become involved in investigating violations of international humanitarian law binding on non-state actors, "specific rules to that effect would have to be drafted."[27] The IACHR observed:

[T]he Commission has often heard the argument that human rights violations are inevitable because they are the consequence of the "war" created by armed groups, who are generally portrayed as terrorists. Thus, human rights violations are being justified as a necessary byproduct of an armed conflict that the authorities and security forces do not admit to having provoked. In the Commission's judgment, this is an invalid argument; consequently, it has repeatedly asserted that unqualified respect for human rights must be a fundamental part of any anti-subversive strategies when such strategies have to be implemented.[28]

The IACHR makes candid judgments in its reports about states' human rights practices and suggests specific recommendations for improvement. Sometimes these judgments are quite condemnatory, as in the case of the Somoza regime in Nicaragua.[29] Criticizing the suspension of Haiti's 1987 Constitution by the military government, the IACHR stated:

A military *coup d'etat* and the summary deportation of the head of state cannot be legitimized by the destruction of the nation's fundamental charter or by

---

INTER-AMERICAN COMMISSION ON HUMAN RIGHTS 1990–1991, OEA/Ser.L/V/II.79 doc. 12, rev. 1., at 504–5 (1991).

24. *Id.* at 504.

25. *Id.* at 505.

26. *Id.* at 508.

27. *Id.* at 509.

28. *Id.* at 512.

29. The report condemned a variety of "serious, persistent and generalized violations." REPORT ON THE SITUATION OF HUMAN RIGHTS IN NICARAGUA, OEA/Ser.L/V/II.45, doc. 16, rev. 1, at 77 (1978). The Permanent Council went further and in an extraordinary resolution in June 1979 called for the "immediate and definitive replacement of the Somoza regime." REPORT ON THE SITUATION OF HUMAN RIGHTS IN THE REPUBLIC OF NICARAGUA, OEA/Ser.L/V/II.53, doc. 25, at 20–23 (1981).

unsupportable claims, made under the threat of the use of force, that one is acting in the name of democracy and human rights.[30]

Even after essentially friendly visits to Colombia[31] and Nicaragua[32] in 1980, the IACHR, while praising efforts to respect human rights, made selective findings of violations and recommendations for change. When an on-site visit discloses an unusually grave situation, the IACHR may also make specific "preliminary recommendations" to the government, which are published only in the final report.[33] These reports seem to indicate an almost complete unanimity among IACHR members as to the propriety of these actions.[34]

The comprehensiveness of the reports, however, does vary. The 1983 visit to Suriname, precipitated essentially by a single barbaric act, was much shorter and yielded a more cursory and unusually pessimistic report.[35] In stark contrast is the 1985 report on Chile, which surveys and analyzes all significant factual and legal developments since September 1973 and sharply criticizes the Government's basic outlook, its

---

30. 1988 REPORT ON HAITI, *supra* note 10, at 51.

31. The Colombian visit was rather unusual, even aside from the dramatic hostage rescue. The Government invited the IACHR to visit certain military trials of civilians accused of security offenses, but when the IACHR delegation arrived in April 1980 it found the proceedings closed. The IACHR decided to leave several staff members to follow the trials and to return in March 1981. Although mindful of good intentions, the report found occasional violations of the right to life, abuses of authority in arrests and detentions, a failure of the military justice system to provide sufficient guarantees of fair trial, excesses against Indians by military authorities in rural areas, and a failure to punish security force members committing abuses. REPORT ON THE SITUATION OF HUMAN RIGHTS IN THE REPUBLIC OF COLOMBIA, OEA/Ser.L/V/II.53, doc. 22, at 12–13, 21, 219–22 (1981).

32. The IACHR found violations of the right to life, inadequate due process in special courts created to punish "Somocistas," inadequate prison conditions, excessive restrictions on expression and political rights, and "unjustifiable obstacles" in the path of human rights groups. REPORT ON THE SITUATION OF HUMAN RIGHTS IN THE REPUBLIC OF NICARAGUA, OEA/Ser.L/V/II.53, doc. 25, at 168–71 (1981).

33. *See, e.g.*, REPORT ON THE SITUATION OF HUMAN RIGHTS IN ARGENTINA, OEA/Ser.L/V/II.49, doc. 19, corr. 1, at 7–9 (1980).

34. This unanimity is confirmed by former IACHR President Tom J. Farer. T. Farer, *Human Rights and Human Wrongs: Is the Liberal Model Sufficient?* 7 HUM. RTS. Q. 189, 190 (1985).

35. Although the focus was on the torture and summary execution of fifteen community leaders in December 1982, the IACHR found a situation of total lawlessness and intimidation. The report notes the irony which will be apparent to "non-lawyers" in asking high officials to investigate and to punish their own deliberate and grave violations of human rights. REPORT ON THE SITUATION OF HUMAN RIGHTS IN SURINAME, *supra* note 7, at 33–34 (1983). A report on Suriname was also issued following a visit in January 1985. OEA/Ser.L/V/II.65, doc. 11 (1985).

institutionalization of the emergency, and corresponding limits on human rights in the 1980 Constitution.[36] A special report on Paraguay in 1987 questioned whether the lifting of the long-prolonged state of emergency had led to any real improvement in the human rights situation.[37]

Although the IACHR does not hesitate to be judgmental, it appears resistant to viewing itself as a judicial body. As noted, its decision to begin an investigation of and to write a special report on a particular country is triggered by reports of human rights abuses that may, but need not, be associated with the imposition of emergency measures. While each of its reports contains a wealth of findings of violations and may note a lack of proportionality to the threat faced by the government or the fact that a violation was of a non-derogable right, the IACHR generally does not make a careful and explicit application of Article 27 of the American Convention. In the case of states that have not ratified the American Convention and are thus bound only by the American Declaration on the Rights and Duties of Man and customary international law, the IACHR has indicated that emergency measures undertaken by these states can be judged by the standards of the American Convention, "which embodies the most received doctrine on this subject."[38] One unique aspect of the American Convention is the non-derogability of the requirement of public elections, which could provide the IACHR with a basis for restricting the privilege of derogation to states with democratically elected governments.

## c. Individual Complaints

The resistance of the IACHR to being a quasi-judicial body can be seen in its somewhat reluctant handling of the individual communications or "denunciations" it receives under its expanded powers conferred in 1965 or under Article 44 of the American Convention. The

---

36. REPORT ON THE SITUATION OF HUMAN RIGHTS IN CHILE, OEA/Ser.L/V/II.66, doc. 17 (1985). This report was prepared without an on-site visit and against the strong objections of the Chilean Government, which attempted to block it by seeking a ruling on the IACHR's competence from the Inter-American Juridical Committee. *Id.* at 3. Chile was reportedly able to kill a resolution on the report at the OAS General Assembly in late 1985. The model for the report may have been a twenty-five-year survey of human rights conditions in Cuba issued in 1983. OEA/Ser.L/V/II.61, doc. 29, rev. 1 (1983).

37. REPORT ON THE SITUATION OF HUMAN RIGHTS IN PARAGUAY, OEA/Ser.L/V/II.71, doc. 19, rev. 1 (1987).

38. REPORT ON THE SITUATION OF HUMAN RIGHTS IN CHILE, *supra* note 36, at para. 93 (1985); REPORT ON THE STATUS OF HUMAN RIGHTS IN CHILE, OEA/Ser.L/V/II.34, doc. 21, corr. 1, at para. 5 (1974).

IACHR has not taken timely action on many of these communications, and its annual reports often contain a comparatively small number of case "resolutions."[39] While the barrier of admissibility has always been high at the European Commission and may be increasing at the Human Rights Committee, the IACHR sometimes neglects for extended periods even to make a decision on admissibility.[40] It is not clear whether the slow processing of communications is due simply to understaffing or whether it reflects a conscious choice by the IACHR to avoid identification as a quasi-judicial body and to place the bulk of its energies into being a flexible *ad hoc* fact-finding unit. However, the IACHR has sometimes used its authority to adjudicate individual communications to make important pronouncements on legal issues related to states of emergency.

The IACHR regularly makes use of even undecided communications in its special reports (essentially as illustrative incidents), with the caveat that such use does not prejudge the merits.[41] A pattern of denunciations revealing gross abuses may also trigger a decision by the Commission to seek an on-site visit and to write a special report on the particular country's human rights situation.[42]

When the IACHR decides the merits of a communication, it exercises enviable fact-finding capacities. A formal presumption under Article 42 of the IACHR's Regulations specifies that credible allegations to which the government fails to respond will be presumed to be true.[43] This presumption may help explain why there is often a substantial delay before the IACHR publishes its reports on individual cases. The IACHR asks the government several times for a response,

---

39. In each of the annual reports for 1983–1984 and 1984–1985, for example, only seventeen resolutions were published. A dramatic departure from this pattern is seen with the 1990–1991 annual report which includes reports on eighty-six individual cases, including fifty against Peru that concerned allegations of disappearances to which the government had failed to reply despite numerous reminders over a period of several years. 1990–1991 ANNUAL REPORT, OEA/Ser.L/V/II.79, doc. 12, rev. 1, at 251–422 (1991). The IACHR decided to refer to these case dispositions as "reports" rather than "resolutions" in the future. *Id.* at 33.

40. This occurred in a substantial number of Uruguayan cases eventually decided by the Human Rights Committee. *See* Chapter IV *supra.*

41. REPORT OF THE SITUATION OF HUMAN RIGHTS IN ARGENTINA, *supra* note 16, at 10–12 (1980).

42. REPORT ON THE SITUATION OF HUMAN RIGHTS IN GUATEMALA, *supra* note 18.

43. Article 42 states: "The facts reported in the petition whose pertinent parts have been transmitted to the government of the State in reference shall be presumed to be true if, during the maximum period set by the commission under the provisions of Article 34 paragraph 5, the government has not provided the pertinent information, as long as other evidence does not lead to a different conclusion." Regulations of the IACHR, *supra* note 12.

presumably to give the government ample opportunity to avoid the finding of a violation through operation of the presumption.[44] In contrast, the Human Rights Committee and the Working Group on Forced or Involuntary Disappearances have declined to adopt such a formal presumption. The IACHR makes findings of violations of specific provisions of the American Convention or American Declaration, and specific recommendations for redress, which may be published in its annual reports. Dissent by Commission members on specific findings and resolutions is rare, but not unknown.[45]

Even more remarkable is the IACHR's ability to conduct on-site visits for purposes of establishing the facts in an individual case. The IACHR has occasionally applied this fact-finding tool since 1963[46] and has codified it with respect to parties to the American Convention in Article 44 of its Regulations.[47] While this technique is somewhat limited by its expense and the practical necessity of obtaining the government's consent to the visit, it has particular value in cases where the facts are especially murky.[48]

In two remarkable decisions concerning Argentina and Uruguay, the IACHR used two groups of consolidated individual communications to pronounce broadly on the impermissibility of amnesty laws adopted during transition to democratic rule from repressive emer-

44. Violations of the right to life and other rights, for example, were found in fifty Peruvian disappearance cases to which the government had not responded after repeated requests. *Supra* note 39.

45. *See, e.g.,* Case 9178 (Costa Rica), Inter-Am. C.H.R., decided October 3, 1984, *in* ANNUAL REPORT OF THE INTER-AMERICAN COMMISSION ON HUMAN RIGHTS 1984–1985, OEA/Ser.L/V/II.66, doc. 10, rev. 1, at 51–77 (1985) (noting Resolution No. 17/84 including the dissent of Dr. Bruce McColm).

46. R. Norris, *Observations* In Loco: *Practice and Procedure of the Inter-American Commission on Human Rights,* 15 TEX. INT'L L.J. 46, 54 (1980) (case from the Dominican Republic).

47. *See supra* note 12, at 131.

48. *See* Norris, *supra* note 46, at 65–66 (describing an instance in which consent was refused by Brazil concerning a denunciation that did not arise under the American Convention).

One highly unusual case arose out of the massacre of twenty-one peasants in El Aguacate, Guatemala. Word of the massacre first reached the IACHR from the government of Guatemala, which claimed that anti-government guerrillas were responsible. The government also brought two peasants from the region to the United States to tell the story to the IACHR. An NGO questioned the government's account and filed a denunciation of the events, alleging Guatemalan military complicity in the massacre. The Guatemalan government then invited the IACHR to make an on-site visit, which was conducted by two IACHR members and two staff members. After sifting through conflicting versions of the facts, the IACHR concluded that "grounds for the petition do not exist." ANNUAL REPORT 1990–1991, *supra* note 39, at 193–233 (noting Report No. 6/91, Case 10.400).

gency situations. The IACHR found Argentina's and Uruguay's amnesties for emergency-related human rights violations by the military and police to violate the obligation to investigate human rights abuse under Article 1 of the American Convention, the right to trial for the victims under Article 8, and the right to judicial protection under Article 25.[49] Approaching the issues in the abstract, the IACHR signaled its capacity, and in these cases its willingness, to perform what is essentially an advisory opinion role with respect to emergency-related interpretive issues.

*d. Annual Reports*

The IACHR's annual reports also may contain general observations or recommendations that are roughly analogous to the Human Rights Committee's "general comments." Its 1981 discussion of "States of Emergency" and several typically associated rights violations, including detention without due process, expulsion of nationals, and limitations on thought and information, is especially pertinent.[50] In this unusually explicit treatment of the legal limits on states of emergency, the IACHR discussed the general phenomenon of emergencies, made comparisons between particular OAS member states, and addressed such issues as indefinite prolongation of emergencies by governments simultaneously claiming a climate of social peace.

These annual reports also contain short sections updating information on the situation of human rights in several countries and often provide extensive information about and critical commentary on emergency measures in a variety of nations previously subject to special reports, including Chile, El Salvador, Haiti, Nicaragua, and Suriname.[51] The cohesiveness of the IACHR permits it to draw remarkably blunt judgments in these reports. For example, the IACHR characterized limitations on judicial remedies to challenge exercises of emergency powers under transitory provision 24 of the Chilean constitution as "provisions that institutionalize arbitrary political power."[52] With re-

49. Report No. 28/92 of 2 October 1992 (Argentina) *reprinted in* 13 Hum. Rts. L.J. 336 (1992), concerning Law No. 23,492 of 24 December 1986 (*punto final* law) and Law No. 23,521 of 8 June 1987 (due obedience law); and Report No. 29/92 of 2 October 1992 (Uruguay), *reprinted in* 13 Hum. Rts. L.J. 340 (1992), concerning Law No. 15,848 (amnesty law approved by referendum).

50. Annual Report of the Inter-American Commission on Human Rights 1980–1981, OEA/Ser.L/V/II.54, doc. 9, rev. 1, at 114–22 (1981).

51. Inter-American Commission on Human Rights, Annual Report 1986–1987, OEA/Ser.L/V/II.71, doc. 9, rev. 1, at 200–227, 234–67 (1987).

52. *Id.* at 203.

spect to El Salvador, the annual report stated that "the IACHR deplores the enactment of a new emergency procedural law [Decree Law 618], which, like the previous one [Decree Law 50], violates elementary legal principles and guarantees as well as international human rights rules that are binding on the Republic of El Salvador."[53] Judgment of a somewhat different sort is reflected in the IACHR's comment that "facts that are a matter of public knowledge show, in the Commission's view, that the Nicaraguan Government is facing a threat to State security," and that the rights suspended in Nicaragua are "in keeping with the provisions of Article 27.2 [of the American Convention on Human Rights], except with regard to the suspension of the remedy of *amparo* or *habeas corpus*."[54] The IACHR indicated in 1987 that it had received reports of violations of the American Convention by Nicaragua[55] and commented that the unavailability of *amparo* or *habeas corpus* during the state of emergency created a "grave contradiction between the Nicaraguan Constitution and the system of the American Convention."[56] A new constitutional law restoring the availability of *habeas corpus* was favorably noted by the IACHR in 1989.[57]

The IACHR has demonstrated flexibility and imagination in pursuing a variety of activities aimed at setting standards relevant to the control of human rights abuses associated with states of emergency. Noteworthy actions include: (1) the submission of a request for an advisory opinion to the Inter-American Court of Human Rights on the interpretation of Article 27(2) of the American Convention, which will be discussed in detail below;[58] (2) a proposal to elaborate a draft convention on forced disappearance of persons;[59] and (3) securing the adoption of a resolution on "Human Rights and Democracy" by the General Assembly of the OAS.[60]

53. *Id.* at 223.
54. *Id.* at 258.
55. *Id.* at 259.
56. *Id.* at 256.
57. ANNUAL REPORT OF THE INTER-AMERICAN COMMISSION ON HUMAN RIGHTS 1988–1989, OEA/Ser.L/V/II.76, doc. 10, at 194 (1989).
58. *Id.* at 25.
59. *Id.* at 227–84.
60. *Id.* at 19–20. The foreign ministers of the OAS exercised new authority granted in June 1991 "to adopt any measures deemed appropriate" to restore constitutional rule in democratic states, including the imposition of an economic embargo on Haiti following the September 1991 coup. The Secretary-General of the OAS also organized missions to mediate the return of elected President Aristide. J.M. Goshko, *OAS Names Delegation To Press Haiti; Group Plans To Demand Restoration of Aristide*, WASH. POST, Oct. 4, 1991, at A19; P. Constable, *Haiti Negotiators Cite Little Progress*, THE BOSTON GLOBE, Dec. 8, 1991, at 2.

## 2. The Inter-American Court of Human Rights

Established under Articles 52–73 of the American Convention, the Inter-American Court of Human Rights ("Court") has jurisdiction to hear a contentious state-to-state case or an individual case referred by the Commission concerning states of emergency.[61] To date, the Court's involvement with states of emergency under Article 27 of the American Convention, that instrument's derogation provision, has taken the form of advisory opinions. Although requests for advisory opinions are couched in abstract language, questions clearly relating to specific situations may be entertained by the Court,[62] including matters arising in the context of a state of emergency.[63]

Wholly abstract questions may also be addressed by the Court. In two path-breaking advisory opinions, the Court held that the remedies of *amparo* and *habeas corpus* are among "the judicial guarantees essential for the protection of [the] rights" made non-derogable by Article 27(2) of the American Convention,[64] and that these essential judicial guarantees also include judicial proceedings which are inherent in representative democracy as a form of government under Article 29(c) and which must be exercised in the framework of due legal process as defined in Article 8.[65] Because of its express allusion to the non-derogability of

61. Article 61 provides that only states parties and the Commission have the right to submit cases to the Court. Article 62 permits states to recognize the Court's jurisdiction *ipso facto,* upon conditions (*e.g.,* reciprocity or for a limited time), or for the purposes of a single case. *See* American Convention, *supra* note 4, arts. 61, 62.

62. The Court's opinion in Restrictions to the Death Penalty, for example, concerned an interpretation of Guatemala's reservation to Article 4(4) of the American Convention despite Guatemala's objection that it had not accepted the Court's jurisdiction. *Restrictions to the Death Penalty,* Advisory Opinion OC-8/83, 3 Inter-Am. Ct. H.R. (ser. A) 54–56, 65–75 (1983). The Court refused to render an advisory opinion requested by Costa Rica on certain proposed legislation, on grounds that the same issue had been raised in petitions decided by the IACHR but not yet referred to the Court. The Court stated that the victims should be permitted to participate in the resolution of the issue (involving violation of art. 8(2)(h) of the American Convention, *supra* note 4). *Compatibility of Draft Legislation with Article 8(2)(h) of the American Convention on Human Rights,* Advisory Opinion OC-12/91 (1991), *reprinted in Refusal to render an advisory opinion so as not to undermine the contentious jurisdiction of the Court,* 13 Hum. Rts. L.J. 149 (1992).

63. *See* C. Moyer & D. Padilla, *Executions in Guatemala as Decreed by the Courts of Special Jurisdiction in 1982–83: A Case Study,* 6 Hum. Rts. Q. 507 (1984).

64. *Habeas Corpus in Emergency Situations (Arts. 27(2), 25(1) and 7(6) of the American Convention on Human Rights),* Advisory Opinion OC-8/87 of Jan. 30, 1987, Annual Report of the Inter-American Court of Human Rights 1987, OEA/Ser.L/V/III.17, doc. 13, at 17 (1987) [hereinafter Advisory Opinion OC-8/87].

65. *Judicial Guarantees in States of Emergency (Arts. 27(2), 25 and 8 American Convention on Human Rights),* Advisory Opinion OC-9/87 of Oct. 6, 1987, Annual Report of the

essential judicial guarantees, the derogation provision of the American Convention has always appeared to be more restrictive than similar provisions of the Covenant on Civil and Political Rights and the European Convention on Human Rights. But this aspect of Article 27(2) had remained rather unclear until the Court rendered these two advisory opinions. While certain aspects of these opinions are left somewhat indefinite, the clear holdings that *amparo* and *habeas corpus* may never be suspended mark a real advance in the understanding of the Convention and, if respected by the states parties, would signify a substantial change in government behavior and improvement in their respect for human rights during states of emergency.

Advisory Opinion OC-8/87 was requested by the IACHR, which noted in its request that the suspension of *habeas corpus* has been a characteristic aspect of many states of emergency, that the practice of incommunicado detention has been associated with violations of the non-derogable guarantee against torture and inhuman treatment, and that the elimination of a judicial role in determining the reasonableness of orders of administrative detention violates the principle of separation of powers inherent in the democratic rule of law.[66] The Court declared in this opinion that the preservation of democracy was the only legitimate basis for a suspension of rights under the Convention,[67] and that suspension of rights never implies suspension of the rule of law.[68] The derogating government is not completely free of legal restraint, though it may have greater flexibility in imposing rights-restrictive measures than in normal times.[69] The Court said that what the judicial guarantees in Article 27(2) include will depend upon the non-derogable right(s) in issue,[70] but indicated that with respect to the non-derogable rights of life and personal dignity, *habeas corpus* and *amparo* must be available even during states of emergency.[71] The Court further stated that constitutions and laws of states parties that authorize the suspension of *habeas corpus* and *amparo* during emergencies are incompatible with the terms of the Convention.[72]

---

INTER-AMERICAN COURT OF HUMAN RIGHTS 1988, OEA/Ser.L/VI/III.19, doc. 13, at 13 (1988).

66. Advisory Opinion OC-8/87, *supra* note 64, at para. 12.

67. *Id.* at para. 20.

68. *Id.* at para. 24.

69. *Id.*

70. *Id.* at paras. 27–29.

71. *Id.* at paras. 42–44.

72. *Id.*

In an advisory opinion requested by the Government of Uruguay,[73] the Court attempted a more general definition of the phrase "essential judicial guarantees." Noting that the lack of a concrete context was not a barrier to its rendering an opinion, the Court observed that "the question raised in the request of the Government is related to a specific juridical, historical and political context, in that states of exception or emergency, and of human rights and the essential judicial guarantees in those moments, is a critical problem in the Americas."[74]

The Court's rather subtle analysis might be characterized as both textual and structural. The opinion draws a number of interesting deductions from the language of the Convention: that the characterization of remedies as judicial implies independence of the decision-maker from the political actors imposing the emergency;[75] that the requirement of proportionality in Article 27(1) implies national measures of control to insure that strict limits are kept;[76] that the Convention does not permit the suspension of judicial remedies essential to protect either non-derogable rights or other rights not actually suspended;[77] that the non-existence of effective judicial remedies itself constitutes a violation of the Convention.[78] The Court draws from Article 8 the conclusion that due legal process is a requirement of all judicial guarantees under the Convention, including those guarantees mentioned in Article 27(2).[79]

From Article 29(c) the Court deduces that judicial protection, as well as political structures, are essential to the preservation of democracy and the rule of law.[80] In addition to *habeas corpus* and *amparo*, Article 27(2) thus requires the preservation of judicial guarantees that are "necessary to the preservation of the rule of law, even during the state of exception that results from the suspension of guarantees."[81] The Court acknowledges that its advisory opinion is general in nature and makes no effort to specify the precise judicial remedies, in addition to *habeas corpus* and *amparo,* that cannot be suspended. These remedies may vary depending upon the judicial organization of the state concerned and the circumstances of the particular emergency, including the specific rights suspended.[82]

---

73. *Supra* note 65.
74. *Id.* at para. 17.
75. *Id.* at para. 20.
76. *Id.* at para. 21.
77. *Id.* at para. 25.
78. *Id.* at para. 24.
79. *Id.* at para. 29.
80. *Id.* at para. 37.
81. *Id.* at para. 38.
82. *Id.* at para. 40.

These two advisory opinions represent a bold initiative by the Inter-American Court respecting the monitoring process for states of emergency. While the Court's opinions are theoretically sound, it remains to be seen whether, as a practical matter, these opinions can or will exert a significant influence on emergencies within the OAS system. The habit of suspending judicial guarantees during emergencies is fairly well entrenched throughout the hemisphere, and the judiciary in most member states habitually restrain themselves even when formal guarantees remain.

Although the Court has not yet heard any contentious cases concerning states of emergency, it has established promising procedures for handling such cases. In several individual cases concerning disappearances in Honduras, which were referred to the Court by the IACHR,[83] the Court honed its methodology, taking extensive witness testimony and elaborating upon the burden of proof. For example, a violation was found in the *Godínez Cruz* case based, in part, on circumstantial evidence that a pattern and practice of disappearances had been tolerated by the Honduran government.[84] But the Court cautioned in the *Fairen Garbi* case that "in the absence of other evidence, whether circumstantial or indirect, the practice of disappearances is insufficient to prove that a person whose whereabouts is unknown was the victim of that practice."[85] When several witnesses in the cases were killed or threatened during the course of the proceedings, the Court took interim measures requiring the government of Honduras to begin judicial inquiries.[86] The need for such interim measures may be quite great in a major derogation case.[87]

## B. The Council of Europe

### 1. The European Commission of Human Rights

Unlike the IACHR, the European Commission of Human Rights ("Commission") initiates an investigation only when seized of a case upon the formal application of an individual under optional Article 25

---

83. Velásquez Rodríguez Case, Inter-Am. Ct. H.R. (ser. C) No. 4 (1988) (judgment); Godínez Cruz Case, Inter-Am. Ct. H.R. (ser. C) No. 5 (1989) (judgment); Fairen Garbi & Solis Corrales Case, (ser. C) No. 6 (1989) (judgment).

84. *Godínez Cruz, supra* note 83, at paras. 128–45.

85. *Fairen Garbi, supra* note 83, at para. 157.

86. *Godínez Cruz, supra* note 83, at paras. 41–52.

87. Interim measures were also ordered by the Court against the government of Peru, at the request of the IACHR, in the *Bustios-Rojas Case,* even before the case was formally referred to the Court. THE INTER-AMERICAN COURT OF HUMAN RIGHTS, No. CDH-CP2-91 (Jan. 23, 1991) (press release).

or upon inter-state application under Article 24 of the European Convention on Human Rights. The Commission has no authority to monitor derogation notices or to decide on its own initiative to undertake the study of a particular emergency. While the Commission has handled a number of individual and inter-state applications arising out of emergency situations, it has issued only a few public decisions on the merits. Using essentially quasi-judicial processes, the Commission has shown itself to be a competent fact-finder in cases concerning states of emergency, despite the complexity of the factual issues. The Commission has taken the lead among intergovernmental bodies in developing the formal jurisprudence of states of emergency and has made invaluable contributions to the definition of the elements of permissible and impermissible emergencies. Nevertheless, it also has been cautious and somewhat deferential to governments and sometimes has failed to impose consistently strict and objective standards under Article 15 of the European Convention.[88]

The Commission has issued non-confidential reports[89] both in inter-state cases and in response to individual applications challenging emergency measures. Although the Commission has carefully considered the two key criteria of Article 15—that the emergency threaten the life of the nation and that derogation measures be strictly required by the

---

88. *See* J. Hartman, *Derogation from Human Rights Treaties in Public Emergencies,* 22 HARV. INT'L L.J. 1 (1981) (for an extended discussion of the jurisprudence on states of emergency developed by the European Commission).

89. The report in Cyprus v. Turkey (I and II) (Apps. No. 6780/74 and 6750/75) was never officially published but was declassified by the Committee of Ministers in January 1979. 2 Eur. Comm'n H.R. Dec. & Rep. 125 (1975); CYPRUS AGAINST TURKEY, REPORT OF THE COMMISSION, EUR. COMM. OF HUM. RTS. (1976); 1979 Y.B. Eur. Conv. on H.R. 440 (Comm. of Ministers Res. DH (79) 1 of Jan. 20) [hereinafter Committee of Ministers Res. DH (79) 1]. The Commission's report in Cyprus v. Turkey (III) was adopted on 4 October 1983 but not published until 2 April 1992, pursuant to Committee of Ministers Res. DH (92) 12. Cyprus v. Turkey, App. No. 8007/77, 13 Eur. Comm'n H.R. Dec. & Rep. 85 (1979); Committee of Ministers Res. DH (92) 12, *reprinted in Decision to make public, after more than eight years, the 1983 Report of the Commission in the interstate complaint Cyprus v. Turkey,* 13 HUM. RTS. L.J. 181 (1992). The first "Cyprus" case, *Greece v. United Kingdom,* was the subject of a friendly settlement. Greece v. United Kingdom, 1958–59 Y.B. Eur. Conv. on H.R. 182 (Eur. Comm'n of H.R.). The Commission adopted its Report in the case of McGlinchey v. U.K. (Apps. No. 15096/89, 15097/89 and 15098/89) on 7 December 1990, and transmitted it to the Committee of Ministers on 28 January 1991. EUROPEAN COMMISSION OF HUMAN RIGHTS, MINUTES, 218th Sess., Doc. DH (90) 11 para. VIII(g); EUROPEAN COMMISSION OF HUMAN RIGHTS, MINUTES, 220th Sess., Doc. DH (91) 2 para. X(r). The cases concern Articles 5(3) and 5(5), relating to detentions under the Prevention of Terrorism (Temporary Provisions) Act of 1984. The Commission's report in the similar case of Brannigan and McBride v. U.K. (Apps. No. 14553/89 and 14554/89) was adopted on 3 December 1991 and made public when the case was referred to the Court.

exigencies of the situation—it has tended occasionally to defer to government evaluations under its "margin of appreciation" doctrine. In the *Lawless* case, the Commission pronounced an influential definition of "public emergency," holding that the Irish Government could regard the existence of the Irish Republican Army and the potential threat posed by its cross-border raids to relations with the United Kingdom as a threat to the life of the nation.[90]

The Commission's approach in the *Greek* case appeared to be more rigorous, involving careful review of the evidence concerning the Communist threat, a constitutional crisis supposedly posed by the upcoming elections, and disruptions of public order by strikes and demonstrations.[91] Placing the burden of proof on the Greek Government, which had seized power in April 1967 by military coup, the Commission held there was no "threat, imminent in that it would be realized before or soon after the May elections, of such political instability and disorder that the organized life of the community could not be carried on."[92] This decision, rejecting the Greek Government's claim of an emergency justifying derogation measures, is a highly significant precedent for other inter-governmental bodies which are similarly competent to make an independent evaluation as to whether an emergency exists which truly threatens the life of the nation.

The existence of the emergency was not controverted by the parties in two other inter-state applications. For example, in *Ireland v. United Kingdom*, the applicant government raised no issue concerning the existence of an emergency in Northern Ireland during the relevant period, and the Commission explicitly found such an emergency to exist.[93] In *Cyprus v. Turkey*,[94] which concerned the 1974 Turkish invasion of Cyprus and allegations of arbitrary killing, torture, disappearances, and unlawful detention, the Commission did not question the existence of a crisis but specifically asked the parties for their observa-

90. EUR. CT. OF HUMAN RIGHTS, REPORT OF THE EUR. COMM'N OF H.R., "LAWLESS" CASE, (SER. B) 82 (1960). There were vigorous dissents proposing a purely objective standard by Commission members Eustathiades, Susterhenn, Dominedo, and Ermacora. Dissents are far more common on the European Commission than on the Human Rights Committee or the IACHR.

91. "Greek" Case, 1969 Y.B. Eur. Conv. on Human Rights 45–76 (Eur. Comm'n of H.R.) (report).

92. *Id.* at 75.

93. Ireland v. United Kingdom, 1976 Y.B. Eur. Conv. on Human Rights 512, 544. Rather surprisingly, the individual applicants in *Brannigan and McBride, supra* note 89 at para. 16, raised "no dispute" as to the existence of a public emergency in Northern Ireland at the time of their arrests in January 1989.

94. The declassified report, dated 10 July 1976, contains findings of violations of Articles 2, 3, 5, 8, 13, and 14. *See supra* note 89.

tions on the applicability of the Convention during military actions.[95] The Commission, unlike the IACHR in its fact-finding reports, consistently has demonstrated a serious interest in exploring such general questions concerning the application of the Convention to states of emergency.

The Government of Turkey refused to reply to the Commission's request,[96] while Cyprus argued that Turkey's obligations under the European Convention were in addition to its obligations under international humanitarian law.[97] The Commission considered avoiding this question in the *Cyprus* case by establishing a principle that a state which fails to file a notice of derogation may not rely on Article 15, making the substantive privilege of derogation conditional upon compliance with the procedural obligations of Article 15(3).[98] Ultimately, the Commission rejected such a demanding approach, holding instead that a formal and public act of derogation, such as an official domestic proclamation, is a prerequisite for the application of Article 15. Failure to give notice is, of course, a separate breach of Article 15(3). Turkey's notice of martial law in a number of its own provinces was held inapplicable to its actions in Cyprus, even as to prisoners from Cyprus transferred to Turkey.[99] Thus, notices of derogation are strictly construed by the Commission within their explicit limits. One noteworthy fact, which reflects well on the seriousness of the European regional system for protection of human rights, is that there have been no cases revealing a total failure to file a notice of derogation.[100] The Commission also clearly held that Turkey's actions in the territory of Cyprus were governed by the Convention,[101] establishing an important jurisdictional principle concerning the territorial application of the Convention.

The Commission, where it has found an Article 15 emergency to

95. *Id.* at para. 506.

96. Turkey refused to participate on the grounds that the applicant government, which had control over essentially only the Greek Cypriot community after the invasion forced a partition, was no longer a contracting party to the Convention and thus unable to bring an Article 24 application. *Id.* at para. 518.

97. *Id.* at para. 509.

98. This procedural argument was also considered in the first "Cyprus" Case, but the issue remains unresolved. *Id.* at paras. 526–528.

99. *Id.* at paras. 529–531.

100. Although, as the discussion of administrative detention in Chapter II indicated, the European Court's rejection of the United Kingdom's justification for the seven-day denial of access to judicial supervision for persons detained under the Prevention of Terrorism Act prompted the government to enter a new notice of derogation, rather than amend the law. Brogan v. United Kingdom, 145 Eur. Ct. H.R. (ser. A) (1989).

101. *Id.* at paras. 525–526. The so-called "Turkish Federated State" in portions of Cyprus was ignored by the Commission.

exist, also has applied its deferential "margin of appreciation" doctrine to the derogating government's selection of particular emergency measures. In the *Lawless* case, the Commission accepted, by a narrow margin, the government's evaluation that detention without trial was more efficacious than trials in ordinary civilian courts, military courts, or special criminal courts.[102] The Commission, however, particularly emphasized the need for safeguards against abusive use of administrative detention.[103] The Commission's deference to government discretion was even greater in *Ireland v. United Kingdom*. There the Commission did not examine the necessity of evolving emergency measures at each point in the changing crisis; rejected efficacy as a measure of necessity on the grounds that this approach involved unfair use of hindsight; downplayed the absence of safeguards against abuse; and rejected the argument that discriminatory application of emergency measures against Catholics disproved the strict necessity of those measures.

Aside from its handling of the *Greek* case, the Commission has eschewed adopting a purely objective standard. The tendency of national judiciaries to shrink from the task of second-guessing government decisions in emergencies frequently has been noted as a contributing factor to unchecked human rights abuses.[104] The Commission's "margin of appreciation" doctrine expresses a judicial reticence that arises not from fear but from a perceived disparity in institutional competence to make the fact-specific determinations necessary to determine whether a crisis truly threatens the life of the nation and whether particular measures are strictly required by the exigencies of the crisis.

The Commission's undemanding approach to the proportionality element of Article 15(1) under the "wide margin of appreciation" is illustrated in the *Brannigan and McBride* case.[105] The crucial issue was not whether investigative detention for up to seven days was necessary

102. "Lawless" Case, *supra* note 90, at 114. The vote on this issue was eight to six. Some dissenters, such as Mr. Ermacora, urged that a standard of "absolutely essential" be applied. *Id.* at 155.

103. The safeguard was an administrative Detention Commission, which could review detention orders. *Id.* at 121–24.

104. *See* G. Alexander, *The Illusory Protection of Human Rights by National Courts during Periods of Emergency,* 5 HUM. RTS. L.J. 1 (1984).

105. *Supra* note 89. The Commission also dismissed objections that the U.K.'s notice of derogation concerning length of investigative detention had not been filed until December 1988, though the practice dated back to 1974. The delay was found justified on the basis that the U.K. did not realize the incompatibility of its practices with Article 5(3) until the Court issued its judgment in the *Brogan* case. *Id.* at para. 56.

to combat terrorism in Northern Ireland, but whether extension beyond an initial two-day period should be subject to judicial rather than purely executive supervision.[106] On this issue, the Commission majority opined that "it is not the Commission's function to substitute its view for the Government's assessment of what might be the most prudent or expedient policy to combat terrorism."[107] The Commission deferentially accepted the United Kingdom's assertion that the small Northern Ireland judiciary might be compromised by involvement in decisions to extend detention where confidential information served as the basis for the determinations.[108] Several dissenting members challenged this reasoning in light of judicial involvement in other sensitive matters, and stressed that "some judicial control is better than none."[109]

The Commission is handicapped in coping with emergencies within the Council of Europe by structural limitations as well as its attitudes of self-restraint. It also lacks authority to examine derogation notices or other reliable information and to commence reviews of emergency measures on its own initiative.[110] Moreover, the Commission depends upon the Committee of Ministers for final resolution of cases not referred to the European Court of Human Rights.

The settlement of the inter-state applications against Turkey[111] casts some doubt upon the prospects for the Commission to develop further its derogation jurisprudence in major inter-state derogation cases. Turkey has been for decades under an almost perpetual state of emergency,[112] although its scope has fluctuated, and the oppressiveness of the associated measures sharply escalated in September 1980. The Commission could take no action to investigate these allegations of

106. *Id.* at para. 58.

107. *Id.* at para. 60.

108. *Id.* at paras. 61–63.

109. *Id.* at 24 (dissenting opinion of Mr. Loucaides joined by Mrs. Thune and Mr. Rozakis).

110. The Secretary-General of the Council of Europe is the designated recipient of derogation notices under Article 15(3). States are obliged under Article 15(3) to keep the Secretary-General "fully informed," and under Article 57, upon request of the Secretary-General, to furnish an explanation of the manner in which internal law ensures effective implementation of the Convention. Accordingly, the Secretary-General could play an important role in securing information about states of emergency in Convention states, but to date has played only a passive role.

111. France, Norway, Denmark, Sweden, and the Netherlands v. Turkey, Apps. No. 9940-9944/82, 1985 Y.B. Eur. Conv. on Human Rights 151 (Eur. Comm'n of H.R.) (report of Dec. 7, 1985).

112. Turkey filed forty-eight notices of derogation between 1961 and 1981, for example. *See* HUMAN RIGHTS INFORMATION SHEET No. 27, 5–7, Council of Europe Doc. H/INF (91)1 (1991) (notice of derogation filed by Turkey 6 August 1990) [hereinafter INFORMATION SHEET No. 27].

abuse until five governments chose to bring an inter-state application against Turkey. After several years of delay, which included an on-site visit by a Commission delegation in January and February 1985, the parties chose to settle the case with the approval of the Commission, even though Turkey continued to maintain a state of emergency in many provinces and was accused, *inter alia,* of extensive violations of non-derogable rights. Turkey agreed to make three reports on its efforts to cease the practice of torture and inhuman treatment, but these reports and the Commission staff's comments on them are entirely confidential.[113] The Commission's report on the settlement of the inter-state application appends a list of modified emergency legislation and recites a "hope" by the Prime Minister that martial law would be lifted in eighteen months.[114]

The settlement of the Turkish case illustrates the complications of the Commission's double role as quasi-judicial enforcement body and friendly-settlement or good-offices facilitator. The Commission has played predominantly the latter role in the proceedings against Turkey both with respect to Turkey's own emergency and its invasion of Cyprus. Unrealized hopes for a friendly settlement of the international armed conflict in Cyprus have rendered ineffectual the Commission's efforts to investigate human rights abuses there.[115] The Commission is at the mercy both of applicant governments and the Committee of Ministers of the Council of Europe, who may be satisfied with mere hopes for improvement and may discount the value of vigorous fact-finding, condemnation of violations, and redress for victims. Applicant governments may respond to foreign policy or trade concerns unrelated to human rights in deciding to settle a case. On the other hand, it is extraordinary that there have been inter-state applications at all, given the diplomatic constraints that generally operate to deter such high-profile altruistic activities. In recent debate over restructuring the

113. *Id.* at 8–9. The confidentiality requirement on the Turkish reports appears to transform the Commission staff into a variant of the ICRC, although no provision is made for actually visiting places of detention. In contrast, the European Committee on the Prevention of Torture exercised its authority to reveal the results of its three visits to Turkey in December 1992 in light of Turkey's continuing failure to improve the situation. *Public Statement on Turkey, reprinted in* 14 HUM. RTS. L.J. 49 (1993).

114. INFORMATION SHEET NO. 27, *supra* note 112, at 9 and annex I.

115. The Committee of Ministers delayed nearly three years in declassifying the Commission's Report of 10 July 1976 in the first two inter-state applications by Cyprus against Turkey (Apps. No. 6780/74 and 6950/75). *See* Committee of Ministers Res. DH (79) 1, *supra* note 89. The Commission's October 1983 report on the third Cyprus application (App. No. 8007/77), which was declared admissible in July 1978 and concerns grave allegations about disappearances, was not published until 1992. *Supra* note 89.

Council of Europe human rights organs, the Commission has stressed its friendly-settlement role and the Court has suggested retaining a role for the Committee of Ministers in inter-state cases.[116]

The Turkish Government's sensitivity to criticism of its human rights record eventually led it to recognize the right of individual application under Article 25.[117] Consequently, several interesting cases have been filed against Turkey which involve allegations of deprivation of non-derogable rights, providing the Commission an opportunity to undertake fact-finding hearings both in Strasbourg and in Turkey.[118] Turkey also has ratified the European Convention for the Prevention of Torture and Inhuman or Degrading Treatment or Punishment, which provides for on-site visits by the European Committee for the Prevention of Torture and Inhuman or Degrading Treatment or Punishment.[119]

The Commission has sometimes been reluctant to provide redress to individuals suffering abuses during states of emergency. For example, the *Second Greek* case, which concerned thirty-four persons court-martialed during 1969–1970, was struck off the list after Greece rejoined the Council of Europe and indicated reform in its laws.[120]

116. *Reform of the control system of the European Convention on Human Rights,* 14 HUM. RTS. L.J. 31 (1993).

117. The government of Turkey accepted the jurisdiction of the Commission to hear individual applications on 28 January 1987 for a period of three years, but limited its jurisdiction to events occurring on Turkish territory through the proviso that "the circumstances and conditions under which Turkey, by virtue of Article 15 of the Convention, derogates from her obligations under the Convention in special circumstances must be interpreted, for the purpose of the competence attributed to the Commission under this declaration, in light of Articles 119 to 122 of the Turkish Constitution." A further proviso states that the phrase "democratic society" in the limitations clauses of several articles must also be interpreted in accord with provisions of the Turkish Constitution. EUROPEAN COMMISSION OF HUMAN RIGHTS, MINUTES 185th Sess., Doc. No. DH (87) 2 (def.) at annex VII (1987).

118. *See, e.g.,* Sargin and Yagci v. Turkey, Apps. No. 14116/88 and 14117/88. According to an *Editor's note* in 13 HUM. RTS. L.J. 154 (1992), the Commission's Report in these cases was not yet available as of April 1992. A delegation of three Commission members held hearings in Ankara and Strasbourg, including a confrontation between the applicants and the chief of police allegedly involved in their torture. *See* European Commission of Human Rights Press Communique C(90)276 (Dec. 7, 1990). Three applications alleging torture and challenging the impartiality of the Izmir State Security Court were declared admissible on 11 October 1991. Mr. and Mrs. H. and Mr. A. v. Turkey, Apps. No. 16311-16313/90; *3 applications v. Turkey declared admissible in respect of: torture in policy custody, impartiality of the Izmir State Security Court, and violation of freedom of thought,* 13 HUM. RTS. L.J. 131 (1992).

119. INFORMATION SHEET No. 27, *supra* note 112, at 9; *Public Statement on Turkey, supra* note 113.

120. Second "Greek" Case, App. No. 4448/70, 6 Eur. Comm'n H.R. Dec. & Rep. 5

Furthermore, the Commission belatedly declared inadmissible numerous individual applications brought by persons subjected to emergency measures in Northern Ireland.[121] Although it has proved itself capable of handling masses of evidence in complex derogation cases,[122] the Commission has tended to examine the impact of emergencies on individuals only through "illustrative" cases. Thus, effective redress to individual victims has not been the hallmark of the Commission's success in derogation cases. The possibility of convening chambers to hear applications under Protocol 8 to the Convention would ease the burden of large numbers of applications arising out of an emergency.[123]

## 2. The European Court of Human Rights

The European Court of Human Rights ("Court") has spoken directly on Article 15 only in the *Lawless* case and in *Ireland v. United Kingdom*, where its approach was deferential to the respondent governments. Applying a wide "margin of appreciation," the Court chose to defer to the "better position"[124] of the national authorities both to determine the existence of an emergency and to select measures. The Court generally does not hear new evidence itself, relying on the facts recited in the Commission's report.[125] However, the Court in *Ireland v. United*

---

(1977). This case also was raised as an inter-state application, since Greece had not recognized the Article 25 right of petition.

121. Donnelly v. United Kingdom (Apps. No. 55/77–83/77), declared admissible in April 1973, and declared inadmissible in December 1975, on the grounds of non-exhaustion of domestic remedies in three cases, and in four others where domestic remedies had been invoked, on grounds that compensation had been received. After *Ireland v. United Kingdom* was decided, some three hundred additional applications were struck off the list or declared inadmissible as manifestly ill-founded. STOCKTAKING ON THE EUROPEAN CONVENTION OF HUMAN RIGHTS, THE FIRST THIRTY YEARS: 1954 UNTIL 1984, at 246 (1984). However, in June 1991, thirteen new cases concerning arrest and detention in Northern Ireland were declared admissible. COUNCIL OF EUROPE HUMAN RIGHTS NEWS, INFORMATION NOTE NO. 97, at 2 (June 17, 1991).

122. Thirty-two witnesses were heard on Article 15 issues in the Greek case. 1969 Y.B. Eur. Conv. on Human Rights 49, 60, 66. Over one hundred persons were heard in *Ireland v. United Kingdom* on various issues. 1976 Y.B. Eur. Conv. on Human Rights 528, 532.

123. Protocol No. 8 to the Convention for the Protection of Human Rights and Fundamental Freedoms, *opened for signature* Mar. 19, 1985, 1985 Y.B. Eur. Conv. on H.R. 3.

124. Ireland v. United Kingdom, 1978 Y.B. Eur. Conv. on Human Rights, at paras. 207, 214 (judgment).

125. In the Stocké case, the Court held that the establishment and verification of the facts is primarily a matter for the Commission, and that only in exceptional circumstances (not present in this case) would the Court itself hear testimony. Stocké v. Germany, App. No. 11755/85, Eur. H.R. Rep. 839 (1991) (judgment of Eur. Ct. H.R.). The

*Kingdom* ruled *proprio motu* that the Commission erred in finding the "five techniques" of interrogation in depth to be torture, holding that they were instead inhuman treatment under Article 3.[126] In any case, the fact that these interrogation techniques were being scrutinized by the Commission and Court may well have contributed to the decision of the United Kingdom Government to cease their use, indicating a concrete measure of effectiveness of the Council of Europe bodies in securing moderation of abuse during emergencies.

Though not technically involving claims of derogation, *Brogan*[127] and *Fox, Campbell and Hartley*[128] have implications for the Court's approach to emergency issues. As described in Chapter II,[129] these cases involved challenges to aspects of the United Kingdom's "criminalisation" policy for handling the separatist threat in Northern Ireland, following Britain's termination of the formal derogation under Article 15. By adopting a fairly strict approach and granting states only limited flexibility to adopt extraordinary detention measures upon asserted antiterrorist grounds,[130] the Court creates pressures for governments, such as that of the United Kingdom, to enter formal notices of derogation and, thereby, increases the possibility for strict application of Article 15.

The Court's role is somewhat limited by the optional nature of its jurisdiction, though state acceptance has become very widespread, and

---

applicant's request for the Court to hear four new witnesses not heard by the Commission was denied.

126. *Id.* at para. 167.

127. Brogan v. United Kingdom, 11 Eur. H.R. Rep. 117 (1988) (ser. A, No. 145-B) (judgment of Eur. Ct. H.R.).

128. Fox, Campbell and Hartley v. United Kingdom, Apps. No. 12244/86 and 12383/86, 13 Eur. H.R. Rep. 157 (1990) (ser. A. No. 182) (judgment of Eur. Ct. H.R.).

129. *See* Chapter II *supra* notes 75–88.

130. The Court rejected the Commission's finding in *Brogan* that up to four days, eleven hours of detention upon suspicion of involvement in terrorist acts, without access to a magistrate, could be justified as a special antiterrorism measure without formal derogation from Article 5(3). *Brogan, supra* note 127, at paras. 55–62. In *Fox, Campbell and Hartley,* the Court held that Article 5(1)(c) requires an objectively reasonable suspicion of involvement in criminal activity, not just a *bona fide* belief on the part of the arresting officer, and found a violation where the United Kingdom did not provide any information upon which an objectively grounded suspicion in this case could be based. *Supra* note 122, at paras. 33–36. At the same time, the Court stated that Article 5(1)(c) "should not be applied in such a manner as to put disproportionate difficulties in the way of the police authorities of the Contracting States in taking effective measures to counter organised terrorism. . . . It follows that the Contracting States cannot be asked to establish the reasonableness of the suspicion grounding arrest of a suspected terrorist by disclosing the confidential sources of supporting information or even facts which would be susceptible of indicating such sources or their identity." *Id.* at para. 34.

by the necessity for the Commission or a state to refer a case to the Court after the Commission's decision on the merits. The small number of emergency cases adjudicated by the Court reflects these structural limits. Widespread ratification of Protocol No. 9, which permits individuals to refer cases to the Court, could greatly expand its potential to respond to abuses.[131] Other suggestions for improving the capacity of the Council of Europe system rapidly to address violations include merging the Court and Commission into one body that would sit continuously, perhaps complemented by a European "High Commissioner for Human Rights" with powers of initiative.[132] The last of these proposed steps, which also appears the least likely to be implemented, would expand substantially the ability of the Council of Europe organs to cope with abuses of human rights under states of emergency.

## 3. The Committee of Ministers of the Council of Europe

As indicated above, the Committee of Ministers of the Council of Europe ("Committee") has authority to give "effect" to Commission decisions under Article 32 and to supervise the implementation of Court judgments under Article 54 of the Convention. When exercising these powers, the Committee acts as a legal body under the Convention and not as a political body of the Council of Europe. Nevertheless, the tendency of the Committee of Ministers has been to seek friendly settlement even at the cost of delay and where settlement is not an option simply to note the relevant decision or judgment of the Commission or Court.[133] The impetus toward friendly settlement is domi-

131. Protocol No. 9 was adopted by the Committee of Ministers on 23 October 1990 and opened for signature on 6 November 1990. On that date, the Protocol was signed by fourteen states, including Cyprus and Turkey. The document will enter into force when ratified by ten states, but of course will open access to the Court only for persons making applications against states that have accepted Protocol No. 9. Persons filing applications under Article 25 will first have to complete proceedings before the Commission prior to referring their cases to the Court. Cases referred to the Court by individuals will first be reviewed by a panel of three judges of the Court (including the judge from the state involved), who will submit the case to the Court for adjudication only if it involves a "serious question affecting interpretation or application of the Convention" or otherwise warrants consideration. Cases not so forwarded will be sent to the Committee of Ministers for disposition. INFORMATION SHEET No. 27, *supra* note 112, at 3 and app. 1.

132. These three steps were all discussed at the Ministerial Conference on Human Rights in March 1985 in Vienna. *See* COUNCIL OF EUROPE PRESS COMMUNIQUE B (85) 7 (March 1985). *See also, Reform of the control system, supra* note 116.

133. The Ministers noted that in light of Greece's withdrawal from the Council of Europe there was "no basis for further action," other than publishing the Commission's

nant in inter-state cases, where diplomatic tensions are likely to exist and may be especially pronounced in emergency situations, particularly those involving armed conflict. In its actions under the Convention, the Committee relies upon the assistance of the Secretariat of the European Commission of Human Rights and the advice of the Secretary-General of the Council of Europe, who can become an active participant in the promotion of human rights in the Council of Europe.

The Committee of Ministers, in addition to its delegated functions under the European Convention, also possesses a general competence in human rights matters as a body of the Council of Europe. Exercising these general powers, the Committee has adopted a variety of resolutions on human rights topics, including asylum and freedom of expression, though it has not yet spoken in such a general fashion on states of emergency.

## 4. The Parliamentary Assembly of the Council of Europe

Like the Committee of Ministers, the Parliamentary Assembly of the Council of Europe ("Assembly") devotes only a portion of its attention to human rights issues. It nevertheless has shown, especially in recent years, a high level of concern with human rights abuses in Council of Europe states undergoing emergencies. For example, it passed a series of highly critical resolutions relating to the human rights situations in Turkey.[134] The Assembly also has suggested consideration of the expulsion of Turkey under Article 8 of the Statute of the Council of Europe, and has called upon Turkey to lift martial law and end its

---

report. Res. DH (70) 1, *in* 1 EUROPEAN COMMISSION OF HUMAN RIGHTS, REPORT OF THE COMMISSION, THE "GREEK CASE," pt. 1 (1970). With respect to the first and second applications of Cyprus against Turkey, the Ministers urged the parties to resume intercommunal talks, declassified rather than published the report, and viewed the decision "as completing its consideration of the case." Committee of Ministers Res. DH (79) 1, *supra* note 89.

On 30 March 1992, Protocol No. 10 to the European Convention was adopted, providing that decisions by the Committee of Ministers can be taken by simple majority vote, rather than by two-thirds. This may enhance the speed and vigor of the Committee's work. *Reduction of the 2/3 Majority Provided for in Art. 32 ECHR,* 13 HUM. RTS. L.J. 182 (1992).

For a critical view of the Committee's role in cases not referred to the Court, *see* C. Tomuschat, *Quo Vadis, Argentoratum?* 13 HUM. RTS. L.J. 401 (1992).

134. *See, e.g.,* Resolution 794, 1983 Y.B. Eur. Conv. on H.R., ch. IV, 4; Resolution 803, 1983 Y.B. Eur. Conv. on H.R., ch. IV, 17; Resolution 822, 1984 Y.B. Eur. Conv. on H.R., ch. IV, 33; Resolution 985, *reprinted in* 13 HUM. RTS. L.J. 464 (1992).

derogation under Article 15.[135] The Assembly similarly took the initiative of sending fact-finding missions to Turkey in 1984, 1991, and 1992.[136]

The Parliamentary Assembly represents a model of an inter-governmental body engaged in monitoring states of emergency which has no close analogues in any of the other systems analyzed in this study. The involvement of these parliamentarians is quite different in nature from the role of high-level government officials, such as those of the Committee of Ministers; from that of diplomats under governmental instructions who serve on the UN Commission on Human Rights; from the role of independent experts who comprise the Human Rights Committee, the IACHR, or the European Commission; and also from that of the trade union representatives who form an element of the tripartite structure of ILO bodies. The parliamentarians are not bound to the official foreign policy of their governments, but, at the same time, they are not simply private citizens or interest group members. The practice of the Parliamentary Assembly with respect to emergencies in Europe indicates that such a body can effectively voice the democratic concerns of public opinion and NGOs about human rights abuses, can attempt to produce action by diplomatic bodies, and can contribute even to the gathering of facts about excesses under emergency regimes. By so doing, the Assembly supplements the efforts of the fact-finding bodies set up to implement the treaties.

## C. The Future for Europe

The European system for the protection of human rights stands at an important crossroads. The dissolution of the Warsaw Pact and the rise of multiparty democracies in Eastern Europe signal a potentially dramatic transformation in the membership of the Council of Europe.[137]

135. Resolution 794, *supra* note 134, at paras. 18–20.

136. *See* Resolution 822, *supra* note 134; *The situation of human rights in Turkey*, 13 HUM. RTS. L.J. 464 (1992).

137. Czechoslovakia was the first state from Eastern Europe to ratify the European Convention, on 18 March 1992. *Czechoslovakia ratifies the European Convention on Human Rights*, 13 HUM. RTS. L.J. 131 (1992). When the republic divided in December 1992, reapplication for membership was made by both the Czech and Slovak Republics in January 1993. 14 HUM. RTS. L.J. 56 (1993). The former German Democratic Republic fell within the application of the European Convention by virtue of its merger into the Federal Republic of Germany. *Verbal Note from the Federal Republic of Germany*, INFORMATION SHEET NO. 27, *supra* note 112, at app. 2; *Resolution (90) 17 of the Committee of Ministers, 17 October 1990, id.* at app. 21; *Resolution (90) 18 of the Committee of Ministers of 23 October 1990, id.* at app. 22. Hungary ratified the European Convention on 11 May

Nationalist tensions within many of the democratizing states of Eastern Europe increasingly have given rise to violent internal strife, marking Europe as a region potentially afflicted by prolonged *de facto* or formal emergencies.[138] Indeed, the dissolution of the Soviet Union was propelled by the failed coup attempted by the "State Committee for the State of Emergency in the U.S.S.R."[139]

At the same time, the human rights elements of the Conference on Cooperation and Security in Europe (CSCE), popularly known as the Helsinki process,[140] have grown in importance with the adoption of the Copenhagen Document on Human Rights at the Conference on the Human Dimension in June 1990[141] and the 1991 Document of the Moscow Meeting.[142] The Copenhagen Document restates basic principles of international human rights law, including detailed standards on states of emergency.[143] It states in pertinent part:

---

1992 and Bulgaria ratified on 9 July 1992, both accepting the Article 25 petition process and the Court's jurisdiction. However, Poland ratified the European Convention on 19 January 1993 without accepting either individual petition or the Court's jurisdiction. 14 Hum. Rts. L.J. 56 (1993). Nine additional Eastern European states had applied for Council of Europe membership by January 1993. *Id.*

138. The war among the fractionating republics of the former state of Yugoslavia has attracted the peace-keeping efforts of a European Community observer mission, beginning in August 1991. C. Sudetic, *Observers Blame Serb-led Army For Escalating War in Croatia,* N.Y. Times, Dec. 3, 1991, at A8, col. 3. A United Nations peacekeeping force was authorized by the Security Council on 27 November 1991. P. Lewis, *U.N. Is Offering To Send a Force To Yugoslavia,* N.Y. Times, Nov. 28, 1991, at A1, col. 4.

139. The text of the statement issued by the State Committee on the State of Emergency on 19 August 1991 reflected the rhetorical attraction of invoking the imagery of states of emergency, as well as the manipulability of the concept: "Instead of showing concern for the security and well-being of every citizen and all society, persons that have come to positions of power not infrequently use it for interests alien to the people, as a means of unscrupulous self-assertion. . . . We intend to restore law and order straight away, end bloodshed, declare a war without mercy to the criminal world, eradicate shameful phenomena discrediting our society and degrading Soviet citizens." *State of Emergency Committee's Statement: "A Mortal Danger Has Come,"* N.Y. Times, Aug. 20, 1991, at A13, col. 1.

140. The CSCE began in 1973; its activities led to the signing of the Helsinki Final Act in August 1975, and continued with periodic meetings between the countries of Western and Eastern Europe, as well as the United States and Canada. *See, generally, Comment, International Human Rights—Helsinki Accords—Conference on Security and Cooperation in Europe Adopts Copenhagen Document on Human Rights,* 20 Ga. J. Int'l & Comp. L. 645 (1990); F. Newman & D. Weissbrodt, International Human Rights 411–80 (1990).

141. Copenhagen Document on Human Rights at the Conference on the Human Dimension in June 1990, *reprinted in* Information Sheet No. 27, *supra* note 123, at 266–81 [hereinafter Copenhagen Document]. *See* 29 I.L.M. 1305 (1990).

142. *See infra* note 144 (held 10 September to 4 October 1991).

143. Copenhagen Document, *supra* note 141, at para. 25.

The participating States confirm that any derogations from obligations relating to human rights and fundamental freedoms during a state of public emergency must remain strictly within the limits provided for by international law, in particular the relevant international instruments by which they are bound, especially with respect to rights from which there can be no derogation. They also reaffirm that
—measures derogating from such obligations must be taken in strict conformity with the procedural requirements laid down in those instruments;
—the imposition of a state of public emergency must be proclaimed officially, publicly, and in accordance with the provisions laid down by law;
—measures derogating from obligations will be limited to the extent strictly required by the exigencies of the situation;
—such measures will not discriminate solely on the grounds of race, colour, sex, language, religion, social origin or of belonging to a minority.

These standards draw upon norms in both the Covenant on Civil and Political Rights and in the European Convention.

The standards of the Copenhagen document were further elaborated in the Document of the Moscow Meeting, which occurred in the immediate aftermath of the failed coup. The Moscow Document added an unusual and potentially significant emphasis upon the motivation for imposition of emergency measures and the legitimate role of the press in monitoring events during an emergency:

The participating States reaffirm that a state of public emergency is justified only by the most exceptional and grave circumstances. . . . A state of public emergency may not be used to subvert the democratic constitutional order, nor aim at the destruction of internationally recognized human rights and fundamental freedoms. . . .

A state of public emergency may be proclaimed only by a constitutionally lawful body, duly empowered to do so. In cases where the decision to impose a state of public emergency may be lawfully taken by the executive authorities, that decision should be subject to approval in the shortest possible time or to control by the legislature.

. . . .

A *de facto* imposition or continuation of a state of public emergency not in accordance with provisions laid down by law is not permissible.

The participating States will endeavor to ensure that the normal functioning of the legislative bodies will be guaranteed to the highest possible extent during a state of public emergency.

. . . .

The participating States will endeavor to ensure that the legal guarantees necessary to uphold the rule of law will remain in force during a state of public emergency. . . .

The participating States will endeavor to maintain freedom of expression and freedom of information . . . with a view to enabling public discussion on the observance of human rights and fundamental freedoms as well as on the lifting of the state of public emergency. They will . . . take no measures aimed at barring journalists from the legitimate exercise of their profession other than those strictly required by the exigencies of the situation.

When a state of public emergency is *declared* or *lifted* in a participating State, the State concerned will immediately inform the CSCE Institution of this decision, as well as of any derogation made from the State's international human rights obligations. The Institution will inform the other participating States without delay.[144]

Perhaps even more significant than the restatement and development of substantive norms in these documents is continued elaboration of improved measures of implementation within the CSCE process. As Thomas Buergenthal observed about the Copenhagen Document, in recent years:

[T]he conceptual underpinnings of the CSCE underwent a dramatic transformation: an arena for dialogue between warring ideological blocs was on the way to becoming an institution of pan-European cooperation with shared values. The shared values—democratic pluralism, the rule of law and human rights—gave birth to a new and democratic European public order based on these principles.[145]

This new solidarity enabled the participating states to create permanent institutions within the CSCE, including a CSCE Council of Ministers of Foreign Affairs, a Committee of Senior Officials, a Secretariat in Prague, a Conflict Prevention Centre in Vienna, and an Office of Free Elections in Warsaw.[146] The participating states pledged themselves to new implementation measures as well, including a state-to-state mechanism of requests for information, written responses, and bilateral meetings.[147] Potentially most significant for monitoring states of emergency, the participating states agreed in Moscow to create a resource list of experts who could undertake fact-finding missions at the invitation of a participating state, as a sequel to bilateral contacts where six states agree, or at the behest of ten states where "a particularly serious threat to the fulfilment of the provisions of the CSCE human dimension has arisen."[148]

The new monitoring mechanisms of the CSCE were brought to bear upon the deteriorating human rights situation within the former terri-

144. Document of the Moscow Meeting, 30 I.L.M. 1670, paras. 28.1, 28.2, 28.4, 28.5, 28.8, 28.9, 28.10 (1991) [hereinafter Moscow Document].

145. T. Buergenthal, *CSCE Human Dimension: The Birth of a System*, Collected Courses of the Academy of European Law, bk. 2, 163, 190 (1992).

146. *Id.* at 195–98 (discussing the Charter of Paris for a New Europe of 21 November 1990).

147. Copenhagen Document, *supra* note 141, at para. 42; Moscow Document, *supra* note 138, at para. 2.

148. Moscow Document, *supra* note 144, at paras. 3–16. The Committee of Senior Officials may also initiate a mission on the request of a participating state. *Id.* at para. 13.

tory of Yugoslavia. In October 1991 the Committee of Senior Officials authorized the establishment of a human rights rapporteur mission and in March 1992 authorized a follow-up mission.[149] This action was in addition to the CSCE's efforts to establish a monitor mission to assist in establishing a ceasefire and peaceful settlement of the armed conflicts.[150]

The creation of new monitoring bodies within the CSCE understandably aroused concern within the Council of Europe. As the President of the European Court of Human Rights cautioned:

[T]he idea has been floated in some quarters of establishing a system of individual protection of human rights within the framework of the CSCE process. This idea, undoubtedly inspired by laudable reasons, nevertheless gives cause for serious concern. There is indeed a real danger in having on a permanent basis in Europe two parallel human rights systems, two parallel sets of standards and fundamental values, one perhaps less demanding than the other. It is in the interests of all of us in this part of the world not to see the unique and hard-earned system of enforcement under the European Convention diluted in the long term.[151]

While the CSCE offers the advantage of broader membership, including two non-European states (Canada and the United States), the Council of Europe benefits from decades of experience and a proven inclination toward progressive development of its monitoring techniques.[152]

149. Decision of the Committee of Senior Officials of October 22, 1991, *reprinted in* 3 U.S. DEPARTMENT OF STATE DISPATCH, No. 6 at 37 (1992); Decision of the Committee of Senior Officials of March 2, 1992, *id.* at 38. *See also, Prague Document on Further Development of CSCE Institutions and Structures,* 13 HUM. RTS. L.J. 174 (1992).

150. Decision of the Committee of Senior Officials of July 4, 1991, *id.* at 34; Decision of Senior Officials of August 9, 1991, *id.* These actions were taken in collaboration with the peacekeeping efforts by the European Community and the United Nations.

151. Rolv Ryssdal, address at a colloquy entitled "Europe: The Roads to Democracy," Council of Europe Doc. Cour (90) 223, Sept. 18–19, 1990, at 2.

152. *See* E. Schlager, *The Procedural Framework of the CSCE: From the Helsinki Consultations to the Paris Charter,* 1972–1990, 12 HUM. RTS. L.J. 221 (1991).

# Chapter VII
# The Role of Non-Governmental Organizations

## A. Introduction

Non-governmental organizations (NGOs) play an active and vital role in creating public awareness of human rights violations occurring during states of emergency, often supplying the basic data that fuel the inter-governmental mechanisms profiled in the previous chapters. Although of central importance, the NGO role is neither well defined nor efficiently coordinated. The attention given by NGOs to monitoring abuses during states of emergency may be episodic, with the internal dynamics of each group determining its priorities without particular regard to coordination with others or to sustained and comprehensive monitoring of emergencies as a discrete phenomenon.

The more formal the monitoring mechanism of an inter-governmental body, the less likely it is to rely or at least to acknowledge its reliance on NGO data. For example, the European Commission and Court of Human Rights hear only from the parties before them, whether states or individual applicants.[1] The Inter-American Court in contentious cases does not even provide a formal role for counsel for the petitioners, much less NGOs with which they may be associated.[2] Of course, NGO documentation on human rights abuses can be used by state or individual applicants invoking these formal proceedings, and NGOs may provide counsel to the victims or *amicus* briefs. Less

---

1. *See supra* Chapter VI (for a discussion of these organs).
2. Claudio Grossman has described his experiences as counsel with Juan Mendez of Americas Watch for the victims in the first contentious cases heard by the Inter-American Court of Human Rights and noted that the Inter-American Commission on Human Rights (IACHR) agreed to appoint them as agents to permit them to participate in the Court proceedings. C. Grossman, *Proposals to Strengthen the Inter-American System of Protection of Human Rights,* 32 GERM. Y.B. INT'L L. 264, 277 (1990).

judicially oriented mechanisms for handling individual communications, such as Resolution 1503, UNESCO's individual communication procedure, and the IACHR's petition process, all permit communications to be filed directly by NGOs themselves, without prior authorization by the victim.[3]

The special rapporteurs and working groups of the UN Commission on Human Rights tend to be very candid about their reliance on NGO data. The Sub-Commission's Special Rapporteur on States of Emergency frankly acknowledged his heavy reliance on information supplied and organized by NGOs, especially Amnesty International.[4] The Human Rights Committee in its reviews of state reports has adopted a middle position; some members rely on NGO-supplied information in framing questions to state representatives without revealing the source of the data, while other members have questioned the propriety of referring to non-state information.[5] Given the inadequate resources of the United Nations Centre for Human Rights, the proliferation of treaty, thematic, and *ad hoc* bodies, and the Sub-Commission's continual authorization of additional abstract studies of human rights issues, the reliance of UN bodies on NGOs for basic information concerning human rights practices can only be expected to increase.

Thus, it is a matter of some concern in devising an effective and efficient system for emergency-specific monitoring that the NGO community is so complex and its fact-finding methodology so poorly defined. As Diane Orentlicher notes, although the "credibility of their fact-finding is their stock in trade . . . the leading NGOs have not adopted uniform methodological standards; most have not even adopted comprehensive, formal standards for use by their own staffs."[6] In essence, more reporting is better in this rather chaotic world. "[H]uman rights reporting is a haphazard enterprise. . . . [T]o date, the chief antidote to unreliable information . . . derives from the multiplicity of independently published assessments by non-governmental organizations . . . [w]hile reliable taken in their entirety, they do not provide systematic and comprehensive coverage of human rights violations."[7]

This lack of uniform methodology stems from two understandable causes, the diversity in mandate and resources among NGOs and the

---

3. *See* discussion *supra* Chapters V and VI (concerning these three procedures).

4. U.N. Doc. E/CN.4/Sub.2/1987/19/Rev.1, at para. 36 (1988).

5. *See supra* Chapter IV.

6. D. Orentlicher, *Bearing Witness: The Art and Science of Human Rights Fact-Finding*, 3 Harv. Hum. Rts. J. 83, 85, 92 (1990). *See* International Law and Fact-Finding in the Field of Human Rights (B.G. Ramcharan ed., 1981).

7. Symposium, *Statistical Issues in the Field of Human Rights: Introduction*, 8 Hum. Rts. Q. 551, 555 (1986).

multiple uses even a single NGO may have for information concerning a particular state or situation. As David Weissbrodt and James McCarthy observe:

In some respects, [NGO] fact-finding processes resemble the methods of investigative journalism. In other ways, these organizations function in a quasi-adjudicative mode. On most occasions, human rights organizations collect information only at their central offices or secretariats. At other times, they send fact-finding missions to perform on-site interviews and observations. . . .

. . . .

NGOs use the results of these fact-finding efforts in very different ways . . . for example, (a) diplomatic contacts, (b) limited or massive letter-writing campaigns, (c) issuance of limited circulation reports, (d) distribution of press releases, (e) publication of detailed reports in pamphlet or book format, (f) printing brief statements in organization periodicals or annual reports, (g) filing communications or lobbying in international human rights bodies, (h) testimony before United Nations organs and national legislative bodies, (i) lobbying certain governments to raise human rights issues with other governments, (j) lobbying with governments or corporations to take trade, aid, or other measures against violating nations, and (k) a combination of several techniques.[8]

There is no constant or compelling reason why such divergently oriented NGOs using such diverse techniques to gather information should pay special attention to the emergency context within which human rights abuses are occurring. Only where the competence of an IGO monitor to which the information is being supplied is defined in specific emergency terms are NGOs likely to organize their material under the rubric of derogation norms, such as the principle of severity or the principle of proportionality.[9] Yet, aside from the treaty organs considering breaches of derogation clauses or the Sub-Commission's Special Rapporteur on States of Emergency, few of the monitoring bodies profiled in this study create a demand for precise analysis of human rights situations in terms of the legality of states of emergency.

## B. The Role of the Press

The extreme diversity among NGOs both increases the need for and impedes the possibility of efficiently coordinating their efforts. The local and international press, for instance, serve as a major source of information on a particular government's exercise of emergency powers, as well as a vital amplifying device for the information disseminated by human rights groups and the evaluations of monitoring

---

8. D. Weisbrodt & J. McCarthy, *Fact-Finding by Nongovernmental Organizations, in* INTERNATIONAL LAW AND FACT-FINDING, *supra* note 6, at 186.

9. *See supra* Chapter III (for a discussion of these principles).

IGOs. Yet the attention of the press may be fickle, and its reliability difficult to verify. Where systematic abuses of human rights are most severe, there may be no local independent press to gather the basic data.[10] Headlines may sprout when a formal emergency is imposed or terminated without any great consequence for the enjoyment of human rights, while long-standing *de facto* emergencies with severe consequences in remote areas may go unreported. Partly out of suspicion of bias or sloppiness, international petition processes often condition the admissibility of a communication on its not being exclusively based on "reports disseminated by mass media."[11]

## C. The Roles of International and National NGOs

Though a basic distinction can be drawn between national NGOs, which work within and focus their concerns upon a single state, and international NGOs, which either operate within several states and direct their attention to human rights issues in more than one state, or focus upon international human rights norms and structures, it is not simple to determine when a group is a human rights NGO. For example, the fact that a group's work makes use of international human rights norms rather than exclusively national law, is not necessarily a dispositive criterion.[12] Many groups based within a single state that have a trade union, religious, or development focus may be the best sources of timely and reliable information concerning the actual impact of emergency measures or the extent of gross human rights abuse. Yet these groups may have no links with the international NGOs, which could repackage and more effectively disseminate their data to the international community, and no direct access to the IGOs with authority to monitor the abuses.

The experience of Servicio Paz y Justicia (SERPAJ) in Uruguay is instructive. Like many national NGOs outside North America and Europe, SERPAJ had a broad view of human rights as embracing economic and social equity as well as civil and political rights. During the period of military rule in Uruguay, however, SERPAJ found itself working "full time to protect rights to personal security."[13] With a return to democratic government, SERPAJ again redefined its goals,

10. Orentlicher, *supra* note 6, at 95.

11. *See, e.g., Sub-Commission Res. 1 (XXIV),* U.N. Doc. E/CN.4/1070, at 50–51, para. (3)(d) (1971) (stating the admissibility standards imposed by the Sub-Commission on communications under Resolution 1503).

12. H. Steiner, Diverse Partners: Non-Governmental Organizations in the Human Rights Movement 5–8 (1991).

13. *Id.* at 52.

only to find itself not only without the same intense attention from international NGOs, but also with eroding support even within Uruguay's middle class.[14]

While a healthy symbiosis would seem to be the ideal prescription for the interaction between international and national NGOs, jealousies and disparate interests may interfere with such cooperative links.[15] For example, during states of emergency international NGOs may forge strong informational links to national NGOs with access to information on emergency measures and details of abuses. To preserve their own credibility, however, the international NGOs may attempt to filter the information they receive to eliminate the possible biases of the source.[16] These biases may consist of deliberate exaggeration of the scope of abuse or simple sloppy reporting in the heat of the moment, or, conversely, efforts to picture reported abuses as relatively moderate "in context."[17]

The imprecise nature of human rights fact-finding compounds the risks of misunderstanding and suspicion, not only among NGOs but between them and their various audiences. And even with respect to the most straightforward aspect of fact-finding in emergency contexts, compiling information on violations on non-derogable rights, the truth of reported events may be murky:

The facts surrounding reported violations . . . are rarely beyond dispute, in large part because the violations themselves are often deliberately shrouded in

14. *Id.*

15. Suggestions for better coordination among NGOs often meet with skepticism, based on a candid acknowledgment that resources (money and publicity) for even the largest and best-known groups are always insufficient to meet their self-imposed goals. As one participant in the seminar described stated: "NGOs 'hated' coordination, prized their autonomy of decision making, and rarely came together to divide responsibilities or to arrange jointly a mission or campaign. This . . . was explained by the importance of egotistical struggles for power and for public recognition among leaders of many organizations. Those struggles led to fights over jurisdiction and strategies rather than to planning within a unified human rights movement." *Id.* at 67.

16. Weissbrodt & McCarthy, *supra* note 8, at 187. Orentlicher suggests a number of relevant factors that must be assessed by an international NGO that relies on data from domestic human rights monitors, including whether the local group reports only violations against its own members or, more generally, whether it relies on the local press and, if so, what the prevailing journalistic standards are; how the domestic monitor may define terms such as "massacre"; whether it confines its reporting to urban rather than rural areas; whether it is linked with insurgent groups and, if so, whether the link seriously damages its credibility. *Supra* note 6, at 126–29.

17. The Israel National Section of the International Commission of Jurists, for example, offered a report that was consciously designed as an answer to criticism of Israeli use of emergency regulations in the Occupied Territories. Rule of Law in the Areas Administered by Israel (Tel Aviv 1981).

secrecy: military forces organize anonymous "death squads" to kill political opponents under cover of darkness; agents of the state seize suspected political opponents without judicial warrant and torture their victims in unauthorized, secret detention centers.[18]

The very context of the emergency may impede the ability of national NGOs to function or to disseminate their information, no matter how eager the audience outside the state. "Protection against torture . . . [and] prevention against massacres all start with information in the hands of a few who are themselves in peril."[19] One of the greatest benefits of a linkage between international NGOs, with steady access to the international press and to IGOs, and local NGOs in crisis-torn states is some degree of "insurance" against arrest or assassination for members of the latter, through the threat of rapid publicity that may harm the government's image in the world community.[20]

International NGOs also may enjoy consultative status with IGOs and have greater familiarity and sophistication in handling IGO processes. They may provide a platform for local human rights figures to address IGOs directly, although this carries a risk of lending credence to claims by target governments that the criticism of its human rights record is politically motivated. For example, the widow of President Salvador Allende of Chile spoke as a special representative of the International Association of Democratic Lawyers and the Women's International Democratic Federation to the UN Commission on Human Rights in 1974, shortly after the military coup.[21] The International Commission of Jurists lent the benefit of its consultative status at the Sub-Commission in 1976 to Rodolfo Matarollo of the Argentine Human Rights Commission, who provided a firsthand account of the gross abuses occurring under the Argentine state of siege.[22]

While the well-established international NGOs thus can provide

18. Orentlicher, *supra* note 6, at 94.

19. Statement of Martin Ennals, *quoted by* Tobin, *infra* note 31, at 977.

20. As participants at the retreat described by Steiner found: "[T]hreats to human rights activists that sometimes culminate in detention or killings have become more common—so much so that, in the words of one participant, 'what we need is not an umbrella of protection but a bullet-proof vest.' Publicity by INGOs [international NGOs] about threats, and mobilization of strong protests against a government intimidating human rights workers, have been helpful. A government may be deterred if aware of the political costs of harming workers." STEINER, *supra* note 12, at 69.

21. D. Weissbrodt, *The Contribution of International Nongovernmental Organizations to the Protection of Human Rights,* in 2 HUMAN RIGHTS IN INTERNATIONAL LAW: LEGAL AND POLICY ISSUES 403, 418 (Theodor Meron ed., 1984).

22. IAIN GUEST, BEHIND THE DISAPPEARANCES: ARGENTINA'S DIRTY WAR AGAINST HUMAN RIGHTS AND THE UNITED NATIONS 111–15 (1990).

assistance and access to national NGOs, there is an obvious risk of resented patronization.[23] The insular and esoteric world of IGO work can create a certain detachment and arrogance in prominent NGOs that may impede their ability to forge mutually beneficial links to local groups: "Among the organizations which attend [UN meetings] most assiduously, and tend to appoint the same delegates repeatedly, there has grown up an international 'corps' of observers reflecting some of the characteristics of the corps of professional diplomats."[24]

On the other hand, the closer involvement such NGOs have with IGOs may facilitate their participation in standard-setting relevant to states of emergency. For example, the Geneva-based Association of International Consultants on Human Rights organized a session in 1991 to assist Special Rapporteur Leandro Despouy with his task of drawing up model emergency laws, as requested by the Sub-Commission.[25] More legally oriented NGOs, such as the International Commission of Jurists and Amnesty International, have played a prominent role in drawing attention by IGOs to the human rights problems posed by emergencies and in suggesting appropriate norms.[26] On the other hand, local or regional human rights groups also can provide the primary impetus for development of new standards, such as the Declaration on the Protection of All Persons from Enforced or Involuntary Disappearances and a proposed convention on the same subject.[27]

Many NGOs are international not only in the sense of relying upon international human rights norms in their work and in directing their monitoring activities to more than one country, but also in themselves having a multinational structure. One of the older major NGOs, for example, is the International League for Human Rights, which operates as a confederation of national civil liberties organizations.[28] The scarcity of such bodies outside Western Europe and the Americas

---

23. STEINER, *supra* note 12, at 65.

24. P. Archer, *Action by Unofficial Organizations on Human Rights, in* THE INTERNATIONAL PROTECTION OF HUMAN RIGHTS 170 (Evan Luard ed., 1967).

25. U.N. Doc. E/CN.4/Sub.2/1991/28 Annex I (1991).

26. *See, e.g.,* INTERNATIONAL COMMISSION OF JURISTS, STATES OF EMERGENCY: THEIR IMPACT ON HUMAN RIGHTS (1983); AMNESTY INTERNATIONAL, STATES OF EMERGENCY: TORTURE AND VIOLATIONS OF THE RIGHT TO LIFE UNDER STATES OF EMERGENCY, AI INDEX: POL 30/02/88 (1988).

27. *See Report of the Sub-Commission on Prevention of Discrimination and Protection of Minorities on its Forty-Second Session,* U.N. Doc. E/CN.4/1991/2, at 63 (1990); *Report of the Working Group on Enforced and Involuntary Disappearances,* U.N. Doc. E/CN.4/1985/15 Annex III (1985) (Draft Convention on Enforced Disappearances prepared by FEDEFAM, the Latin American Federation of Associations of Relatives of Disappeared Detainees).

28. L. Wiseberg & H. Scoble, *The International League for Human Rights: The Strategy of a Human Rights NGO,* 7 GA. J. INT'L & COMP. L. 289 (1977).

places limits on the possibility that such a structure could provide in itself the coordination that would produce a comprehensive monitoring program for states of emergency. Likewise, Amnesty International and the International Commission of Jurists also have active membership structures in numerous countries, but tend to centralize their research and to be driven by mandate concerns that extend beyond states of emergency.[29] Multinational lawyers groups, such as the International Law Association, have limited resources, an almost exclusively volunteer structure, and an agenda that extends far beyond human rights.

For a truly comprehensive monitoring project on states of emergency to come into existence, effective coordination and compatible technology would have to be devised. A pilot project at Queen's University in Belfast, Northern Ireland, has made a promising start in developing a computer program that organizes data in a usable format that could reasonably be made accessible to a wide range of groups. Its full-scale implementation, however, would require establishing ongoing links with local human rights groups to gather and update the pertinent information. Although some human rights clearinghouses have been established[30] and some steps have been taken to create standardized bibliographic formats,[31] there does not exist a "standard

29. Amnesty International has hundreds of thousands of individual members throughout the world and national sections in over forty countries, but it generally imposes "work on own country rules" that direct members' activities away from human rights abuses committed by their home governments and toward human rights abuses committed abroad. The aim is to maintain AI's impartial and non-political image as well as to protect the safety of members. Research is centralized at the professional International Secretariat in London. *See* E. LARSON, A FLAME IN BARBED WIRE: THE STORY OF AMNESTY INTERNATIONAL (1979); AMNESTY INTERNATIONAL, HANDBOOK 68–70, 77–80 (1983).

The ICJ itself consists of forty eminent jurists, a vestige of the older-style NGO composed of a tightly knit elite group. But others may join as associates and the ICJ has national sections and affiliated legal organizations in more than sixty countries. The professional staff in Geneva includes research experts for different regions as well as the Centre for the Independence of the Judiciary. *See* INTERNATIONAL COMMISSION OF JURISTS, OBJECTIVES, ORGANIZATIONS, ACTIVITIES (1965).

30. The most prominent of these is Human Rights Internet which publishes the HUMAN RIGHTS INTERNET REPORTER, informing readers of texts of new human rights instruments, recent decisions of IGOs, calendars of upcoming events, news on NGO activities and articles on human rights issues, as well as directories of NGOs in different regions. Internet is currently located at the University Human Rights Centre at the University of Ottawa.

31. The Human Rights Information and Documentation System (HURIDOCS), for example, was created in 1982 to facilitate information-sharing among NGOs by promoting a standard bibliographic format for storing and retrieving information. *See* J. Tobin,

format for the recording of events constituting human rights violations . . . and situations that constitute patterns of violations,"[32] nor even for recording the more formal aspects of emergencies, such as proclamations and terminations.

## D. The International Committee of the Red Cross

Deserving separate and extended consideration is the International Committee of the Red Cross (ICRC), not only because it is the oldest body involved in the monitoring process[33] but also because of its distinctive structure, methodology, and legal competence. The situations within which the ICRC acts, from international armed conflict to internal armed conflict to internal strife, might all be categorized as states of emergency. It seems strange even to speak of the ICRC, given its unusual mode of operation, as a human rights NGO, though this aspect of its identity is growing in visibility both internally and externally.[34] The ICRC is unique among NGOs in its operational capacity and its special entitlement to act under the Geneva Conventions of 1949 and the Additional Protocols of 1977.[35] On the other hand, the ICRC often

---

*Book Note*, 81 Am. J. Int'l L. 977 (1987) (reviewing B. Stormorken, HURIDOCS Standard Formats for the Recording and Exchange of Information on Human Rights (1985)).

32. *Id.* at 979.

33. The ICRC came into existence in 1863 and was instrumental in the successful conclusion of a conference organized by the Swiss government to draw up the first Geneva Convention on international humanitarian law in 1864. The inspiration for the conference came from Henri Dunant's book, A Memory of Solferino, which chronicled his experiences at the 1859 battle of Solferino in Italy, at which he organized relief, with the help of local residents, to assist thousands of unattended wounded soldiers on both sides. Annual Report of the International Committee of the Red Cross 1990, at 3; P. Boissier, From Solferino to Tsushima (1985); D. Forsythe, *Human Rights and the International Committee of the Red Cross*, 12 Hum. Rts. Q. 265, 266 (1990).

34. Forsythe, *supra* note 33, at 265.

35. States ratifying the Geneva Conventions of 1949 recognize the right of the ICRC to visit prisoners of war and civilian detainees and to take initiatives to secure compliance with other treaty provisions by parties to the conflict. Detained foreign combatants and civilian detainees "have a right to communicate directly and privately with the ICRC about their conditions of detention." Forsythe, *supra* note 33, at 270. *See* G. Peirce, *Humanitarian Protection for the Victims of War: The System of Protecting Powers and the Role of the ICRC*, 90 Mil. L. Rev. 89 (1980). However, in internal armed conflict "fighting parties are not legally obligated . . . to admit the ICRC to territory they control for prisoner visits . . . [though the] ICRC is authorized to request such access" under 1977 Protocol II. Forsythe, *supra* note 33, at 271. The Statutes of the International Red Cross and Red Crescent Movement also permit the ICRC to offer its services in the event of internal disturbance and tension, without the offer constituting interference in a state's in-

consciously eschews framing its approach in legal terms, contributing to its image "as a charitable organization, perhaps even as a humanitarian do-gooder."[36] Indeed, the ICRC's role is constantly evolving, generally following a distinct pattern: "[T]he invariable sequence of events has seen an ad hoc action of the ICRC develop into a general practice that later achieved the status of a customary norm in international law and was finally codified by treaties and conventions."[37]

Other characteristics that distinguish the ICRC from the remainder of the NGO world are its unusual organization and funding. The ICRC is an all-Swiss organization. Its Assembly is composed of prominent Swiss, traditionally drawn from the elite of business and government, who themselves are generally amateurs motivated by *noblesse oblige* in their humanitarian work.[38] Following restructuring in the 1970s, ICRC operations became much more professionalized, and its work today is carried on by more than six hundred headquarters staff, more than five hundred "delegates" in the field, and thousands of local employees of many nationalities.[39]

But the ICRC is only one component of the Red Cross and Red Crescent "movement" and must maintain sometimes tense relationships with national societies and a League that may either have inconvenient agendas or be too closely identified with home governments.[40] Participation at the quadrennial conferences of the movement extends not only to the ICRC and the national societies, but also to governments of states that have ratified the Geneva Conventions. The interjection of politics into this otherwise humanitarian movement created

---

ternal affairs. INTERNATIONAL COMMITTEE OF THE RED CROSS, ANNUAL REPORT 1988, at 7 (1989); *ICRC Protection and Assistance Activities in Situations Not Covered by International Humanitarian Law*, 28 INT'L REV. RED CROSS 9, 13–18 (1988) [hereinafter *ICRC Protection*].

36. Forsythe, *supra* note 33, at 265.

37. J.D. Armstrong, *The International Committee of the Red Cross and Political Prisoners*, 39 INT'L ORG. 615, 621 (1985).

38. Forsythe, *supra* note 33, at 278–79.

39. INTERNATIONAL COMMISSION OF THE RED CROSS, 1988 ANNUAL REPORT 123 (1989).

40. Forsythe describes the awkward crisis that arose in Ethiopia in 1988, when the ICRC decided to withdraw because it could not obtain adequate assurances from the government that food relief in the conflicted north would be distributed equitably to persons on all sides. The Ethiopian Red Cross was closely allied with the government and could not be trusted to distribute the aid neutrally. But the League of Red Cross Societies, without consulting the ICRC, undertook to distribute the aid without insisting on guarantees from the Ethiopian government. Forsythe indicates that ICRC officials were privately incensed by this action, although they agreed to cooperate with it. *Supra* note 33, at 268.

difficulties for the ICRC in 1986 when the conference voted to exclude the government of South Africa from participation. The South African government retaliated by temporarily suspending ICRC access to political detainees.[41] This unusual government involvement in the affairs of an NGO is further complicated by the fact that the bulk of the ICRC's regular and special budgets are derived from government contributions rather than from private fund-raising.[42]

Nevertheless, the ICRC has succeeded in carving out a distinct niche for itself within the Red Cross movement and also within the NGO world. While national Red Cross and Red Crescent societies concentrate upon disaster relief and related work, the ICRC performs its unique role of humanitarian initiative in international and internal armed conflicts and continues its unusual program of prison visits to political detainees. Sensitivity to sovereignty concerns caused the ICRC's role in internal armed conflict and internal strife to evolve slowly, but in 1919 the ICRC began to develop a program of visiting prisoners detained because of their involvement in civil war or internal strife.[43] Since then, the ICRC has visited over a half a million political detainees in ninety-five countries.[44]

While other NGOs, such as Amnesty International, are not entirely averse to the attractions of quiet diplomacy where it holds some prospect for ameliorating a particular human rights situation, none have made this approach so central to their mission as has the ICRC. The ICRC uses publicity as a very selective tool in its work, both to promote respect for international humanitarian law during armed conflicts and in its prison-visit and tracing activities.[45] Ironically, one key bit of leverage the ICRC sometimes uses against recalcitrant governments is to threaten publicly to withdraw its operations in the country, an action that carries the implicit suggestion that the government is committing

41. While the government later restored partial access, the ICRC itself later withdrew because the access was inadequate. Forsythe, *supra* note 33, at 267; INTERNATIONAL LAW ASSOCIATION, SECOND INTERIM REPORT OF THE COMMITTEE ON THE ENFORCEMENT OF HUMAN RIGHTS LAW, SIXTY-THIRD CONFERENCE 169 (Warsaw 1988).

42. In 1990, of a budget of about 385 million Swiss francs, approximately 270 million francs were donated by governments (the leaders in donations were Switzerland at 72 million and the United States at 50 million). ANNUAL REPORT OF THE INTERNATIONAL COMMITTEE OF THE RED CROSS 1990 26–28 (1991).

43. The first visits occurred in the USSR and in Hungary. Armstrong, *supra* note 37, at 623; *ICRC Protection*, *supra* note 35, at 14.

44. Forsythe, *supra* note 33, at 272.

45. The ICRC also engages in a great deal of promotional and educational work, however, for which wide dissemination is centrally important. *See, e.g.*, M. Harroff-Tavel, *The Principle of Neutrality*, DISSEMINATION, April 1992, at 14.

and seeking to conceal gross abuses of detainees or others.[46] In contrast, the lifeblood of other major NGOs is high-profile publicity for their detailed reports on human rights abuse, and their offering to go away would be warmly welcomed by many governments.

The confidentiality of the ICRC's work is sometimes overestimated, as information concerning the countries in which it is operating, the number of detainees visited, and so forth, can easily be gleaned from its annual reports and other publications. Indeed, because the ICRC's work takes place largely in emergency situations, these public reports describing ICRC operations serve as a good source of basic information on the occurrence of emergencies. But the details of the conditions discovered and formally reported by ICRC delegates in detention centers largely remain confidential, unless the government chooses selectively to release portions of the report.[47] ICRC discretion creates a risk that the government may manipulate its cooperation with the ICRC to bolster its internal or external legitimacy or to justify non-cooperation with IGOs and NGOs using more public methods of inquiry.[48] The ICRC's policy is to continue its visits as long as it is satisfied that its presence may provide benefits to the detainees. One commentator concludes:

If the ICRC were the only voice to be heard on the issue of political prisoners, the morality of its refusal to criticize governments or reveal its findings might be more tenuous. It is because other NGOs (and governments) are actively involved in trying to bring about the release of political prisoners and condemning the detaining governments that the ICRC is able to play its more restricted role without serious qualms of conscience.[49]

The ICRC's involvement in standard-setting is also distinct from that of the other key NGOs concerned with human rights during states of emergency. The ICRC does not work like Amnesty International or the International Commission of Jurists within UN or other IGO structures to shape the content of international human rights law. On the other hand, it does prepare draft texts for the international diplomatic conferences that draw up new instruments of humanitarian law and actively promotes ratification of such instruments. Hans-Peter Gasser of the ICRC floated a proposal to draw up a code of conduct for states

46. Forsythe cites as examples South Vietnam, Portuguese Mozambique, South Africa, and El Salvador. Forsythe, *supra* note 33, at 275.

47. *Id.* at 275; Armstrong, *supra* note 37, at 638–39.

48. Armstrong, *supra* note 37, at 638–39 (citing example of interaction with Greek junta in 1967–70).

49. *Id.* at 642.

involved in internal strife, drawing upon strands of customary and codified human rights and humanitarian law, as well as basic principles of humanity,[50] but this code was never formally adopted by the ICRC or the Red Cross Conference. Nevertheless, it has served as a useful model for further discussion of the potential core of non-derogable rights of detainees in emergency situations.[51]

In recent years major human rights NGOs have shown an increasing interest in the relevance of international humanitarian law to their work, particularly with respect to abusive actions by non-governmental entities during periods of armed conflict. Amnesty International broadened its concerns with respect to such violations at its 1991 International Council Meeting,[52] and groups such as Americas Watch have increasingly drawn on the standards of international humanitarian law in their reports on strife-torn states.[53] Thus, an increasing convergence of interests is likely among the ICRC and human rights NGOs.

---

50. H.P. Gasser, *A Measure of Humanity in Internal Disturbances and Tensions: Proposal for a Code of Conduct*, 28 INT'L REV. RED CROSS 38 (1988).

51. *See* discussion *supra* Chapter III.

52. REPORTS AND DECISIONS OF THE 20TH INTERNATIONAL COUNCIL OF AMNESTY INTERNATIONAL, YOKOHAMA, JAPAN, DECISION 5 OF THE 20TH INTERNATIONAL COUNCIL, AUG. 31–SEPT. 7 1991, AI INDEX: ORG 52/01/92 at 31 (1992).

53. *See, e.g.,* AMERICAS WATCH, VIOLATION OF FAIR TRIAL GUARANTEES BY THE FMLN'S *AD HOC* COURTS (1990); HUMAN RIGHTS WATCH, NEEDLESS DEATHS IN THE GULF WAR (1991).

# Chapter VIII
# **Conclusion**

Measuring the effectiveness of the various bodies profiled in this study is difficult because cause and effect relationships in protection of international human rights are inherently elusive[1] and also because there are multiple goals to the monitoring process. As the Committee on the Enforcement of Human Rights Law of the International Law Association (ILA) noted in 1986:

[A]s with "states of emergency" the concept of "effectiveness" is multi-faceted and elusive. At least six possible aspects of effectiveness can be identified, including: exposing the fact of human rights abuses; stopping or moderating abuses during the course of an emergency; providing redress to individual victims through findings of violations, compensation, rehabilitation, release from detention, or clarification of the fate of missing persons; securing the punishment of violators; terminating a state of emergency; and prevention of possible future abuses or invalid imposition of emergency measures.[2]

Examples of small successes in each of these categories can be found scattered throughout this study, but on no count can the existing monitoring system be seen as ideally effective.

Yet moderate goals for improving existing mechanisms can be set and concrete steps taken to improve coordination. At its Sixty-Fourth Conference in Brisbane in 1990, the ILA adopted the Queensland Guidelines for Bodies Monitoring Respect for Human Rights During

---

1. *See, e.g.,* D. Weissbrodt & M.L. Bartolomei, *The Effectiveness of International Human Rights Pressures: The Case of Argentina, 1976–1983,* 75 MINN. L. REV. 1009 (1991).

2. INTERNATIONAL LAW ASSOCIATION, INTERIM REPORT OF THE COMMITTEE ON THE ENFORCEMENT OF HUMAN RIGHTS LAW, SIXTY-SECOND CONFERENCE OF THE INTERNATIONAL LAW ASSOCIATION 112 (Seoul 1986).

States of Emergency,[3] whose primary drafter was the author of this study. These Guidelines are reprinted in the Appendix.

The Queensland Guidelines remain pertinent and timely. No simple or single answer exists to the question whether all human rights monitors should devote special attention to the phenomenon of human rights abuse during states of emergency. Rather, the linkage between a certain pattern of human rights abuse and the occurrence of a particular form of emergency will be of varying significance for different components of the international human rights monitoring system. Each monitor could improve its effectiveness against abuse associated with states of emergency by responding to the Guidelines' recommendations most pertinent to its work, without necessarily undertaking a major redirection of its operations specifically toward states of emergency. By maximizing the impact of the existing complex, but patchy, system of international monitoring of states of emergency, reducing inconsistency and redundancy, and improving coordination, scarce resources can be made to stretch further. Many years of additional incremental improvements by all participants are likely to be required before a comprehensive monitoring system with real and rapid influence on governments facing or claiming an emergency emerges.

Several issues demand priority attention or stand on the brink of major developments. With respect to the interpretation of the derogation clauses of human rights treaties, these issues include: (1) clarification of the threshold of severity to meet the definition of a public emergency justifying suspension of rights; (2) stricter and more purely objective application by treaty implementation bodies of the principle of proportionality to suspensions of derogable rights; (3) identification of rights that are functionally non-derogable, either because their suspension is never strictly required by the exigencies of any emergency or because their violation would breach other obligations under international law; and (4) development of criteria for determining when reservations to derogation clauses or to non-derogable provisions are impermissible. Greater effort must also be made to reach consensus concerning a core of rights that are non-derogable as a matter of customary law, particularly with respect to limits on arbitrary detention and for fair trial during emergencies.

The greater involvement of the United Nations Security Council in emergency situations with important human rights dimensions poses a

---

3. QUEENSLAND GUIDELINES FOR BODIES MONITORING RESPECT FOR HUMAN RIGHTS DURING STATES OF EMERGENCY, *reprinted in* 85 AM. J. INT'L L. 716 (1991).

challenge and an opportunity to the bodies described in this study. The use of forceful measures to promote human rights and the deployment of large numbers of on-site monitors with a human rights protection mission may become increasingly common techniques of international response to certain visible emergencies. Integration of the specialized human rights organs as active participants, along with the political and humanitarian assistance authorities, in these multilateral efforts is crucial.

# Appendix: The Queensland Guidelines for Bodies Monitoring Respect for Human Rights During States of Emergency

## Treaty Implementation Bodies

### A. Treaties Containing Derogation Clauses

1. Treaty implementation bodies with responsibility to review periodic state reports should carefully scrutinize those reports for their adequacy in describing emergency provisions in national law and especially for their description of and justification for any emergency measures actually imposed. In any dialogue with state representatives in the context of report reviews, the treaty implementation body should insist upon receiving adequate information about emergency laws and practices, requesting supplemental reports if necessary.

2. Treaty implementation bodies with the authority to request additional reports from states parties (*e.g.*, the Human Rights Committee under article 40(1)(b) of the International Covenant on Civil and Political Rights; the Secretary-General of the Council of Europe under article 57 of the European Convention on Human Rights and Fundamental Freedoms) should institute a procedure by which they automatically require a supplemental report, within a reasonable period of time, from any state party which has filed a notice of derogation under the treaty, or as to which reliable reports from credible sources indicate that the state party is either undergoing a *de facto* emergency with great consequences for protection of human rights or has recently substantially increased its use of such measures as detention without trial under "ordinary" security laws or trial of civilians by military courts.

3. Treaty implementation bodies with report review responsibilities may consider information from sources other than the state party, such as information provided by non-governmental human rights organiza-

tions (NGOs) or other intergovernmental organizations (IGOs), and media reports. Treaty implementation bodies should actively seek out such information and, in particular, should create effective systems of information-sharing with other IGOs.

4. States parties to treaties requiring formal notification of emergency measures must ensure that their derogation notices include a description of the emergency measures, their expected duration, the provisions of national law being suspended or invoked and the treaty provisions affected. The derogation notice should also include a summary of the facts indicating the existence of a public emergency of the necessary magnitude. The notice should be provided promptly (generally within a week of the imposition of emergency measures) and should be regularly updated as conditions change. Prompt notice of the termination of an emergency should also be made.

5. Implementation bodies under treaties requiring notification should develop a procedure by which the depositary of the notices or the head of the implementation body scrutinizes derogation notices as they are received and immediately requests the state party to cure any deficiencies in the notice. To assist in this process, the implementation body might consider the creation of a "model" derogation notice that sets out defined categories of essential information.

6. Treaty implementation bodies with the authority to hear applications by one state party that another state party has breached its treaty obligations in the context of a state of emergency should make full use of their authorized powers to find the facts, including whenever possible on-site visits and examination and cross-examination of all feasible and relevant witnesses. In mediating a friendly settlement between the parties to a contentious case, the treaty implementation body should seek maximum assurances that respect for human rights will be concretely promoted by such settlement.

7. Treaty implementation bodies with jurisdiction to receive individual applications alleging that the terms of the treaty have been breached during a state of emergency also should undertake to find the facts as thoroughly as possible. The powers of such bodies should be defined so that the individual applicant may submit oral as well as written testimony and pleadings. Provision of legal aid should be made wherever possible.

8. In contentious cases arising out of both inter-state and individual applications, the treaty implementing body should not extend a broad "margin of appreciation" to the derogating state but should make an objective determination whether a public emergency as defined in the treaty actually existed, whether the measures taken were proportional

to the emergency and non-discriminatory, whether the proper procedures (under both the treaty and national law) for lawful derogation were followed, and whether any non-derogable rights were violated.

9. Treaty implementing bodies with authority to issue general interpretations or advisory opinions under the treaty should make creative and effective use of this authority to inform the states parties of their obligations under the derogation clauses.

## B. Other Treaty Implementation Bodies

10. Bodies set up to implement human rights treaties that do not contain an explicit derogation clause should nevertheless be guided in their work by fundamental principles of proportionality and necessity. Such bodies should take note that certain rights are regarded as being non-derogable, including those rights mentioned in the ILA's Paris Minimum Standards of Human Rights Norms in a State of Emergency, Section (C).

11. In construing limitation clauses, treaty implementation bodies should not approve restrictions on rights more severe than would be permitted in time of emergency under derogation clauses.

12. Bodies with authority to undertake on-site investigations of human rights abuses that tend to be associated with states of emergency, such as the European Committee for the Prevention of Torture and Inhuman or Degrading Treatment or Punishment, should be strongly encouraged as a model for preventative measures to reduce the level of human rights abuse, especially in the case of non-derogable rights.

## Charter Organs and Subsidiary Bodies

13. General and parliamentary assemblies of universal and regional inter-governmental organizations should support studies of the impact on human rights of states of emergency, both in specific countries and as a general matter. Adequate resources should be made available for these studies.

14. Inter-governmental assemblies and subsidiary bodies empowered to adopt resolutions concerning human rights practices in specific member states should adopt resolutions condemning human rights violations associated with formal and *de facto* emergencies whenever credible evidence of such violations is brought to their attention.

15. Programs of advisory services in human rights that include training in the preparation of periodic reports on compliance with human rights treaties should emphasize adequate attention to emergency de-

rogations from treaty obligations. Advisory services aimed at assisting reform of national laws should include attention to emergency provisions of such laws to ensure consistency with international standards.

16. *Ad hoc* working groups or special rapporteurs delegated responsibility to examine certain types of human rights abuse and to act on a humanitarian basis in response to reports of individual instances of such abuse (*e.g.*, disappearance, torture, summary execution) should analyze, where possible, the data they have collected to determine whether there appears to be any correlation between the level of abuse and the existence of some type of state of emergency.

17. Human rights bodies with a general authority to issue country reports and *ad hoc* working groups or special rapporteurs delegated authority to study the human rights situation in particular countries should include, where appropriate, an analysis of any observed relationship between human rights abuse in the particular country and the existence of some type of state of emergency. In making recommendations to the subject country, these bodies should address as a matter of priority compliance with international standards concerning the violation of emergency powers.

18. Initiatives such as that undertaken by the Sub-Commission on the Prevention of Discrimination and the Protection of Minorities of the United Nations Commission on Human Rights under the Economic and Social Council resolution 1985/37, to authorize a Special Rapporteur on States of Emergency, deserve high praise and adequate support services. The following aspects of the Special Rapporteur's programme of work in particular represent a positive model for such undertakings:

(1) the initiative shown in gathering data from a wide variety of sources, including governments, other inter-governmental organizations (such as the derogation notices filed with the Organization of American States), non-governmental organizations and the press;

(2) the systematic listing of states of emergency proclaimed or terminated;

(3) systematic scrutiny of formal derogation notices and requests to the relevant governments for additional information;

(4) efforts to analyze thoroughly the context and consequences of a particular state of emergency, through exchanges of information with non-governmental organizations and the state concerned;

(5) efforts to analyze the general phenomenon of states of emergency and their relation to respect for human rights;

(6) emphasis upon measures to prevent violation of non-derogable rights;

(7) plans to develop model legal provisions to promote continued respect for fundamental rights during states of emergency; and

(8) plans to devote further attention to *de facto* states of emergency and to administrative detention under internal security laws without proclamation of an emergency, so as to avoid the potentially negative consequences of an exclusive focus on formal emergencies.

## Non-Governmental Organizations

19. Given the variety of NGOs in terms of structure, mandate and resources, it is neither possible nor desirable to prescribe particular methods of work not the priority to be given to states of emergency and their impact on human rights. NGOs tend to specialize by region or by the types of human rights abuse they seek to expose and prevent, and this specialization has the advantage of enhancing the depth of information they are able to develop, promotes long-term work against particular abuses and tends to reduce duplication of effort among NGOs.

20. NGOs should continue to enhance their collaborative efforts at information-sharing and the development of more sophisticated information technology in connection with states of emergency. Institutions with resources for issuing grants for human rights work should be encouraged to support collaborative efforts among NGOs, academic institutions, learned societies, and IGOs (including the UN's Centre for Human Rights) for systematic data-gathering and analysis of patterns of human rights abuse, including those associated with states of emergency.

21. NGOs should continue to provide information, within the limits of their resources, on a regular and sustained basis to IGOs monitoring human rights abuse during states of emergency.

22. Established international NGOs should strive to promote direct links between relevant IGO monitoring bodies and smaller, more localized NGOs which may have access to timely and accurate information on human rights abuse associated with states of emergency.

# Bibliography

## BOOKS

Blaustein, Albert and Gisbert Flanz, Constitutions of the Countries of the World (1986).

Boissier, Pierre, From Solferino to Tsushima (1985).

Boyle, Kevin, Tom Hadden and Paddy Hillyard, Law & State: The Case of Northern Ireland (1975).

Boyle, Kevin, Tom Hadden and Paddy Hillyard, Ten Years in Northern Ireland: The Legal Control of Political Violence (1980).

Buergenthal, Thomas and Robert Norris, eds., Human Rights: The Inter-American System (1982).

Chowdhury, Subrata Roy, Rule of Law in a State of Emergency: The Paris Minimum Standards of Human Rights Norms in a State of Emergency (1989).

Country Reports on Human Rights Practices for 1988, Report to the Committee on Foreign Relations of the U.S. Senate and the Committee on Foreign Relations of the House of Representatives, by the U.S. Department of State, S.Prt. 101–3, 101st Cong., 1st Sess. (1989).

Country Reports on Human Rights Practices for 1989, Report to the Committee on Foreign Relations of the U.S. Senate and the Committee on Foreign Affairs of the House of Representatives, by the U.S. Department of State, 101st Cong., 2d Sess. (1990).

Country Reports on Human Rights Practices for 1990, Report to the Committee on Foreign Relations of the U.S. Senate and the Committee on Foreign Affairs of the House of Representatives, by the U.S. Department of State, S.Prt. 102–5, 102d Cong., 1st Sess. (1991).

Ellmann, Stephen, In a Time of Trouble: Law and Liberty in South Africa's State of Emergency (1992).

Fairman, Charles, The Law of Martial Rule (1943).

Garcia, Ed, ed., Human Rights Reader: Towards a Just and Humane Society (1990).

Guest, Iain, Behind the Disappearances: Argentina's Dirty War against Human Rights and the United Nations (1990).

Hadden, Tom, Colm Campbell and K.S. Venkateswaran, A Database on States of Emergency: Report of a Feasibility Study (1992).

Humphrey, John, Human Rights and the United Nations: A Great Adventure (1984).

INTERNATIONAL COMMISSION OF JURISTS, STATES OF EMERGENCY: THEIR IMPACT ON HUMAN RIGHTS (1983).

JELLINEK, W., GESETZ UND VERORDNUNG (1887).

KOHLER, JOSEF, NOT KENNT KEIN GEBOT (1915).

LARSON, E., A FLAME IN BARBED WIRE: THE STORY OF AMNESTY INTERNATIONAL (1979).

LEROY, PAUL, L'ORGANISATION CONSTITUTIONNELLE ET LES CRISES (1966).

LILLICH, RICHARD, INTERNATIONAL HUMAN RIGHTS: PROBLEMS OF LAW, POLICY AND PRACTICE (2d ed. 1991).

MCGOLDRICK, DOMINICK, THE HUMAN RIGHTS COMMITTEE (1991).

MEDINA QUIROGA, CECILIA, THE BATTLE OF HUMAN RIGHTS: GROSS, SYSTEMATIC VIOLATIONS AND THE INTER-AMERICAN SYSTEM (1988).

MERON, THEODOR, HUMAN RIGHTS IN INTERNAL STRIFE: THEIR INTERNATIONAL PROTECTION (1987).

NEWMAN, FRANK AND DAVID WEISSBRODT, INTERNATIONAL HUMAN RIGHTS (1990).

ORAA, JAIME, HUMAN RIGHTS IN STATES OF EMERGENCY IN INTERNATIONAL LAW (1992).

PLAYFAIR, EMMA, ADMINISTRATIVE DETENTION IN THE OCCUPIED WEST BANK (1986).

RAMCHARAN, B.G., ed., INTERNATIONAL LAW AND FACT-FINDING IN THE FIELD OF HUMAN RIGHTS (1981).

RAMCHARAN, B.G., THE INTERNATIONAL LAW AND PRACTICE OF EARLY-WARNING AND PREVENTIVE DIPLOMACY: THE EMERGING GLOBAL WATCH (1991).

ROSSITER, CLINTON, CONSTITUTIONAL DICTATORSHIP: CRISIS GOVERNMENT IN THE MODERN DEMOCRACIES (1948).

STEINER, HENRY, DIVERSE PARTNERS: NON-GOVERNMENTAL ORGANIZATIONS IN THE HUMAN RIGHTS MOVEMENT (1991).

TIMERMAN, JACOBO, PRISONER WITHOUT A NAME, CELL WITHOUT A NUMBER (1981).

TOLLEY, HOWARD, THE U.N. COMMISSION ON HUMAN RIGHTS (1987).

VASAK, KAREL AND PHILIP ALSTON, eds., THE INTERNATIONAL DIMENSIONS OF HUMAN RIGHTS (1982).

VOISSET, MICHELE, L'ARTICLE 16 DE LA CONSTITUTION DU 4 OCTOBRE 1958 (1969).

## ARTICLES

Alexander, George, *The Illusory Protection of Human Rights by National Courts During Periods of Emergency*, 5 H.R.L.J. 1 (1984).

Alston, Philip, *The Security Council and Human Rights: Lessons to Be Learned from the Iraq-Kuwait Crisis and Its Aftermath*, 13 AUST. Y.B. INT'L L. 107 (1992).

———, *UNESCO's Procedures for Dealing with Human Rights Violations*, 20 SANTA CLARA L. REV. 665 (1980).

Archer, Peter, *Action by Unofficial Organizations on Human Rights*, in THE INTERNATIONAL PROTECTION OF HUMAN RIGHTS 170 (Evan Luard ed., 1967).

Armstrong, J.D., *The International Committee of the Red Cross and Political Prisoners*, 39 I.O. 615 (1985).

Bossuyt, Marc, *The Development of Special Procedures of the United Nations Commission on Human Rights*, 6 HUM. RTS. L.J. 179 (1985).

Brody, Reed, *The United Nations Creates a Working Group on Arbitrary Detention*, 85 Am. J. Int'l L. 709 (1991).

Brody, Reed, Maureen Convery and David Weissbrodt, *The 42nd Session of the Sub-Commission on Prevention of Discrimination and Protection of Minorities*, 13 Hum. Rts. Q. 260 (1991).

Brody, Reed, Penny Parker and David Weissbrodt, *Major Developments in 1990 at the UN Commission on Human Rights*, 12 Hum. Rts. Q. 559 (1990).

Brookfield, F.M., *The Fiji Revolutions of 1987*, 1988 N.Z.L.J. 250.

Buergenthal, Thomas, *CSCE Human Dimension: The Birth of a System*, Collected Courses of the Academy of European Law, Volume I, Book 2 163 (1992).

Buergenthal, Thomas, *To Respect and to Ensure: State Obligations and Permissible Derogations*, in The International Bill of Rights: The Covenant on Civil and Political Rights 72 (Louis Henkin ed. 1981).

Claude, Richard and Thomas Jabine, *Symposium: Statistical Issues in the Field of Human Rights: Introduction*, 8 Hum. Rts. Q. 551 (1986).

Comment, *International Human Rights—Helsinki Accords—Conference on Security and Cooperation in Europe Adopts Copenhagen Document on Human Rights*, 20 Ga. J. Int'l & Comp. L. 645 (1990).

Comment, *The United Kingdom's Obligation to Balance Human Rights and Its Anti-Terrorism Legislation: The Case of Brogan and Others*, 13 Fordham Int'l L.J. 328 (1989–1990).

Dugard, John, *A Bill of Rights for South Africa?* 23 Cornell Int'l L.J. 441 (1990).

Dumont, Georges-Henri, *Discreet Dialogue*, UNESCO Sources No. 16 at 11 (1990).

Ellmann, Stephen, *A Constitution for All Seasons: Providing Against Emergencies in a Post-Apartheid Constitution*, 21 Col. Hum. Rts. L. Rev. 163 (1989).

Farer, Tom, *Human Rights and Human Wrongs: Is the Liberal Model Sufficient?*, 7 Hum. Rts. Q. 189 (1985).

Fischer, Dana, *Reporting under the Covenant on Civil and Political Rights*, 76 Am. J. Int'l L. 142 (1982).

Fitzpatrick, Joan, *UN Action With Respect to "Disappearances" and Summary or Arbitrary Executions*, in The Universal Declaration of Human Rights 1948–1988: Human Rights, the United Nations and Amnesty International 35 (Amnesty International USA 1988).

Forsythe, David, *Human Rights and the International Committee of the Red Cross*, 12 Hum. Rts. Q. 265 (1990).

Franck, Thomas and H. Scott Fairley, *Procedural Due Process in Human Rights Fact-Finding by International Agencies*, 74 Am. J. Int'l L. 308 (1980).

Gardeniers, Ton, Hurst Hannum and Janice Kruger, *The U.N. Sub-Commission on Prevention of Discrimination and Protection of Minorities: Recent Developments*, 4 Hum. Rts. Q. 368 (1982).

Garibaldi, Oscar, *General Limitations on Human Rights: The Principle of Legality*, 17 Harv. Int'l L.J. 503 (1976).

Gasser, Hans Peter, *A Measure of Humanity in Internal Disturbances and Tensions: Proposal for a Code of Conduct*, Int'l Rev. Red Cross, Jan.–Feb. 1988 at 38.

Gemalmaz, Mehmet Semih, *State of Emergency Rule in the Turkish Legal System: Perspectives and Texts*, 11–12 Turk. Y.B. Hum. Rts. 115 (1989–90).

Ghandhi, P.R., *The Human Rights Committee and Derogation in Public Emergencies*, 32 Germ. Y.B. Int'l L. 321 (1990).

Green, L.C., *Derogation of Human Rights in Emergency Situations*, 16 CAN. Y.B. INT'L L. 92 (1978).

Greer, D.S., *Admissibility of Confessions and the Common Law in Times of Emergency*, 24 NO. IRE. L.Q. 199 (1973).

Grossman, Claudio, *Proposals to Strengthen the Inter-American System of Protection of Human Rights*, 32 GERM. Y.B. INT'L L. 264 (1990).

Hartman, Joan, *Derogation from Human Rights Treaties in Public Emergencies*, 22 HARV. INT'L L.J. 1 (1981).

———, *"Unusual" Punishment: The Domestic Effects of International Norms Restricting the Application of the Death Penalty*, 52 CINN. L. REV. 655 (1983).

———, *Working Paper for the Committee of Experts on the Article 4 Derogation Provision*, 7 HUM. RTS. Q. 89 (1985).

Hassan, Farooq, *A Juridical Critique of Successful Treason: A Jurisprudential Analysis of the Constitutionality of Coup d'etat in the Common Law*, 20 STAN. J. INT'L L. 191 (1984).

Hatchard, John, *The Implementation of Safeguards on the Use of Emergency Powers: A Zimbabwean Perspective*, 9 OXFORD J. LEGAL STUDIES 116 (1989).

Haysom, Nicholas, *States of Emergency in a Post-Apartheid South Africa*, 21 COL. HUM. RTS. L. REV. 139 (1989).

Higgins, Roslyn, *Derogations under Human Rights Treaties*, 48 BRIT. Y.B. INT'L L. 281 (1976–77).

Jackson, J.D., *The Northern Ireland (Emergency Provisions) Act 1987*, 39 NO. IRE. L.Q. 235 (1988).

Jhabvala, Farrokh, *The Practice of the Covenant's Human Rights Committee, 1976–82: Review of State Party Reports*, 6 HUM. RTS. Q. 81 (1984).

Kamminga, Menno, *The Thematic Procedures of the UN Commission on Human Rights*, 34 NETH. INT'L L. REV. 299 (1987).

Lillich, Richard, *The U.N. and Human Rights Complaints: U Thant as Strict Constructionist*, 64 AM. J. INT'L L. 610 (1970).

Livingstone, Stephen, *A Week Is a Long Time in Detention: Brogan and Others v. United Kingdom*, 40 NO. IRE. L.Q. 288 (1989).

Lobel, Jules, *Emergency Power and the Decline of Liberalism*, 98 YALE L.J. 1385 (1989).

Lowry, David, *Terrorism and Human Rights: Counter-Insurgency and Necessity at Common Law*, 53 NOTRE DAME L.REV. 49 (1977).

Marks, Stephen, *The Complaint Procedure of the United Nations Educational, Scientific and Cultural Organization (UNESCO)*, in GUIDE TO INTERNATIONAL HUMAN RIGHTS PRACTICE 94 (Hurst Hannum ed., 1984).

Marks, Stephen, *Principles and Norms of Human Rights Applicable in Emergency Situations: Underdevelopment, Catastrophes and Armed Conflicts*, in THE INTERNATIONAL DIMENSIONS OF HUMAN RIGHTS 175 (Karel Vasak and Philip Alston eds., 1982).

Meron, Theodor, *Draft Model Declaration on Internal Strife*, INT'L REV. RED CROSS, Jan.–Feb. 1988 at 59.

———, *The Geneva Conventions as Customary Law*, 81 AM. J. INT'L L. 348 (1987).

———, *On the Inadequate Reach of Humanitarian and Human Rights Law and the Need for a New Instrument*, 77 AM. J. INT'L L. 589 (1983).

———, *Towards a Humanitarian Declaration on Internal Strife*, 78 AM. J. INT'L L. 859 (1984).

Miller, Arthur Selwyn, *Constitutional Law: Crisis Government Becomes the Norm*, 39 OHIO ST. L.J. 736 (1978).

Montealegre, Hernan, *The Compatibility of a State-Party's Derogation under Human Rights Conventions with its Obligations under Protocol II and Common Article 3*, 33 AM. U. L. REV. 41 (1983).

Moyer, Charles and David Padilla, *Executions in Guatemala as Decreed by the Courts of Special Jurisdiction in 1982–83: A Case Study*, 6 HUM. RTS. Q. 507 (1984).

Nagan, Winston, *Law and Post-Apartheid South Africa*, 12 FORDHAM INT'L L.J. 399 (1989).

Nariman, Fali, *The Judiciary under Martial Law Regimes*, 14 C.I.J.L. BULLETIN 41 (1984).

Norris, Robert, *Observations* In LOCO: *Practice and Procedure of the Inter-American Commission on Human Rights*, 15 TEX. INT'L L.J. 46 (1980).

Norris, Robert and Paula Reiton, *The Suspension of Guarantees: A Comparative Analysis of the American Convention of Human Rights and the Constitutions of the States Parties*, 30 AM. U.L. REV. 189 (1981).

O'Boyle, Michael, *Emergency Situations and the Protection of Human Rights: A Model Derogations Provision for a Northern Ireland Bill of Rights*, 28 No. IRE. L.Q. HUM. RTS. 160 (1977).

O'Boyle, Michael, *Torture and Emergency Powers under the European Convention on Human Rights*, 71 AM. J. INT'L L. 674 (1977).

O'Donnell, Daniel, *States of Exception*, 21 INT'L COMM. OF JURISTS REV. 52 (1978).

Orentlicher, Diane, *Bearing Witness: The Art and Science of Human Rights Fact-Finding*, 3 HARV. HUM. RTS. J. 83 (1990).

Parker, Penny and David Weissbrodt, *Major Developments at the UN Commission on Human Rights in 1991*, 8 AMNESTY INTERNATIONAL LEGAL SUPPORT NETWORK NEWSLETTER 19 (1991).

Parker, Penny and David Weissbrodt, *Major Developments at the UN Commission on Human Rights in 1991*, 13 HUM. RTS. Q. 573 (1991).

Partsch, K.J., *Experiences Regarding the War and Emergency Clause (Article 15) of the European Convention on Human Rights*, 1971 ISRAEL Y.B. HUM. RTS. 327.

Peirce, George, *Humanitarian Protection for the Victims of War: The System of Protecting Powers and the Role of the ICRC*, 90 MIL. L. REV. 89 (1980).

Prémont, Daniel, *United Nations Procedures for the Protection of All Persons Subjected to Any Form of Detention or Imprisonment*, 20 SANTA CLARA L. REV. 603 (1980).

Robertson, A.H., *The Implementation System: International Measures*, in THE INTERNATIONAL BILL OF RIGHTS: THE COVENANT ON CIVIL AND POLITICAL RIGHTS 332 (Louis Henkin ed. 1981).

Rudolph, Harold, *The Judicial Review of Administrative Detention Orders in Israel*, 14 ISRAEL Y.B. HUM. RTS. 148 (1984).

Saltman, Michael, *The Use of the Mandatory Emergency Laws by the Israeli Government*, 10 INT'L J. SOC. L. 385 (1982).

Schlager, Erika, *The Procedural Framework of the CSCE: From the Helsinki Consultations to the Paris Charter, 1972–1990*, 12 HUM. RTS. L.J. 221 (1991).

Schreuer, Christoph, *Derogation of Human Rights in Situations of Public Emergency: The Experience of the European Convention on Human Rights*, 9 YALE J. WORLD PUB. ORDER 113 (1982).

Shetreet, Shimon, *A Contemporary Model of Emergency Detention Laws: An Assessment of the Israeli Law*, 14 ISRAEL Y.B. HUM. RTS. 182 (1984).

Simpson, A.W. Brian, *Detention Without Trial in the Second World War: Comparing the British and American Experiences,* LAW QUADRANGLE NOTES Vol. 34 No. 3 at 48 (1990) (Published by the University of Michigan).

Stavros, Stephanos, *The Right to Fair Trial in Emergency Situations,* 41 INT'L & COMP. L.Q. 343 (1992).

Steinberg, Robert, *Judicial Independence in States of Emergency: Lessons from Nicaragua's Popular Anti-Somocista Tribunals,* 18 COL. HUM. RTS. L. REV. 359 (1987).

Tardu, M.E., *United Nations Response to Gross Violations of Human Rights: The 1503 Procedure,* 20 SANTA CLARA L. REV. 559 (1980).

Tobin, Jack, *Book Review* (HURIDOCS STANDARD FORMATS FOR THE RECORDING AND EXCHANGE OF INFORMATION ON HUMAN RIGHTS, by Bjørn Stormorken), 81 AM. J. INT'L L. 977 (1987).

Tolley, Howard, *The Concealed Crack in the Citadel: The United Nations Commission on Human Rights' Response to Confidential Communications,* 6 HUM. RTS. Q. 420 (1984).

Tomuschat, Christian, *Quo Vadis, Argentoratum?* 13 HUM. RTS. L.J. 401 (1992).

Van Hoff, F., *The Protection of Human Rights and the Impact of Emergency Situations under International Law, with Special Reference to the Present Situation in Chile,* 11 HUM. RTS. L.J. 213 (1979).

Walkate, Jaap, *The Human Rights Committee and Public Emergencies,* 9 YALE J. WORLD PUB. ORDER 133 (1982).

Warbrick, Colin, *The Protection of Human Rights in National Emergencies,* in HUMAN RIGHTS, PROBLEMS, PERSPECTIVES, AND TEXTS 89 (F.E. Dowrick ed., 1979).

Weissbrodt, David, *The Contribution of International Nongovernmental Organizations to the Protection of Human Rights,* in HUMAN RIGHTS IN INTERNATIONAL LAW: LEGAL AND POLICY ISSUES 403 (Theodor Meron ed., 1984).

———, *The Three "Theme" Special Rapporteurs of the UN Commission on Human Rights,* 80 AM. J. INT'L L. 685 (1986).

Weissbrodt, David and Maria Luisa Bartolomei, *The Effectiveness of International Human Rights Pressures: The Case of Argentina, 1976–1983,* 75 MINN. L. REV. 1009 (1991).

Weissbrodt, David and James McCarthy, *Fact-Finding by Nongovernmental Organizations,* in INTERNATIONAL LAW AND FACT-FINDING IN THE FIELD OF HUMAN RIGHTS 186 (B.G. Ramcharan ed., 1981).

Wiseberg, Laurie and Harry Scoble, *The International League for Human Rights: The Strategy of a Human Rights NGO,* 7 GA. J. INT'L & COMP. L. 289 (1977).

## NGO DOCUMENTS

AMERICAS WATCH, VIOLATION OF FAIR TRIAL GUARANTEES BY THE FMLN'S *AD HOC* COURTS (1990).

AMNESTY INTERNATIONAL, A GUIDE TO THE UNITED NATIONS BODY OF PRINCIPLES FOR THE PROTECTION OF ALL PERSONS UNDER ANY FORM OF DETENTION OR IMPRISONMENT, AI Index: IOR 52/04/89 (1989).

AMNESTY INTERNATIONAL, CONTINUING DETENTIONS UNDER THE INTERNAL SECURITY ACT: FURTHER EVIDENCE OF THE TORTURE AND ILL-TREATMENT OF DETAINEES, AI Index: ASA 36/09/88 (1988).

AMNESTY INTERNATIONAL, EGYPT: ARBITRARY DETENTION AND TORTURE UNDER EMERGENCY POWERS (1989).

AMNESTY INTERNATIONAL, HANDBOOK (1983).

AMNESTY INTERNATIONAL, JORDAN: HUMAN RIGHTS PROTECTION AFTER THE STATE OF EMERGENCY (1990).

AMNESTY INTERNATIONAL, PROTECTING HUMAN RIGHTS: INTERNATIONAL PROCEDURES AND HOW TO USE THEM, PART 3, AI Index: IOR 30/01/89 (1989).

AMNESTY INTERNATIONAL, RECENT DETENTIONS UNDER THE INTERNAL SECURITY ACT: REPORT OF AN AMNESTY MISSION IN SINGAPORE, AI Index: ASA 36/11/87 (1987).

AMNESTY INTERNATIONAL, REPORT 1985 (1985).

AMNESTY INTERNATIONAL, REPORT 1987 (1987).

AMNESTY INTERNATIONAL, REPORT 1988 (1989).

AMNESTY INTERNATIONAL, STATES OF EMERGENCY: TORTURE AND VIOLATIONS OF THE RIGHT TO LIFE UNDER STATES OF EMERGENCY, AI Index: POL 30/02/88 (1988).

AMNESTY INTERNATIONAL, TORTURE IN THE EIGHTIES (1984).

AMNESTY INTERNATIONAL, WHEN THE STATE KILLS . . . THE DEATH PENALTY: A HUMAN RIGHTS ISSUE (1989).

AMNESTY INTERNATIONAL, WORLD CONFERENCE ON HUMAN RIGHTS, AI Index: IOR 41/16/92 (1992).

ASSOCIATION OF INTERNATIONAL CONSULTANTS ON HUMAN RIGHTS, MODEL LEGAL PROVISIONS CONCERNING STATES OF EMERGENCY (1991), reprinted in UN Doc. E/CN.4/Sub.2/1991/28 Annex I (1991).

ASSOCIATION OF THE BAR OF THE CITY OF NEW YORK, CRIMINAL JUSTICE AND HUMAN RIGHTS IN NORTHERN IRELAND (1988).

CAMBODIA DOCUMENTATION COMMISSION, HUMAN RIGHTS, FUNDAMENTAL FREEDOMS AND THE UN PEACE PLAN FOR CAMBODIA (1991).

COHEN, ROBERTA, HUMAN RIGHTS AND HUMANITARIAN EMERGENCIES: NEW ROLES FOR U.N. HUMAN RIGHTS BODIES (Refugee Policy Group 1992).

DECLARATION OF MINIMUM HUMANITARIAN STANDARDS, reprinted in 85 AM. J. INT'L L. 375 (1991).

HUMAN RIGHTS WATCH, NEEDLESS DEATHS IN THE GULF WAR (1992).

INTERNATIONAL COMMISSION OF JURISTS, ISRAEL NATIONAL SECTION, THE RULE OF LAW IN THE AREAS ADMINISTERED BY ISRAEL (TEL AVIV 1981).

INTERNATIONAL COMMISSION OF JURISTS, OBJECTIVES, ORGANIZATION, ACTIVITIES (1965).

INTERNATIONAL COMMISSION OF JURISTS, UN SUB-COMMISSION ON THE PREVENTION OF DISCRIMINATION AND THE PROTECTION OF MINORITIES (1990), THE REVIEW (No. 45) (1990).

INTERNATIONAL COMMISSION OF JURISTS, UNESCO's SPECIAL COMMITTEE ON HUMAN RIGHTS: AN UNFORTUNATE CASE, THE REVIEW (No. 24) (1982).

INTERNATIONAL COMMITTEE OF THE RED CROSS, ANNUAL REPORT 1988 (1989).

INTERNATIONAL COMMITTEE OF THE RED CROSS, ANNUAL REPORT 1990 (1991).

INTERNATIONAL HUMAN RIGHTS LAW GROUP, WORKING SEMINAR ON UNESCO's HUMAN RIGHTS PROCEDURES (WASHINGTON, D.C. 1984).

INTERNATIONAL LAW ASSOCIATION, FINAL REPORT ON MONITORING STATES OF EMERGENCY: GUIDELINES FOR BODIES MONITORING RESPECT FOR HUMAN RIGHTS DURING STATES OF EMERGENCY, REPORT OF THE COMMITTEE ON THE ENFORCEMENT OF HUMAN RIGHTS LAW, SIXTY-FOURTH CONFERENCE OF THE INTERNATIONAL LAW ASSOCIATION, QUEENSLAND (1990), reprinted in 85 AM. J. INT'L L. 716 (1991).

INTERNATIONAL LAW ASSOCIATION, INTERIM REPORT OF THE COMMITTEE ON

THE ENFORCEMENT OF HUMAN RIGHTS LAW, SIXTY-SECOND CONFERENCE OF THE INTERNATIONAL LAW ASSOCIATION, SEOUL (1986).

INTERNATIONAL LAW ASSOCIATION, PARIS MINIMUM STANDARDS OF HUMAN RIGHTS NORMS IN A STATE OF EMERGENCY, REPORT OF THE COMMITTEE ON THE ENFORCEMENT OF HUMAN RIGHTS LAW, SIXTY-FIRST CONFERENCE OF THE INTERNATIONAL LAW ASSOCIATION, PARIS (1984), reprinted in 79 AM. J. INT'L L. 1072 (1985).

INTERNATIONAL LAW ASSOCIATION, SECOND INTERIM REPORT OF THE COMMITTEE ON THE ENFORCEMENT OF HUMAN RIGHTS LAW, SIXTY-THIRD CONFERENCE OF THE INTERNATIONAL LAW ASSOCIATION, WARSAW (1988).

INTERNATIONAL LEAGUE FOR HUMAN RIGHTS, URUGUAY'S HUMAN RIGHTS RECORD (1982).

LAWYERS COMMITTEE FOR HUMAN RIGHTS, ABANDONING THE VICTIMS—THE UN ADVISORY SERVICES PROGRAM IN GUATEMALA (1980).

OSLO STATEMENT ON NORMS AND PROCEDURES IN TIMES OF PUBLIC EMERGENCY OR INTERNAL VIOLENCE, reprinted in 5 MENNESKER OG RETTIGHETER—NORDIC J. HUM. RTS. 2 (1984) and UN Doc. E/CN.4/Sub.2/1987/31 (1987).

SIRACUSA PRINCIPLES ON THE LIMITATION AND DEROGATION PROVISIONS IN THE INTERNATIONAL COVENANT ON CIVIL AND POLITICAL RIGHTS, reprinted in 7 HUM. RTS. Q. 3 (1985), 36 REV. INT'L COMM'N. JURISTS 47 (1986) and UN Doc. E/CN.4/1985/4 (1985).

## INTERGOVERNMENTAL ORGANIZATION PUBLICATIONS

### OAS Documents

INTER-AMERICAN COMMISSION ON HUMAN RIGHTS, ANNUAL REPORT OF THE INTER-AMERICAN COMMISSION ON HUMAN RIGHTS 1979–1980, O.A.S. Doc. OEA/Ser.L/V/II.50, doc. 13 rev. 1 (1980).

INTER-AMERICAN COMMISSION ON HUMAN RIGHTS, ANNUAL REPORT OF THE INTER-AMERICAN COMMISSION ON HUMAN RIGHTS 1980–1981, O.A.S. Doc. OEA/Ser.L/V/II.54, doc. 9 rev. 1 (1981).

INTER-AMERICAN COMMISSION ON HUMAN RIGHTS, ANNUAL REPORT OF THE INTER-AMERICAN COMMISSION ON HUMAN RIGHTS 1984–1985, O.A.S. Doc. OEA/Ser.L/V/II.66, doc. 10 rev. 1 (1985).

INTER-AMERICAN COMMISSION ON HUMAN RIGHTS, ANNUAL REPORT OF THE INTER-AMERICAN COMMISSION ON HUMAN RIGHTS 1986–1987, O.A.S. Doc. OEA/Ser.L/V/II.71, doc. 9 rev. 1 (1987).

INTER-AMERICAN COMMISSION ON HUMAN RIGHTS, ANNUAL REPORT OF THE INTER-AMERICAN COMMISSION ON HUMAN RIGHTS 1988–1989, O.A.S. Doc. OEA/Ser.L/V/II.76, doc. 10 (1989).

INTER-AMERICAN COMMISSION ON HUMAN RIGHTS, ANNUAL REPORT OF THE INTER-AMERICAN COMMISSION ON HUMAN RIGHTS 1989–1990, O.A.S. Doc. OEA/Ser.L/V/II.77 rev. 1 doc. 7 (1990).

INTER-AMERICAN COMMISSION ON HUMAN RIGHTS, ANNUAL REPORT OF THE INTER-AMERICAN COMMISSION ON HUMAN RIGHTS 1990–1991, O.A.S. Doc. OEA/Ser.L/V/II.79 rev. 1 doc. 12 (1991).

INTER-AMERICAN COMMISSION ON HUMAN RIGHTS, HANDBOOK OF EXISTING RULES PERTAINING TO HUMAN RIGHTS IN THE INTER-AMERICAN SYSTEM, O.A.S. Doc. OEA/Ser.L/V/II.65, doc. 6 (1985).

INTER-AMERICAN COMMISSION ON HUMAN RIGHTS, REPORT ON THE SITUATION OF HUMAN RIGHTS IN ARGENTINA, O.A.S. Doc. OEA/Ser.L/V/II.49, doc. 19 corr. 1 (1980).

INTER-AMERICAN COMMISSION ON HUMAN RIGHTS, REPORT ON THE SITUATION OF HUMAN RIGHTS IN BOLIVIA, O.A.S. Doc. OEA/Ser.L/V/II.53, doc. 6 (1981).

INTER-AMERICAN COMMISSION ON HUMAN RIGHTS, REPORT ON THE STATUS OF HUMAN RIGHTS IN CHILE, O.A.S. Doc. OEA/Ser.L/V/II.34, doc. 21 (1974).

INTER-AMERICAN COMMISSION ON HUMAN RIGHTS, SECOND REPORT ON THE SITUATION OF HUMAN RIGHTS IN CHILE, O.A.S. Doc. OEA/Ser.L/V/II.37, doc. 19 corr. 1 (1976).

INTER-AMERICAN COMMISSION ON HUMAN RIGHTS, REPORT ON THE SITUATION OF HUMAN RIGHTS IN CHILE, O.A.S. Doc. OEA/Ser.L/V/II.66, doc. 16 (1985).

INTER-AMERICAN COMMISSION ON HUMAN RIGHTS, REPORT ON THE SITUATION OF HUMAN RIGHTS IN THE REPUBLIC OF COLOMBIA, O.A.S. Doc. OEA/Ser.L/V/II.53, doc. 22 (1981).

INTER-AMERICAN COMMISSION ON HUMAN RIGHTS, REPORT ON THE SITUATION OF HUMAN RIGHTS IN EL SALVADOR, O.A.S. Doc. OEA/Ser.L/V/II.46, doc. 23 rev. 1 (1978).

INTER-AMERICAN COMMISSION ON HUMAN RIGHTS, REPORT ON THE SITUATION OF HUMAN RIGHTS IN THE REPUBLIC OF GUATEMALA, O.A.S. Doc. OEA/Ser.L/V/II.53, doc. 21 rev. 2 (1981).

INTER-AMERICAN COMMISSION ON HUMAN RIGHTS, REPORT ON THE SITUATION OF HUMAN RIGHTS IN HAITI, O.A.S. Doc. OEA/Ser.L/V/II.77, rev. 1 doc. 18 (1981).

INTER-AMERICAN COMMISSION ON HUMAN RIGHTS, REPORT ON THE SITUATION OF HUMAN RIGHTS IN HAITI, O.A.S. Doc. OEA/Ser.L/V/II.74, doc. 9 rev. 1 (1988).

INTER-AMERICAN COMMISSION ON HUMAN RIGHTS, REPORT ON THE SITUATION OF HUMAN RIGHTS IN HAITI, O.A.S. Doc. OEA/Ser.L/V/II.77, rev. 1 doc. 18 (1990).

INTER-AMERICAN COMMISSION ON HUMAN RIGHTS, REPORT ON THE SITUATION OF HUMAN RIGHTS IN NICARAGUA, O.A.S. Doc. OEA/Ser.L/V/II.45, doc. 16 rev. 1 (1978).

INTER-AMERICAN COMMISSION ON HUMAN RIGHTS, REPORT ON THE SITUATION OF HUMAN RIGHTS IN NICARAGUA, O.A.S. Doc. OEA/Ser.L/V/II.45, doc. 16 rev. 1 (1981).

INTER-AMERICAN COMMISSION ON HUMAN RIGHTS, REPORT ON THE SITUATION OF HUMAN RIGHTS IN NICARAGUA, O.A.S. Doc. OEA/Ser.L/V/II.53, doc. 25 (1981).

INTER-AMERICAN COMMISSION ON HUMAN RIGHTS, REPORT ON THE SITUATION OF HUMAN RIGHTS OF A SEGMENT OF THE NICARAGUAN POPULATION OF MISKITO ORIGIN, O.A.S. Doc. OEA/Ser.L/V/II.62, doc. 10 rev. 3 (1983).

INTER-AMERICAN COMMISSION ON HUMAN RIGHTS, REPORT ON THE SITUATION OF HUMAN RIGHTS IN PANAMA, O.A.S. Doc. OEA/Ser.L/V/II.44, doc. 38 rev. 1 (1978).

INTER-AMERICAN COMMISSION ON HUMAN RIGHTS, REPORT ON THE SITUATION OF HUMAN RIGHTS IN PARAGUAY, O.A.S. Doc. OEA/Ser.L/V/II.10, doc. 2 (1964).

INTER-AMERICAN COMMISSION ON HUMAN RIGHTS, REPORT ON THE SITUATION

OF HUMAN RIGHTS IN PARAGUAY, O.A.S. Doc. OEA/Ser.L/V/II.13, doc. 5 (1965).

INTER-AMERICAN COMMISSION ON HUMAN RIGHTS, REPORT ON THE SITUATION OF HUMAN RIGHTS IN PARAGUAY, O.A.S. Doc. OEA/Ser.L/V/II.43, doc. 13 corr. 1 (1978).

INTER-AMERICAN COMMISSION ON HUMAN RIGHTS, REPORT ON THE SITUATION OF HUMAN RIGHTS IN PARAGUAY, O.A.S. Doc. OEA/Ser.L/V/II.71, doc. 19 rev. 1 (1987).

INTER-AMERICAN COMMISSION ON HUMAN RIGHTS, REPORT ON THE SITUATION OF HUMAN RIGHTS IN SURINAME, O.A.S. Doc. OEA/Ser.L/V/II.61, doc. 6 rev. 1 (1983).

INTER-AMERICAN COMMISSION ON HUMAN RIGHTS, REPORT No. 28/92 and REPORT No. 29/92 of 2 OCTOBER 1992, *reprinted in* 13 HUM. RTS. L.J. 336 (1992).

LA PROTECCIÓN DE LOS DERECHOS HUMANOS FRENTE A LA SUSPENSIÓN DE LAS GARANTÍAS CONSTITUCIONALES O "ESTADO DE SITIO," O.A.S. Doc. OEA/Ser.L/V/II.15, doc. 12 (1966).

INTER-AMERICAN COURT OF HUMAN RIGHTS, ANNUAL REPORT OF THE INTER-AMERICAN COURT OF HUMAN RIGHTS 1987, O.A.S. Doc. OEA/Ser.L/V/III.17, doc. 13 (1987).

INTER-AMERICAN COURT OF HUMAN RIGHTS, ANNUAL REPORT OF THE INTER-AMERICAN COURT OF HUMAN RIGHTS 1988, O.A.S. Doc. OEA/Ser.L/V/III.19, doc. 13 (1988).

## UN Documents

HUMAN RIGHTS COMMITTEE

*Reports of the Human Rights Committee:*

33 U.N. GAOR Supp. (No. 40), U.N. Doc. A/33/40 (1978)
34 U.N. GAOR Supp. (No. 40), U.N. Doc. A/34/40 (1979)
35 U.N. GAOR Supp. (No. 40), U.N. Doc. A/35/40 (1980)
36 U.N. GAOR Supp. (No. 40), U.N. Doc. A/36/40 (1981)
37 U.N. GAOR Supp. (No. 40), U.N. Doc. A/37/40 (1982)
38 U.N. GAOR Supp. (No. 40), U.N. Doc. A/38/40 (1983)
39 U.N. GAOR Supp. (No. 40), U.N. Doc. A/39/40 (1984)
40 U.N. GAOR Supp. (No. 40), U.N. Doc. A/40/40 (1985)
42 U.N. GAOR Supp. (No. 40), U.N. Doc. A/42/40 (1987)
44 U.N. GAOR Supp. (No. 40), U.N. Doc. A/44/40 (1989)
45 U.N. GAOR Supp. (No. 40), U.N. Doc. A/45/40 (1990)
46 U.N. GAOR Supp. (No. 40), U.N. Doc. A/46/40 (1991)
47 U.N. GAOR Supp. (No. 40), U.N. Doc. A/47/40 (1992)

*Summary Records of the Human Rights Committee:*

U.N. Docs. CCPR/C/SR. 65, 67, 82, 84, 84, 87 (1978); 128, 181 (1979); 260 (1980); 308 (1981); 334, 349, 351, 404, 414 (1982); 420, 430, 442, 443, 446, 463, 468, 477 (1983); 492, 499, 513, 520, 527, 528, 529, 530, 531, 541, 546, 547, 548 (1984); 575, 599, 603, 604, 609 (1985); 713, 765, 771, 776 (1987); 952, 973, 1062/Add.1 (1990).

SELECTED DECISIONS UNDER THE OPTIONAL PROTOCOL, U.N. Doc. CCPR/C/
OP/1 (1985).
SELECTED DECISIONS OF THE HUMAN RIGHTS COMMITTEE UNDER THE OPTIONAL
PROTOCOL VOLUME 2, U.N. Doc. CCPR/C/OP/2 (1990).


COMMITTEE AGAINST TORTURE

REPORT OF THE COMMITTEE AGAINST TORTURE, 45 U.N. GAOR Supp. (No. 44),
U.N. Doc. A/45/44 (1990).
47 U.N. GAOR Supp. (No. 44), U.N. Doc. A/47/44 (1992).


COMMISSION ON HUMAN RIGHTS

*Reports of the Commission on Human Rights:*

Fourth Session, U.N. Doc. E/600 (1948).
Sixth Session, U.N. Doc. E/1681 (1950).


*Summary Records of the Commission on Human Rights:*

Fifth Session, U.N. Docs. E/CN.4/SR.89, 126, 127 (1949)
Sixth Session, U.N. Docs. E/CN.4/SR.195, 196 (1950)
Eighth Session, U.N. Docs. E/CN.4/SR.330, 331 (1952)
Tenth Session, U.N. Docs. E/CN.4/SR.427, 428 (1954)
Thirtieth Session, U.N. Docs. E/CN.4/SR.1272, 1279, 1287 (1974)
Thirty-fourth Session, U.N. Docs. E/CN.4/SR.1440, 1446, 1449, 1466, 1468,
1469 (1978)
Thirty-fifth Session, U.N. Docs. E/CN.4/SR.1510, 1515 Add. 1, 1516 (1979)
Thirty-seventh Session, U.N. Docs. E/CN.4/SR.1592, 1593, 1594, 1616, 1617,
1635 (1981)
Thirty-eighth Session, U.N. Docs. E/CN.4/1982/SR.14, 15, 27 (1982)
Fortieth Session, U.N. Docs. E/CN.4/1984/SR.57, 59 (1984)
Forty-first Session, U.N. Docs. E/CN.4/1985/SR.19, 28, 31, 32, 34, 41, 45, 46,
48 (1985)
First special session, U.N. Docs. E/CN.4/1992/S-1/SR.2/Add.1 and SR.3
(1992).


*Documents Relating to the Drafting of the Covenant:*

U.N. Doc. A/2929 (1955)
U.N. Doc. E/CN.4/AC.1/4 (1947)
U.N. Doc. E/CN.4/AC.1/19 (1948)
U.N. Docs. E/CN.4/170 and Add. 1 (1949)
U.N. Doc. E/CN.4/187 (1949)
U.N. Doc. E/CN.4/188 (1949)
U.N. Doc. E/CN.4/324 (1949)
U.N. Doc. E/CN.4/325 (1949)
U.N. Doc. E/CN.4/365 (1950)
U.N. Doc. E/CN.4/528 (1951)
U.N. Doc. E/CN.4/530/Add.1 (1952)

*Ad Hoc Reports on Human Rights Situations and Advisory Services:*

Afghanistan
  U.N. Doc. E/CN.4/1985/21 (1985)
  U.N. Doc. A/40/843 (1985)
  U.N. Doc. E/CN.4/1986/24 (1986)
  U.N. Doc. A/42/667 (1987)
  U.N. Doc. A/45/664 (1990)
  U.N. Doc. E/CN.4/1990/25 (1990)
  U.N. Doc. E/CN.4/1992/33 (1992)
  U.N. Doc. A/47/656 (1992)
Bolivia
  U.N. Doc. E/CN.4/Sub.2/459 (1980)
  U.N. Doc. E/CN.4/1441 (1980)
  U.N. Doc. E/CN.4/1500 (1981)
  U.N. Doc. E/CN.4/1983/22 (1983)
  U.N. Doc. E/CN.4/1984/46 (1984)
Cambodia
  U.N. Doc. E/CN.4/1437 (1981)
  U.N. Doc. E/CN.4/1491 (1981)
Chile
  U.N. Doc. E/CN.4/Sub.2/412 (1978)
  U.N. Doc. E/CN.4/1188 (1976)
  U.N. Doc. E/CN.4/1221 (1977)
  U.N. Doc. E/CN.4/1266 (1978)
  U.N. Doc. E/CN.4/1310 (1979)
  U.N. Doc. E/CN.4/1986/2 (1986)
  U.N. Doc. A/42/556 (1987)
  U.N. Doc. E/CN.4/1988/7 (1988)
  U.N. Doc. E/CN.4/1989/7 (1989)
  U.N. Doc. A/44/635 (1989)
  U.N. Doc. E/CN.4/1990/5 (1990)
China
  U.N. Doc. E/CN.4/1990/52 (1990)
Cuba
  U.N. Doc. E/CN.4/1989/46 (1989)
El Salvador
  U.N. Doc. E/CN.4/1475 (1981)
  U.N. Doc. E/CN.4/1502 (1982)
  U.N. Doc. E/CN.4/1983/20 (1983)
  U.N. Doc. E/CN.4/1984/25 (1984)
  U.N. Doc. A/40/818 (1985)
  U.N. Doc. E/CN.4/1986/22 (1986)
  U.N. Doc. E/CN.4/1987/21 (1987)
  U.N. Doc. A/42/641 (1987)
  U.N. Doc. A/45/630 (1990)
  U.N. Doc. E/CN.4/1991/34 (1991)
  U.N. Doc. E/CN.4/1992/32 (1992)
Equatorial Guinea
  U.N. Doc. E/CN.4/1371 (1980)

U.N. Doc. E/CN.4/1985/9 (1985)
U.N. Doc. E/CN.4/1990/42 (1990)
Guatemala
U.N. Doc. E/CN.4/1438 (1981)
U.N. Doc. E/CN.4/1501 (1981)
U.N. Doc. E/CN.4/1984/30 (1984)
U.N. Doc. E/CN.4/1985/19 (1985)
U.N. Doc. A/40/865 (1985)
U.N. Doc. E/CN.4/1986/23 (1986)
U.N. Doc. E/CN.4/1987/24 (1986)
U.N. Doc. E/CN.4/1988/42 (1987)
U.N. Docs. E/CN.4/1990/45 and Add.1 (1989)
U.N. Docs. E/CN.4/1991/5 and Add.1 (1991)
U.N. Doc. E/CN.4/1992/5 (1992)
Haiti
U.N. Doc. E/CN.4/1988/38 (1988)
U.N. Doc. E/CN.4/1989/40 (1989)
U.N. Docs. E/CN.4/1990/44 and Add.1 (1990)
U.N. Docs. E/CN.4/1992/50 and Add.1 (1992)
U.N. Doc. A/47/621 (1992)
Iran
U.N. Doc. E/CN.4/1985/20 (1985)
U.N. Doc. A/40/874 (1985)
U.N. Doc. E/CN.4/1986/25 (1986)
U.N. Doc. E/CN.4/1987/23 (1987)
U.N. Doc. A/42/648 (1987)
U.N. Doc. E/CN.4/1988/24 (1988)
U.N. Doc. E/CN.4/1990/24 (1990)
U.N. Doc. E/CN.4/1992/34 (1992)
Iraq
U.N. Doc. E/CN.4/1992/31 (1992)
Kuwait
U.N. Doc. E/CN.4/1992/26 (1992)
Poland
U.N. Doc. E/CN.4/1983/18 (1983)
U.N. Doc. E/CN.4/1984/26 (1984)
Romania
U.N. Docs. E/CN.4/1990/28 (1989) and Add.1 (1990)
Yugoslavia (former)
U.N. Docs. E/CN.4/1992/S-1/9 and 10 (1992)


*Theme Mechanisms:*

Working Group on Enforced and Involuntary Disappearances
U.N. Doc. E/CN.4/1435 (1981)
U.N. Doc. E/CN.4/1492 (1981)
U.N. Doc. E/CN.4/1983/14 (1983)
U.N. Doc. E/CN.4/1984/21 (1984)
U.N. Doc. E/CN.4/1985/15 (1985)

U.N. Docs. E/CN.4/1986/18 and Add.1 (1986)
U.N. Docs. E/CN.4/1988/19 (1988) and Add.1 (1987)
U.N. Doc. E/CN.4/1990/13 (1990)
U.N. Docs. E/CN.4/1991/20 and Add.1 (1991)
U.N. Doc. E/CN.4/1992/18 (1991)
Special Rapporteur on Extrajudicial, Summary or Arbitrary Executions
U.N. Doc. E/CN.4/1984/29 (1984)
U.N. Doc. E/CN.4/1985/15 (1985)
U.N. Doc. E/CN.4/1986/21 (1986)
U.N. Docs. E/CN.4/1988/22 and Add.1 (1988)
U.N. Docs. E/CN.4/1990/22 and Add.1 (1990)
U.N. Doc. E/CN.4/1991/36 (1991)
U.N. Doc. E/CN.4/1993/46 (1992)
Special Rapporteur on Torture
U.N. Doc. E/CN.4/1986/15 (1986)
U.N. Docs. E/CN.4/1988/17 and Add.1 (1988)
U.N. Docs. E/CN.4/1990/17 and Add.1 (1990)
U.N. Doc. E/CN.4/1991/17 (1991)
U.N. Docs. E/CN.4/1992/17 and Add.1 (1992)
Special Rapporteur on Religious Intolerance
U.N. Doc. E/CN.4/1988/45 (1988)
Special Rapporteur on Mercenaries
U.N. Doc. E/CN.4/1990/11 (1990)
Working Group on Arbitrary Detention
U.N. Doc. E/CN.4/1993/24 (1993)

*Other Commission Documents:*

Report of the Working Group on the Declaration on the protection of all persons from enforced disappearances, U.N. Doc. E/CN.4/19/Rev.1 (1992)

SUB-COMMISSION ON PREVENTION OF DISCRIMINATION AND PROTECTION OF MINORITIES

Study of the implications for human rights of recent developments concerning situations known as states of siege or emergency, U.N. Doc. E/CN.4/Sub.2/ 15 (1982) (Questiaux Report).
Explanatory paper on the best way of undertaking the drawing up and updating of a list of countries which proclaim or terminate a state of emergency each year, U.N. Doc. E/CN.4/Sub.2/1985/19 (1985).
First annual report and list of states which, since 1 January 1985, have proclaimed, extended or terminated a state of emergency, U.N. Docs. E/CN.4/ Sub.2/1987/19 (1987) and Rev.1 (1988) (Despouy Report).
Second annual report and list of states which, since 1 January 1985, have proclaimed, extended or terminated a state of emergency, U.N. Docs. E/ CN.4/Sub.2/1988/18 and Add.1 and Rev.1 (1988).
Third annual report and list of states which, since 1 January 1985, have proclaimed, extended or terminated a state of emergency, U.N. Docs. E/CN.4/ Sub.2/1989/30 and Add.2/Rev.1 (1989), and Rev.1 and Rev.2 (1990).
Question of human rights and states of emergency, working paper, U.N. Docs. E/CN.4/1990/33 and Add.1 (1990).

Fourth annual report and list of states which, since 1 January 1985, have proclaimed, extended or terminated a state of emergency, U.N. Doc. E/CN.4/Sub.2/1991/28 (1991).

Fifth annual report and list of states which, since 1 January 1985, have proclaimed, extended or terminated a state of emergency, U.N. Doc. E/CN.4/Sub.2/1992/23 (1992).

Explanatory paper on the practice of administrative detention without charge or trial, U.N. Doc. E/CN.4/Sub.2/1987/16 (1987).

Preliminary report on the right to freedom of opinion and expression, U.N. Doc. E/CN.4/Sub.2/1990/11 (1990).

Report on the practice of administrative detention, U.N. Doc. E/CN.4/Sub.2/1989/27 (1989) and U.N. Docs. E/CN.4/Sub.2/1990/29 and Add.1 (1990).

Study on the right to a fair trial, U.N. Doc. E/CN.4/Sub.2/1990/34 (1990).

Study on the right to a fair trial: Current recognition and measures necessary for its strengthening, Addendum: Right to amparo, habeas corpus, and similar procedures, U.N. Doc. E/CN.4/Sub.2/1992/Add.3 (1992).

The Individual's Duties to the Community and the Limitations on Human Rights and Freedoms under Article 29 of the Universal Declaration of Human Rights, U.N. Doc. E/CN.4/Sub.2/432/Rev.2 (1983).


UNESCO

UNESCO Doc. 104 EX/Decision 3.3 (1978).

UNESCO Doc. 110 EX/Decisions (1980).


SECRETARY-GENERAL

Note verbale dated 14 August 1990 from the Chargé d'affaires a.i. of the Permanent Mission of El Salvador, U.N. Doc. A/44/971, S/21541 (1990).

Central America: Efforts towards Peace, U.N. Doc. S/224494 (1991).

Report of the Secretary-General on the Work of the Organization, U.N. Doc. A/47/1 (1992).


INTERNATIONAL LABOUR ORGANISATION

ILO OFFICIAL BULLETIN (Special Supplement), Vol. XLIX, 1966, No. 3.

ILO OFFICIAL BULLETIN (Special Supplement), Vol. LIV, 1971, No. 2.

ILO OFFICIAL BULLETIN Series B, Vol. LXVI, 1983, No. 3.

ILO OFFICIAL BULLETIN Series B (Special Supplement), Vol. LXVII, 1984.

REPORT OF THE COMMITTEE OF EXPERTS ON THE APPLICATION OF CONVENTIONS AND RECOMMENDATIONS, 52nd Session of the International Labour Conference, Report III (Part 4) (1968).

REPORT OF THE COMMITTEE OF EXPERTS ON THE APPLICATION OF CONVENTIONS AND RECOMMENDATIONS (Articles 19, 22, and 35 of the Constitution), Volume B, 69th Session of the International Labour Conference, Report III (Part 4B) (1983).

REPORT OF THE COMMITTEE OF EXPERTS ON THE APPLICATION OF CONVENTIONS AND RECOMMENDATIONS (Articles 19, 22 and 35 of the Constitution), 72nd Session of the International Labour Conference, Report III (Part 4A) (1986).

Council of Europe

[1958–59] Y.B. Eur. Conv. on Human Rights
[1969] Y.B. Eur. Conv. on Human Rights
[1976] Y.B. Eur. Conv. on Human Rights
[1978] Y.B. Eur. Conv. on Human Rights
[1985] Y.B. Eur. Conv. on Human Rights
Human Rights Information Sheet No. 27, Doc. H/INF (91)1 (1991)
Reform of the Control System of the European Convention on Human Rights, *reprinted in* 14 Hum. Rts. L.J. 31 (1993).
Stocktaking on the European Convention on Human Rights, The First Thirty Years: 1954 until 1984 (1984).
Stocktaking on the European Convention on Human Rights, Supplement 1988 (1989).
Brannigan and McBride v. U.K., Report of the European Commission of Human Rights, adopted 3 December 1991.
European Committee on the Prevention of Torture, Public Statement on Turkey, *reprinted in* 14 Hum. Rts. L.J. 49 (1993).
Parliamentary Assembly, The Situation of Human Rights in Turkey, *reprinted in* 13 Hum. Rts. L.J. 464 (1992).

# Table of Cases

# Index

## Procedural Aspects of International Law Series

Richard B. Lillich, Editor (1964–1977)
Robert Kogod Goldman, Editor (1977–)

(Asterisks denote volumes published by the University of Pennsylvania Press.)

1. Richard B. Lillich. *International Claims: Their Adjudication by National Commissions.* 1962
2. Richard B. Lillich and Gordon A. Christenson. *International Claims: Their Preparation and Presentation.* 1962
3. Richard A. Falk. *The Role of Domestic Courts in the International Legal Order.* 1964
4. Gillian M. White. *The Use of Experts by International Tribunals.* 1965
5. Richard B. Lillich. *The Protection of Foreign Investment: Six Procedural Studies.* 1965
6. Richard B. Lillich. *International Claims: Postwar British Practice.* 1967
7. Thomas Buergenthal. *Law-Making in the International Civil Aviation Organization.* 1969
8. John Carey. *UN Protection of Civil and Political Rights.* 1970
9. Burns H. Weston. *International Claims: Postwar French Practice.* 1971
10. Frank Griffith Dawson and Ivan L. Head. *International Law, National Tribunals, and the Rights of Aliens.* 1971
11. Ignaz Seidl-Hohenveldern. *The Austrian-German Arbitral Tribunal.* 1972
12. Richard B. Lillich and Burns H. Weston. *International Claims: Their Settlement by Lump Sum Agreements.* 1975
13. Durward V. Sandifer. *Evidence Before International Tribunals* (Revised Edition). 1975
14. Roger Fisher. *Improving Compliance with International Law.* 1981
15. Richard B. Lillich and Burns H. Weston, eds. *International Claims: Contemporary European Practice.* 1982
16. Frederic L. Kirgis, Jr. *Prior Consultation in International Law: A Study of State Practice.* 1983
17. David Harris. *The European Social Charter.* 1984
18. Richard A. Falk. *Reviving the World Court.* 1986
*19. Joan Fitzpatrick. *Human Rights in Crisis: The International System for Protecting Rights During States of Emergency.* 1994